T0391415

CAUSATION IN COMPETITION LAW DAMAGES ACTIONS

Competition law damages actions are often characterized by the uncertainty of the causal connection between the infringement and the harm. The damage consists in a pure economic loss flowing from an anticompetitive conduct. In such cases, the complexity of the markets' structures, combined with the interdependence of individuals' assets, fuel this causal uncertainty. In this work, Claudio Lombardi elucidates the concept of causation in competition law damages actions and outlines its practical implications in competition litigation through the comparative analysis of the relevant statutory and case law, primarily in the European Union. This book should be read by practitioners, scholars, and graduate students with experience in competition law, as well as those interested in analyzing economic torts and causation in general.

CLAUDIO LOMBARDI is an assistant professor at KIMEP University's School of Law. He previously served as a visiting research fellow at University College London and at the University of Cambridge, Faculty of Law. Before that, he was a postdoctoral research fellow at the Max Planck Institute for Comparative and International Private Law and the Europa-Kolleg, Hamburg and a visiting lecturer at the International University College of Turin and at Trinity College Dublin, School of Law.

GLOBAL COMPETITION LAW AND ECONOMICS POLICY

This series publishes monographs highlighting the interdisciplinary and multijurisdictional nature of competition law, economics, and policy. Global in coverage, the series should appeal to competition and antitrust specialists working as scholars, practitioners, and judges.

General Editors: Ioannis Lianos, University College London; Thomas Cheng, University of Hong Kong; Simon Roberts, University of Johannesburg; Maarten Pieter Schinkel, University of Amsterdam; Maurice Stucke, University of Tennessee

Causation in Competition Law Damages Actions

CLAUDIO LOMBARDI
KIMEP University

CAMBRIDGE
UNIVERSITY PRESS

University Printing House, Cambridge CB2 8BS, United Kingdom

One Liberty Plaza, 20th Floor, New York, NY 10006, USA

477 Williamstown Road, Port Melbourne, VIC 3207, Australia

314–321, 3rd Floor, Plot 3, Splendor Forum, Jasola District Centre, New Delhi – 110025, India

79 Anson Road, #06–04/06, Singapore 079906

Cambridge University Press is part of the University of Cambridge.

It furthers the University's mission by disseminating knowledge in the pursuit of education, learning, and research at the highest international levels of excellence.

www.cambridge.org
Information on this title: www.cambridge.org/9781108428620
DOI: 10.1017/9781108552509

© Claudio Lombardi 2020

This publication is in copyright. Subject to statutory exception and to the provisions of relevant collective licensing agreements, no reproduction of any part may take place without the written permission of Cambridge University Press.

First published 2020

A catalogue record for this publication is available from the British Library.

Library of Congress Cataloging-in-Publication Data
NAMES: Lombardi, Claudio, 1983– author.
TITLE: Causation in competition law damages actions / Claudio Lombardi, KIMEP University.
DESCRIPTION: Cambridge, United Kingdom ; New York, NY, USA : Cambridge University Press, 2020. |
Based on author's thesis (doctoral - Università degli studi di Trento, 2015) issued under title:
Causation in private enforcement of competition law : a comparative analysis of divergent national approaches. | Includes bibliographical references and index.
IDENTIFIERS: LCCN 2019035493 (print) | LCCN 2019035494 (ebook) |
ISBN 9781108428620 (hardback) | ISBN 9781108450805 (paperback) |
ISBN 9781108552509 (epub)
SUBJECTS: LCSH: Antitrust law–European Union countries. | Antitrust law. |
Damages–European Union countries. | Damages. | Actions and defenses–European Union countries. | Actions and defenses.
CLASSIFICATION: LCC KJE6530 .L66 2020 (print) | LCC KJE6530 (ebook) |
DDC 343.2407/21–dc23
LC record available at https://lccn.loc.gov/2019035493
LC ebook record available at https://lccn.loc.gov/2019035494

ISBN 978-1-108-42862-0 Hardback

Cambridge University Press has no responsibility for the persistence or accuracy of URLs for external or third-party internet websites referred to in this publication and does not guarantee that any content on such websites is, or will remain, accurate or appropriate.

For Andrea

Contents

Acknowledgements		*page* ix
Table of Cases		xi
	Introduction	1
1	**Causation in Competition Law**	3
	1.1 Causation: A Primer	5
	1.2 Theories of Causation	7
	1.3 Nature and Conditions of the Antitrust Harm	11
	1.4 The Causal Connection in Competition Damages Actions	16
	1.5 Causation in Fact	19
	1.6 Legal Causation	25
2	**Causation Rules in National Courts**	34
	2.1 English Law	34
	2.2 German Law	38
	2.3 French Law	40
	2.4 Italian Law	43
	2.5 US Law	45
3	**Causation in the European Union Competition Law and Decisions**	50
	3.1 Causation in the Court of Justice of the European Union Decisions	51
	3.2 Causation in the European Union Competition Law	53
	3.3 The (Positive) Limits to the National Rules on Causation	55
	3.4 The Objectives of the Damages Directive and of Articles 101 and 102	56
	3.5 The Right to Full Compensation in the Directive on Antitrust Damages Claims	60
	3.6 Scope of Competition Law Damages Actions	61

vii

viii   *Contents*

3.7 Convergence of Different Causation Regimes and
    the Effects of a Diverse Set of Legal Frameworks   64
3.8 Causation and EU Law   66

4   Causal Uncertainty in Competition Law Damages Claims   69

4.1 Sources of Causal Uncertainty   70
4.2 Use of Probabilities in National Courts   74
4.3 Causal Proportional Liability and Multiple Defendants   77
4.4 Causal Proportional Liability   89
4.5 Loss of Chance   91
4.6 Lost Chances in Domestic Antitrust Case Law   93
4.7 Claimant Indeterminacy and Collective Redress   103
4.8 Preemption and Duplicative Causes   104

5   Proof Rules of Causation   106

5.1 The Burden of Proof   109
5.2 The Standards of Proof   110
5.3 Proof of Causation in EU Law   112
5.4 Standards of Proof, Judges' Persuasion and Causal Uncertainty in
    Competition Law   114
5.5 Proving Causation in EU Competition Law   118
5.6 Proving Causation in National Courts   119
5.7 Econometrics and the 'Calculation' of Causation in EU
    Competition Law   131

6   Proving the Uncertain Causation   141

6.1 Relaxation of Proof Rules   142
6.2 Use of Causal Presumptions by EU Courts   147
6.3 Causal Presumptions in the Damages Directive   148
6.4 Lowering the Standard of Proof for Causation   151
6.5 The Moral Justification of the Standards of Proof for Causation 160

7   Causation in Indirect and Secondary Antitrust Damages   164

7.1 Indirect Purchasers' Claims   167
7.2 The Regulatory Framework in the EU   180
7.3 Indirect Purchasers Aggrieved by Umbrella Effects   188

Conclusion   192

Bibliography   197
Index   219

Acknowledgements

This book is based on a doctoral thesis I defended at the University of Trento in March 2015. Since then, many people and places have contributed to its development.

I am deeply indebted to Peter Behrens for hosting me at the Europa-Kolleg Institute for European Integration in Hamburg and for the many inspiring conversations.

I also thank Jürgen Basedow for giving me the opportunity to conduct most of my research at the Max Planck Institute for Comparative and International Private Law, Hamburg, and for sharing with me his ideas on the book's topic. I am very grateful to Okeoghene Odudu for hosting me at the University of Cambridge and for our inspiring conversations, and I thank Andelka Phillips for having me as visiting professor at Trinity College Dublin and for being a stimulating colleague. Similarly, I would also like to thank Ioannis Lianos for hosting me at the UCL in London. All these universities and hosts have provided a perfect environment to conduct research and write this book. In this vein, I want to thank Martins Paparinskis and Meagan Wong for the continuous encouragement and for their friendship inside and outside the walls of the UCL in London. My gratitude goes also to Alexey Ivanov for the period I spent at the HSE in Moscow and for our friendship afterwards. Moreover, I would like to thank Saira Mian for her uplifting example as a researcher and as a person and for the many inspiring conversations, and Marina Chang for being a similarly stimulating colleague in London.

I am also deeply indebted to Joseph Luke, dean of the Faculty of Law of KIMEP University for his comments on the first draft of this book, for his support, and for the motivation to move faster when I needed it most.

Finally, I would like to thank my family and my wife for their encouragement and support throughout my writing. Without them, it would not even make sense to write a book.

x   Acknowledgements

Cover image used with permission. Caravaggio (Merisi, Michelangelo), The Cardsharps, c. 1594. © 2019. Kimbell Art Museum, Fort Worth, Texas /Art Resource, NY/Scala, Florence.
© Photo SCALA, Florence

Table of Cases

European Union

C-362/95 P Blackspur DIY Ltd, Steven Kellar, JMA Glancy and Ronald Cohen v Council of the European Union and Commission of the European Communities [1997] ECR I-04775 118

C-49/92 P Commission v Anic Partecipazioni (1999) ECR I-4125

C-89/85 Ahlström Osakeyhtiö and Others v Commission [1994] ECR I-99

C-192/95 Comateb and Others v Directeur général des douanes and droits indirects ECR I-00165

C-199/92 P Hüls v Commission (1999) ECR I-4287

C-208/90 Emmott v Minister for Social Welfare [1991] ECR I-4269

C-222/84 Johnston v the Chief Constable of the Royal Ulster Constabulary [1986] ECR 1651

C-231/11 P a C-233/11 Commission v Siemens Österreich and Others ECLI: EU:C:2014:256

C-238/78 Ireks-Arkady v Council and Commission ECR 01719

C-256/80 Birra Wührer v Council and Commission ECR 00789

C-293/13 P e C-294/13 P Fresh Del Monte

C-331/85 Bianco and Girard v Directeur général des douanes and droits indirects [1988] ECR 1988 01099

C-382/12 P MasterCard Inc and Others v European Commission (2014) not yet published

27/76 United Brands Co v Commission ECLI:EU:C:1978:22

C-33/76, Rewe-Zentralfinanz eG and ReweZentral AG v Landwirtschafts-kammer für das Saarland ECR 1976-1989

C-44/76 Milch-, Fett- und Eier-Kontor GmbH v Council and Commission of the European Communities [1977] ECR 393

C-45/76 Comet BV v Produktschap voor Siergewassen 1976-02043

Table of Cases

C-61/80 Coöperatieve Stremsel- en Kleurselfabriek *v* Commission ECLI: EU:C:1981:75

C-96/82 IAZ International Belgium NV *v* Commission [1989] [1983] ECR – 3369

C-199/82 Amministrazione delle Finanze dello Stato *v* SpA San Giorgio ECR 1983 03595

C-74/14 Eturas and Others ECLI:EU:C:2016:42

C-7/95 P Deere (John) Ltd *v* Commission [1998] ECR I-3111

C-8/08 T-Mobile *v* Raad van bestuur van de Nederlandse Mededinging-sautoriteit [2009] ECR I-4529

C-12/03 P Commission of the European Communities *v* Tetra Laval BV ECR [2005] I-987

C-14/83 Von Colson and Kamann *v* Land Nordrhein-Westfalen [1984] ECR 1891

C-22/71 Béguelin Import *v* GL Import Export [1971] ECR 00949

C-35/09 Speranza [2010] ECR I-6581

C-55/06 Arcor [2008] ECR I-2931

C-56/65 Société Technique Minière *v* Maschinenbau Ulm GmbH [1966] ECR 235

C-73/95 P Viho Europe BV *v* Commission of the European Communities [1996] ECR I-5457

C-94/00 Roquette Frères SA *v* Directeur général de la concurrence, de la consommation et de la répression des fraudes, and Commission of the European Communities [2002] ECR I-09011

C-94/10 Danfoss A/S and Sauer-Danfoss ApS *v* Skatteministeriet ECR I-09963

C-97/08 P Akzo Nobel and Others *v* Commission [2009] ECR I-08237

C-105/04 P Nederlandse Federatieve Vereniging voor de Groothandel op Elektrotechnisch Gebied (FEG) *v* Commission, ECLI:EU:C:2005:751

C-128/92 H J Banks & Co Ltd *v* British Coal Corporation [1994] ECR I-01209

C-147/83 Münchener Import-Weinkellerei Herold Binderer GmbH *v* Commission of the European Communities [1985] ECR 257

C-199/11 Europese Gemeenschap *v* Otis NV and Others [2012] ECLI:EU: C:2012:684

C-205/03 P – FENIN *v* Commission [2006] I–06295

C-222/86 UNECTEF *v* Heylens [1987] ECR 4097

C-224/02 Pusa [2004] ECR I-5763

C-228/98 Dounias [2000] ECR I-577

C-234/89 Stergios Delimitis *v* Henninger Bräu AG [1991] ECR I-935

C-250/92 DLG [1994] ECR 1-5641

C-250/92 Gøttrup-Klim [1994] ECR I-564

Table of Cases

C-271/91 Marshall *v* Southampton and South West Area Health Authority II [1993] ECR I-4367

C-398/09 Lady & Kid A/S and Others *v* Skatteministeriet ECR I-07375

C-440/12 Metropol Spielstätten Unternehmergesellschaft (haftungsbeschränkt) *v* Finanzamt Hamburg-Bergedorf not yet published

C-453/99 Courage Ltd *v* Bernard Crehan and Bernard Crehan v Courage Ltd and Others [2001] ECR I-06297

C-470/03 AGM-COSMET Srl *v* Suomen valtio ECR I-2749

C-472/00 Commission *v* Fresh Marine Company A/S [2003] ECR 7541

C-526/04 Laboratoires Boiron [2006] ECR I-7259

C-526/04 Laboratoires Boiron [2006] ECR I-7259

C-536/11 Donau Chemie and Others [2013] ECLI:EU:C:2013:366

C-557/12 Kone AG and Others *v* ÖBB-Infrastruktur AG, 5 June 2014 ECLI: EU:C:2014:1317

C-681/11Bundeswettbewerbsbehörde, Bundeskartellanwalt *v* Schenker & Co and Others ECLI:EU:C:2013:404

C-332/11 ProRail BV *v* Xpedys NV and Others EU:C:2013:87

Commission Decision Carbonless Paper Cartel [2001] OJ L 115, 21.04.2004

Commission Decision Case COMP/36545/F3 – Amino Acids OJ L 152, 762001, p 24–72

Commission Decision Choline Chloride Case COMP/E-2/37533, 9122004

Commission decision Kali and Salz, MdK, Treuhand 14 December 1993, Case IV/M308 [1994] OJ L 316/1

Continental Ore Co *v* Union Carbide & Carbon Corp 370 US 690

Conwood Co *v* US Tobacco Co, 290 F3d 768

European Commission Case COMP/F/38638 29 November 2006 – Butadiene Rubber and Emulsion Styrene Butadiene Rubber

Joined Cases C-5/66, 7/66 and 13/66 to 24/66 Kampffmeyer *v* Commission ECR 245

Joined Cases C-64 and 113/76, 167, and 239/78, 27–28 and 45/79 Dumortier Frères *v* Commission [1979] ECR 3091

Joined Cases C-6/90 and C-9/90, Andrea Francovich and Danila Bonifaci and Others *v* Italian Republic [1991] ECR 5357

Joined Cases C-46/93 and C-48/93 Brasserie du Pêcheur SA *v* Bundesrepublik Deutschland and The Queen *v* Secretary of State for Transport, ex parte: Factortame Ltd and Others [1996] ECR I-01029

Joined Cases C-104/89 and C-37/90 Mulder *v* Council and Commission ECR I-3061

Joined Cases C-204/00 P, C-205/00 P, C-211/00 P, C-213/00 P, C-217/00 P and C-219/00 P Aalborg Portland and Others *v* Commission ECLI:EU: C:2004:6

xiv *Table of Cases*

Joined Cases C-295/04 to C-298/04 Vincenzo Manfredi *v* Lloyd Adriatico Assicurazioni SpA [2006] ECR I-6619
Lundkvist *v* Sweden (dec), no 48518/99 ECHR 2003-XI
Opinion of Advocate General Jääskinen in Case C-536/11 Bundeswettbewerbsbehörde *v* Donau Chemie AG and Others ECLI:EU:C:2013:67
Opinion of Advocate General Jääskinen in Case C-559/12 P French Republic *v* Commission ECLI:EU:C:2013:766
Opinion of Advocate General Kokott Case C-557/12 Kone AG and Others *v* ÖBB-Infrastruktur AG ECLI:EU:C:2014:45
Opinion of AG Kokott, Case C-105/04 P Nederlandse Federatieve Vereniging voor de Groothandel op Elektrotechnisch Gebied (FEG) *v* Commission ECLI:EU:C:2005:751
Opinion of Mr Van Gerven Case C-128/92 ECR I-01209
Ringvold *v* Norway, no 34964/97, ECHR 2003-II
T-24/93 Compagnie Maritime Belge Transports and Others *v* Commission
T-112/07 Hitachi Ltd, Hitachi Europe Ltd and Japan AE Power Systems Corp *v* European Commission II-03871
T-461/07 Visa Europe and Visa International Service *v* Commission [2013] ECR II-01729
T-11/89 Shell International Chemical Company *v* Commission [1992] ECR II-757
T-44/02 Dresdner Bank AG and Others *v* Commission of the European Communities II-3567
T-67/00, JFE Engineering *v* Commission ECLI:EU:T:2004:221
T-193/02 Piau *v* Commission [2005] ECR II-209
T-201/04 Microsoft Corp *v* Commission, ECR [2007] II-3601
T-216/13 Telefónica *v* Commission, ECLI:EU:T:2016:369
T-286/09 Intel *v* Commission [2014] ECLI:EU:T:2014:547
T-328/03 O2 (Germany) GbmH & Co OHG *v* Commission (2006) ECR II-1231
T-478/93 Wafer Zoo *v* Commission ECR II-1479

England

AB & Ors *v* British Coal Corporation & Anor [2004] EWHC 1372 (QB)
Allied Maples Group Ltd *v* Simmons & Simmons [1995] 1 WLR 1602
Allied Maples Group Ltd *v* Simmons & Simmons [1995] EWCA Civ 17
Alphacell Ltd *v* Woodward [1972] UKHL 4
Arkin *v* Borchard Lines Ltd & Ors [2003] EWHC 687 (Comm)
Arkin *v* Borchard Lines Ltd & Ors [2005] EWCA Civ 655
Attheraces Ltd & Anor *v* British Horse Racing Board & Anor [2005] EWHC 3015 (Ch)

Table of Cases

Baker *v* Willoughby [1969] UKHL 8, [1969] 3 All ER 1528
Barker *v* Corus (UK) Plc [2006] UKHL 20
Barnett *v* Chelsea & Kensington Hospital Management Committee [1968] 1 All ER 1068
BCL Old Co Ltd & Ors *v* BASF SE & Ors [2008] 24 (CAT)
Bookmakers Afternoon Greyhound Services Ltd *v* Amalgamated Racing Ltd [2009] EWCA Civ 750
Bradford *v* Robinson Rentals Ltd [1967] 1 All ER 267
Caswell *v* Powell Duffryn Associated Collieries [1940] AC 152, 165
CAT JJB Sports Plc *v* Office of Fair Trading, 17 [2005] Comp. A.R. 29
Chaplin *v* Hicks [1911] 2 KB 786, CA
Cooper Tire & Rubber Co & Ors *v* Shell Chemicals UK Ltd & Ors [2009] EWHC 2609 (Comm)
Cooper Tire & Rubber Company Europe Limited *v* Dow Deutschland Inc [2010] EWCA Civ 864
Corr *v* IBC Vehicles Ltd [2008] UKHL 13 (UKHL [2008])
Crehan *v* Inntrepreneur Pub Company CPC [2004] EWCA Civ 637
Devenish Nutrition Ltd *v* Sanofi-Aventis SA [2008] EWCA Civ 1086
DHN Food Distributors *v* London Borough of Tower Hamlets [1976] 3 All ER 852
Doughty *v* Turner Manufacturing Company [1964] 1 QB 518
Emerald Supplies Ltd & Anor *v* British Airways Plc [2010] EWCA Civ 1284
Emerson Electric Co & Ors *v* Mersen UK Portslade Ltd & Anor [2012] EWCA Civ 155
English Welsh & Scottish Railway Ltd *v* Enron Coal Services Ltd [2009] EWCA Civ 647
Enron Coal Services Ltd (In Liquidation) *v* English Welsh & Scottish Railway Ltd [2011] EWCA Civ 2
Enron Coal Services *v* English Welsh and Scottish Railways [2003] EWHC 687
Fairchild *v* Glenhaven Funeral Services Ltd [2002] UKHL 22
Fulton Shipping Inc of Panama *v* Globalia Business Travel SAU of Spain [2014] EWHC 1547
Gabriel *v* Kirklees Metropolitan Council [2004] EWCA Civ 345
Garden Cottage Foods Limited *v* Milk Marketing Board [1984] AC 130
Gregg *v* Scott [2005] UKHL 2
H & Ors (minors), Re [1995] UKHL 16
Healthcare at Home *v* Genzyme Ltd [2006] CAT 29
Hedley Byrne *v* Heller [1964] AC 465
Holtby *v* Brigham & Cowan (Hull) Ltd [2000] 3 All ER 421
Hotson *v* East Berkshire Area Health Authority [1988] UKHL 1, [1987] AC 750

xvi *Table of Cases*

Hughes *v* Lord Advocate [1963] AC 837
Inntrepreneur Pub Company (CPC) and others *v* Crehan [2006] UKHL 38
Jayasena *v* R [1970] AC 618, 623
JJB Sports Plc *v* Office of Fair Trading [2004] CAT 17, [2005] Comp AR 29
Jobling *v* Associated Dairies Ltd [1981] UKHL 3
Liyama (UK) Ltd *v* Samsung Electronics Co Ltd Court of Appeal (Civil Division) [2018] 4 CMLR 23
Mallett *v* McMonagle [1970] AC 166
McGhee *v* National Coal Board [1972] UKHL 7
Miller *v* Minister of Pensions [1947] 2 ALL ER
Napp Pharmaceuticals Holdings Ltd *v* Director General of Fair Trading [2002] CAT 1
Overseas Tankship (UK) Ltd *v* Morts Dock & Engineering Company Ltd [1961] UKPC 2
Overseas Tankship (UK) Ltd *v* The Miller Steamship Co Pty (The Wagon Mound No2) [1966] UKPC 10
Provimi Ltd *v* Roche UK [2003] EWHC 961 (Comm)
Re Polemis and Furness, Withy & Co [1921] 3 KB 560
Roche Products Ltd & Ors *v* Provimi Ltd [2003] EWHC 961 (COMM)
Sainsbury's Supermarkets Ltd *v* MasterCard Incorporated and Others [2016] CAT 11
Sienkiewicz *v* Greif (UK) Ltd [2009] EWCA Civ 1159 (EWCA (Civ))
Smith *v* Leech Brain & Co [1962] 2 QB 405
Vattenfall AB *v* Prysmian SpA [2018] EWHC 1694 (Ch)
WH Newson Holding Ltd & Ors *v* IMI Plc & Ors [2013] EWCA Civ 1377 (EWCA (Civ))
2 Travel Group PLC (in liquidation) *v* Cardiff City Transport Services Ltd [2012] CAT 19 CAT

Germany

BGH 15.6.1993, XI ZR 111/92, NJW 1993, 3073
BGH 28.6.2011, KZR 75/10 NJW 2012, 928
BGH 8.6.2010, KZR 45/09
BGH NJW 2004, 777; BGH NJW 2008, 1381
BGH, 04.11.2003, KZR 2/02 GRUR 2004, 351
BGH, 12.05.1998, KZR 23/96 NJW-RR 1999, 189
BGH, 12.7.2016, KZR 25/14, NZKart 2016, Lottoblock II
BGH, 17.2.1970, 53 BGHZ 245
BGH, 17.6.1998, XII ZR 206/95, WM 1998, 1787
BGH, 24.06.1965, KZR 7/64 1965 BHGZ 44, 279

Table of Cases

BGH, 25.01.1983, KZR 12/81 NJW 1984, 2819
BGH, 6.7.1993, VI ZR 228/92 , NJW 1993, 2673
BGH, 8.10.2008 XII ZR 84/06 NJW 2008, 3772
BGH 06.11.2012, II ZR 111/12.
Bundeskartellamt, 23.08.2006, B10–148/05.
KG 1.10.2009, 2 U 10/03 Kart NZG 2010, 420
KG Berlin, 01.10.2009, 2 U 17/03 Kart
LG Berlin, 27.06.2003, 102 O 155/02 Kart
LG Dortmund 01.04.2004, 13 O 55/02 KartWuW/E DE-R, 1352
LG Dusseldorf, 9 April 2014, VI-U (Kart) 10/12
LG Mainz, 15.1.2004, 12 HKO 52/02 Kart NJW-RR 2004, 478
LG Mannheim 22 O 74/04 Kart EWiR 2005, 659
LG Mannheim 11.7.2003, 7 O 326/02 GRUR 2004, 182
LG Mannheim 29.4.2005, 22 O 74/04 Kart EWiR 659
LG Stuttgart, 6.6.2019, 30 O 38/17
OLG (Higher Regional Court) Karlsruhe 6 U 118/05 (Kart) 21
OLG Dortmund WuW/E DE-R 1352
OLG Düsseldorf 9.4.2014, VI-U (Kart) 10/12
OLG Karlsruhe 11 June 2010, 6-U 118/05 (Kart)
OLG Karlsruhe 11062010, 6-U 118/05 Kart
OLG Karlsruhe 2812004, 6 U 183/03 NJW 2004, 2243
OLG Stuttgart, 22.05.1998, 2 U 223/97 NZV 1999, 169
OLG Wien, 14 December 2007 Az. 25 Kt 12/07

France

Cour d'Appel Paris, SNC Doux Aliments Bretagne etc *v* SAS Ajinamoto Eurolysine, 27 February 2014 no 07/10478
Cour d'Appel Paris, M Merhi Bassam *v* SNC Société Presse Paris Services – SPPS, 27 April 2011, no 08/21750
Cour d'Appel Paris, JCB Ltd *v* Central Parts, 26 June 2013, no 1204441
Cour d'Appel Versailles, SA Concurrence *v* SA Aiwa France, 9 December 2003, no 01/08413
Cour d'Appel Versailles, SA Verimedia *v* SA Mediametria SA Secodip Gie Audipub, no 2002 07434, 24 June 2004
Cour de Cassation civ., 24 September 20091, 2492009, Bull I, no 187, D 2010, 49, note P B, Revue trimestrielle de droit civil (RTD Civ) 2010, 111
Cour de Cassation comm., 18 April 2000, no 97-22604
Cour de Cassation comm., 15 February 2011, no 09-16779
Cour de Cassation comm., 15 February 2011, no 10-11614
Cour de Cassation comm., 15 June 2010, no 09-15816

xviii   *Table of Cases*

Cour de cassation comm., 15 September 2009, no 08-14398
Cour de Cassation comm. Ajinomoto Eurolysine *v* SNC Doux Aliment
  Bretagne and Others 15 June 2010, no 09/15816
Cour de Cassation, JCB Services et al. *v* Central Parks, 6 October 2015,
  no 13-24854
Cour de Cassation Le Gouessant 15 May 2012, no 11-18495
Cour de Cassation Orange *v* Cowes, 25 March 2014, no 1313839
Tribunal de Commerce Nanterre SA Les Laboratoires Pharmaceutiques
  Arkopharma *v* Ste Roche etc, 11 May 2006, no 02004F02643
Tribunal de Commerce Paris Eco System/Peugeot, 22 October 1996, not
  published
Tribunal de Commerce Paris, Société les Laboratoires Juva Production v
  SAS Roche, 10 September 2003, no RG2003048044

Italy

Autorità Garante della Concorrenza e del Mercato, 16 November 2004,
  A351 no 13752
Autorità Garante della Concorrenza e del Mercato, 28 July 2000, no
  8546 I377
Cassazione civile sez II, 1 December 2000, no 15385
Corte Costituzionale, 21 April 2000 no 114
Corte d'Appello Cagliari, Unimare S.r.l *v* Geasar S.p.a, 23 January 1999, in
  Giur it 2000, 346
Corte d'Appello Milan, Telecom Italia SpA *v* Brennercom SpA, 2 January
  2017 no 1/2017
Corte d'Appello Turin, Indaba Incentive co *v* società Juventus FC S.pA,
  6 July 2000, in Danno e Resp. 2001
Corte di Cassazione civ, Telecom *v* Sign and Others, 16 May 2007, no 11312
Corte di Cassazione, 1 December 2000, no 15385
Corte di Cassazione, 10 October 2001, no 13533
Corte di Cassazione, 14 May 2006, no 11755/2006
Corte di Cassazione, 16 January 2009, no 975, in Giustizia Civile
  Massimario, 2009, 68
Corte di Cassazione, 16 October 2007, no 21619, in Danno e Responsabilità,
  2008, 1, 43 note by R Pucella
Corte di Cassazione, 18 April 2005, no 7997/2005
Corte di Cassazione, 18 July 1987, no 6325, in Massimario Giuridico
  italiano 1987, 54
Corte di Cassazione, 21 July 2011, no 15991, in Giustizia Civile Massimario,
  2011, 1098
Corte di Cassazione, 22 September 2011 no 19262

Table of Cases

Corte di Cassazione, 23 December 2010, no 26042 (rv 615614), in CED Cassazione
Corte di Cassazione, 27 April 2010, no 10060/2010
Corte di Cassazione, 28 May 2014, no 11904/2014, in Foro it, 2014, I, 1729
Corte di Cassazione, 3 June 1980, no 3622, in Massiamario Giustizia civile 1980, 6
Corte di Cassazione, 4 June 2015, no 11564 /2015
Corte di Cassazione, 9 April 1963, no 910, in Giuriprudenza italiana, I 490
Corte di Cassazione, Allianz v Tagliaferro, 26 May 2011, no 11610, in Giust civ Mass 2011, 5, 808
Corte di Cassazione, Blasi v Az. Cons. Trasp. Pubbl. Napoli, 22 April 1993, no 4725, in Giust civ Mass 1993, 720
Corte di Cassazione, Fonsai v Nigriello, 2 February 2007, no 2305, in Foro it., I, 2007
Corte di Cassazione, Montani et al v Lloyd Adriatico, 25 September 1998, no 9598, in Studium Juris 1999, 81 Danno e resp 1999, 534
Corte di Cassazione, s.u., 11 January 2008, no 581, in Danno e resp, 2009, 667
Corte di Cassazione, Sara Assicurazioni v GV, 30 May 2013, n 13667
Corte di Cassazione, Sez Un, 4 February 2005, no 2207, in Riv dir proc, 2006, I, 375
Corte di Cassazione, Pen., Sez. Un., 11.09.2002, n 30328
Tribunale Milan, Brennercom Spa v Telecom Italia Spa, 27122013 no 22423/2010
Tribunale Milan, Brennercom Spa v Telecom Italia Spa, 332014 no 14802/2011
Tribunale Milan, OK Com Spa v Telecom Italia SpA, 13 February 2013, RG 76568/2008
Tribunale Milan, Teleunit Spa v Vodafone Omnitel Spa, no 75623/2008

United States

Brunswick Corp v Pueblo Bowl-O-Mat, Inc 429 US 477 (1977)
City of Long Beach v Standard Oil Co of California 872 F2d 1401
Costner v Blount National Bank n52 578 F2d 1192
District Court of Columbia, In Re: Vitamins Antitrust Litigation, (2001) Lexis 12114; 2001-2 Trade Cas (CCH) P73, 339
Ferebee v Chevron Chemical Company 21 ERC 1688, 237 USAppDC 164, 14 (1983) F2d 1529
Gatt Communications, Inc v PMC Associates LLC 711 F3d 68, 76 (2d Cir 2013)
Geneva Pharmaceuticals Tech v Barr Laboratories 201 F Supp 2d 236 (SDNY 2002)

xx *Table of Cases*

Geneva Pharmaceuticals Technology Corp *v* Barr Laboratories, Inc et al 98 CIV 961 RWS, 99 CIV 3607 RWS

Hanover Shoe, Inc *v* United Shoe Machinery Corp 392 US 481 (1968)

Hayes *v* Solomon 597 F2d 958, 978

Illinois Brick Co *v* Illinois, 431 US 720 (1977)

In re Methyl Tertiary Butyl Ether (MTBE) Products Liability Litigation (2010) 739 F. Supp. 2d 576 (SDNY)

Lohrmann *v* Pittsburgh Corning Corp Gaf Ac S & Hk 782 F 2d 1156

McClure *v* Undersea In dus, Inc, 671 F2d 1287, 1289

Nat'l Indep Theatre Exhibitors, Inc *v* Buena Vista Distrib Co, 748 F2d 602

Rambus Inc *v* FTC 522 F3d 456

Sindell *v* Abbott Laboratories 26 Cal 3d 588; 2 ALR (4th) 1061; 163 Cal Rptr 132; 607 P 2d 924 (Cal, 1980)

Tele Atlas NV *v* NAVTEQ Corp, No C-05-01673, 2008 WL 4809441

United States *v* Microsoft 253 F3d 34

US District Court, SD New York, Gross *v* New Balance Athletic Shoe, 11 February 11, 1997, Inc n 96 CIV 4921 (RWS), MDL-1154

Watson Laidlaw & Co Ltd *v* Pott, Cassells and Williamson 31 RPC 104

Zenith Radio Corp *v* Hazeltine Research, Inc 395 US 100

Introduction

Competition law infringements may cause economic losses which are protected by EU and national laws. Liability for compensation of private damages in EU competition law is the result of the judicial interpretation of Articles 101 and 102 TFEU. The Court of Justice of the European Union (CJEU), with the two seminal cases *Courage*[1] and *Manfredi*,[2] introduced the principle of right to compensation for violation of competition law, stating that 'any individual can claim compensation for the harm suffered where there is a causal relationship between that harm and an agreement or practice prohibited'.[3] Article 3 of Directive 104/2014 (the 'Damages Directive') on competition damages actions has then imposed the transposition of this principle into national laws.[4]

The compensatory principle is based on a corrective justice regime whereby the duty to repair the damage burdens only the subjects that have caused it. A fundamental element of responsibility for such harms is causation, as it attributes responsibility to a specific person for a specific harm. An antitrust infringement restricts or distorts competition in a relevant market, and it potentially may affect all individuals active in the same market. Direct purchasers may claim the disgorgement of overcharges paid and indirect purchasers the compensation of the overcharge passed through the supply chain, while competitors aggrieved by exclusionary conducts may claim compensation for market foreclosure and lost chances, to mention just a few. The consumers or undertakings who see their assets

---

[1] Case C-453/99 *Courage Ltd v Bernard Crehan* and *Bernard Crehan v Courage Ltd and Others* ECR I-06297.

[2] Joined Cases C-295/04 to C-298/04 *Vincenzo Manfredi v Lloyd Adriatico Assicurazioni SpA* [2006] ECR I-06619.

[3] Ibid., para 61.

[4] Directive 2014/104/EU of the European Parliament and of the Council of 26 November 2014 on Certain Rules Governing Actions for Damages under National Law for Infringements of the Competition Law Provisions of the Member States and of the European Union, OJ L 349 2014.

diminished in value would base their claims on a loss of welfare caused by the antitrust infringement. Accordingly, they will have to prove that the economic loss was caused by the antitrust infringement and not by other contextual market factors. The problem of causation in domestic laws has a long and diverse history that shaped different approaches in the legal doctrines of the European member states. Hence, national courts tend to assess the causal link adopting different standards and approaches.

The European Union law, however, provides little guidance to the judge in the assessment of the causal connection. The CJEU's decisions together with the Damages Directive confer the right to stand to any individual harmed by the infringement but do not deal with the instantiation of causation. It follows that, in accordance with Article 3, Regulation 1/2003, national courts have to apply their domestic laws of obligations within the limits drawn by the principles of effectiveness and equivalence. The claimant in actions for damages has, therefore, to prove the breach of law, the damage and the causal connection between the two, mainly relying on the applicable national laws of substance and procedure.

The analysis of antitrust litigation in Europe reveals that only a minority of cases are based on claims for compensation of damages. Of these cases, a very small proportion is initiated by indirect purchasers or subjects aggrieved by dead-weight losses. The common thread connecting these situations is the causal uncertainty of the claim that makes the assessment of liability particularly complex. Surprisingly, both scholars and the Damages Directive have devoted little attention to the study of the causal connection between the infringement of competition law and the damage.[5]

This book first addresses the concept of causation in claims for damages for infringement of competition law, discussing the main and more relevant approaches in tort law theory (Chapter 1). Therefore, it discusses the different approaches for the assessment of causation in competition law in national courts (Chapter 2). It then describes and critically analyzes the approach to causation adopted by EU law and courts (Chapter 3). In the fourth chapter, the book delves into the fundamental issues of causal uncertainty in competition law damages actions (Chapter 4), to which follows the analysis of the standards of proof for causation (Chapter 5). It then focuses on particular cases of causal uncertainty that may justify the relaxation of proof rules in competition law (Chapter 6). Finally, it explores the causal proof requirements for indirect and secondary antitrust damages (Chapter 7). A conclusion follows.

---

[5] See Ioannis Lianos, 'Causal Uncertainty and Damages Claims for the Infringement of Competition Law in Europe' [2015] 34 *Yearbook of European Law* 170, and Hanns A Abele, Georg E Kodek and Guido K Schaefer, 'Proving Causation in Private Antitrust Cases' [2011] 7 *Journal of Competition Law and Economics* 847.

1

Causation in Competition Law

A competition law infringement may cause economic harm simultaneously to several market participants. Economic harms may indeed flow from an antitrust infringement in the form of price overcharges or other economic loss – for instance, lost profits or lost chances. Tort laws generally establish the liability of the infringer through the principle of corrective justice, based on which the wrongdoer has a duty to repair only the wrongful losses that their conduct has caused. Along these lines, the principle of corrective justice dispenses a general rule whereby a person harmed by a tort must be able to recover damages to restore the same situation, at least from an economic perspective, existing before the breach.[1] The tortfeasor will be condemned, when possible, to the *restitutio ad integrum* or, alternatively, to pay a financial reparation that restores in its economic equivalent the situation existing before the breach.[2] To obtain the compensation of damages, the claimant has to substantiate the infringement, the prejudice suffered and the causal connection between the two.[3]

---

[1]   Ernest Joseph Weinrib, *Corrective Justice* (Oxford University Press, 2012) 17; Allan Beever, *Rediscovering the Law of Negligence* (Hart, 2009) 45 ff; Simon Deakin, Angus Johnston, and Basil Markesinis, *Markesinis and Deakin's Tort Law* (Oxford University Press, 2012) 38.

[2]   This principle was, for example, reiterated in *Devenish Nutrition v Sanofi Aventis* [2007] EWHC 2394, where the court stated that compensation has to 'place a person who has suffered harm in the position in which that person would have been had the infringement of competition law not been committed'.

[3]   For a comparative overview of causation in European tort laws, see Cees Van Dam, *European Tort Law* (Oxford University Press, 2013) 308 ff; Marta Infantino and Eleni Zervogianni, *Causation in European Tort Law* (Cambridge University Press, 2017); Christian von Bar, *The Common European Law of Torts*, vol II (Oxford University Press, 2000) 433–498; Isabel C Durant, 'Causation' in Helmut Koziol and Reiner Schulze (eds), *Tort Law of the European Community* (Springer, 2010).

4 *Causation in Competition Law*

The European Union law grants the right to claim for damages to anyone harmed by an antitrust infringement, be they consumers, undertakings or public authorities.[4] This is the legacy of the *Courage*[5] and *Manfredi*[6] cases and also the text of the Directive 104/2014.[7] However, this should not be considered a rule setting unlimited responsibility on antitrust infringers. The claimant, in each specific instance, has to prove the 'causal relationship between the harm suffered and the prohibited arrangement'.[8] It is, indeed, through the filter of causation that national courts establish the responsibility of the wrongdoer and select the damages that are compensated for the infringement of EU competition law. Despite this, scholars have generally focused on the right to stand and the quantification of damages rather than causation.[9] The 2014 Damages Directive solved, once and for all, the doubts regarding the right to stand, according it to any legal or natural person who has suffered harm caused by a violation of competition law. However, the Directive avoids dealing with causation and leaves its definition to the laws of obligation of the member states. On the other hand, competition law damages actions show a marked causal uncertainty. In this vein, the impact study ordered by the European Commission in 2007 pointed out that 'it seems that the success of a claim in the EU would be dependent on whether the plaintiff is actually able to prove causation'.[10] Despite this, causation in competition law litigation continues to be one of the most underexplored topics on both sides of the Atlantic.[11] From this comes the need to identify a proper theory of causation and

---

[4] Article 1 Directive 2014/104/EU of the European Parliament and of the Council of 26 November 2014 on Certain Rules Governing Actions for Damages under National Law for Infringements of the Competition Law Provisions of the Member States and of the European Union, OJ L 349; Joined Cases C-295/04 to C-298/04 *Vincenzo Manfredi v Lloyd Adriatico Assicurazioni SpA* [2006] ECR I-6619.

[5] Case C-453/99 *Courage Ltd v Bernard Crehan* and *Bernard Crehan v Courage Ltd and Others* [2001] ECR I-06297.

[6] Joined Cases C-295/04 to C-298/04 *Vincenzo Manfredi*.

[7] *Directive* 2014/104/EU.

[8] Joined Cases C-295/04 to C-298/04 *Manfredi v Lloyd*, para 17.

[9] Ever since the adoption of Regulation 1/2003, academic research has tried to analyze and define such requirements. Scholars have tried to explain the proof of the antitrust infringement to smooth the hurdles for the quantification of the damages and to proposed solutions to several procedural rules. The quantification of damages may become particularly complex in antitrust litigation because of the deep use of econometrics and economic theories. However, judges generally have the power to estimate the amount of damages, therefore avoiding their precise calculation.

[10] Andrea Renda, Roger J van den Bergh and Roberto Pardolesi, 'Making Antitrust Damages Actions More Effective in the EU: Welfare Impact and Potential Scenarios: Final Report' (2007) Contract DG COMP/2006/A3/012 36, available at http://ec.europa.eu/competition/antitrust/actionsdamages/files_white_paper/impact_study.pdf.

[11] See, in the United States, Michael A. Carrier, 'A Tort-Based Causation Framework for Antitrust Analysis', [20011] 77 *Antitrust Law Journal* 991; similarly observe, for the EU, Ioannis Lianos, 'Causal Uncertainty and Damages Claims for the Infringement of Competition Law in Europe' [2015] 34 *Yearbook of European Law* 170, 172.

coherent rules for the proof of causation in antitrust litigation.[12] European jurisdictions apply the general rules on non-contractual liability to the illicit antitrust behaviour.[13] However, damages for infringements of competition law have shown peculiarities which distinguish them from other torts. Antitrust infringements often impact on sophisticated supply chains active in complex market structures,[14] which make the establishment of causative links difficult. Moreover, national laws of obligations have to be interpreted in accordance with the EU law that they trigger (i.e., duty of consistent interpretation),[15] whereby one has to determine if the EU law has developed any independent concept or interpretative canon.

1.1 CAUSATION: A PRIMER

1.1.1 *The Function of Causation*

The law continuously applies causal ideas to establish connections between events. Causal ideas are embodied in the language of the legislation and are an integral part of the reasoning of judicial decisions to attribute responsibility for wrongful conducts.[16] They are, in other words, the backbone of corrective justice.[17] According to the principle of corrective justice, the tort law system provides remedies that apply when a person's wrongful conduct interferes with another person's rights and property.[18] The aim of corrective justice is indeed to restore the position of the victim before the wrong took place. Thus, this criterion places responsibility upon the injurer as both a moral and a legal duty to compensate.[19] And it does so by connecting the victim to the injurer,[20] as it burdens the injurer for compensating the victim, blaming the former for the harm caused to the latter. In other words, according to this principle, p has to compensate d if p has caused an economic harm to d, and the compensation has to be limited to the damage inflicted. The corrective justice criterion comprises first-order

---

[12] This is the observation made in one of the very few papers published on the topic: Hanns A Abele, Georg E Kodek and Guido K Schaefer, 'Proving Causation in Private Antitrust Cases' [2011] 7 *Journal of Competition Law and Economics* 847

[13] See further Chapter 2 and Section 5.6 for a comparative overview of the different approaches.

[14] David Ashton and David Henry, Competition Damages Actions in the EU: Law and Practice (Edward Elgar Publishing, 2013), 39.

[15] Damian Chalmers, Gareth Davies, and Giorgio Monti, European Union Law: Cases and Materials (Cambridge University Press, 2010), 296.

[16] For an analysis of how causal ideas are used in the law, see Michael S Moore, *Causation and Responsibility: An Essay in Law, Morals, and Metaphysics* (Oxford University Press, 2010).

[17] Tort laws also have a deterrent function; on this aspect, see Section 1.4.

[18] David Miller, 'Justice' in Edward N Zalta (ed), *The Stanford Encyclopedia of Philosophy*, Fall 2017 Edition. (Metaphysics Research Lab, Stanford University, 2017) https://plato.stanford.edu/archives/fall2017/entries/justice/, accessed 1 February 2019.

[19] Moore (n 16). Who observes that the principle of corrective justice mandates that 'legal liability tracks moral responsibility', at 4.

[20] Miller (n 18).

duties, which prohibits a conduct or inflicts an injury, and second-order duties, which impose an obligation to repair harm arising upon the breach of a first-order duty.[21] Between first and second order duties there is a causal link.

Causation has, therefore, the function of linking the victim to the tortfeasor. Let us assume that p allegedly harmed d while performing the action x. In order to place responsibility for the harm on p, the first causal question to solve will be if the harm (y) would have happened had p's action not occurred. Causation therefore attributes responsibility for the harm by linking two events (x and y) and attributing them to a person (d). But causation is also said to be able to predict a certain outcome on the basis of its preconditions. For this reason, it is common to ascribe three functions to causation, whereby causation is (1) forward looking, (2) backward looking and explanatory and (3) attributive.[22] According to the first function, causation studies the conditions that lead to certain results, allowing the formulation of predictions and thus fostering prevention.[23] This forward-looking quality is appreciated, for example, in policy analysis, philosophy and economics. The second function relates instead more closely to the language and reasoning of law. Here, causation serves to spot from a set of conditions the one that can explain an event or a class of events.[24] It explains the connection between two events – a harm and a prior action – that would otherwise be independent from each other. The third function is attributive and – together with the second – ascribes responsibility to a specific agent.[25]

1.1.2 *General Causation and Specific Causation*

When we refer to events, we mean either a general class of events or specific events.[26] By the same token, causation may be general, meaning that it considers an abstract event and its outcome, or specific, which asks whether outcome x was caused by action y.[27] General causation asks whether a type of action can produce an outcome. For instance, can a cartel on car parts cause an economic harm to final customers (car buyers)? The question is usually answered through causal associations between the alleged cause and the damage.[28] Often, in competition law, statistics and econometrics

---

[21] Jules Coleman, Scott Hershovitz and Gabriel Mendlow, 'Theories of the Common Law of Torts' in Edward N Zalta (ed), *The Stanford Encyclopedia of Philosophy*, Winter 2015 Edition (Metaphysics Research Lab, Stanford University, 2015) https://plato.stanford.edu/archives/win2015/entriesort-theories/, accessed 1 February 2019.

[22] Antony Honoré, 'Causation in the Law' in Edward N Zalta (ed), *The Stanford Encyclopedia of Philosophy*, Winter 2010 Edition (Metaphysics Research Lab, Stanford University, 2010), available at http://plato.stanford.edu/archives/win2010/entries/causation-law/, accessed 30 August 2014.

[23] Ibid.

[24] Ibid.

[25] Ibid.

[26] HLA Hart and Tony Honoré, *Causation in the Law* (Oxford University Press, 1985) 41 ff.

[27] For an analysis of general and specific causation, see John Leslie Mackie, *The Cement of the Universe: A Study of Causation* (Clarendon Press, 1980) 29 ff.

[28] Lara Khoury, *Uncertain Causation in Medical Liability* (Bloomsbury Publishing, 2006) 50.

1.2 Theories of Causation

establish the link between the abstract action (a cartel) and a general consequence (economic damage). On the other hand, specific causation asks whether action x caused harm y. Did the cartel on car parts x cause the economic harm to the consumer-claimant y? In this case, it is indispensable to establish a factual and legal connection between the action and the damage on a specific occasion.[29]

Judges take their decisions according to specific causation, in theory. What matters for the attribution of liability is whether the defendant's action caused the actual damage, not if potentially it is able to do so. However, the role of general causation is to provide an important part of the evidence for specific causation. If the former is not possible, neither will be the latter. By the same token, in order for the latter to be possible, the former also has to be proven when this is not already of common knowledge.[30] Disputes over general and specific causation hence arise in case of causal uncertainty, which is when it is unclear whether a class of events can cause a certain damage (uncertainty over general causation) and, by consequence, it is not possible or particularly difficult to prove that the defendant caused the claimed harm (uncertainty over specific causation). As it will be better explained in Chapter 4, competition damages actions often rely, to a large extent, on the proof of general causation to infer specific causation. The following chapter analyses the main theories of causation and their importance for competition law enforcement.

1.2 THEORIES OF CAUSATION

One can approach causation as a unitary topic from an epistemological point of view, for it defines the tools to establish connections between events.[31] But, as already remarked in philosophy, causation is 'one word [but] many things'.[32] Every field of knowledge engages – in a way or another – with establishing causality links between events. Philosophy, mathematics, physics, economics, medicine and the law are only some examples. In this vein, a meta approach to causation aims at the creation of general rules able to identify appropriate links for any relation of agency effect.[33] However, a link between a cause and its effect, drawn to the satisfaction of one of them, does not necessarily satisfy the requirements of the other. While exact sciences approach causation from a deterministic perspective, meaning that they seek full certainty about the relationship of cause and effect, for other areas of

---

[29] Sandy Steel, *Proof of Causation in Tort Law* (Cambridge University Press, 2015) 6.
[30] On proof of causation in competition damages actions, see Chapters 5 and 6.
[31] Helen Beebee, Christopher Hitchcock and Peter Menzies, *The Oxford Handbook of Causation* (Oxford University Press, 2009); Jon Williamson, 'Causal Pluralism versus Epistemic Causality' [2006] 77 *Philosophica-Gent* 69.
[32] Nancy Cartwright, 'Causation: One Word, Many Things' [2004] 71 *Philosophy of Science* 5 (2004) 805–820.
[33] Julian Reiss, 'Causation in the Social Sciences: Evidence, Inference, and Purpose' [2009] 39 *Philosophy of the Social Sciences* 1, 20–40.

8 *Causation in Competition Law*

knowledge, it suffices to establish a probable causal link.[34] That is because causal connections often follow irregular paths, and there is only limited knowledge allowing one to understand them. For example, science demonstrated that smoking is a cause of lung cancer, but some smokers do not develop this cancer.[35] By the same token, in competition law, exploitative conducts are supposed to cause economic harm to buyers or suppliers, but this harm does not always materialize. Causal uncertainty is therefore the result of limited information that the fact-finder often faces in the application of the law.[36] The impossibility of establishing perfectly regular patterns for causation in the law imposes to depart from fully deterministic approaches.[37] Moreover, the law is not only concerned with finding a factual connection between events; it also aims to establish responsibility for that harm. Causation in law additionally asks whether there is a legal link between the harm and the action, thus determining responsibility.

Causation in the law is a particularly elusive concept whose definition is influenced by the extent and importance of the other elements of the non-contractual obligation, in particular the tortious conduct and the harm. Question arises on whether a specific agency is cause of some other events, only their occasion, a mere condition or part of the circumstances in which the cause operated.[38] In this regard, Hart and Honoré asked if there is any principle governing the selection of the set of conditions of events or if it is arbitrary, irrational, the mere survival of the metaphysical beliefs in the superior 'potency' possessed by some events.[39] While causal uncertainty cannot be fully displaced, correct use of causation theories can help unravel the connections between infringements and their harmful effects. Without any pretention to be exhaustive, this chapter aims to present these theories and the approaches to causation that are particularly relevant for the analysis of antitrust infringements.

1.2.1 *Approaches to Causation*

Outside the law, two seminal approaches have founded the entire scientific and philosophical speculation on causation: the empirical method of Hume and the metaphysical forged by Kant.[40] Of them, only the former has become part of the

---

[34] Carl Hoefer, 'Causal Determinism' [2016] Stanford encyclopedia of philosophy https://plato.stanford.edu/entries/determinism-causal/.

[35] Christopher Hitchcock, 'Probabilistic Causation' in Edward N Zalta (ed), *The Stanford Encyclopedia of Philosophy*, Fall 2018 Edition (Metaphysics Research Lab, Stanford University, 2018), available at https://plato.stanford.edu/archives/fall2018/entries/causation-probabilistic/, accessed 4 February 2019.

[36] On the different sources of causal uncertainty, see also Steel (n 29) 5 ff.; Khoury (n 28) 5 ff.

[37] For a more in-depth analysis of determinism, probabilities and causation in competition law, see Chapter 5.

[38] HLA Hart and Tony Honoré, *Causation in the Law* (Oxford University Press, 1985) 112.

[39] Ibid., 17.

[40] Michael S Moore, *Causation and Responsibility: An Essay in Law, Morals, and Metaphysics* (Oxford University Press, 2010) 41 ff.

1.2 Theories of Causation

legal discourse.[41] For Hume, causation can only be established in terms of empirical regularities involving classes of events by calling 'to mind their constant conjunction in all past instances'.[42] John Stuart Mill further built on this elaboration of regularity theories expounding a system of inductive inferences for causal reasoning.[43] The subsequent philosophical and scientific doctrine developed on these bases a number of other theories and definitions – such as the counterfactual, for which it is a cause 'something that makes a difference, and *the* difference it makes must be a difference from what would have happened without it'.[44] In addition to this, scholars developed the statistical model,[45] the 'structural equation modelling'[46] and several others.[47] While these approaches differ in the means of research and the description of causation that they provide, they all have in common the research of an explanation of existing links between facts.

Put differently, the lawyer is not content with finding any factual connection between events, as only a legally relevant antecedent can determine the event and therefore become a cause of it.[48] Compared to other disciplines,[49] causation in law requires the analysis of only some of the circumstances of the case, which are relevant to determine the causal connection. As such, only some items of the event are legally relevant to the causation of the damage. For instance, in the case of a cartel, the fact that the tortfeasor sold the good subject to infringement to the claimant and that an overcharge was applied to the price are relevant aspects of the agency, while information about – for instance – the characteristics of the products may have no standing for establishing causation. Since Collingwood,[50]

---

[41] Despite the attempt to create comprehensive theories of causation explaining its function in order to attribute responsibility in history, law and other disciplines, lawyers have doubted that such definitions can be effective; see ibid., 90.

[42] In this well-known excerpt, Hume observed that 'Without further ceremony, we call the one cause and the other effect, and infer the existence of one from that of the other', David Hume, *A Treatise of Human Nature* (Clarendon Press, 1817), 87/61.

[43] The most diffuse canon advanced by Mill is the 'Direct Method of Difference' for which 'If an instance in which the phenomenon under investigation occurs, and an instance in which it does not occur, have every circumstance save one in common, that one occurring only in the former; the circumstance in which alone the two instances differ, is the effect, or cause, or a necessary part of the cause, of the phenomenon'. John Stuart Mill, *A System of Logic, Ratiocinative and Inductive: Being a Connected View of the Principles of Evidence and the Methods of Scientific Investigation* (Harper & Brothers, 1858), 455.

[44] David Lewis, 'Causation' [1973] 70(17) *The Journal of Philosophy* 556–567.

[45] See, in particular, the 'Neyman-Rubin Model': Donald B. Rubin, 'Causal Inference Using Potential Outcomes' [2005] 100 *Journal of the American Statistical Association* 469.

[46] Roy J Epstein, *A History of Econometrics* (North-Holland Amsterdam, 1987).

[47] John Losee, *Theories of Causality: From Antiquity to the Present* (Transaction Publishers, 2012).

[48] The fact that the widgets sold by the antitrust infringer were of red colour will rarely be of legal significance for the determination of causation in an antitrust action, despite being a factual aspect that may result relevant for other causal enquiries.

[49] Included economics that in competition law plays a fundamental role, see further Section 6.6.

[50] RG Collingwood, 'Causation in Practical Natural Science' [1937] 38 *Proceedings of the Aristotelian Society* 85.

the quest for a specific notion of causation related to legal responsibility has become independent. According to this view, the role of the legal theory of causation is to define the meaning of the word cause (and its several synonyms) in statutes, regulations and judicial decisions.[51]

The difficulty to define causation is exacerbated by the different legal traditions of civil and common law countries, which use different approaches to material and legal causation. This problem partly explains the reason for the adoption of a broad definition of causation in the Draft Common Frame of Reference (DCFR) on Principles, Definitions and Model Rules of European Private Law;[52] an only slightly more detailed definition in the Principles of European Tort Law (PETL);[53] and the refusal to define causation in the Damages Directive.

Despite the different legal backgrounds, both civil law and common law countries adopt a multistage inquiry approach to causation, whereby the judge establishes the existence of material causation between the events submitted to the court and their effects. In addition, the judge has to select the causes which are legally relevant for the causation of the harm,[54] delimiting the damages that the defendant is bound to compensate. To do so, however, it is fundamental to first determine the nature of the harm that has to be compensated. As the following chapter explains, the nature of antitrust harms has an important impact on the definition of the causal conditions and on causal uncertainty.

---

[51] Ibid.

[52] Article 4:101 'General rule (1) A person causes legally relevant damage to another if the damage is to be regarded as a consequence of that person's conduct or the source of danger for which that person is responsible. (2) In cases of personal injury or death the injured person's predisposition with respect to the type or extent of the injury sustained is to be disregarded'. Draft Common Frame of Reference (DCFR) on Principles, Definitions and Model Rules of European Private Law, available at http://ec.europa.eu/justice/policies/civil/docs/dcfr_out line_edition_en.pdf.

[53] Helmut Koziol and others, *Principles of European Tort Law (PETL): Text and Commentary* (Springer, 2005).

[54] For an introduction to the two-stage causation framework, see, among the others, Cees Van Dam (n 3) 310 ff, *European Tort Law* (Oxford University Press, 2013); Richard W Wright, 'Causation in Tort Law' [1985] 73 *California Law Review* 1735–1828; Håkan Andersson and Bénédict Winiger, *Digest of European Tort Law* (Springer, 2007) 1, 1; William Lloyd Prosser, *Prosser and Keeton on the Law of Torts* (West Pub. Co., 1984); Simon Deakin, Angus Johnston, and Basil Markesinis, *Markesinis and Deakin's Tort Law* (Oxford University Press, 2012); Fowler Vincent Harper, Fleming James, and Oscar S. Gray, *The Law of Torts* (Little, Brown, 1986); Robert E. Keeton, *Legal Cause in the Law of Torts* (University Microfilms, 1986); Walter Gerven, Jeremy Lever, and Pierre Larouche, *Tort Law* (Hart, 2000); Forschungsstelle für Europäisches Schadenersatzrecht Wien and Österreichische Akademie der Wissenschaften Forschungsstelle für Europäisches Schadenersatzrecht, *Digest of European Tort Law* (Springer, 2007); Jaap Spier, Francesco Donato Busnelli, and European Centre of Tort and Insurance Law, *Unification of Tort Law: Causation* (Kluwer Law International, 2000); Steven Shavell, 'An Analysis of Causation and the Scope of Liability in the Law of Torts' [1980] 9(3) *The Journal of Legal Studies* 463–516; William M. Landes and Richard A. Posner, 'Causation in Tort Law: An Economic Approach' [1983] 12(1) *The Journal of Legal Studies* 109–134.

1.3 NATURE AND CONDITIONS OF THE ANTITRUST HARM

An antitrust infringement causes a pure economic loss that the victim is entitled to recover – depending on the jurisdiction – on the basis of a statutorily protected interest[55] or a subjective right,[56] under EU law.[57] Here, two elements are particularly relevant to the analysis of causation: (1) the nature of the damage and (2) the legal basis for the claim.

1.3.1 *The Nature of the Antitrust Damage*

The antitrust damage is a pure economic loss, as it does not involve any harm to persons or property but only a financial loss flowing from the anticompetitive conduct of one or more undertakings. The tort law landscape is relatively new to including pure economic losses among the harms subject to compensation for the causal uncertainty that characterizes them.[58] Tort laws usually refer to the harm to a person or to tangible property and establish the compensation of the economic damages only when they are consequent upon the infliction of such harm. Hence, as a general idea, tort laws traditionally protect fundamental rights pertaining to the security of person and property.[59] Since Gaius, who first categorized legal obligations as contracts and wrongs, in the absence of a contractual relationship between the parties, a person has to compensate the damages inflicted on another person only when the former is in breach of a duty or obligation. And, for a long time, tort laws have exclusively referred to a duty to protect the property or the body of a person.[60] The twentieth-century economic analysis reinforced this idea by pointing

---

[55] This is in common law jurisdictions – more precisely – a sui generis statutorily protected interest; see infra, Section 2.1.

[56] Some of the civil law jurisdictions, such as France and Italy, prefer focusing on the violation of a subjective right, along the lines of the *Manfredi* and *Courage* cases.

[57] See infra Chapter 2.

[58] See, for instance, liability for misleading information in offering documents and other financial statements, whereby, in theory, anyone is entitled to sue for damages, provided that there is causal connection between the damage and the provision of misleading or false information in a prospectus. Despite this, EU countries have generally restricted the spectrum of possible claimants. So, for instance, in Germany, Italy and UK, only investors have the right to claim damages. ESMA, 'Comparison of Liability Regimes in Member States in Relation to the Prospectus Directive' (2013) 619 13, www.esma.europa.eu/document/comparison-liability-regimes-in-member-states-in-relation-prospectus-directive, accessed 19 October 2017.

[59] Coleman, Hershovitz and Mendlow (n 21).

[60] For an examination of pure economic losses and their evolution in the jurisprudence of different coutries, see Efstahios K Banakas, *Tortious Liability for Pure Economic Loss: A Comparative Study* (Hellenic Institute of International and Foreign Law, 1989); Vernon V Palmer and Mauro Bussani, *Pure Economic Loss: New Horizons in Comparative Law* (Taylor & Francis, 2009); Annual International Colloquium of the United Kingdom National Committee of Comparative Law and Efstahios K Banakas (eds), *Civil Liability for Pure Economic Loss: Proceedings of the Annual International Colloquium of the United Kingdom National*

out that tort law has the function of maximizing social welfare and that, in case of pure economic losses, markets should be the preferred institutions.[61] The answer to the question of their compensability – according to this scholarship – was that tort law should generally refrain from offering remedies against pure financial losses, as it would otherwise generate inefficient outcomes.[62] A bodily or property damage causes a social welfare loss that tort law should aim to remedy and deter.[63] If someone damages the property of a neighbour, there is no transfer of welfare but only a loss of welfare for society as a whole. From here, the need of imposing the compensation of the so-called social cost of accidents.[64] On the other hand, pure economic losses, in most cases, concern a redistribution of welfare among different persons. The economic loss of the harmed person usually enriches another person, therefore only shifting resources from one to the other.[65] Also for this reason, an ongoing debate discusses the recoverability of pure economic losses, with contrasting outcomes.[66]

Traditionally, pure economic losses were conceived as a *damnum sine iniura* (or a damage without wrongful act) and, therefore, not enforceable. During the last part of the twentieth century, however, this paradigm was questioned both in courts and in academia.[67] The detractors of the liability for pure economic losses mainly point out that property and assets are interconnected and that, therefore, economic losses are 'an inevitable incident of being active in the world'.[68] The conduct of a person in the market will most likely impact other persons operating in the same market – for instance, the builder who obstructs the entrance to a shop due to a fallen crane[69] or the auditor who misleads an investor who – finding the auditor's report which overestimates the value of a company – pays double the real value of the company's shares.[70] However, as pure economic losses became more

---

Committee of Comparative Law Held in Norwich, September 1994 (Kluwer Law International, 1996).

[61] Richard A Posner, 'Common-Law Economic Torts: An Economic and Legal Analysis' [2006] 48 *Arizona Law Review* 735.

[62] Ibid.

[63] William M Landes and Richard A Posner, 'The Positive Economic Theory of Tort Law' [1980] 15 *Georgia Law Review* 851, 868.

[64] Ibid.

[65] More similarly to what happens in an action of restitution for wrong, also called actions for unjust enrichment, which is not based on the violation of a duty of the tortfeasor but, rather, on a specific obligation to restore to an innocent party gains received unjustly.

[66] Banakas, *Tortious Liability for Pure Economic Loss* (n 60); Annual International Colloquium of the United Kingdom National Committee of Comparative Law and Banakas (n 60); Mauro Bussani and Vernon Valentine Palmer, *Pure Economic Loss in Europe* (Cambridge University Press, 2003); Palmer and Bussani (n 60).

[67] *Hedley Byrne v Heller* [1964] AC 465; Banakas, *Tortious Liability for Pure Economic Loss* (n 60).

[68] Peter Benson, 'The Basis for Excluding Liability for Economic Loss in Tort Law' in David G Owen (ed), *Philosophical Foundations of Tort Law* (Oxford University Press, 1995) 443.

[69] Posner (n 61) 736.

[70] Palmer and Bussani (n 60) 2.

1.3 Nature and Conditions of the Antitrust Harm

and more important in market economies, legislators in different jurisdictions introduced special statutes sanctioning the compensability of such financial harm.[71]

Among these rules, in the EU, we find those granting the right to claim antitrust damages. Competition law infringements cause a pure economic harm that – in the absence of special norms – would fail to be restored in many jurisdictions. Whereas there is no doubt about their compensability today, thanks to EU and domestic laws, the nature of this damage remains important for antitrust actions because it explains some of the difficulties in defining the liability criteria and in proving causation.[72] Pure economic losses taking place in the market show special characteristics of causal uncertainty.[73] Some elements, which will be analyzed in later chapters, include the unobservability of the cause of the event, which consists in a financial loss and not in a breaking or a smashing; the concurrence of multiple possible causes, as a company's losses may be caused by an antitrust infringement as well as by other market factors; and the indeterministic nature of economic processes, which are not controlled by law of physics, thus making it impossible to foresee with full certainty the state of the world in the future. Economics usually explains connections between events through counterfactuals,[74] whereby they create a hypothetical scenario in which an alleged cause x of a harm y did not occur. All these conditions together contribute to explain the causal uncertainty for pure economic losses and antitrust damages too.

Despite the many uncertainties regarding the responsibility for economic loss in tort, the cases of enforceable rights to compensation have multiplied, and antitrust damages actions are among them. However, while there is extensive guidance on how to define and prove anticompetitive conducts of any kind and how to reckon the damages, very little has been said on how to determine the causal connection between the two.

1.3.2 The Legal Basis for the Claim

The claimant's right to recover damages derives from the violation of an interest or a right protected under competition law. In *Manfredi*, the referring judge asked whether third parties having a relevant legal interest may rely on the invalidity of a prohibited agreement and claim damages. In replying positively, the ECJ observed that the principle of invalidity sanctioned by Article 101(2) 'can be relied on by

---

[71] There are jurisdictions that already adopt a very broad definition of harm, which includes also financial harm, such as France. See Palmer and Bussani (n 60).

[72] See infra Chapters 5 and 6.

[73] On this aspect, see Chapter 4.

[74] See infra Section 5.8.

anyone'[75] and that this norm creates rights for individuals who can claim the invalidity of the agreement and the damages causally connected to the antitrust infringement. One may observe, therefore, that competition law is the 'law of the subjects of the market', which is all market players (both firms and consumers), as they have an interest to the preservation of the competitive character of the market.[76] However, the language concerned by the violation of a protected interest is familiar only to a restricted number of member states' jurisdictions;[77] indeed, the ECJ has always preferred speaking about right to full compensation of all market players rather than violation of a protected interest.

In the same vein, the Damages Directive sanctioned the right to full compensation of any person harmed by anticompetitive conduct.[78] The compensatory principle is based on a corrective justice regime in which the duty to repair the damage burdens only the subjects that have caused the damage and that the law holds responsible. The principle of corrective justice stipulates that any claimant, including victims of these indirect damages, has to prove to the satisfaction of the court that he or she would be better off but for the unlawful conduct of the defendant.[79] This approach has two main consequences for the award of damages. Firstly, it is not possible for instance to attribute liability to the person 'best placed' to avoid the damage most cheaply.[80] Secondly, the law burdens only the subject that, as a matter of fact, caused the harm and, as a matter of law, is held responsible.

The duty not to create restrictions or distortions within the internal market is complemented by the obligation of avoiding damages to private parties caused by the same restrictions. This duty is, moreover, detailed by domestic rules on civil liability and, where present, on competition law liability.

The scope of the rule is therefore to ensure compensation of damages that are caused by such infringements. This is in line also with previous case law of the CJEU where, with regard to state liability, the European judges noted that the aim of state liability is compensation, not deterrence or punishment.[81] The lack of

---

[75] Para 57.

[76] See, in this sense, Italian Court of Cassation civ. Sez. Un., 4 February 2005, n 2207, in *Riv. dir. proc.*, 2006, I, 375.

[77] See for a comparative analysis in the EU, Christian von Bar, Ulrich Drobnig and Guido Alpa, *The Interaction of Contract Law and Tort and Property Law in Europe: A Comparative Study* (Sellier, 2004) 27.

[78] See Article 3(1) of Directive 104/2014/EU.

[79] Weinrib (n 1) 17; Beever (n 1) 45 ff; Deakin, Johnston and Markesinis (n 1) 38.

[80] William M Landes and Richard A Posner, 'Causation in Tort Law: An Economic Approach' [1983] 12(1) *The Journal of Legal Studies* 109.

[81] Case C-470/03 A.G.M.-COS.MET *Srl v Suomen valtio* [2007] ECR I-2749.

punitive scope is one of the main reasons for the exclusion of punitive or exemplary damages from the Damages Directive.[82]

Yet compensation is not the only function of tort laws. In its long history, tort law has served disparate aims, such as 'punishment, appeasement, deterrence, compensation, and efficient loss spreading of the cost of accidents'.[83] As has been noted with reference to these objectives: 'None offers a complete justification; all are important, though at different stages one may have been more prominent than the rest'.[84] As of today, punishment is generally left to criminal laws and exceptionally to torts through punitive or exemplary damages, which are, however, explicitly excluded from competition damages actions in the EU.

Deterrence, instead, aims at preventing future illegal behaviours of the same kind. The economic analysis of law has long focused on this aspect of tort law, observing that deterrence involves 'what the accident costs of activities are and letting the market determine the degree to which, and the ways in which, activities are desired given such costs. Similarly it involves giving people freedom to choose whether they would rather engage in the activity and pay the costs of doing so, including accident costs, or, given the accident costs, engage in safer activities that might otherwise have seemed less desirable'.[85] However, it implies rationality of human behaviours and the capacity to discern the causes of an accident. Hence, in case of causal uncertainty, the decision to engage in a certain activity is not an informed one, and, therefore, burdening that person with the risk of harm that may take place would be unfair. As Basil Markesinis observes, tort law pursues broader objectives of fairness and justice than mere efficiency, and it sometimes includes the application policy-based reasoning – for instance, in collective redress actions – that may even be in contrast with cost–benefit analysis.[86] Also for this reason, outside the United States, economic analysis of law has found little application in courts.

Finally, in EU competition law enforcement, the law has drawn a line between the formal functions of private and public enforcement. The Damages Directive states that the main objective of competition damages actions is to ensure that any person harmed by an anticompetitive behaviour is able to obtain compensation for that harm, leaving to the public enforcement of competition law to punish anticompetitive

---

[82] Directive 2014/104/EU OJ L 349 (n 4).

[83] Basil Markesinis, 'Tort Law', *Encyclopædia Britannica* www.britannica.com/topic/tort, accessed 1 February 2019.

[84] Ibid.

[85] Guido Calabresi, *The Costs of Accidents: A Legal and Economic Analysis* (Yale University Press, 1970) 63.

[86] Markesinis (n 83).

16 *Causation in Competition Law*

behaviours and, to a certain extent, deter the same conduct in the future.[87] The corrective justice criterion gives central importance to responsibility for the causation of a harm, therefore putting causation at the core of the analysis.

1.4 THE CAUSAL CONNECTION IN COMPETITION DAMAGES ACTIONS

1.4.1 *Causation and the Anticompetitive Harm*

A bundle of national and EU legal provisions determines the assessment of causation in competition damages actions. Infringements of Articles 101 and 102 TFEU may cause two different kinds of effects. Firstly, they may bring about the imposition of a price overcharge on the products sold. Secondly, they may cause the so-called lost-volume effect or other present or future dead-weight welfare losses.[88] The Damages Directive allows the compensation of both types of damages as actual loss and lost profits. In addition to this, the Directive recognizes the compensability of lost opportunities.[89] Hence, both the harm for price overcharge and for lost-volume effect oblige the tortfeasor to compensate actual loss and loss of profits, plus the payment of interest.[90] These harms may be caused by either exploitative abuses or exclusionary practices. Both types of harm may generate causal uncertainty. Exploitative abuses, for instance, have been discussed in this sense especially for the passing-on effect of the price overcharge that they may entail. Exclusionary abuses pose unique challenges in proving causation, as they often cause lost profits or loss of chances whereby the causal link has to be determined using hypothetical scenarios.[91]

1.4.2 *Causation and the Anticompetitive Conduct*

From the point of view of the offence causing harm, it is possible to differentiate between harm from exclusionary conduct and harm from exploitative abuses and cartels.[92]

---

[87] Although it is undeniable that, to a certain extent, the prospect of civil liability should – in theory – have a bearing on the behavior of a firm, therefore deterring future illegal actions.

[88] For a description of loss-volume effect in competition law, see Kai Hüschelrath and Heike Schweitzer, *Public and Private Enforcement of Competition Law in Europe: Legal and Economic Perspectives* (Springer, 2014) 127.

[89] Recital (13).

[90] Article 3(2).

[91] See Section 4.4.

[92] For a thorough overview of both types of harm, see Eleanor M Fox, 'What Is Harm to Competition-Exclusionary Practices and Anticompetitive Effect' [2002] 70 *Antitrust Law*

1.4.2.1 Exploitative Behaviours

An exploitative offence is an anticompetitive agreement or an abuse of dominant position which typically raises prices to buyers or worsens the conditions for buyers or sellers and consumers in that market.[93] The damage usually consists in a price overcharge multiplied by the number of purchases. Depending on the type and length of the supply chain, the anticompetitive conduct can involve different subjects. As the good may be resold or used for the production of other goods,[94] the number of damaged parties can increase even beyond the mere vertical chain of distribution, from direct purchasers of the goods or services to indirect purchasers and, for instance, umbrella and counterfactual buyers. But since nobody can be responsible *ad inifinitum* for the consequences of their wrongful conduct, it is important to determine what characteristics define the principle of causation for such type of antitrust offence. Exploitative offences mainly generate actual losses but they can potentially bring about lost volume effects and certain types of hypothetical harms, such as to counterfactual buyers. Most of these harms will flow from a price overcharge or other similar types of conditions.[95] Goods are purchased and resold, used as input of production, while services become part of the cost structure of a firm. The overcharge or the output reduction may therefore cause a welfare loss not only to downstream firms but also upstream – for instance, in the form of reduced demand of the product[96] – and to firms operating outside the value chain.[97] For the sake of simplicity, the harm caused by an exploitative abuse is usually imagined as a token overcharge which can be passed on. The last person to receive this token has the right to claim damages, as they are causally connected to the antitrust infringement that generated that overcharge. However, this approximation fails to identify heads of damages flowing from the same exploitative offence other than the overcharge.[98]

Journal 371; Phillip Areeda and Herbert Hovenkamp, *Fundamentals of Antitrust Law* (Aspen Publishers Online, 2011), 6–23; Jürgen Basedow and Wolfgang Wurmnest, *Structure and Effects in EU Competition Law: Studies on Exclusionary Conduct and State Aid* (Kluwer Law International, 2011); Robert Pitofsky, *How the Chicago School Overshot the Mark: The Effect of Conservative Economic Analysis on U.S. Antitrust* (Oxford University Press, 2008), 142 ss; Gustavo Ghidini, Marcello Clarich, Fabiana Di Porto e Piergaetano Marchetti, *Concorrenza e mercato. Rassegna degli orientamenti dell'autorità garante (2009)* (Giuffrè, 2010), 21.

[93] Such effects generally bring about a diminution in the output of production or in the quality of the goods.

[94] See Sections 7.1 and 7.3.

[95] Such as buyers cartels or bid rigging.

[96] Frank Maier-Rigaud and Ulrich Schwalbe, 'Quantification of Antitrust Damages', in David Ashton (ed), *Competition Damages Actions in the EU* (Edward Elgar, 2018) 413–414.

[97] For instance, purchasers of goods and services of other firms in the value chain. For more details on indirect effects, see Chapter 7.

[98] See Section 7.2.5.

18   *Causation in Competition Law*

1.4.2.2 Exclusionary Offence

This type of anticompetitive conduct aims at foreclosing the market to other competitors and potential market entrants.[99] This is a target that both cartel participants and dominant players want to achieve, especially when they are at the same time adopting exploitative practices.[100] This happens because artificially reducing market outputs or raising prices generally creates the conditions for new competitors to enter the market.[101]

Exclusionary conducts therefore affect those who, as a consequence of the unlawful behaviour, have been excluded or foreclosed from the market. However, a number of different causes can concur to the exit of such undertakings from the relevant market. Causation has to establish with a certain degree of certainty or probability that it is the antitrust infringement that caused the foreclosure of the competitor, not other concurring factors. Exclusionary practices pose exceptional problems in determining causation, if one considers the complex patterns that lead to the erosion of the competitors' market shares and ultimately to their foreclosure. There are at least three different phases[102] generally leading to the foreclosure of a competitor: (1) the competitor loses market share, (2) the incumbent recoups the benefits of the abuse and (3) the competitor recoups market shares. Fumagalli et al. call these three phases 'attrition', 'recoupment' and 'growth'.[103] Although economic harm to the competitor arises in each phase, the illegal behaviour is limited to the infringement period.[104] Moreover, especially in the first phase, exclusionary abuses such as predatory pricing or tying may entail positive effects in the short term.[105] From a causative perspective, it therefore will be fundamental to determine if there is economic harm flowing from the infringement taking place after the infringement period. This will depend also on the type of harm caused. While a classic foreclosure comprises the three phases illustrated, an exclusionary abuse culminating in the prevention of the entry of a competitor or the prevention of the expansion of a competitor would start from the end of the first phase.[106] Exclusionary practices directly affect competitors by endangering their market position and thereby the

---

[99] Basedow and Wurmnest (n 92).
[100] Michele Roma 'Abuso escludente mediante contratto' in Antonio Catricalà, *I contratti nella concorrenza* (UTET Giuridica, 2011), chapter 6, 246 ff.
[101] Fox (n 92).
[102] See Chiara Fumagalli, Jorge Padilla and Michele Polo, 'Damages for Exclusionary Practices: A Primer' in I. Kokkoris and F. Etro (eds), *Competition Law and the Enforcement of Art. 102* (Oxford University Press, 2010), 203–220.
[103] Ibid., 206.
[104] Ibid., 207.
[105] See Frank Maier-Rigaud and Ulrich Schwalbe (n 96), 425–426.
[106] Ibid., 208.

1.5 Causation in Fact 19

level of competition in the market. By consequence, such practices may cause harm to customers by way of higher prices or reduced choice, quality or innovation.[107]

In this connection, causation responds also to the need of avoiding that the injured party is unjustly enriched by the claim. For instance, a competitor may claim that its exit from the market has flown from the exclusionary offence of another undertaking when, instead, it would have happened anyway. Other events may also 'break the chain of causality', making the antitrust infringement ineffectual for the causation of the damage. In these cases, the damages should not be awarded, given the compensatory nature of the tort and the lack of a direct causal link between the unlawful behaviour and the damage. Moreover, the risk embedded in the exercise of an economic activity cannot be reversed on the antitrust infringer[108] in absence of a causal connection (i.e., in those cases in which, even in the absence of a cartel, the damage would have happened). However, there might be cases of high causal uncertainty in which the law prefers to burden the defendant with the risk of proving the uncertain causation or compensate the damages on the basis of a causal proportionate system.[109] These exceptional circumstances may justify departures from the general rules of causation and proof of causation and will be analyzed in Chapter 6.

The following sections sort out the analysis of causation into three parts. Firstly, it examines the different theories used for assessing the causative link in competition law. Since European competition law jurisdictions draw these principles from domestic tort laws, the analysis will be initially centred on the explanation of the most relevant aspects of these approaches. Secondly, the causation in antitrust law is revised with reference to the anticompetitive behaviour. Here it is described the link connecting the behaviour to the damage (cause in fact or material cause). In this regard, the chapter also considers the different categories of conditions used in the causal inquiry. Thirdly, it comments on the different approaches to legal causation. This part concerns the analysis of the types of damages that can be linked to the antitrust infringement. In other words, the analysis here tends to frame the concept of causation in order to find the limits of the potentially vast recoverable damages that might flow from the antitrust infringement.

1.5 CAUSATION IN FACT

The material or factual connection between an alleged cause and its alleged consequence is the first step to find causation. As events never happen in isolation

---

[107] See the Commission Staff Working Document, Practical Guide Quantifying Harm in Actions for Damages Based on Breaches of Article 101 or 102 of the Treaty on the Functioning of the European Union (2013) 3440, para 182.

[108] Pietro Trimarchi, *Causalità e danno* (Giuffrè, 1967) 451.

[109] See Chapter 6.

from the real world, the cause-in-fact analyzes the conditions of the harm and, amongst them, finds the condition that is factually connected to it. It is possible to distinguish at least two different approaches to causation in fact. The first and most used by courts and scholars is based on conterfactual tests, whereby the judge has to assess the causal link on the basis of a but-for scenario. If the claimant proves the test, it will receive full compensation for the harm (all-or-nothing approach). On the other hand, other approaches to causation use probabilities and proportional causal theories in order to recognize the right to recover a portion of the damages.

1.5.1 *Counterfactual Theories*

Most courts establish the factual connection between the defendant's conduct and the harm based on the *conditio sine qua non* or but-for test. This test is the predominant approach in all the jurisdictions analyzed, and it entails the ruling out of the fact under scrutiny to determine if that action caused the harm.[110] An action is the cause of a harm if the harm would not have happened, but for the defendant's conduct.[111] Given the action x and the damage y, the but-for test asks whether 'would y have occurred had x not occurred'. In other words, the but-for test 'asks the question – would the accident have occurred but for the defendant's negligence? If the answer is that the accident would have occurred even without the defendant's negligence, there is no causation'.[112] The but-for test therefore aims to find the action that is necessary to the harm.[113]

Despite its clarity, this test sometimes gives solutions contrary to common sense in case of overdetermined and jointly determined causes.[114] By overdetermined we mean multiple causes that are independently sufficient for the causation of a harm.[115] Jointly determined causes are instead individually insufficient, as one event is causally dependent on the other to bring about the harm.[116] One common example to show this downside is the case of the 'two hunters'. Here, two hunters

---

[110] Weinrib (n 1) 17; Beever (n 1) 45 ff; Deakin, Johnston and Markesinis (n 1) 235; William Lloyd Prosser, *Prosser and Keeton on the Law of Torts* (West Pub Co, 1984); Cees van Dam (n 3) 310; Håkan Andersson and Bénédict Winiger, *Digest of European Tort Law* (Springer, 2007) 1, 1.

[111] Wright (n 54) 1776.

[112] *Supreme Court Bow Valley Husky (Bermuda) Ltd. v Saint John Shipbuilding Ltd.* [1997] 3 S.C.R. 1210

[113] Hart and Honoré (n 26) 109.

[114] For an examination of overdetermined causation and its effects, see Jonathan Schaffer, 'Overdetermining Causes' [2003] 114 *Philosophical Studies* 23; Jane Stapleton, 'Factual Causation' [2010] 38 *Federal Law Review* 467.

[115] Hart and Honoré (n 26) 123.

[116] Consider, for instance, two exclusionary behaviors independently insufficient to exclude a competitor but jointly sufficient to achieve this objective.

1.5 Causation in Fact

shoot at the same time at the victim, a third hunter, who dies. Given that both shots would alone be fatal, the application of the but-for test brings to the paradoxical result for which neither the first nor the second shot would be cause of the victim's death. The same problem would arise in other instances of pre-empted and overdetermined cause. In competition law damages actions, it may happen, for instance, that the exclusionary conducts of two undertakings are each of them individually capable of foreclosing a competitor.

In order to cope with the shortcomings of the but-for test, scholars have developed other theories of factual causation. Hart and Honoré divided them into individualizing and generalizing theories.[117] Individualizing theories explain the occurrence of a specific harm as caused by a certain event. On the other hand, generalizing theories posit that it if sufficient to observe connections between classes of events and type of harms to infer causation.[118] However, individualizing theories often imply, to a certain extent, generalizations, as the next chapter on the NESS test explains. On the other hand, generalizing theories, such as adequate causation, have to explain the causative link in the individual occurrence. Hence, this distinction seems to be useful to highlight two fundamental characteristics of causal tests, but less so to distinguish between different tests although this would leave out the scalar or quantitative theories of causation and the probabilistic theories. For this reason the following sections analyze the main tests to determine the cause in fact, without a strict distinction between generalizing and individualizing theories. However, this book posits that generalizations are a powerful instrument to circumvent the proof of specific causation and that their use should be limited to a strict number of cases.[119]

1.5.1.1 The NESS Test

The NESS (necessary element of a sufficient set) test has been designed by Hart and Honoré,[120] and later refined by Wright,[121] who pointed out that an act is a cause of an injury if it is a 'necessary element of a set of conditions jointly sufficient for the result'.[122] This test 'states that a particular condition was a cause of a specific consequence if and only if it was a necessary element of a set of antecedent actual

---

[117] Hart and Honoré (n 26) 431 ff.

[118] Ibid., 435.

[119] See Chapters 4 and 5.

[120] Hart and Honoré (n 26) 547.

[121] This is the same Wright who acknowledges about the creation of the theory by Hart and Honoré (see 'Causation in Tort Law' [n 35], p. 1774) but then changes his view stating that 'The NESS account often is erroneously equated with Hart and Honoré's account of a "causally relevant factor" and John Mackie's account of an INUS condition', Richard W Wright, 'The NESS Account of Natural Causation: A Response to Criticisms' in R Goldberg (ed), *Perspectives on Causation* (Hart, 2011), 285 ff.

[122] Wright (n 54).

conditions that was sufficient for the occurrence of the consequence'.[123] While the but-for test requires the condition to be necessary, in the NESS test, x contributed to y if x is a necessary factor of a group of conditions sufficient for causing y.

The NESS test draws on JS Mill's notion of a jointly sufficient set of conditions and uses the logic of conditions, using sufficient and necessary elements to select the material cause of the event. Based on the causal laws of nature, the latter test instantiates the immediate effects of the selected factors.[124] The NESS test solves most cases of overdetermination, as none of the multiple conditions need to be necessary, but only sufficient to be a cause of the harm.[125] In application of the NESS theory, the harm is factually linked to the anticompetitive conduct, if the exploitative abuse or the exclusionary conduct was a necessary element among all the market conditions contributing to the causation of the damage. Put differently, for this theory, it is enough to state that the anticompetitive conduct contributed to a certain extent to the damage.

A primary limitation of the NESS approach comes from its main author who acknowledged that the test is limited to the causal laws of nature.[126] Most of the rules and dynamics according to which persons interact on markets are not law of nature, but they form part of the set of conditions causing the harm. Hence, in competition law, economics often has to determine whether a condition is necessary, according to this test.

Other scholars observe that this approach, as well as the other 'counterfactual' theories based on causal generalizations or abstractions,[127] are flawed.[128] They note that the NESS test hinges on 'causal laws' which are generalizations[129] that cannot

---

[123] Ibid., 1774.

[124] Wright (n 122) 289.

[125] Cf. Wright (n 54) 1735. However, for a critical overview of the limitations of the NESS approach see Steel (n 29) 26 ff; Jane Stapleton, 'Unpacking Causation' in Peter Cane, Anthony M Honoré and John Gardner (eds), *Relating to Responsibility: Essays for Tony Honoré on His Eightieth Birthday* (Hart, 2001).

[126] Wright (n 122) 309 ff.

[127] On this equation of the NESS test to counterfactual theories, Wright responds noting that 'the analysis is (or should be) a real-world "covering law" matching of actual conditions against the required elements of the relevant causal generalizations rather than a counterfactual "possible worlds" exploration of what might have occurred in the absence of the condition at issue', Wright (n 122) 302.

[128] See, among others, Moore (n 40); John David Collins, Edward Jonathan Hall and Laurie Ann Paul, *Causation and Counterfactuals* (MIT Press, 2004).

[129] Generalizing theories are effectively explained by Hart and Honoré who note that

the generalizing theories insist that, if a particular act or event is a cause of something, its status as a cause is derived from the fact that it is of a kind believed to be generally connected with an event of some other kind" therefore they differ from individualizing theories because they "concentrate on the selection of one from among a set of conditions of an event as its cause, they select a particular condition as the cause of an event because it is of a kind which is connected with such events by a generalization or statement of regular sequence.

(Hart and Honoré [n 23] 465)

1.5 *Causation in Fact*

be applied when organic processes, such as the decision-making activity by human beings, are at stake, since such processes do not conform to settled patterns.[130] The result is that the decision maker will utilize causal generalizations in order to assert the singular causal judgment, although the causal generalization is not able to explain the connection between the events, due to a lack of information.[131] Moreover, the test generates false positives when it uses abstract processes to determine the set of conditions, sometimes finding causes when they do not exist.[132]

The NESS test is an all-or-nothing account of causation, as each set of conditions can be a cause or not of a specific event, while it admits no gradation or proportional appraisal of causation. Hence, it would not be possible to apportion liability based on the causal contribution of each agent.[133]

1.5.1.2 The Quantitative or Scalar Approaches

Other scholars propose the adoption of quantitative or scalar approaches which measure the extent of causation of an event in terms of causal contribution to the harm.[134] In particular, for cases of multiple causes coexisting in the causation of the same event, according to these scholars, an agency is a cause of a harm if it is involved in[135] or contributes to[136] the damage to a greater or lesser extent. Based on this theory, the agency must be a substantial factor of the damage in order to be a cause of it.[137] Whether the agency is substantial or not, has to be established on the basis of probability, statistics or other scientific laws. For more in-depth analysis on the use of probabilities to prove causation in national courtrooms, see Section 4.2.

---

[130] Moore (n 40).

[131] In this regard, Wright observes that

> Contrary to Hart and Honoré's account, the NESS account insists that singular instances of causation always consist of the complete instantiation on a particular occasion of one or more causal laws, and that identification of a singular instance of causation always implies that such complete instantiation has occurred. The implication may be based on direct particularistic evidence of the existence of one or more of the required conditions, or, as is always true for the unknown conditions in the causal laws and generally true for many (sometimes all) of the known conditions, is inferred from particularistic evidence of the network of causal relationships that encompasses the particular occasion.
>
> (n 121, 289)

[132] Steel (n 29) 29 ff.

[133] Section 4.3.

[134] Ibid.

[135] Jane Stapleton, 'Choosing What We Mean by Causation in the Law' [2008] 73 *Missouri Law Review* 433, 441.

[136] Moore (n 40).

[137] Honoré (n 26) para 3.1.

1.5.1.3 Adequate Causation

While the but-for and NESS approaches use causal laws to determine specific causation, the adequate cause theory examines the probability of an event to occur based on generalizations.[138] According to this theory, an action causes a harm if it significantly increases the probability of a certain outcome to ensue. This approach considers the type of harm to which the specific harm belongs, and determines if the defendant's action generally brings about that type of harm. The connection between an action and an outcome hinges on the study of the regularity of the occurrence of a certain type of events. This approach is often defined as the quintessential form of generalizing theory of causation.[139] The adequate causation aims at finding causation by abstracting the harm and its condition, as a type of harm caused by a general set of conditions. On the basis of this, it determines the alteration of risk and calculates the probability of that class of conditions to generate the harm.[140] If this fits within the increase in probability required, then causation is established.[141]

1.5.2 *Risk Theories and Probability Theories*

The theories mentioned above apply an all-or-nothing approach whereby the claimant has the right to full compensation if he or she successfully proves causation. An alternative account to the all-or-nothing approaches has been provided by the causal proportional theories of liability.[142] A first account determines responsibility in relation to the probability of the action to cause the specific harm. The trier of fact determines probability ex post and establishes the causal contribution of the defendant's action on a scale of 1 to 100, accordingly attributing responsibility.[143] Thus, if the defendant's causal contribution to the damage is 50, he or she will be responsible for the compensation of half of the total harm.

A second approach examines the creation of risk of causation of future harm. This account posits that it is possible to examine the ex ante increase in risk caused by the defendant's action to determine their responsibility for the 'derivative harms', such as the prevention costs, but also for the lost chances.[144]

---

[138] Moore (n 40) 171; Hart and Honoré (n 26) 472.
[139] Hart and Honoré (n 26) 547.
[140] Ibid., 560.
[141] For a more in-depth analysis of the requirements of the adequate causation theory, see infra Section 1.6.
[142] Israel Gilead and others, *Proportional Liability: Analytical and Comparative Perspectives* (De Gruyter, 2013).
[143] Ibid., 50.
[144] Ibid., 51 ff.

1.6 Legal Causation

The theories examined in the previous section, although differing in the description of the conditions of the causal requirements, adopt a counterfactual approach to causation whereby either the defendant's action is cause of the harm or it is not.[145] By contrast, the causal proportional liability theories that this section describes depart from a counterfactual assessment of causation and also avoid the all-or-nothing approach to causation. They indeed analyze the causal contribution of an action to the harm without ruling out its causal force according to pre-stated conditions.[146]

Causation in fact establishes the mechanical connection between the events that brought about the harm. However, causation has the function of determining not just scientific connections between events but legally relevant ones. For this reason, each legal system details the characteristics that this link needs to have to place responsibility on the defendant. Factual causation alone is not sufficient to determine the responsibility of the defendant, as the harm may be too remote, not adequately connected or not direct.[147] In other words, although the defendant's action contributed – as a matter of fact – to the causation of the harm, the legal system has to determine whether that contribution gives rise to responsibility.

The next chapter explores the current formulations of legal causation.

1.6 LEGAL CAUSATION

A competition law infringement is capable of damaging different subjects at the same time, virtually all the market players that are directly or even indirectly connected to the business of the competition law infringer.[148] For instance, an abuse of a dominant position causing the unlawful foreclosure of a competitor may equally impact the business partners of that competitor, its employees and the consumers of both markets, causing loss of profits and actual losses. Moreover, these harmed parties may attribute many of their economic losses to the antitrust infringement whilst they might be caused by other market factors, such as the entry of a new competitor in the market. Causation therefore determines the factual link between the infringement and the damage (causation in fact) and also delimits the compensable damages to those legally relevant (causation in law).[149] In the

---

[145] Chapter 5 will contrast the different theories of factual causation with the degree of certainty required by the standard of proof for causation.

[146] See Section 4.3 for an analysis of causal proportional liability theories for the proof of causation.

[147] Depending on the jurisdiction.

[148] Directive 104/2014/EU mainly considers the case of passing-on of the overcharge when considering the 'indirect purchasers' harmed by an antitrust infringement (see Article 2 (24) for the definition of indirect purchaser according to the Directive). Chapter 7 of this book defines all the types of damages and the parties that may be indirectly involved in an antitrust action, observing that indirect purchasers are only one of the many categories of potential harmed parties.

[149] See, for a critical introduction to this bipartition, Cees Van Dam (n 3) 310 ff.; Christian von Bar (n 3) 449; Richard W Wright, 'The Grounds and Extent of Legal Responsibility' [2003] 41 *San Diego Law Review* 1425.

26 *Causation in Competition Law*

mechanical chain of events that links the action to the harm, a very remote action can be still considered a *conditio sine qua non* of the harm. For instance, consider the harm to the workers of a counterfactual buyer that goes out of business because not able to purchase at umbrella pricing from a non-cartelist. In the absence of the cartel, the workers would not have been displaced, thus confirming the existence of a factual link. Furthermore, not all the damages encountered by the claimant may be causally connected to the action of the defendant.

The second stage of the causal enquiry has exactly the function of limiting the responsibility of the tortfeasor to the damages that are – depending on the jurisdiction – reasonably foreseeable, adequately connected or sufficiently direct, given the circumstances of the case.[150] It is clear, therefore, how responsibility and causation are strictly connected to each other; in a sense, causation is an instrument for the attribution of responsibility in legal systems based on the corrective justice criterion.[151] Far from being a mere legal technicality, the concept of legal causation has, therefore, a fundamental role in determining responsibility and selecting the harms that will be compensated. Also for this reason, some scholars and judges prefer calling causation only the inquiry on factual causation, while they call 'scope of responsibility' the second step of the attribution of liability, which entails the analysis of legal policy reasons.[152] However, causation in fact, causation in law and legal responsibility norms (such as the duty of care rule) partly rely on the same factual enquiry, thus making often difficult to draw a clear line between these elements.[153]

A harm caused by an antitrust infringement is a pure economic loss, recoverable – depending on the jurisdiction – on the basis of a statutorily protected interest or a subjective right, under EU law. In addition to this, an indirect damage, as here defined, includes the action of a third party, which intervenes without 'breaking the causal chain',[154] for instance, due to passing-on of a price overcharge or to 'umbrella effects'. The sheer number of different persons connected to a specific market – such as buyers, sellers, service providers and counterfactual buyers – exponentially multiplies the number economic harms that may occur. However, as observed in the tort law literature 'no defendant is responsible ad infinitum for all the

---

[150] See Chapter 2 for a comparative analysis of the different causal concepts utilized in the selected jurisdictions.

[151] Although it is debated whether this attribution of responsibility should rest on a positivistic interpretation of the law, on principles based on 'expediency, justice, or social policy' or, as Hart and Honoré believe, on 'common-sense principles of causation': see Hart and Honoré (n 23) 91–92, and for a critical review, see Richard W. Wright 'The Grounds and Extent of Legal Responsibility' (2003) 41 *San Diego Law Review* 1425; cf. Stapleton (n 136), 449 ff.

[152] Stapleton (n 135) 449–450.

[153] Von Bar (n 3) 440; Stapleton (n 135) 440–441.

[154] That is to introduce an independent and sufficient cause of the damage.

1.6 Legal Causation

consequences of his wrongful conduct, however remote in time and however indirect the process of causation, for otherwise human activity would be unreasonably hampered. The law must draw a line somewhere, some consequences must be abstracted as relevant, not on grounds of pure logic, but simply for practical reasons'.[155] This line is usually drawn through the assessment of 'legal causation', which the ECJ recalled in the *Kone* case[156] by loosely referring to the concept of foreseeability.[157]

The effects originating from a specific agency are different and possibly diverse. All of them may be de facto linked to the agency but not necessarily should be attributed to the agent. The legal causation is the second stage of the causal enquiry and has the function of limiting the compensable damages.[158] The criteria for delimiting such responsibilities vary across jurisdictions. While some jurisdictions refer to the concept of remoteness, others focus on specific characteristics of the damages[159] or at the scope of the infringed rule. Hence, while in English law the cause should not be too remote,[160] in the United States, the leading principle for courts is the one of a proximate causation.[161] Civil law countries show a wide range of approaches, which span from the direct and adequate causes to the scope of the rule theory and the 'causal regularity' theory.[162]

Although these jurisdictions tend to use the two-stage approach in most of the cases, it is not always possible to determine the difference between factual and legal causation with certainty.[163] The factual nexus between the action and the harm and the legal responsibility that arises from it are connected and sometimes difficult to disentangle. Moreover, some authors argue that the concept of legal causation hides public policy reasons behind a curtain of 'generalizing theories'. This was the view of the so-called legal realists,[164] also called causal minimalist,[165] who stated that there is only one causal issue in tort law that is the causation-in-fact, while all other aspects are mere instruments in the hands of

---

[155] James Coudkamp, Sir Percy Henry Winfield and John Anthony Jolowicz, *Winfield und Jolowicz on Tort* (Sweet & Maxwell, 2014) 334.

[156] Case C-557/12 *Kone AG and Others v ÖBB-Infrastruktur AG*, 5 June 2014 ECLI:EU:C:2014:45, para 30.

[157] For a comparative analysis of foreseeability, see Section 1.7.

[158] Roberto Pucella, *La causalità 'incerta'* (Giappichelli, 2007).

[159] Honoré, 'Causation in the Law', reports proximate, adequate, direct, effective, operative, legal and responsible causes.

[160] Deakin, Johnston and Markesinis (n 1) 254 ff.

[161] John CP Goldberg and Benjamin Charles Zipursky, *The Oxford Introductions to U.S. Law: Torts* (Oxford University Press, 2010).

[162] See Section 1.6. See also Wien and Schadenersatzrecht (n 54); Van Dam (n 3) 313 ff.

[163] Alex Broadbent, 'Fact and Law in the Causal Inquiry' [2009] 15 *Journal Legal Theory* 173–178.

[164] For an overview of the different positions, see Wright, 'Causation in Tort Law' (n 54), 1738 ff.

[165] Stapleton (n 135) 455–458.

28   *Causation in Competition Law*

judges to exercise broad discretion in their own decisions.[166] Stapleton suggests therefore to replace the 'legal cause' with an approach that considers the 'scope of liability for consequences'.[167]

The responses to these critiques, in defence of the two-stage causal test, have been of two types. Firstly, facing the failure of courts to deal with causation as a mere material and policy-neutral account, some authors noted that causation-in-fact is also permeated by policy considerations.[168] Secondly, Hart and Honoré noted that common-sense judgments are characterized by non-legal causal language, which is fundamental not only for the description of the cause-in-fact but also for most of the proximate-cause issues.[169] Therefore, theorists such as Hart and Honoré[170] and Moore,[171] believe that legal causation can fruitfully borrow from other disciplines the items and reasoning, respectively ordinary usage and metaphysics of causation, to delimit the causal grounds. Since causation has to attribute the responsibility for a harm, they believe that limits to this attribution, if not present in nature, have to be found in common sense or, alternatively, in the broader scope that the rule of law intends to pursue. Legal causation is, therefore, a legal instrument influenced by legal policy objectives and fairness concerns.[172]

In conclusion, the division between factual and legal causation is not a neat one. However, if we think of factual and legal causation as two phases of a process rather than two independent concepts, this division is relatively easier to implement in the decision-making mechanisms. Moreover, in this regard, we should think that causation is a link between facts, not a fact itself. Hence, the two-stage process is a method useful to test under different perspectives the relevance of the conditions of the harm. It is often said that compensation is limited to the harm foreseeable at the time it occurred. However, the function of this test depends on the jurisdiction in which it is enforced.

---

[166] Causal minimalists, in other words, believe that the only causal theory is the one that finds the straight connection between agency and damage, while all the others comprehend policy reasoning that are unknown to causal connection. See Leon Green, *Rationale of Proximate Cause* (Rothman Reprints, 1927); Leon Green, *Judge and Jury* (Vernon Law Book Company, 1930); Fowler Vincent Harper, Fleming James, and Oscar S Gray, *The Law of Torts* (Little, Brown 1986) Vol 4, 29 ff; Henry W Edgerton, 'Legal Cause' *University of Pennsylvania Law Review and American Law Register*, 1924, 211–244; Charles O Gregory, 'Proximate Cause in Negligence: A Retreat from "Rationalization"' [1939] *The University of Chicago Law Review*, 1938, 36–61; Clarence Morris, 'On the Teaching of Legal Cause' [1939] 39 *Columbia Law Review* 1087–1109.

[167] Jane Stapleton, 'Cause-in-Fact and the Scope of Liability for Consequences' [2003] 119 *Law Quarterly Review* 388.

[168] Wex S Malone, 'Ruminations on Cause-in-Fact' [1956] 9(1) *Stanford Law Review*, 60–99.

[169] Hart and Honoré (n 26) 26; Wright (n 54) 1740.

[170] Hart and Honoré (n 26) 93.

[171] Moore (n 40).

[172] Khoury (n 28) 17.

1.6.1 *Foreseeability and Other Tests for Legal Causation*

The expression 'foreseeability of the harm' evokes a vague concept, which moreover has different functions in domestic laws across Europe. While in some EU jurisdictions it refers to an element of the negligent conduct, in others it forms part of the assessment of the causative link.[173] In England and Germany, for instance, causation in tort law depends on the assessment of the foreseeability of the occurrence of the event.[174] By contrast, in France, foreseeability seems to play a role only in contract while it is excluded in tort.[175] In Italy, instead, foreseeability is a condition for the assessment of negligence and is sometimes considered – following a different standard – for the assessment of causation. Rather than comparing the legal instrument according to their *nomen iuris*, it is preferable in this case to compare them according to the functional equivalence existing between the different legal tools.[176]

Especially in the analysis of causation and liability for uncertain torts (involving, therefore, a complex examination of foreseeability and remoteness of the damages), adopting a comparative approach that focuses on a specific expression and on not the function of the legal instrument can be misleading, as foreseeability – per se – may refer to different stages of the assessment of liability for damages. From a functional perspective, therefore, foreseeability in England would become adequate causation in Germany, a direct causal link in France and 'regular causality' in Italy. However, a common ground for the assessment of the role of foreseeability in competition law litigation across Europe seems to be the relationship it has with the probability to cause a certain damage and, therefore, with the degree of likelihood that the law requires for proving the causal connection between the antitrust infringement and the harm.

Every anticompetitive conduct, be it an abuse of dominant position or a cartel, may bring about several different effects on the assets of market actors, all of them factually linked to the infringement but not necessarily legally compensable. For instance, an exploitative conduct, which effects into a price overcharge, may cause an actual loss together with a possible loss of profits for a reduction in sales, to the undertaking that uses those products as part of its output. Possibly, the damaged purchaser might complain about a lost chance caused by the higher cost of its outputs or by a missed purchase of a particular good, due to the higher expenditure

---

[173] For a comparative overview, see Cees Van Dam (n 3) 313; Infantino and Zervogianni (n 3).

[174] Infantino and Zervogianni (n 3) 85 ff.

[175] See ibid., 92. Quézel-Ambrunaz, *Essai sur la causalité*, 450–452; Viney and Jourdain, *Les conditions de la responsabilité*, 266.

[176] Konrad Zweigert and Hein Kötz, *Introduction to Comparative Law* (Oxford University Press, 1998) 34; Ralf Michaels, 'The Functional Method of Comparative Law' [2005] *The Oxford Handbook of Comparative Law* https://papers.ssrn.com/sol3/papers.cfm?abstract_id=839826, accessed 31 May 2017.

30 *Causation in Competition Law*

caused by the cartel. Moreover, due to the lost profits, the purchaser would foreseeably reduce the production and the purchase of other goods from her suppliers. The supplier of this undertaking would be, by consequence, damaged by the infringement as well, as but for the overcharge, they would have sold more units. Now, the level of factual causation in all the different heads of damages listed is theoretically the same since the competition law infringement is a necessary cause of the damage. However, there are sound reasons to divide, from a causal perspective, the damages due to the overcharge paid on the price to, for instance, damages caused to the direct purchasers for buying alternative goods or for lost chances.

To this problem, the European member states' tort law regimes respond with different solutions, which the next Chapter 2 analyzes with reference to the four selected jurisdictions.

1.6.2 *Intervening Events*

In Kone, the ECJ observed that 'even if the determination of an offer price is regarded as a purely autonomous decision',[177] the causal chain is not interrupted, for the non-cartelist has determined the selling price based on the market price distorted by the cartel.[178] It follows that the buyer of the distributor unrelated to the illegal agreement has the right to seek compensation for the damage caused by the overcharge just as the direct or indirect purchasers of the cartelists. Since the action of the non-cartel members had to be foreseen, both the AG Kokott and the ECJ agreed in saying that this action could not be an intervening cause of the harm.

Every time an event, subsequent to the one which infringed the law, intervenes in the causal chain, there is a possibility that it interrupted the causal connection between the damage and the tort. Tort law generally refer to it as a *novus actus interveniens*, which is a superseding cause of the damage.[179] There are three dimensions of intervening events: (1) the one of a third party; (2) the one caused by the claimant; (3) the one caused by natural events. In the case of umbrella effects, but also of passing on of price overcharges, and other 'indirect antitrust damages',[180] if the defendant's breach of competition law has only provided the occasion for a third party's independent action, which has a direct connection to the harm, the defendant will not be liable.[181] On the contrary, the *novus actus* is not breaking the causal chain if it was reasonably foreseeable to the defendant. All the tests for the

---

[177] Case C-557/12 Kone AG and Others v ÖBB-Infrastruktur AG, 5 June 2014 Para 29.
[178] Ibid., para 29–30.
[179] This is the definition preferred by US courts.
[180] For a definition of this kind of damages, See Section 5.5, n 68 and Chapter 7.
[181] Goudkamp, Winfield and Jolowicz (n 155) 196.

1.6 Legal Causation

assessment of causation in fact and in law in theory utilize scientific laws for proving causal connections. However, limited knowledge of scientific processes explaining causal connections often impose the use of common sense. The following section explores the function and use of common sense in causation.

1.6.3 Common Sense

National courts have generally avoided delving into the conceptualization of causation, following a more pragmatic approach.[182] Judges have developed solutions that are mainly founded on the proof rules of causation and therefore on the assessment of facts that can substantiate the existence of a causal connection.[183] However, it is still necessary to define causation as the object of this proof. Since the nature of causation seems to be the subject of an endless debate in the philosophical, legal and scientific doctrine, often judges recur to common sense to circumvent the impasse created by the conceptualization of causation in uncertain cases.[184] Courts recur to common sense in particular to establish legal causation.[185] In common law, Lord Salmon famously observed that 'The nature of causation has been discussed by many eminent philosophers and also by a number of learned judges in the past. I consider, however, that what or who has caused a certain event to occur is essentially a practical question of fact which can be best answered by ordinary common sense rather than by abstract metaphysical theory'.[186] On the other hand, in civil law jurisdictions, the judge often draws on its *intime conviction* to determine the existence of a causal connection, based on the observation of facts.[187]

While Wright and Stapleton have posited that legal causation is a matter of legal policy,[188] Hart and Honoré observed that it is often common sense to guide the judge in the selection of the relevant legal causes.[189] However, they also acknowledged that the lack of a definition of the elements of 'common sense' rendered courts decisions often unpredictable or difficult to interpret.[190] For this reason, the

---

[182] Von Bar (n 153) 412; Khoury (n 28) 14.

[183] See Chapters 5 and 6.

[184] A. Summers, 'Common-Sense Causation in the Law' [2018] 38 *Oxford Journal of Legal Studies* 793. Khoury (n 28) 15; Jane Stapleton, 'Law, Causation and Common Sense' [1988] 8 *Oxford Journal of Legal Studies* 111.

[185] Hart and Honoré (n 26) 26; Stapleton (n 184); Andrew Summers, 'Common-Sense Causation in the Law' [2018] 38 *Oxford Journal of Legal Studies* 793, 795.

[186] *Alphacell Ltd v Woodward* [1972] UKHL 4 (UKHL [1972]) 847.

[187] See Chapter 5.

[188] Wright, 'Causation in Tort Law' (n 54); Richard W Wright and Ingeborg Puppe, 'Causation: Linguistic, Philosophical, Legal and Economic' [2016] 91 *Chicago-Kent Law Review* 461; Jane Stapleton, 'Choosing What We Mean by Causation in the Law' [2008] 73 *Missouri Law Review* 433; Stapleton, 'Factual Causation' (n 135).

[189] Hart and Honoré (n 26) 26 ff.

[190] Ibid 27.

two authors defined the characteristic elements of common sense in causation, examining also from a linguistic perspective the language of cause-and-effect in ordinary life. Based on this, they developed a definition of common sense for causation in law by analyzing how causal language is used in the case law.[191] They therefore found out that the causal language generally distinguishes between normal and abnormal conditions.[192] And although normality and abnormality are relative to the context, the analysis of the case law resurfaces distinct definitions of both concepts.[193] Secondly, Hart and Honoré noted that common-sense causal language distinguishes between voluntary and involuntary causes. They noted that causation in law is not always the result of a natural chain of events but rather of a 'man's motive'.[194]

By observing the law in action, Hart and Honoré concluded that 'it is the plain man's notions of causation (and not the philosopher's or the scientist's) with which the law is concerned'.[195] Contra, a body of scholarly literature against this vision of causation, as embedding common sense, posits that common sense is 'an empty slogan ... so indeterminate that it is effectively worthless as an analytical guide'.[196] This scholarship also acknowledged the important use of common sense in the case law, however objecting to its vagueness and proposing to replace it with different tests, generally hinging on policy considerations, such as the purpose or the scope of the norm. Stapleton also observed that judicial decisions are based on the prescriptive value of a norm even when there are 'normal departures' from the description of events.[197] However, policy-based principles entail to a certain extent interpretation

---

[191] Ibid 36.

[192] Ibid 34. This approach is also adopted by French and Italian law, whereby causation in law is generally determined on the basis of the 'normal course of events', see Chapter 2.

[193] According to Hart and Honoré, 'normal conditions (and hence in causal inquiries mere conditions) are those conditions which are present as part of the usual state or mode of operation of the thing under inquiry: some of such usual conditions will also be familiar, pervasive features of the environment: and many of them will not only be present alike in the case of disaster and of normal functioning, but will be generally known to be present by those who make causal inquiries' whereas 'What is abnormal in this way "makes the difference" between the accident and things going on as usual'. Ibid., 36.

[194] They argued that 'It is to be noted that, despite what is commonly said by philosophers, causal relationships are not always "transitive": a cause of a cause is not always treated as the cause of the "effect", even when the cause of the cause is something more naturally thought of as a cause than a man's motive is', ibid., 44.

[195] Ibid., 1.

[196] Jane Stapleton, 'Reflections on Common Sense Causation in Australia' in Simone Degeling and James Edelman (eds), *Torts in Commercial Law* (Thomson Reuters, 2011) 350. See also Richard W Wright, 'The Nightmare and the Noble Dream: Hart and Honore on Causation and Responsibility' in Matthew Kramer and others (eds), *The Legacy of H.L.A. Hart: Legal, Political and Moral Philosophy* (Oxford University Press, 2008) 170; AS Burrows, *Remedies for Torts and Breach of Contract* (Oxford University Press, 2004) 97. For a general analysis of the different scholarly views on common sense causation, see Summers (n 185).

[197] Jane Stapleton, 'Causation in the Law' in Helen Beebee, Christopher Hitchcock and Peter Menzies (eds), *The Oxford Handbook of Causation* (Oxford University Press, 2009) 758.

based on external sources of knowledge, which do not directly belong to the prescriptive norm. Moreover, according to empirical research, common-sense decisions include the simultaneous evaluation of prescriptive and descriptive knowledge, statistical and moral principles.[198] Thus, common sense distills and conflates elements of general knowledge about causal processes, fairness considerations, and a policy-based application of the law. When it is still disputed the attribution of liability based on the prescriptive or descriptive norms violated, judges tend to attribute causation on the basis of what is 'normal' according to ordinary people. The use of common sense allows the judge to adjust the outcome of the tests on legal causation to have a fair decision.

[198] Adam Bear and Joshua Knobe, 'Normality: Part Descriptive, Part Prescriptive' (2017) 167 *Cognition* 25, 25–26; Christopher Hitchcock and Joshua Knobe, 'Cause and Norm' [2009] 106 *The Journal of Philosophy* 587, 598; Summers (n 185) 811.

2

Causation Rules in National Courts

National courts have generally embraced a multifold account for causation in virtually all member states.[1] However, the different national tort law systems structure the multistage accounts differently. National judges enforce competition law rules largely relying on their domestic laws of obligations. For this reason, this chapter examines the bundle of tort law and competition law that applies to establish causation in competition damages actions before national courts of England, Germany, France and Italy. These four jurisdictions were selected because of the size of their economies, the amount of litigation and the fact that they show four different, almost paradigmatic, approaches to causation.

2.1 ENGLISH LAW

In England and Wales, claims for damages for infringement of competition law are based on the defendant's failure to comply with a statutory obligation. This is, therefore, a tort conceptually separate from the general tort of negligence.[2] When the claimant invokes a breach of statutory duty, they have to prove that they belong to a class of persons that the statutes protect.[3] Lord Wright, in *London Passenger*

---

[1] For an overview of the different tort law systems in Europe, see Cees Van Dam, *European Tort Law* (Oxford University Press, 2013) 308 ff; Marta Infantino and Eleni Zervogianni, *Causation in European Tort Law* (Cambridge University Press, 2017); Christian von Bar, *The Common European Law of Torts*, vol II (Oxford University Press, 2000) 433–498; Isabel C Durant, 'Causation' in Helmut Koziol and Reiner Schulze (eds), *Tort Law of the European Community* (Springer, 2010); Marta Infantino and Eleni Zervogianni, *Causation in European Tort Law* (Cambridge University Press, 2017).

[2] Simon Deakin, Angus Johnston and Basil Markesinis, *Markesinis and Deakinea Tort Law* (Oxford University Press, 2012) 294.

[3] Cf. *Liyama (UK) Ltd v Samsung Electronics Co Ltd Court of Appeal (Civil Division)* [2018] 4 C.M.L.R. 23, and *Crehan v Inntrepreneur Pub Company CPC* [2004] EWCA Civ 637; *Inntrepreneur Pub Company (CPC) and Others v Crehan* [2006] UKHL 38.

Transport Board v *Upson*, laid down the formula that still finds application in most courts, whereby the breach of a statute is 'a special common law right which is not to be confused in essence with a claim for negligence. The statutory duty right has its origin in the statute, but the particular remedy of an action for damages is given by the common law in order to make effective for the benefit of the injured party his right to the performance by the defendant of the defendant's statutory duty. It is not a claim in negligence in strict or ordinary sense'.[4]

As a consequence, common law does not set a standard of care (e.g., reasonable man) which the defendant has to conform to, because this will be established by the particular statute that was breached.[5] The scope of the duty of care is relevant for establishing the claim, as well as for determining causation and the defences that find application. In *X and Others (Minors)* v *Bedfordshire County Council*,[6] the court held that there are four categories of breach of statutory duty: (1) strict liability; (2) careless performance; (3) statutory duty of care; (4) misfeasance in public office. When the statutory duty cause of action protects the rights of individuals, the responsibility is without negligence. For this reason, competition law infringements have been framed as strict liability breaches of statutory duty. However, depending on the statute, the defendant may still be able to avoid liability showing that they were not at fault. On 9 March 2017, entered into force the Regulations 2017 on *The Claims in Respect of Loss or Damage Arising from Competition Infringements*[7] implementing the Damages Directive in the United Kingdom. Besides adopting the prescribed EU rules on damages claims, the UK Directive Regulation 2017 did not introduce new or different accounts for determining causation.[8]

Three conditions are relevant to establish whether the claimant's action falls within the scope of the civil remedy: 'i) the defendant's conduct has infringed the standard set by the Act; ii) the claimant was a member of the class protected by the Act; iii) the damage occurred in the manner against which the Act was meant to guard'.[9] Hence, the usual two-stage approach to causation combines with the analysis of the scope of the statute violated, setting the policy standards for legal causation. Courts tend to establish the lack of causation when, despite the breach of statutory duty, the damage would have happened anyway for a claimant's act, which is an independent cause of the damage.

The factual connection is generally established on the basis of the but-for test[10] and the standard for its proof is 'more probable than not'.[11] The contiguity of the

---

[4] *London Passenger Transport Board* v *Upson* [1949] AC 155 177–178.
[5] Deakin, Johnston and Markesinis (n 2) 295.
[6] [1995] 2 AC 633.
[7] Competition Act 1998 and Other Enactments (Amendment), SI 2017/385.
[8] However, see further, Section 5.6 for its impact on the proof of causation.
[9] Deakin, Johnston and Markesinis (n 2), 304.
[10] Ibid. 223. *Barnett* v *Chelsea & Kensington Hospital Management Committee* [1968] 1 All ER 1068.
[11] Richard Goldberg, *Perspectives on Causation* (Hart, 2011) 23, see infra Chapter 5.

but-for factors to the damage have to be intended as absence of intervening events that can sever the link between event and damage.[12] When it is said that a superseding cause 'broke the causal chain', there is an intervention in the course of events. It might also happen that an action with adequate causal effect on the damage is overtaken by a subsequent event unrelated to the initial tort. In this case, the defendant is responsible only for the injury caused regardless of the consequences created by the subsequent event.[13] In case of multiple causal conditions, instead, English case law resorts to the use of scientific laws which have to ascertain which action in fact caused the damages.[14] Some approaches derive the determination of the causal link from common sense that would justify the limitation of legal responsibility to certain damages. Some authors oppose that this theory is too uncertain.[15] The criteria set out for determining causation through common sense consist in decision about limitation of liability rather than assessment of de facto causality.[16]

With reference to legal causation, English judges use different accounts to determine responsibility and recoverable damages. English law firstly resorts to the concept of remoteness,[17] for which the defendant is responsible only if the damage was a foreseeable consequence of the breach of duty irrespective to its extent.[18] As long as the damage is foreseeable, it does not matter the form it takes, even if it is unusual.[19] By consequence, the law requires the damage to be of the same type of the one described by the rule, no matter how severe it is. The cause is too remote when it was not foreseeable to a 'reasonable man'.[20] The reasonable foreseeability of damages test can be used at the same time backward to determine causation and forward to determine responsibility, as they are both elements for the determination of responsibility of the defendant.[21] In other words, while causation determines the connection existing between the harm and a past action that caused it, culpability has to establish whether the agent has foreseen or had to foresee the causation of

---

[12] William Lloyd Prosser, *Handbook of the Law of Torts* (West Pub Co, 1971) 244 ff; Michael S Moore, *Causation and Responsibility: An Essay in Law, Morals, and Metaphysics* (Oxford University Press, 2010) 102 ff.

[13] *Baker* v *Willoughby* [1969] UKHL 8, [1969] 3 All ER 1528.

[14] *McGhee* v *National Coal Board*, [1972] 3 All E.R. 1008, 1 W.L.R. 1.

[15] See Section 1.7.3; William Lucy, *Philosophy of Private Law* (Oxford University Press, 2007) 199.

[16] Jeremy Waldron, 'Moments of Carelessness and Massive Loss' in David G Owen (ed), *The Philosophical Foundations of Tort Law* (Oxford University Press, 1997).

[17] See Anthony M Honoré, 'Causation and Remoteness of Damage' in A Tunc (ed), *International Encyclopedia of Comparative Law*, vol 6 (Mohr Siebeck, 1983) 26 ff.

[18] *Re Polemis and Furness, Withy & Co* [1921] 3 KB 560; *Overseas Tankship (UK) Ltd* v *The Miller Steamship Co Pty (The Wagon Mound No2)* [1966] UKPC 1 (UKPC [1966]); *Overseas Tankship (UK) Ltd* v *Morts Dock & Engineering Company Ltd* [1961] UKPC 1 (UKPC [1961]).

[19] *Bradford* v *Robinson Rentals Ltd* [1967] 1 All ER 267; *Hughes* v *Lord Advocate* [1963] AC 837; *Doughty* v *Turner Manufacturing Company* [1964] 1 QB 518; *Smith* v *Leech Brain & Co* [1962] 2 QB 405; *Gabriel* v *Kirklees Metropolitan Council* [2004] EWCA Civ 345.

[20] Sarah Green, *Causation in Negligence* (Bloomsbury Publishing, 2015) 134.

[21] This does not mean that the examination should be ex ante or ex post but only reflects the direction that the analysis of the remoteness of the damage has to take.

2.1 *English Law*

a future harm and negligently or intentionally failed to do so. Albeit expounding different functions, therefore, causation and culpability both contribute to placing responsibility on one or more specific agents. Especially in competition law infringements, in which a number of different economic actors may intervene or contribute to the causation of a damage, determining responsibility is the legal ground to justify the generation of a moral and legal duty to compensate.

English courts have also referred to the adequate causal theory which relies on laws of probability to establish causation.[22] The agency is cause of the event, in legal terms, only if it considerably increases the objective probability of the outcome.[23] This theory utilizes an objective standard, which is, however, subdue to an 'assumed epistemic base'.[24] Pursuant to this alternative approach, the harm must be 'within the risk', meaning that the harm has to fall into the type of risk that the liability rule protects.[25] The scope of the infringed rule defines the risk, therefore delimiting the responsibility for harm through causation.[26]

Finally, there are cases where it is not possible to define if the case has a single material causation or multiple causes. Here the House of Lords in *Fairchild* v *Glenhaven Funeral Services Ltd*[27] stated that when it is scientifically impossible to show which of several negligent employers in fact caused the death of the victim, it is sufficient for the claimant to demonstrate that the defendant's negligence materially increased the risk of contracting the disease. In the case *Barker* v *Corus (UK) plc*,[28] the House of Lords added that the liability of the tortfeasors has to be proportionate to the increase in the risk they caused. Moreover, the House of Lords in *McGhee* stated that there is a presumption of liability of the person that materially increased the risk of injury, who also has the right of proving the contrary.[29]

The judicial application of these principles is effectively described by Justice Popplewell in *Fulton Shipping Inc* v *Globalia Business Travel*, observing that 'The principle does not, however, mean that a claimant always recovers for the amount of the losses which arise from the breach. Principles of causation mean that his losses may be factually too remote from the breach to be recoverable despite the fact that they would not have been suffered but for the breach. His losses may be too remote

---

[22] Guido Calabresi, 'Concerning Cause and the Law of Torts: An Essay for Harry Kalven, Jr.' (1975) *The University of Chicago Law Review* 69.

[23] *Jobling* v *Associated Dairies Ltd* [1981] UKHL 3 (UKHL [1981]).

[24] Therefore, introducing an element of discretionality in determining the cause; see Moore (n 12) 180.

[25] Robert E Keeton, *Legal Cause in the Law of Torts* (Ohio State University Press, 1963); Warren A Seavey, 'Mr. Justice Cardozo and the Law of Torts' [1939] 48(3) *Yale Law Journal* 390; Glanville Williams, 'The Risk Principle' (1961) 77 *Law Quarterly Review* 179.

[26] A theory espoused in Germany by Joseph Georg Wolf, *Der Normzweck im Deliktsrecht: Ein Diskussionsbeitrag* (Schwartz, 1962).

[27] [2002] UKHL 22.

[28] [2006] UKHL 20.

[29] *McGhee* v *National Coal Board*; for more details on the use of causal presumptions, see Chapter 6.

38   *Causation Rules*

in law. Conversely, he may end up better off as a result of the breach than he would otherwise have been, without having to give credit for such benefit against his recoverable loss'.[30]

2.2 GERMAN LAW

The German law of obligations has been defined as 'narrow in tort but wide in contract'.[31] This definition refers in particular to the ban of pure economic losses as compensable damages, unless they are not consequence of the infringement of a statutorily protected interest. This is one of the reasons explaining the early adoption of a specific statute on private antitrust enforcement.[32] The law was then amended in 2005 with the adoption of the 7th Amendment to the Law Against Restraints of Competition[33] (ARC), which introduced important modifications to the legal basis for the damages claims. Article 33(1) of the ARC provided that whoever causes harm by intentional or negligent infringement of competition law shall be liable for compensation. The ARC, however, had no special rules on the assessment of causation. Therefore, the general principles of tort law continued to apply. In order to implement the Damages Directive, the German law has been enriched with the 9th Amendment introducing several departures from the general proof rules of causation.[34] Despite these latest additions, also the last amendment to the law omits a definition of causation that has to be found in the civil law.

German law determines the existence of factual causation through the *conditio sine qua non* formula (*Äquivalenztheorie*).[35] According to German scholarship, the broad recognition of the requirement of causation has to be attributed to the fact that it determines liability on the basis of a factual responsibility for one's actions. As Schulin observes, 'If the person liable to pay damages did not have any means of preventing the loss for which the claim against him is asserted, then neither can he

---

[30] *Fulton Shipping Inc of Panama v Globalia Business Travel SAU (formerly Travelplan SAU) of Spain* (2014) EWHC 1547 (Comm).

[31] Mauro Bussani and Vernon Valentine Palmer, *Pure Economic Loss in Europe* (Cambridge University Press, 2003) 148.

[32] See, in particular, the version promulgated on 26 August 1998 (*Federal Gazette I*, 2546), Section 33, stating that 'Whoever violates a provision of this Act or a decision taken by the cartel authority shall, if such provision or decision serves to protect another, be obliged vis-à-vis the other to refrain from such conduct; if the violating party acted wilfully or negligently, it shall also be liable for the damages arising from the violation. The claim for injunction may also be asserted by associations for the promotion of trade interests provided the association has legal capacity'. Translation provided by German Law Archive, available at https://germanlawarchive.iuscomp.org/?p=820#33.

[33] Siebtes Gesetz zur Änderung des Gesetzes gegen Wettbewerbsbeschränkungen, Bundesgesetzblatt (BGBL) 2005, Part I, 1954–1969, 2005.

[34] See Chapter 6.

[35] Helmut Koziol, *Basic Questions of Tort Law from a Germanic Perspective* (Jan Sramek Verlag Vienna, 2012) 133–134; Marta Infantino and Eleni Zervogianni, *Causation in European Tort Law* (Cambridge University Press, 2017) 103.

2.2 German Law

be held liable to that extent'.[36] However, as in other systems, the German scholarship has acknowledged the limitations of the but-for test, especially when alternative, cumulative and superseding causal events intervene.[37]

As for legal causation, the jurisprudence has developed other tests to restrict the liability of the tortfeasor. Firstly, German scholars formulated the adequate causal theory approach[38] (*Adäquanztheorie*), in order to select the compensable damages after the application of the *conditio sine qua non test*. A cause is therefore adequate 'if it has in a general and appreciable way enhanced the objective possibility of a consequence of the kind that occurred. In making the necessary assessment account is to be taken only of (a) all the circumstances recognisable by an "optimal" observer at the time the event occurred (b) the additional circumstances known to the originator of the condition'.[39] In the case law, the 'enhancement' of objective possibility of damage soon has become an objective probability of causation of a certain event.[40] Thus, the test builds on the proof of general causation to infer causation in the specific case. Although this approach has been often criticized for excessively relying on the proof of general rather than specific causation, it nonetheless produced a useful intuition that the cause has to be alone sufficient for generating the damage. Moreover, German courts have deemed the adequate liability test insufficient in situations of scarce probability or proof about causation – as, for example, for unforeseeable events in cases of strict liability.[41]

Challenged by the downsides of the *Adäquanztheorie*, German theorists formulated another approach, then called the 'scope of the rule'[42] theory or 'legal policy theory'[43] (*Schutzzweck der Norm*). This approach maintains that the injury claimed, in order to be compensable, should be protected by the specific rule of law that was

---

[36] Bertram Schulin, 'Der Natürliche, Vorrechtliche Kausalitätsbegriff Im Zivilen Schadensersatzrecht' 27, translated by Koziol (n 44) 134.

[37] Ibid., 134, also citing Spickhoff, Folgenzurechnung im Schadensersatzrecht: Gründe und Grenzen, in E. Lorenz (ed), Karlsruher Forum 2007 (2008) 15 ff; Mirjam Annika Frei, *Der Rechtlich Relevante Kausalzusammenhang Im Strafrecht Im Vergleich Mit Dem Zivilrecht* (Schulthess Juristische Medien AG, 2010) 35 ff.

[38] Initially postulated by Carl Ludwig von Bar, *Zur Lehre von Versuch und Theilnahme am Verbrechen* (Hahn, 1859), and Johannes Von Kries, *Die Principien Der Wahrscheinlichkeitsrechnung* (JCB Mohr-Siebeck, 1886) – later developed by Träger, Ludwig, *Der Kausalbegriff Im Straf- Und Zivilrecht* (Keip, 1904), and refined by Guido Calabresi, 'Concerning Cause and the Law of Torts: An Essay for Harry Kalven, Jr '[1975] 49 *The University of Chicago Law Review* 69–108.

[39] BS Markesinis and Hannes Unberath, *The German Law of Torts: A Comparative Treatise* (Hart Publishing, 2002) 107.

[40] Honoré (n 17) para 80.

[41] Infantino and Zervogianni (n 44) 114 and 411.

[42] This theory is applied within the framework of § 823 II BGB (breach of statutory duty); § 839 (governmental liability); and § 823 I as regards safety duties (*Verkehrspflichten*), the right to business (*das Recht am Gewerbebetrieb*) and the general personality right (*allgemeine Persönlichkeitsrecht*).

[43] In particular, this second definition was given by HLA Hart and Tony Honoré, Causation in the Law (Oxford University Press, 1985), 291.

40 *Causation Rules*

infringed.[44] For instance, bad maintenance of a public street triggers the responsibility of the authority which owes a specific duty of care for damages to persons who are involved in a car accident caused by the bad maintenance. On the other hand, the authority is not liable, for instance, for claims based on pure economic losses incurred by persons who suffer a delay because of bad maintenance.[45] This is because the scope of the rule is to impose to the highway authority a duty of care of the safety of road users and not a protection against any sort of loss the highway users might incur in. The 7th Amendment to the ARC broadened the scope of Section 33(1) on damages claims, replacing the word 'protected parties' with the more all-embracing 'affected parties',[46] therefore impacting on the extent of legal causation. Thanks to this modification, not only the parties that are directly protected by the statute but any party affected by the antitrust infringement is within the scope of the rule.

German courts now tend to apply a three-stage approach, whereby they firstly use the but-for test, then they determine whether the action is an adequate cause of the event, and finally they have to confirm that the protective scope of the rule covers the harm caused.

2.3 FRENCH LAW

The French liability system for competition law damages actions is based on general tort law rules complemented by the Ordinance No. 2017-303 of 9 March 2017 (Ordinance) and its implementing decree (Decree) modifying the French Commercial Code (FCC). Parties harmed by antitrust infringements can therefore claim damages under Article 1382 of the French Civil Code[47] for which 'Any act of a person which causes damage to another makes him by whose fault the damage occurred to make reparation for the damage'.[48] This provision states a general

---

[44] It is defined, within the notes to the art. 4:101 of DCFR as 'an obligation to make reparation will only arise, if the damage claimed, according to its type and its origin, stems from a sphere of danger which the infringed norm was enacted to protect against'; see Christian von Bar, *Non-Contractual Liability Arising Out of Damage Caused to Another (PEL Liab. Dam.)* (Sellier, 2009) 759.

[45] Van Dam (n 1) 314.

[46] The actual formulation of Section 33(1) recites: 'Whoever violates a provision of this Part or Articles 101 or 102 of the Treaty on the Functioning of the European Union (infringer) or whoever violates a decision taken by the competition authority shall be obliged to the *person affected* to rectify the harm caused by the infringement and, where there is a risk of recurrence, to desist from further infringements', emphasis added.

[47] The statutory basis for damages actions under French law is the general regime for torts – i.e., Article 1382 of the French Civil Code. It states the general principle that whoever anyone who caused a damage by his fault shall be liable and compensate the victim for the loss incurred, which implies three general elements: a fault, a direct and certain damage and a causal link between the fault and the damage.

[48] In the original version, 'Tout fait quelconque de l'homme, qui cause à autrui un dommage, oblige celui par la faute duquel il est arrivé, à le réparer'.

2.3 French law

principle whereby any act which causes damages by fault obliges the tortfeasor to repair it. Additionally, Article L 481-1 of the Code de Commerce sanctions the liability of undertakings for antitrust damages. Following the entry into force of the Damages Directive, the French Ministry of Justice has implemented an ordinance adding to the book IV of the Commercial Code a new title VIII on Damages actions for anticompetitive practices.[49] In addition to these amendements, the Ministry of Justice has provided additional guidance publishing the 'Circulaire' of 23 March 2017 and the Paris Court of Appeal has issued a set of guidelines.[50] However, causation is still largely regulated by general tort law. The French system is characterized by a determined reluctance to conceptualize causation, which remains a vague concept both in case law and in scholarly papers.[51]

From a factual perspective, French judges tend to apply the same but-for test used by other national courts. French civil courts apply the general account of the 'direct cause' of the harm, based on Article 1382 of the French Civil Code. The legal causal link is defined in Article 1151 of the Code Civil which – although referring to contracts – has long since been applied to non-contractual obligations.[52] This norm prescribes that only the 'immediate and direct consequences' of the breach of law are subject to compensation. However, as it is subject to interpretation as to what is an immediate and direct consequence of a breach of the law, courts have developed two main tests. The German theory of adequate causation strongly influenced the French laws of obligations at the beginning of the twentieth century, to the extent that French courts often apply a version of the adequate theory often deprived of its probabilistic calculation.[53] Other courts adopt a stricter interpretation of the law requiring the causal link to be certain and direct.[54] However, there is no consensus on the definition of such characteristics of causation.

The causal connection between the breach of law and the damage has to be therefore 'direct and certain', where these characteristics do not refer to specific abstract categories but rather tend to limit the judicial application of causation.[55] Generally, French lawyers revert to the common-sense and 'normal course of things' standard in order to determine

---

[49] Section VIII of chapter IV of the French Commercial Code, 'Des actions en dommages et intérêts du fait des pratiques anticoncurrentielles'.

[50] The 'Fiches méthodologiques' of 19 October 2017.

[51] Geneviève Viney and Patrice Jourdain, *Les conditions de la responsabilité* (LGD, 2006) 335, who refer to 'le refus systématique de tout effort de définition'.

[52] François Terré, Philippe Simler and Yves Lequette, *Droit civil: Les obligations* (Dalloz, 1999) 592; Viney and Jourdain (n 51) 348; Duncan Fairgrieve and Florence G'Sell-Macrez, 'Causation in French Law: Pragmatism and Policy' in Richard Goldberg (ed), *Perspectives on Causation* (Hart Publishing, 2011) 113.

[53] Jacques Ghestin and others, *Traité de droit civil: Les conditions de la responsabilité* (LGDJ, 1998).

[54] Walter Van Gerven, Jeremy Lever, and Pierre Larouche, *Cases, Materials and Text on National, Supranational and International Tort Law* (Hart, 2000) 424; Van Dam (n 1) 319.

[55] Duncan Fairgrieve and Florence G'Sell-Macrez, 'Causation in French Law: Pragmatism and Policy' in Richard Goldberg (ed) *Perspectives on Causation* (Hart, 2011) 113.

the adequacy of a single causal element.[56] These characteristics have to be matched with a particularly strict standard adopted in competition law cases. The requirement of the direct causal link in competition law has been defined as 'the main obstacle on which the right to reparation stumbles'.[57] This situation may explain the reason why the majority of competition law claims concern contractual disputes and the claims for damages are often based on loss of chance allegations.[58] Causation is indeed the main instrument of the French judge to determine responsibility for the harm. While Article 1240 c.c. requires the finding of fault on the side of the tortfeasor, for the purpose of the application of competition law, this requirement is satisfied by the mere infringement of the law. This is usually defined as objective fault, and it requires only the finding of illegality.[59]

French scholars have proposed two projects of reform of the laws of obligations.[60] The first project was submitted to the French Minister of Justice in 2005, and it was coordinated by Prof. Pierre Català (*Català Project*).[61] The second was coordinated by Prof. François Terré and was divided into two draft projects, one devoted to the law of contracts and the other to non-contractual liability (*Terré Project*).[62] Both the Català project and Terré project only cursorily deal with causation, although they do it in different manners. While the Català draft simply suggests that the causal link must be proven, the Terré draft devotes Article 10 to the definition of causation. However, also in the latter case, the draft offers a particularly loose definition which introduces the concept of the 'ordinary course of things and without which it would not have occurred' in order to determine the causal regularity of the link.[63] Both drafts opted for the introduction of more flexibility in the civil liability systems, leaving to the judge ample discretion in the investigation of the causal nexus.[64]

---

[56] Ibid., 119. See infra Chapter 5.

[57] Louis Vogel, *Les Actions Civiles de Concurrence. Union Européenne, France, Allemagne, Royaume-Uni, Italie, Suisse, États-Unis* (EPA, 2013) 43.

[58] See Section 4.4. Cf Ioannis Lianos, 'Causal Uncertainty and Damages Claims for the Infringement of Competition Law in Europe' [2015] 34 *Yearbook of European Law* 170, 204.

[59] See David Ashton, *Competition Damages Actions in the EU: Law and Practice*, Second Edition (Edward Elgar Publishing, 2018) 34, citing SARL Philippe Streiff Motorsport/SAS Speedy (25ème chambre A, judgment of 28 June 2002, JCP E. 2003, JP n° II 1018, 2091), 'The Paris Cour d'appel ruled that a breach of Articles L. 420-1 and L. 420-2 of the *code de commerce* gave standing for an action on the basis of Article 1382 of the *code civil*'. Moreover, in Eco System/ Peugeot (judgment of 22 October 1996, not published, but mentioned by Fasquelle, D in 'La réparation des dommages causés par les pratiques anticoncurrentielles', RTD com, n° 4/1998, p 772), the Paris Tribunal de commerce the finding of an infringement of Article 101 (1) TFEU by the Commission, automatically determines the fault of the infringer in a damages action.

[60] Olivier Moréteau, 'France: French Tort Law in the Light of European Harmonization' [2013] 6 *Journal of Civil Law Studies* 2, 15.

[61] Pierre Català, 'Avant-Projet de Réforme du Droit des Obligations et du Droite de la Prescription' (Documentation française, 2005), available at www.ladocumentationfrancaise.fr/rapports-publics/054000622/.

[62] François Terré (ed), *Pour une réforme du droit de la responsabilité civile* (Dalloz, 2011).

[63] Article 10(1): 'Constitue la cause du dommage tout fait propre à le produire selon le cours ordinaire des choses et sans lequel il ne serait pas advenu'.

[64] Moréteau, 'France: French Tort Law in the Light of European Harmonization' (n 65) 770.

2.4 Italian law

This wide definition of causation in law justifies the rather flexible approach adopted by French courts that have used in some cases also the causal proportional liability approach to determine causation.[65] The assessment of causation in competition law damages actions remains, however, the thorniest element of the tort to prove for French lawyers.[66] This situation explains the frequent recourse to the doctrine of loss of chance (*perte de chance*), which permits overcoming the proof of the certain and direct causal link between the infringement and the damage.[67] Moreover, the ordinance has introduced presumptions to facilitate the claimant's action, especially in cases of causal uncertainty.[68]

2.4 ITALIAN LAW

In the Italian system, the obligation to compensate antitrust injuries is based on the combination of Article 2043 of the Civil Code and Article 33 of the Law 287/90 (Law on the Protection of Competition).[69] According to Article 2043 C.C., 'Any intentional or negligent act that causes a wrongful injury to another obliges the person who has committed the act to pay damages'. The norm synthesizes the French model based on the formula of the *neminem laedere* and the German-inspired addition of the requirement of a 'wrongful injury'.[70] However, the Italian legislator has avoided defining either principle of civil responsibility, leaving it to the courts and the scholars to conceptualize all its aspects, including causation.

The Italian theoretical background related to causation has been at the centre of important doctrinal discussions and brisk changes in the case law, with seminal decisions in competition law damages actions that defined the extent of causation. The causal assessment consists of a two-stage process[71] whereby, firstly, the judge has

---

[65] Olivier Moréteau, 'Causal Uncertainty and Proportional Liability in France' in Israel Gilead, Michael D Green and Bernhard A Koch (eds), *Proportional Liability: Analytical and Comparative Perspectives*, Tort and Insurance Law 33 (De Gruyter, 2013) 141.

[66] Jacques Buhart and Lionel Lesur, 'France: Private Antitrust Litigation' [2014] *Global Competition Review* 60.

[67] See infra Section 5.3.

[68] See Chapter 6.

[69] Law No 287 of 10 October 1990 containing Rules on Protection of Competition (*Norme per la tutela della concorrenza e del mercato*) G U 13 October 1990, no. 240.

[70] Rodolfo Sacco, 'Legal Formants: A Dynamic Approach to Comparative Law (Installment II of II)' [1991] 39 *The American Journal of Comparative Law* 343, 366; Infantino and Zervogianni (n 44) 94.

[71] Gino Gorla, 'Sulla Cosiddetta Causalità Giuridica: Fatto Dannoso E Conseguenze' [1951] I (11) *Rivista Di Diritto Commerciale* 405; Angelo Luminoso, 'Possibilità O Necessità Della Relazione Causale' [1991] *Rivista Giuridica Sarda* 533; Francesco Realmonte, *Il problema del rapporto di causalità nel risarcimento del danno* (Giuffrè, 1967); Francesco Donato Busnelli and Salvatore Patti, *Danno e responsabilità civile* (G Giappichelli Editore, 2013); Umberto Breccia, *Le obbligazioni* (Giuffrè, 1991); Eugenio Bonvicini, *La responsabilità civile: Responsabilità da accadimento tipico. Parte speciale: Il danno a persona* (A. Giuffrè, 1971); SM Carbone, 'Il Rapporto Di Causalità', in Alpa-Bessone (eds), *La Responsabilità Civile* vol II

44 Causation Rules

to assess the 'natural causality'[72] or cause-in-fact, which is the material link between the event and the damage, generally through the adoption of the *conditio sine qua non* test.[73] Secondly, the judge determines the legal causation for detecting and limiting the damages subject to compensation.[74]

With regard to the second moment of the causal enquiry, Italian judges have transitioned from an account similar to the adequate cause to a more complex rule of 'causal regularity' (*regolarità causale*), although both are still in use today. Article 1223 of the Civil Code literally limits the compensable damage to the direct and immediate effects of the action.[75] This restrictive definition was interpreted extensively by proponents of a broader approach who described Article 1223 C.C. as a mere application of the theory of adequacy of the causal conditions.[76] The prevalent opinion supports this view, although some scholars have put forward dissenting and alternative approaches.[77] The predominant theoretical approach reframed the provision of Article 1223 C.C. going back to its historical roots.[78] The contextualization of the norm permitted one to go beyond the precise wording of the law[79] and even to clearly point out that Italian law admits the award of indirect damages.[80]

(Giuffrè, 1980) 55 f.; Vincenzo Carbone, *Il fatto dannoso nella responsabilità civile* (Jovene, 1969); Valente, 'Appunti in Tema Di Fatto, Nesso Causale E Danno' (1955) *Diritto E Giurisprudenza*, 372; Pietro Trimarchi, *Causalità e danno* (Giuffrè, 1967).

[72] The Italian Civil Code does not define the cause-in-fact whose definition is borrowed from the Articles 40 and 41 of the Criminal Code; see Guido Alpa, *La responsabilità civile. Parte generale* (Wolters Kluwer Italia, 2010) 326; Marco Capecchi, *Il Nesso Di Causalità: Dalla Condicio Sine qua Non Alla Responsabilità Proporzionale* (CEDAM, 2012) 18.

[73] Other authors dissent from this view maintaining that the assessment of causation has a unitary nature and is operated before the selection of the compensable damages; see Paolo Forchielli, *Il rapporto di causalità nell'illecito civile* (CEDAM, 1960); Francesco Carnelutti, 'Perseverare Diabolicum (a Proposito Del Limite Della Responsabilità per Danni)' (1952) *Il Foro Italiano* 97–98; Mario Barcellona, *Inattuazione dello scambio e sviluppo capitalistico: Formazione storica e funzione della disciplina del danno contrattuale* (Giuffrè, 1980); Roberto Pucella, *La causalità 'incerta'* (Giappichelli, 2007).

[74] Nicolò Lipari and others, *Diritto civile* (Giuffrè, 2009); Gorla, Gino (n 71).

[75] Article 1223 Civil Code: 'Il risarcimento del danno per l'inadempimento o per il ritardo deve comprendere così la perdita subita dal creditore come il mancato guadagno, in quanto ne siano conseguenza immediata e diretta'.

[76] Paolo Forchielli, Responsabilità civile (CEDAM, 1983) 45 ff.

[77] The first minority view maintains that the Article 1223 does not set any limit to legal causation and to responsibility; see Adriano De Cupis, *Il danno: Teoria generale della responsabilità civile* (Giuffrè, 1979) 122; Giovanni Valcavi, 'Sulla causalità giuridica nella responsabilità civile da inadempienza e da illecito' (2001) *Rivista di diritto civile* II 409. A second alternative view, developed by Trimarchi, asserts that the Article 1223 demands the analysis of the interest protected by the rule violated in order to determine legal causation, see Trimarchi (n 71) 3.

[78] In particular, using the concept of 'necessary damage' formulated by Pothier: Robert Joseph Pothier, *Traité des obligations, selon les règles, tant du for de la conscience que du for extérieur* (Letellier, 1805).

[79] Forchielli (n 76) 50.

[80] Adriano De Cupis, *Il danno: Teoria generale della responsabilità civile* (Giuffrè, 1979) 235.

The approach of Italian courts to Article 1223 C.C. is unanimous in stating that it is impossible to establish a unique criterion for the 'immediate and direct effects'.[81] Relying on an extensive interpretation of the law, judges normally consider both direct and indirect damages as covered by Article 1223 C.C.[82] The predominant case law follows the principle of causal regularity, whereby legal causation is established when damages are a normal or regular consequence of the event.[83] This approach entails a logic or probabilistic judgement based on which the judge has to rely on 'covering laws' (*leggi di copertura*) that consist in sufficient scientific or economic evidences which can support the allegation of causation.[84]

The Italian case law on causation is sweeping and ambivalent, to the extent that in cases of causal uncertainty, especially due to multiple causes, some courts have swore by an all-or-nothing approach[85] and others by a causal proportional liability system.[86] Therefore, while approaches to uncertain causation have been highly conceptualized, it is often difficult to determine in advance what approach or causal rule a court will decide to adopt. Due to this uncertainty, some scholars have observed that 'causation is one of the main battlefields where the liability game is played' in Italy.[87]

The Legislative Decree 19 January 2017, n 3 (GU n 15 del 19-1-2017), transposing Directive 2014/14 in Italian law, has done little to solve this uncertainty. The decree, for the most part, transposes the Directive without major additions. It therefore grants standing to sue to any person harmed by an antitrust infringement[88] and, similarly to the Directive, the decree omits any definition of the causal requirements leaving it to the general tort law.

2.5 US LAW

Causation has been defined in the United States as 'one of the most underexplored areas in antitrust law'.[89] Contrary to what is observed in Europe, the US judge refers

---

[81] Laura Castelli, 'La Causalità Giuridica Nel Campo Degli Illeciti Anticoncorrenziali' (2013) 18 *Danno E Responsabilità* 11 1051.

[82] For a description of the early case law, see Alessandra Pinori, 'Il Criterio Legislativo Delle Conseguenze Immediate E Dirette' in Giovanna Visintini (ed), *Il Risarcimento Del Danno Contrattuale Ed Extracontrattuale* (Giuffrè, 1984).

[83] Corte di Cassazione civ., 23 December 2010, n 26042 (rv 615614), in CED Cassazione (2010); Corte di Cassazione civ., 16 October 2007, n 21619, in Danno e Responsabilità, 2008, 1, 43 commented by R. Pucella [2008]; Corte di Cassazione, 9 April 1963, n 910, in Giurisprudenza italiana, I, 490 [1964], Corte di Cassazione, 3 June 1980, n 3622, in Massimario Giustizia civile, 6 [1980]; Corte di Cassazione civ., 18 July 1987, n 6325, in Massimario Giuridico italiano [1987].

[84] See infra Chapter 5.

[85] Corte di Cassazione, civ., 16 January 2009, n 975, in Giustizia Civile Massimario, 2009, 68.

[86] Corte di Cassazione civ., 21 July 2011, n 15991, in Giustizia Civile Massimario, 2011, 1098; Infantino and Zervogianni (n 44) 95.

[87] Ibid.

[88] Article 1(1).

[89] Michael A Carrier, 'A Tort-Based Causation Framework for Antitrust Analysis' [2011] 77 *Antitrust Law Journal* 991, on which is based most of the following case law analysis.

46   *Causation Rules*

to the antitrust regulation in order to define each single aspect of the unlawful behaviour, and causation makes no exception. Therefore, no references (at least direct references) to general tort law are made. However, several tests are borrowed from tort law[90] with some variations, allowed mainly by the lack of specific regulation.[91]

This premise is fundamental to understand the differing, sometimes even contrasting, approaches adopted by US and EU courts in assessing antitrust causation.

2.5.1 *Material Causation*

Causation tests can vary from a 'sole proximate cause' to a mere 'substantial factor'. It is not possible to find a principle which enjoys priority over the others in the case law because, from a chronological viewpoint, they have been bundling up without the subsequent dismissal of the prior.

In *Zenith Radio Corp.*,[92] the Supreme Court opened to what is still the most common approach in cartel litigation, which is to require the plaintiff to substantiate that the agency is a 'material cause of the injury'.[93] In the more recent *Methyl* and *Tele Atlas* cases, courts stated, respectively, that the conduct has to be a 'substantial factor of the injury'[94] and that the plaintiff does not need to 'exhaust all possible alternative sources of injury'.[95] Additionally, some courts require that the conduct has to be the 'sole proximate cause' of the harm.[96] These obiter dicta have been also inflected with different formulations, such as that the conduct has 'materially contributed' to the plaintiff's harm or that the plaintiff must show 'with a fair degree of certainty'[97] that the 'defendant's illegal conduct materially contributed to the injury'.[98]

Factual causation in abuse of monopoly power cases has shown a similar pattern. In *Microsoft*, the court alleged that it is sufficient for the plaintiff to show that there is a reasonable connection between the conduct and the injury suffered.[99] Whereas in the following *Broadcom* case, the court adopted a particularly flexible causation test since it merely required that the harm has to 'increase the likelihood that patent

---

[90] Such as '"but for" causation, proximate cause, sole causation, reasonable connection, and increased possibility of harm', ibid., 992.

[91] Ibid., 1002.

[92] *Zenith Radio Corp.* v *Hazeltine Research, Inc.* 395 U.S. 100 [1969].

[93] Ibid., 114 n 9.

[94] *In re Methyl Tertiary Butyl Ether (MTBE) Products Liability Litigation* [2010] 739 F. Supp. 2d 576 (SDNY) 596.

[95] *Tele Atlas N.V.* v *NAVTEQ Corp.*, No. C-05-01673, 2008 WL 4809441, at *22 [N.D. Cal. 2008].

[96] *Conwood Co.* v *U.S. Tobacco Co.*, 290 F.3d 768, 791 [6th Cir. 2002]; *Nat'l Indep. Theatre Exhibitors, Inc.* v *Buena Vista Distrib. Co.*, 748 F.2d 602, 607 [11th Cir. 1984].

[97] *Continental Ore Co.* v *Union Carbide & Carbon Corp.* 370 U.S. 690, 702 [1962].

[98] *Hayes* v *Solomon* 597 F.2d 958, 978 [5th Cir. 1979] (quotation omitted); see also *McClure* v *Undersea In dus., Inc.*, 671 F.2d 1287, 1289 [11th Cir. 1982].

[99] *United States* v *Microsoft* 253 F.3d 34 [D.C. Cir. 2001].

rights will confer monopoly power'.[100] Finally, in the subsequent *Rambus* case, the court applied a higher standard of causation adopting a 'but-for' exclusive test.[101] The claim was rejected on the basis that since it was at least possible that the defendant would have selected plaintiff's technology, causation was not proven.

In *Costner*, instead, the court dealt with the problem of multiple causes, in particular when antitrust and non-antitrust causes concur in the causation of the damage.[102] The judge accepted the claim even though '[t]here was evidence that general economic conditions and poor management caused a decline in plaintiff's business', and taking into consideration that there also was 'evidence that the illegal tying arrangements contributed to the decline'.[103] However, the Sixth Circuit concluded, since there was also evidence of causal contribution to the harm, the jury and the district court's verdict was not 'unfair' and therefore could not be set aside.[104] In *City of Long Beach v Standard Oil Co. of California*, the Ninth Circuit has adopted a stricter view of the requirements for the definition and proof of causation, rejecting the claim for lack of causation since '[t]he establishment of price ceilings" did "not in itself mean that the companies' conduct could not have caused the injuries'.[105]

According to Carrier, there are three mainstream approaches to causation in the US antitrust panorama: *Microsoft* with its flexible approach, *Rambus* with its strict requirements and *Broadcom* with its particularly lax rule.[106] These are only the main and better explained of the many different canons developed so far. American case law on antitrust causation is indeed drifting in a sea of different approaches. The problem depends firstly on the refusal to build the civil antitrust framework on the more solid basement of tort law.[107] Carrier observes that private antitrust law should gain 'insights by turning to tort law, the law with the most developed causation framework'.[108] He also proposes to adapt the general tort law rules in a way that echoes the newly approved European Directive on damages actions, since he suggests an inversion of the burden of proof when there is a 'reasonable connection between the challenged conduct and the anticompetitive effects'.[109] The plaintiff would have to provide prima facie evidence showing the anticompetitive effects flowing from the unlawful behaviour, and the damage would be presumed.

---

[100] *Broadcom Corp. v Qualcomm Inc* 501 F.3d 297 [3rd Cir. 2007].
[101] *Rambus Inc. v FTC.* 522 F.3d 456 [D.C. Cir. 2008].
[102] *Costner v Blount National Bank* n 52 578 F.2d 1192 [6th Cir. 1978].
[103] Ibid., 1195.
[104] Ibid., 1196.
[105] 872 F.2d 1401 [9th Cir. 1989], 1408.
[106] Carrier (n 89).
[107] See, in this regard, ibid. (n 89) 1001.
[108] Ibid., 1001.
[109] Ibid., 1006.

2.5.2 *The Antitrust Damage*

According to the US case law, the claimant has to show to have suffered an 'antitrust injury'. The Supreme Court defined this harm as 'injury of the type the antitrust laws were intended to prevent and that flows from that which makes the defendant's acts unlawful'.[110] This landmark case concerned a bowling equipment manufacturer, Brunswick, which started acquiring failing bowling centres in the 1960s. After a few years, Brunswick had acquired 222 centres, some of them close or in competition with the plaintiff, Pueblo. The latter sued Brunswick, alleging, inter alia, that these acquisitions might have substantially lessened competition or anyway lead to monopolization of the market in violation of § 7 of the Clayton Act, 15 U.S.C. § 18.[111] The Supreme Court rejected the claim, holding that the plaintiff claimed the compensation of an injury that did not fall into the types of harm that antitrust law was designed to protect.[112] The following judgments have considered the antitrust damage an issue of 'standing'.[113] In the case *Gatt* v *PMC*, the Court of Appeal decided that Gatt had no standing to sue the defendants due to a lack of antitrust damage.[114] Gatt intended to recover the damages caused by an alleged bid-rigging scheme of the defendants, which forced Gatt out of the market. In this connection, the court observed that 'this harm only supports antitrust injury, however, if it flows from that which makes the bid-rigging scheme unlawful'.[115] The Second Circuit court observed that 'The doctrine of antitrust standing prevents private plaintiffs from recover[ing] damages under § 4 . . . merely by showing injury causally linked to an illegal presence in the market'[116] rather in order to establish antitrust injury, the plaintiff must demonstrate that its injury is 'of the type the antitrust laws were intended to prevent and that flows from that which makes [or might make] defendants' acts unlawful'.[117] On this basis, the court established that the claimant's injuries were at best an indirect result of the alleged antitrust violation.[118] The price-fixing scheme through bid-rigging, as perpetuated by termination of the Dealer Agreement, had the possible effect of generating a loss of opportunity for Gatt, which was not enough, according to the court to prove causation: 'Gatt was

---

[110] *Brunswick Corp.* v *Pueblo Bowl-O-Mat, Inc.*
[111] Ibid.
[112] Ibid.
[113] Pier Luigi Parcu, Giorgio Monti and Marco Botta, *Private Enforcement of EU Competition Law: The Impact of the Damages Directive* (Edward Elgar Publishing, 2018) 44.
[114] *Gatt Communications, Inc.* v *PMC Associates, L.L.C.* 711 F.3d 68, 76 [2nd Cir. 2013].
[115] Ibid., 76.
[116] *Citing Atlantic Richfield Co.* v *USA Petroleum Co.*, 495 U.S. 328, 334, 110 S.Ct. 1884, 109 L.Ed.2d 333 [1990].
[117] Referring to *Daniel* v *American Bd. of Emergency Medicine*, 428 F.3d 408 [2d Cir. 2005] 438.
[118] They refer to the case *International Bus. Machs. Corp.* v *Platform Solutions, Inc.*, 658 F.-Supp.2d 603, 611 (SDNY, 2009) establishing that 'Directness in the antitrust context means close in the chain of causation'; see also Associated General Contractors, 459 U.S. at 540–541, 103 S.Ct. 897.

only incidentally harmed by the conspiracy . . . It did not pay higher prices by virtue of the conspiracy; it merely lost the right to sell one brand of radio. If there are direct victims of the alleged conspiracy, they are the state agencies, not Gatt'.[119]

As European jurisdictions did not develop a similar concept of 'antitrust damage', most of the issues pertaining to whether the loss is related to the antitrust offence would be solved through legal causation. German law would address similar problems to those in *Brunswick* and *Gatt* by referring to the 'scope of the norm' principle, whereby the harm has to be within the protective scope of the rule infringed in order to be compensated.[120] In England, the judge would have to consider if claimant was a member of the class protected by the Act and if the damage occurred in the manner against which the Act was meant to guard.[121] However, this analysis of the scope of the national legislation should never result in a violation of the principle of effectiveness of EU law, denying standing to claimants that would otherwise be allowed under EU law. Italian law would determine the existence of causation through the principle of causal regularity and in French law by application of the theory of a *perte d'une chance*.[122]

European jurisdictions would also deal with those issues of 'antitrust damages' by referring to the foreseeability of the damage (England, Italy and Germany) or to the adequate test of causation (Italy and Germany). Although EU competition law grants standing to anyone harmed by an antitrust infringement, if the harm is not related to the norm breached, it will not be subject to compensation.[123]

[119] *Gatt v PMC* (n 114) 79.
[120] See supra, Section 2.2.
[121] Section 2.1.
[122] Section 2.3.
[123] Section 1.6 for the differences in the formulation of such rules on legal causation.

3

Causation in the European Union Competition Law and Decisions

The Directive on Damages Actions 104/2014 (the Damages Directive)[1] has laid down a common European framework for the regulation of competition damages actions. It establishes fundamental principles, such as the right to compensation and the joint liability of antitrust infringers for such compensation. However, it explicitly avoids defining causation, thus leaving it to the domestic laws of member states. The main limit set by the EU law is the observance of the principles of equivalence and effectiveness, in line with what was already disposed by the CJEU in *Manfredi*.[2] However, there are some principles addressing causation that can be found in European law and case law.

Article 3 of the Damages Directive establishes the principle for which the right to stand in a claim for infringement of Articles 101 and 102 TFEU belongs to 'any natural or legal person who has suffered an harm caused by an infringement of competition law'.[3] From a procedural perspective, therefore, there is no limitation to the standing to sue by subjects harmed in an antitrust infringement. These claimants cannot be selected on the basis of individual characteristics – for instance, differentiating between direct and indirect purchasers. However, the trier of facts has to make sure that the claim for compensation is well founded and has to verify the existence of a 'causal relationship between the harm suffered and the prohibited arrangement'.[4] Therefore, there is no selection of compensable parties but only of

---

[1] Directive 2014/104/EU of 26 November 2014 on Certain Rules Governing Actions for Damages under National Law for Infringements of the Competition Law Provisions of the Member States and of the European Union, [2014] OJ L349/1.

[2] Joined Cases C-295/04 to C-298/04 *Vincenzo Manfredi v Lloyd Adriatico Assicurazioni SpA* [2006] ECR I-6619.

[3] See also ibid., para 60; Case C-453/99 *Courage Ltd v Bernard Crehan* and *Bernard Crehan v Courage Ltd and Others* [2001] ECR I-06297, para 26; Case C-199/11 *Europese Gemeenschap v Otis NV and Others* [2012] ECLI:EU:C:2012:684, para 41; Case C-536/11, Donau Chemie and Others [2013] ECLI:EU:C:2013:366, para 21; Article 3 *Directive 2014/104/EU.*

[4] Joined Cases C-295/04 to C-298/04 *Vincenzo Manfredi* (n 2), para 17.

3.1 *Causation in the Court of Justice of the European Union Decisions* 51

compensable damages. In other words, as for the actual formulation of European law principles, no one can be denied access to damages action for antitrust infringement as a matter of standing, but the limitation to compensation can be found as a matter of lack of causal connection of the harm to the infringement. However, as already mentioned, the Directive omits any conceptualization of the causal link. On the other hand, it contains some rules that realize a piecemeal harmonization of the proof rules of causation, which are analyzed in this section and in Chapters 5 and 6.

The diverse set of approaches to causation in the European Union did not suffice to the adoption of a common rule, although several voices urged for a clarification of the issue of causation in competition law.[5] However, some common interpretative principles can be found in the case law of the European courts and in the legislative acts and papers of the European Union institutions, although both showed visible reluctance to give unequivocal definitions and to deepen into the interpretation of causation.

3.1 CAUSATION IN THE COURT OF JUSTICE OF THE EUROPEAN UNION DECISIONS

The European Union courts have not developed any precise definition of causation or causal link. However, from the case law, it is possible to glean important information on the minimum requirements of causation for civil liability. Albeit some authors argue that the ECJ has formulated an autonomous theory of causation,[6] the definition(s), if existing, seem to lack a consistent and comprehensive approach that would suffice to create an independent account of causation and its proof.

The ECJ's case law on causation is abundant with regard to state liability for infringement of EU Treaties' norms. The approach to causation developed by this case law has been used also in cases of horizontal application of EU competition law,[7] making it especially useful to analyse with reference to competition law.

---

[5] Centre for European Policy Studies (CEPS), Erasmus University Rotterdam (EUR) and Luiss Guido Carli (LUISS), 'Making Antitrust Damages Actions More Effective in the EU. Welfare Impact and Potential Scenarios', 21 December 2007, available at http://ec.europa.eu/competi tion/antitrust/actionsdamages/files_white_paper/impact_study.pdf; *Study on the Conditions of Claims for Damages in Case of Infringement of EC Competition Rules*, 2004, available at http:// ec.europa.eu/competition/antitrust/actionsdamages/comparative_report_clean_en.pdf; Commission Staff Working Paper Accompanying the White Paper on Damages Actions for Breach of the EC Antitrust Rules, 2008.

[6] Wolfgang Wurmnest, *Grundzüge eines europäischen Haftungsrecht: Eine vergleichende Untersuchung des Gemeinschaftsrechts* (Mohr Siebeck, 2003); Klaus Bitterich, 'Elements of an Autonomous Concept of Causation in European Community Law Concerning Liability' vol 1 [2007] *Zeitschrift für vergleichende Rechtswissenschaft* 12.

[7] Joined Cases C-295/04 to C-298/04 *Vincenzo Manfredi* (n 2).

52 *Causation in the European Union Competition Law and Decisions*

Chronologically, the leading case is *Roquettes Frères*,[8] in which the court, facing a case of state liability, pointed out that the claimant has to prove the 'causal connexion' between the damage to its business and the measures adopted by the European community to seek redress.[9] Moreover, the court argued that, in order to substantiate the causal link, it is not sufficient for the applicant to supplement its claim with statistical evidence about market conditions[10] even in a claim for nominal damages.[11] In the *Dumortier Frères* case, the court pointed out that the consequence of the misconduct causing the damage has to be 'direct'.[12] The following case law, however, has not applied this particular requirement of the causal link. Indeed, the *Fresh Marine* decision[13] as well as the landmark *Francovich* decision[14] required only the proof of a causal link, without demanding it to be direct.

However, this element was resuscitated in *Brasserie du Pêcheur*, where the court set out three requirements for conferring the right to damages: (1) a rule of law which confers rights on individuals; (2) a sufficiently serious breach of that rule and (3) a direct causal link between the breach of the obligation resting on the state and the damage sustained by the injured parties.[15]

The court never expounded the nature of the direct causal nexus that it required. There is no clear definition of it either in the EU legislation or in the case law interpreting it. The court has, in various instances, applied a *conditio sine qua non* test[16] and also added that, in addition, the claimant has to prove the existence of a sufficient proximity between the illegal act and the loss suffered.[17] However, the court also admitted that this way of assessing causation is not sufficient to create an independent principle of causation and that it needs to be complemented by national laws.[18] In this vein, some advocate generals argued for the introduction of an adequate causation test, but it has never become law.[19]

---

[8] Case 26/74 Société Roquette *Frères* v *Commission of the European Communities*, 21 May 1976, ECR 677.

[9] Ibid., para 23.

[10] In particular, in this case, the applicant produced statistics showing the increase in importations of amyloid products in France, which, in turn, should have demonstrated the competitive advantage of its foreign competitors; see paras 16–17.

[11] Ibid., 687–688.

[12] Joined Cases 64/76, 113/76, 167/78, 239/78, 27/79, 28/79 and 45/79 *Dumortier Frères* v *Council* [1979] ECR 3091.

[13] Case C-472/00 *Commission* v *Fresh Marine Company A/S* [2003] ECR 7541.

[14] Joined Cases C-6/90 and C-9/90, *Andrea Francovich and Danila Bonifaci and Others* v *Italian Republic* [1991] ECR 5357.

[15] Brasserie du Pêcheur and Factortame, para 51.

[16] Case T-478/93 *Wafer Zoo* v *Commission* [1995] ECR II-1479, 49.

[17] *Dumortier Frères* v *Council* [1979] ECR 3091.

[18] Joined Cases C-104/89 and C-37/90 *Mulder* v *Council and Commission* [1992] ECR I-3061; C-238/78 *Ireks-Arkady* v *Council and Commission* [1981] ECR 01719.

[19] Opinion of Mr Van Gerven, Case C-128/92 [1994] ECR I-01209, I–1256; Opinion of Advocate General Kokott Case C-557/12 *Kone AG and Others* v *ÖBB-Infrastruktur* AG ECLI:EU: C:2014:45.

The CJEU, when dealing with private enforcement of competition law, appears to be even more reluctant to define rules pertaining to the law of obligations. In *Manfredi*, the CJEU clearly stated that causation is a fundamental element of the compensation claim but that it rests with the applicable law to determine the characteristics of this element of civil responsibility.[20] The court further specified that the application of domestic law has to be subordinated to the observance of principles of equivalence[21] and effectiveness[22] of EU law.[23]

This decision however, beyond the formulation of the horizontal effect principle, confirms another important principle for the following private antitrust enforcement. The court, indeed, by referring to the requirements of liability developed by previous case law, confirms that the criteria pointed out for state liability are applicable also in competition law. For the first time, it was AG Van Gerven, in *Brasserie du Pêcheur*, to observe that the three conditions for liability laid down by the CJEU should find application also in actions for breach of competition law.[24] However, it was only with the *Manfredi* case that this 'jurisprudential *renvoi*' was crystallized also in competition law.

3.2 CAUSATION IN THE EUROPEAN UNION COMPETITION LAW

In 2005, the EC commissioned the drafting of a Green Paper on competition damages actions.[25] This report mentioned causation as a necessary requirement of any damages claim. It acknowledged that proof of a causal link between the infringement and a loss 'may be particularly difficult to achieve due to the economic complexity of the issues involved', and it concluded that the application of the

---

[20] At para 64, see *Manfredi* (n 2), the court points out that 'In the absence of Community rules governing the matter, it is for the domestic legal system of each Member State to prescribe the detailed rules governing the exercise of that right, including those on the application of the concept of "causal relationship", provided that the principles of equivalence and effectiveness are observed'.

[21] As explained in the Case C-45/76 *Comet v Produktschap* [1976] ECR 2043.

[22] See Joined Cases C-6/90 and C-9/90 *Francovich v Italian Republic*.

[23] The European legislator confirmed this approach, stating that 'In the absence of Union law, actions for damages are governed by the national rules and procedures of the Member States', Recital (11) of Directive 2014/104/EU.

[24] Opinion of AG Van Gerven, Case C-128/92, *H. J. Banks & Co. Ltd v British Coal Corporation* [1994] ECR I-01209, para 50:

> In its decisions concerning the second paragraph of Article 215 of the EEC Treaty, the Court has inferred from the general principles common to the legal systems of the Member States that the liability of the Community depends on fulfilment of three conditions, namely the existence of damage, a causal link between the damage claimed and the conduct alleged against the institution, and the illegality of such conduct. In my view, those conditions for liability apply as such to actions for breach of directly effective provisions of Community competition law.

[25] Green Paper – Damages Actions for Breach of the EC Antitrust Rules SEC (2005) 1732 COM/ 2005.

causation requirement 'should not lead to exclusion of those who have suffered losses arising from an antitrust infringement from recovering those losses'.[26] This position was based on the outcome of the 'Study on the Conditions of Claims for Damages in Case of Infringement of EC Competition Rules' (the so-called *Ashurst* study), which observed that the proof of causation was one of the main obstacles to an efficient use of competition damages actions.[27] The *Ashurst* comparative study also took note of the fact that in the different jurisdictions, most reporters observed that the '[p]roof of causal link is considered as a great obstacle to plaintiffs. This will particularly be the case as regards plaintiffs who are indirect purchasers'.[28]

However, the diversity of approaches to the notion of causal link in the member states, together with a case-by-case approach to causation adopted by most courts in antitrust litigation, limited an in-depth comparative analysis of causation. Most probably, this aspect discouraged the European legislator to take a position on the issue of causation that, indeed, was only cursorily mentioned in the following White Paper.[29] Even the Commission Staff Working Paper attached to it mentioned nothing but the usual warning reported by the Green Paper and the Ashurst study about the particularly complex nature of the proof of causation.[30]

These pieces of legislation acknowledge that causation remains one of the thorniest issues in competition law damages actions, and they also call for major harmonization. The Proposal Directive, in particular, highlighted with unprecedented persistence the problem of the diversity of the liability standards in the EU, especially for matters related to the assessment and quantification of damages.[31] The Proposal Directive pointed out that this diversity of approaches may cause legal uncertainty for all parties involved in actions for antitrust damages and that 'has created a markedly uneven playing field in the internal market' and that it 'may cause legal uncertainty for all parties involved in actions for antitrust damages, which in turn leads to ineffective private enforcement of the competition rules, especially in cross-border cases'.[32]

Despite this, even the approved Directive decided not to take an explicit stance on this issue. The Directive mentions the causal link only once at Recital (11) to

---

[26] Ibid., 11.

[27] D Waelbroeck, D Slater and G Even-Shoshan, 'Study on the Conditions of Claims for Damages in Case of Infringement of EC Competition Rules (Ashurst Study)' (2004), available at http://ec.europa.eu/competition/antitrust/actionsdamages/comparative_report_clean_en.pdf.

[28] Ibid.

[29] White Paper on Damages Actions for Breach of the EC Antitrust Rules, SEC (2008) 404–406.

[30] Commission Staff Working Paper Accompanying the White Paper on Damages Actions for Breach of the EC Antitrust Rules 2008 COM (2008) 165 final, SEC (2008) 404, 12.

[31] Observing that 'The differences in the liability regimes may thus negatively affect competition and run a risk of appreciably distorting the proper functioning of the internal market'. Proposal for a Directive of the European Parliament and of the Council on Certain Rules Governing Actions for Damages under National Law for Infringements of the Competition Law Provisions of the Member States and of the European Union, COM (2013) 404, 2013, 10.

[32] Ibid., 4.

confirm the principle that 'All national rules governing the exercise of the right to compensation for harm resulting from an infringement of Article 101 or 102 TFEU, including those concerning aspects not dealt with in this Directive such as the notion of causal relationship between the infringement and the harm, must observe the principles of effectiveness and equivalence'.[33]

Therefore, the limits to the application of the domestic notion of causation are the principles of effectiveness and equivalence of EU law. In addition, the Directive introduced presumptions and legal inferences that also influence the formation of the proof of causation. The following section will address the direct limitations to the application of causation principles set forth with the principles of equivalence and effectiveness.

3.3 THE (POSITIVE) LIMITS TO THE NATIONAL RULES ON CAUSATION

The principle of equivalence consists in the enforcement of rules that are not less favourable than those governing similar domestic actions.[34] The principle of effectiveness, on the other hand, makes sure that domestic rules 'do not render practically impossible or excessively difficult the exercise of rights conferred by Community law'.[35]

The CJEU has often applied these wide concepts,[36] especially to enforce the effectiveness of European laws in order to limit the application of national remedial rules.[37] This interventionist approach of the European Union courts has been described as 'waxing and waning' in the history of EU law,[38] and it seems to be reviving more than ever in competition law remedies. For instance, in the *Kone* case, the CJEU has used the principle of effectiveness in order to determine the illegality of the application of domestic rules governing causation in Austria, as they would have impeded the compensation of damages caused by umbrella prices.[39]

---

[33] Recital (11) Directive 2014/104/EU.

[34] Joined Cases C-295/04 to C-298/04 *Vincenzo Manfredi v Lloyd Adriatico Assicurazioni SpA* ECR [2006] I-06619, para 71.

[35] Ibid., para 71.

[36] Cases C-14/83 *Von Colson und Kamann v Land Nordrhein-Westfalen* [1984] ECR 1891; C-222/84 *Johnston v The Chief Constable of the Royal Ulster Constabulary* [1986] ECR 1651, and C-222/86 *UNECTEF v Heylens* [1987] ECR 4097. See also Rachael Craufurd Smith, 'Culture and European Union Law', in Paul Craig and Gráinne de Búrca (eds) *The Evolution of EU Law* (Oxford University Press, 2011) 300 and 307–310.

[37] Eva Storskrubb, *Civil Procedure and EU Law: A Policy Area Uncovered* (Oxford University Press, 2008); Paul Craig and Gráinne de Búrca, *EU Law: Text, Cases, and Materials* (Oxford University Press, 2011) 228, referring to cases C-271/91 *Marshall v Southampton and South West Area Health Authority* II [1993] ECR I-4367 and C-208/90 *Emmott v Minister for Social Welfare* [1991] ECR I-4269.

[38] Craig and Búrca (n 37) 422.

[39] Case C-557/12 *Kone* (n 19) para 33.

56   *Causation in the European Union Competition Law and Decisions*

The principle of effectiveness has been often applied to guarantee judicial protection to individual right-holders.[40] Since the right to seek redress belongs to anyone harmed by a competition law infringement, the EU law in principle protects any subject lamenting an injury that is causally connected to the infringement. Hence, barring the action of a potential claimant based on his position in relation to the damage would result in a violation of the principle of effectiveness.

In this vein, the position held by the CJEU in *Kone* becomes more evident as to the defence of the individual right to claim for damages. The principle of effectiveness, to a certain extent, becomes a European 'scope of the rule', applied to legal causation. The application of national rules on causation therefore needs to pass this additional test, which, however, has only a positive function. If the domestic rules on causation lead to the rejection of the claim, the judge has to further analyze the claim under the light of the principle of effectiveness and of the European Courts' decisions. Moreover, the effectiveness of EU law always has to conform to the principles of subsidiarity and proportionality, laid down in Article 5 of the Treaty on European Union, for which the involvement of the institutions must be limited to what is necessary to achieve the objectives of the treaties.[41]

The application of these principles has the further aim and consequence of bringing a progressive harmonization of national remedial rules. The principles of effectiveness, equivalence, and proportionality impose on national judges to interpret and modify the applicable law to the extent it is needed to comply with the European rules and principles.[42]

3.4 THE OBJECTIVES OF THE DAMAGES DIRECTIVE AND OF ARTICLES 101 AND 102

The Directive on Antitrust Damages Actions (Damages Directive) was signed into law on 26 November 2014, introducing the adoption of 'certain rules governing actions for damages under national law for infringements of the competition law provisions of the Member States and of the European Union'. The Damages Directive states, in line with the CJEU case law, that anyone can seek full compensation of the damage causally connected to an antitrust infringement.[43] As for the assessment of causation, the harm is legally relevant if the loss results from a violation of a right conferred by the law – in other words, if the infringement has

---

[40] Craig and Búrca (n 37) 424–425.
[41] Article 5 TEU establishes and defines the principles of conferral, subsidiarity and proportionality to determine the limits of the European Union competences.
[42] Walter Van Gerven, 'Harmonization of Private Law: Do We Need It?' [2004] 41 *Common Market Law Review* 505.
[43] Article 3, Directive 2014/104 (n 1).

3.4 The Objectives of the Damages Directive and of Articles 101 and 102 57

resulted in the violation of an interest worthy of legal protection.[44] But what are the protected interests under EU competition law?[45] And what is the function of competition law in relation to its private enforcement?[46]

A clear definition of the boundaries of competition law determines the protective scope of the European and national norms that, at the same time, establish the rights of the claimants and the obligations of the defendants.[47] The protective scope of a law contributes to define the extent of liability but also the damages that are subject to compensation, as this approach asks if the norm was designed to protect against the loss claimed.

Hence, to a certain extent, the goals of competition law define the extent of their protected interests in private enforcement. For instance, if one accepts that competition law also serves wider, non-economic goals, such as environmental concerns and the quality of public health, would patients be allowed to seek compensation for an antitrust infringement bringing about lower quality of public services? And what type of damages causally connected to the alleged infringement would they be allowed to allege?

An ongoing debate in the academic scholarship focuses on the aims of competition law.[48] There is hardly a common ground on which scholars seem to agree, to

---

[44] Christian von Bar, Research Group on the Existing EC Private and Study Group on a European Civil Code, *Principles, Definitions and Model Rules of European Private Law: Draft Common Frame of Reference (DCFR)* (Sellier European Law Publishers, 2009) 3030.

[45] For a general description of the goals of competition law, see Richard Whish, *Competition Law* (Oxford University Press, 2012); ASCOLA Workshop on Comparative Competition Law, *The Goals of Competition Law* (Edward Elgar Publishing, 2012); Areeda and Hovenkamp, *Fundamentals of Antitrust Law* (Aspen Publishers, 2011); Okeoghene Odudu, *The Boundaries of EC Competition Law: The Scope of Article 81* (Oxford University Press, 2006).

[46] Wouter PJ Wils, 'Ten Years of Regulation 1/2003 – A Retrospective' (Social Science Research Network 2013) SSRN Scholarly Paper ID 2274013, available at http://papers.ssrn.com/abstract=2274013, accessed 12 May 2014; Charles Alan Wright, 'The Law of Remedies as a Social Institution' [1954] 18 *University of Detroit Law Journal* 376; Ioannis Lianos, 'Competition Law Remedies in Europe: Which Limits for Remedial Discretion?' [2013] CLES Research Paper No. 2/2013, available at http://papers.ssrn.com/abstract=2235817, accessed 12 May 2014; Ioannis Lianos, 'Some Reflections on the Question of the Goals of EU Competition Law' [2013] CLES Working Paper Series 3/2013, available at http://papers.ssrn.com/abstract=2235875, accessed 12 May 2014; Francesco Denozza and Luca Toffoletti, 'Compensation Function and Deterrence Effects of Private Actions for Damages: The Case of Antitrust Damage Suits', available at http://papers.ssrn.com/abstract=1116324, accessed 12 May 2014; Maurice E Stucke, 'Should Competition Policy Promote Happiness?' [2013] 81 *Fordham Law Review* 2575; Eleanor Fox and Paul Sirkis, 'Antitrust Remedies – Selected Bibliography and Annotations' [2005] American Antitrust Institute Working Paper No. 06-01, available at http://ssrn.com/abstract=1103601 or http://dx.doi.org/10.2139/ssrn.1103601, accessed 12 May 2014.

[47] For an analysis of the protective scope of EU law after Francovich, see Michael Dougan, 'Addressing Issues of Protective Scope within the Francovich Right to Reparation' [2017] 13 *European Constitutional Law Review* 124.

[48] For a global comparative perspective, see OECD, 'The Objectives of Competition Law and Policy and the Optimal Design of a Competition Agency' [2003] 5 *OECD Journal:*

the extent that it is even disputed whether competition law should have one aim,[49] usually consumer welfare, or multiple objectives.[50] Besides what competition law should be or do, antitrust enforcement in the EU has been advancing a number of different objectives, from the protection of market structure and economic freedom to the core market values of the EU – *in primis* market integration.[51] In addition to this, competition authorities have applied economic and non-economic objectives, such as public interest concerns, in the enforcement of their powers, adding further complications (sometimes perhaps needed) to the defin-ition of the liability of undertakings for the violation of competition laws. But these objectives are loosely defined so that even the consumer welfare standard has only been vaguely conceptualized, becoming of uncertain application as a legal instrument.[52]

The Directive clearly states that its main objective is 'to establish rules concerning actions for damages for infringements of Union competition law'.[53] These rules should ensure the full effectiveness of Articles 101 and 102 TFEU and the proper

---

Competition Law and Policy 7; Daniel Zimmer, *The Goals of Competition Law* (Edward Elgar Publishing, 2012).

[49] Easterbrook, 'The Limits of Antitrust' [1984] 63 *Texas Law Review* 1; O Odudu, *The Boundaries of EC Competition Law* (Oxford University Press, 2006) 159. See also R Blair and D Sokol, 'The Rule of Reason and the Goals of Antitrust: An Economic Approach' [2012] 78 *Antitrust Law Journal* 471, 472; In contrast, Stucke argues that a single well-defined objective for competition law is unrealistic: M Stucke, 'Reconsidering Antitrust Goals' [2012] 53 *Boston College Law Review* 551.

[50] According to Ezrachi, competition law has a 'sponge' and 'membrane' composition, which 'acknowledges that the effects of the domestic environment are an integral part of competition law and are echoed in the properties of the law. In doing so it points to the margin for subjective, or at times, arbitrary decision making that may be shielded under the perceived structure of the law and the legitimacy of economic analysis'. Ariel Ezrachi, 'Sponge' [2016] 5 *Journal of Antitrust Enforcement* 49, 74. Lianos, instead, posited that that while the economic welfare approach is inherently flawed, finding the goals of competition law does not solve the problem of what institution is the best placed to solve a specific problem. In this case, Lianos maintains that comparative institutional analysis should inform the choices of decision makers and in particular the selection of the 'least imperfect alternative' institution; see Ioannis Lianos, 'Some Reflections on the Question of the Goals of EU Competition Law' [2013] CLES Working Paper Series 3/2013, available at http://papers.ssrn.com/abstract=2235875, accessed 12 May 2014. More recently, Lianos advanced a model of 'polycentric competition law'. Ioannis Lianos, 'Polycentric Competition Law' [2018] 71 *Current Legal Problems* 161. Finally, Stucke observes that a single objective for antitrust enforcement is unrealistic, and, therefore, it is essential to have a more holistic approach to competition law enforcement; see Maurice E Stucke, 'Reconsidering Antitrust's Goals' [2012] 53 *Boston College Law Review* 551.

[51] Ezrachi (n 50) 54.

[52] Barak Y Orbach, 'The Antitrust Consumer Welfare Paradox' [2010] 7 *Journal of Competition Law and Economics* 133, 137; Maria Ioannidou, *Consumer Involvement in Private EU Compe-tition Law Enforcement* (2016) 22, available at http://oxcat.ouplaw.com/view/10.1093/law:ocl/9780198726432.001.0001/law-ocl-9780198726432, accessed 6 March 2019. ICN, 'Competition Enforcement and Consumer Welfare' (2011).

[53] Recital (49).

3.4 *The Objectives of the Damages Directive and of Articles 101 and 102*   59

functioning of the internal market for undertaking and consumers. The European legislator has doubted that these objectives can be achieved while applying member states' laws of obligation. As pointed out by the European Commission in its *Impact Assessment of the Proposal Directive for Antitrust Damages Actions 2013*, 'the differences in the liability regimes applicable in the Member States may negatively affect competition and risk to appreciably distort the proper functioning of the internal market'.[54] The European parliament held this position also in the Damages Directive.[55] With this in mind, the Directive was designed to pursue this harmonization and uniformity in the application of Articles 101 and 102 for damages actions.[56]

The Directive aims at establishing and giving effect to the compensation principle and to grant it to anyone who suffered a damage caused by an infringement of competition law, as established by the CJEU in *Manfredi*.[57] Moreover, in application of the compensatory principle, a further aim is to avoid overcompensation – through punitive, multiple, or other damages.[58] With regard to the different liability regimes, the Directive makes clear that the intent of the law is to create a 'level playing field' where all the undertakings can compete at the same level, and the internal market is not endangered by inequalities in the application of EU law.[59] Relying on this background, one could say that the assessment of causation in competition law damages actions has to be adapted to a system that aims at (1) compensation, rather than punishment and deterrence and (2) convergence of the different national approaches.

Although there is no consensus on the scope of competition law and on its boundaries, no interpretation of the protective scope of the rule can be used to bar an action from a person that claims damages caused by an antitrust

---

[54] Impact Assessment Report Accompanying the Proposal for a Directive COM (2013) 404, SWD (2013) 203 Final 2013 20.

[55] Directive 2014/104/EU (n 1) Recital (7).

[56] The Directive simply recalls the established case law in defining the principles of effectiveness and equivalence at Article 4:

> In accordance with the principle of effectiveness, Member States shall ensure that all national rules and procedures relating to the exercise of claims for damages are designed and applied in such a way that they do not render practically impossible or excessively difficult the exercise of the Union right to full compensation for harm caused by an infringement of competition law. In accordance with the principle of equivalence, national rules and procedures relating to actions for damages resulting from infringements of Article 101 or 102 TFEU shall not be less favourable to the alleged injured parties than those governing similar actions for damages resulting from infringements of national law.

[57] Joined Cases C-295/04 to C-298/04 *Vincenzo Manfredi v Lloyd Adriatico Assicurazioni SpA*, [2006] ECR I-06619.

[58] Directive 2014/104/EU (n 1) Recital (13).

[59] Ibid., Recitals (7), (9) and (10).

60   *Causation in the European Union Competition Law and Decisions*

infringement. Any other interpretation would conflict with the Article 3 of the Directive, according to which anyone has the right to seek redress for such damages, and with the principle of effectiveness. However, it seems that a restrictive or extensive interpretation of the scope of the competition rules may still influence the judgment of the wrongful conduct and the selection of the compensable damages. As for the latter, after the decision in *Kone*, the courts have received clear instruction to limit the restrictive exegesis of the competition rules that limits the types of compensable damages.[60] However, the decision did leave some room for further interpretation in future cases.[61]

3.5 THE RIGHT TO FULL COMPENSATION IN THE DIRECTIVE ON ANTITRUST DAMAGES CLAIMS

An infringement of competition law often causes injuries to protected interests of individuals. The injury is legally relevant if the loss results from a violation of a right conferred by the law or the violation of an interest worthy of legal protection.[62] This injury therefore gives right to reparation, but against whom and on what basis?

The Damages Directive, as already pointed out, adopts a particularly broad approach with reference to the right of standing. By consequence, the term 'injured party' refers to any person (natural or legal) that has suffered harm caused by an infringement of competition law,[63] and the infringer is broadly defined as 'an undertaking or association of undertakings which has committed an infringement of competition law'.[64] On the basis of Article 3 (1), therefore, any injured party should be able to obtain full compensation unless the harm was caused by an infringement of competition law.[65] Full compensation, for the Damages Directive, includes actual loss and loss of profits, plus interests, as it should 'place a person who has suffered harm in the position in which that person would have been had the infringement of competition law not been committed'.[66] Such economic losses have to be limited to those having an adequate causal connection to the infringement and that are protected by the scope of competition law – however, without this barring, as a matter of principle, the possibility to claim damages to entire classes of claimants.

---

[60] See more in detail infra Section 3.6.
[61] See Section 3.8.
[62] Von Bar, (n 44) 3030.
[63] Article 2(6).
[64] Article 2(2).
[65] Article 3(1): 'Member States shall ensure that any natural or legal person who has suffered harm caused by an infringement of competition law is able to claim and to obtain full compensation for that harm'.
[66] Article 3(2).

3.6 SCOPE OF COMPETITION LAW DAMAGES ACTIONS

Causation in the law is limited in the first place by the same rules that place liability on the tortfeasor. For the damage to be compensable, it is also necessary that the purpose of the infringed rule protects precisely the harmful consequences object of the claim. Once it has been ascertained that the damage corresponds to the legal interests protected by the law, the judge must ensure that that injury is causally connected to the offence.

The antitrust laws have a dual function of protection. On the one hand, they protect the process of competition in the European market.[67] On the other hand, competition law rules ensure the compensation of the damage suffered by those private parties affected by distortions of the market. It follows that, as the European Court of Justice considers in *Kone*,[68] the antitrust harm is not only the one directly caused to buyers of the cartel but also the losses caused to all the other subjects who act in different ways on the same market. Infringers are then responsible toward all persons who have suffered damages causally linked to the anticompetitive behaviour. In causal terms, among the conditions of the event, the judge has to find the ones that are legally relevant and, among them, the conditions that caused a damage which falls into the scope of the rule.[69] The damage, in any possible instance, in order to be compensable, has to be of the type that is protected by the rule of law. Therefore, if the assessment is not part of the causal analysis, it is attributed to the phase of the establishment of responsibility.[70]

In competition law damages actions, the judge has, therefore, to define the scope that European and domestic rules private enforcement pursue. The *Courage* and *Manfredi* decisions explained that European laws and treaties created a legal order which works in parallel with domestic legal systems of the member states. Here '[t]he subjects of that legal order are not only the Member States but also their nationals. Just as it imposes burdens on individuals, Community law is also intended to give rise to rights which become part of their legal assets. Those rights arise not only where they are expressly granted by the Treaty but also by virtue of obligations

---

[67] With the ultimate goal of fostering consumer welfare, see, in this sense, Whish (n 45) 20. Okeoghene Odudu, 'The Wider Concerns of Competition Law' [2010] *Oxford Journal of Legal Studies* 612–613; David Gerber, *Global Competition: Law, Markets, and Globalization* (Oxford University Press, 2010) 164.

[68] Case C-557/12 *Kone AG and Others v ÖBB-Infrastruktur AG* [2014] not yet published, para 33–34.

[69] This passage expressly corresponds to the finding of legal causation in Germany, and is also implied in the assessment of liability in the other systems; for an overview, see Chapter 3.

[70] Guido Alpa, Mario Bessone and Zeno Zencovich, 'I Fatti Illeciti' in Pietro Rescigno (ed), *Trattato di Diritto Privato* (Utet, 1995) 35; Van Dam, (n 1), 321; Simon Deakin, Angus Johnston and Basil Markesinis, *Markesinis and Deakin's Tort Law* (Oxford University Press, 2012) 219.

which the Treaty imposes in a clearly defined manner both on individuals and on the Member States and the Community institutions'.[71]

However, this still does not tell us what is the scope of the norm and the protected private right of the Articles 101 and 102 TFEU. These rules indeed explicitly address the protection of competition, as they punish conducts 'which may affect trade between Member States and which have as their object or effect the prevention, restriction or distortion of competition within the internal market'.[72] The court in *Courage* notes that, given the fact that these norms produce direct effects in relations between individuals, they create rights for those individuals which national courts must safeguard.[73] The full effectiveness of Articles 101 and 102 would be put at risk if such a protection is not granted. The duty not to create restrictions or distortions within the internal market is therefore completed by the obligation of avoiding damages to private parties caused by the same restrictions. This duty is moreover detailed by domestic rules on civil liability and, where present, specifically on competition law liability.

The limits of the scope of the duty placed on firms, as a matter of causation, is better detailed in the cases *Manfredi*[74] and more recently in *Kone*.[75] The scope of the rule is therefore to ensure compensation of damages that are caused by such infringements. The lack of a punitive scope can reasonably be seen as one of the main reasons for the ban of punitive or exemplary damages from the Directive on compensation of damages for infringement of competition law.[76]

Amongst these classes of compensatory damages, what damage falls within the scope of Articles 101 and 102 TFEU, as completed by the domestic rules applicable in each case, is still matter of discussion. The case law of the European courts gives no further clues about the limitation of such damages. What the case law says is that the purpose of private claims under European competition law is compensation. This is in line also with previous jurisprudence of the CJEU whereby, with regard to state liability, whereby the European judges noted that the aim of state liability is compensation, not deterrence or punishment.[77]

---

[71] Case C-453/99 *Courage Ltd* v *Bernard Crehan* and *Bernard Crehan* v *Courage Ltd* and Others [2001] ECR I-06297, para 19, which cites the judgments in Case C-26/62 Van Gend en Loos [1963] ECR 1, Case 6/64 *Costa* v *E.N.E.L.* [1964] ECR 585 and Joined Cases C-6/90 and C-9/90 Francovich and Others [1991] ECR I-5357, para 31.

[72] Articles 101 and 102 TFEU.

[73] Ibid., para 23, cites judgments in Case C-127/73 BRT and SABAM [1974] ECR 51, para 16, (BRT) and Case C-282/95 P *Guérin Automobiles* v *Commission* [1997] ECR 1-1503, para 39.

[74] Joined Cases C-295/04 to C-298/04 *Vincenzo Manfredi* v *Lloyd Adriatico Assicurazioni SpA* [2006] ECR I-06619.

[75] Case C-557/12 *Kone AG and Others* v *ÖBB-Infrastruktur AG* [2014] not yet published, available at http://curia.europa.eu/juris/liste.jsf?language=en&num=C-557/12.

[76] Directive 2014/104/EU (n 1).

[77] Case C-470/03 *A.G.M.-COS.MET Srl* v *Suomen valtio* [2007] ECR I-2749.

3.6 Scope of Competition Law Damages Actions

In *Kone*, the Court of Justice broadened the classes of damages subject to compensation, arguing again on the principle of effectiveness of EU law.[78] We know, therefore, that umbrella effects not only are (potentially) linked to the event, but the damages arising from them are, by principle, falling within the scope of European law and may be subject to compensation. Similarly, in *Courage v Crehan*, the European Court of Justice stated that the English law rule *ex turpi causa non oritur actio* violated the principle of effectiveness of EU law because it impeded a subject damaged by an anticompetitive agreement from obtaining compensation of such losses.[79]

In *Manfredi*, the court referred to the definition of effectiveness reported in the *Courage* case and added that ensuring full effectiveness of European competition law means also to guarantee full compensation of the losses caused by the antitrust infringement.[80] Domestic laws of substance and procedure should not deter the lodging of meritorious cases.[81]

Actually, this right is can be found into two different principles – the first being *stricto sensu*, the principle of effectiveness, limited exclusively to the protection of Treaty norms, and the second being the principle of effective judicial protection which concerns 'the effectiveness of subjective rights enjoyed by individuals under the Treaty as they are enforced against Member States or private parties'.[82] However, the Court of Justice's principle of effectiveness tends to encompass both principles, sometimes making it rather ambiguous.[83] On the other hand, the same case law of the CJEU did not develop a definition of the content of the rights that have to be enforced within the principle of effectiveness, of their function, scope and content.[84] Therefore, the principle of effectiveness should draw the limits of the right to compensation for infringement of EU competition law, showing the domestic laws of obligations when a right to compensation has to be conferred under EU law. But the definition of such right is left to the member states' laws, as far as they abide by a partially defined EU principle of full compensation, creating a self-contradictory statement rather than a principle, an oxymoron rather than a rule. An efficient solution, although not fully resolving, is the one suggesting that the legal basis of the right to compensation which 'determines function and content of the right under

---

[78] Case C-557/12 *Kone AG and Others v ÖBB-Infrastruktur AG* [2014] not yet published.

[79] Case C-453/99 *Courage Ltd v Bernard Crehan* and *Bernard Crehan v Courage Ltd and Others* [2001] ECR I-06297, para 26.

[80] Joined Cases C-295/04 to C-298/04 *Vincenzo Manfredi v Lloyd Adriatico Assicurazioni SpA*, [2006] ECR I-06619, 95.

[81] Renato Nazzini, 'Potency and Act of the Principle of Effectiveness: The Development of Competition Law Remedies and Procedures in Community Law' in Catherine Barnard and Okeoghene Odudu (eds), *The Outer Limits of European Union Law* (Hart, 2009) 425.

[82] Michael Dougan, *National Remedies before the Court of Justice: Issues of Harmonisation and Differentiation* (Hart, 2004) 27.

[83] Nazzini (n 81) 436.

[84] Ibid.

64   *Causation in the European Union Competition Law and Decisions*

Community law and the existence and scope of the remedy' should be analyzed 'in conjunction with the principle of effective judicial protection'.[85] The reach of the principles of effectiveness and equivalence, however, appear to be determined by principles enclosed in ephemeral boundaries that tend more to the expansion of the EU right to compensation, as in *Kone,* rather than to its restriction. Accordingly, restrictive interpretations of the principles of causation, especially with relation to the scope of the competition law rules, would hardly fulfil the requirements of the new rules of antitrust civil responsibility.

3.7 CONVERGENCE OF DIFFERENT CAUSATION REGIMES AND THE EFFECTS OF A DIVERSE SET OF LEGAL FRAMEWORKS

The diversity of causal approaches throughout the EU is evidence of the fact that the endeavour of the EU institutions to harmonize the private enforcement of competition law is only at its inception. The application of Regulation 1/2003 highlighted the underlying issue of the parallel application of national laws when domestic courts enforce Articles 101 and 102 TFEU. Article 3, Regulation 1/2003, introduced the principle of parallel application of national competition laws, whereby domestic rules are used in order to integrate the application of EU competition law. Given the numerous and important differences among national laws of substance and procedure, the European Commission argued that this parallel application of national rules endangers the uniform enforcement of EU laws across the member states.[86] As pointed out by the European Commission in its Impact Assessment of the Proposal Directive for Antitrust Damages Actions 2013, the 'undertakings established and operating in different Member States are exposed to significantly different risk of being held liable for infringements of competition law'.[87] Therefore, the Commission has clung to the argument by stating that 'the differences in the liability regimes applicable in the Member States may negatively affect competition and risk to appreciably distort the proper functioning of the internal market'.[88] The process of convergence sponsored by the European institutions aims, in this vein, at harmonizing national private enforcement rules in order to ensure a more level playing field for both infringers and victims of the illegal conduct. It may be argued, in this vein, that the harmonization process backed by the European institutions should respond

---

[85] Ibid.

[86] Proposal for a Directive of the European Parliament and of the Council on Certain Rules Governing Actions for Damages under National Law for Infringements of the Competition Law Provisions of the Member States and of the European Union COM (2013) 404, 4.

[87] Impact Assessment Report Accompanying the Proposal for a Directive COM (2013) 404, SWD (2013) 203 Final, 2013, 20, para 54.

[88] Ibid.

3.7 Convergence of Causation Regimes and Effects of Diverse Legal Frameworks 65

also to the EU Treaties' aims and guiding principles. The wider concern of the process of convergence is to ensure equivalence[89] and effectiveness[90] of EU law, which together – in turn – foster the sound functioning of the internal market. It is worth observing that the divergent substantive and procedural standards of liability in Europe may also endanger the application of the constitutional principle of non-discrimination.[91] Moreover, national competition laws have to be checked under Article 3 TFEU establishing that '[t]he Union shall have exclusive competence in the following areas: (b) the establishing of the competition rules necessary for the functioning of the internal market'.

As pointed out by the Commission, two different undertakings might be judged differently by national courts, even when they are accused of pursuing the same anticompetitive behaviour.[92] In this regard, it has to be observed that the same undertaking operating in more than one member state and affecting evenly their markets might be held liable in one member state but not in the other.[93] This situation is, according to the Commission, particularly advantageous for deep-pocketed competitors that can use the opportunities of 'forum shopping' given by the European legislation to choose the court that would be more 'favourable' to them.[94] By contrast, injured parties with smaller claims or fewer resources will tend to choose the domestic court or, more often, to drop the case. Causation, as seen in Chapter 1, being one of the main obstacles in proving the claim, directly bears on the decision of the jurisdiction where the claimant intends to litigate the case. The uneven playing field created by such diversity can result in a competitive advantage for some undertaking and a disincentive to the exercise of the rights of establishment and provision of goods and services.[95] Moreover, it may negatively affect competition and the proper functioning of internal market. As a result, undertakings are discouraged from settling in countries where the right to compensation is more effectively enforced.[96]

This conclusion is, however, a moot point. In fact, the countries where competition law is more effectively applied are also those where companies are moving their seats.[97] Moreover, the Damages Directive did not clearly initiate such convergence,

---

[89] As explained in Case 45-76 Comet BV v Produktschap voor Siergewassen [1976] ECR I-02043.

[90] Which requires EU law to be interpreted in such a way as to fulfil the Treaty's objectives, see para 4.3, also intended as full effectiveness of EU law or 'effet utile', see Case 199/82 Amministrazione delle Finanze dello Stato v SpA San Giorgio [1983] ECR 3595, para 14.

[91] Case C-208/90 Theresa Emmott v Minister for Social Welfare and AG [1991] ECR I-4269.

[92] Proposal for a damages directive (n 86) 9.

[93] Ibid.

[94] Notable cases being, amongst the others, Cooper Tire & Rubber Co Europe Ltd v Shell Chemicals UK Ltd [2010] EWCA Civ 864 and Devenish Nutrition Ltd v Sanofi-Aventis SA (France) & Ors (Rev 1) [2008] EWCA Civ 1086.

[95] Proposal for a damages directive (n 86) 9.

[96] Impact Assessment Report Accompanying the Proposal for a Directive (n 54) para 115.

[97] See, for instance, the results of a study on the freedom of establishment in the UE, Gerner-Beuerle C and others, 'Study on the Law Applicable to Companies – Final Report' (2016),

66 Causation in the European Union Competition Law and Decisions

preferring a more cautious approach. As a result, undertakings operating in the European territory are subject to different standards of liability for competition law infringements, despite the presence of common antitrust rules. This situation may support, on one hand, a process of regulatory competition among domestic laws of obligation and, on the other hand, a partial inconsistency of judgments across the European Union.

3.8 CAUSATION AND EU LAW

The harmonization process of the rules establishing liability for compensation of antitrust damages involves also the causative link that is recalled several times by the Commission and remains one of its unresolved major concerns. Some empirical studies on antitrust litigation in Europe demonstrate that there is a widespread uncertainty over the substantiation of the causal connection.[98] This uncertainty is common to all the jurisdictions analyzed. However, a closer inspection of causal theories and principles adopted by national courts tells that the uncertainty often hinges on different bases. National courts are accustomed to different ways of approaching the proof of causation, although they adopt similar solutions, as in the case of the passing-on of price overcharges. These solutions are also oriented to the pursuit of the principle of effectiveness of EU law and of the obligation to interpret national law in conformity with community law[99] as established by the EU courts.[100] By consequence, there is a natural, although limited, process of convergence of the solutions regarding the causal enquiry, supported by national courts.

Advocate General Kokott went further than this, maintaining in her opinion on the *Kone* case that 'the issue of the civil liability of cartel members for umbrella pricing is a matter of European Union law, not national law'[101] and that the legal conditions for the finding of the causal link have to be found under EU law.[102] Her opinion focuses specifically on the problem of causation, and, in this analysis, she embraces the concerns of the European Commission related to the diversity

---

https://publications.europa.eu/en/publication-detail/-/publication/259a1dae-1a8c-11e7-808e-01aa75ed71a1/language-en, accessed 8 July 2019, 41–42.

[98] See, for instance, the Green Paper – Damages Actions for Breach of the EC Antitrust Rules SEC (2005) 1732 COM/2005, 672 2005, and the national reports within the AHRC Project on Competition Law: Comparative Private Enforcement and Consumer Redress, led by Prof. Barry Rodger, available at www.clcpecreu.co.uk/.

[99] See, inter alia, Joined Cases C-397/01 to C-403/01 Pfeiffer and Others [2004] ECR I-8835, para 113, and the case law cited.

[100] Case C-453/00 *Kühne & Heitz NV v Produktschap voor Pluimvee en Eieren* [2004] I-00837.

[101] Opinion of Advocate General Kokott Case C-557/12 *Kone AG and Others v ÖBB-Infrastruktur AG* [2014] ECLI:EU:C:2014:45, para 45.

[102] Ibid.

3.8 Causation and EU Law

of civil liability standards in Europe.[103] In practice, this situation should justify the formulation of a common concept of causation. AG Kokott takes the view that, in the context of non-contractual liability of the EU institutions, under Article 340 TFEU, European Union law developed an independent notion of causation that '[f]or the sake of consistency' should be applied also in competition law litigation.[104] This criterion, as she acknowledges, is the 'sufficiently direct causal nexus between the harmful conduct and the damage alleged'.[105] She admits that, given the open-endedness of this concept, it would need further specification by the domestic judge.[106] However, the AG Kokott observes that it is possible to design a causal account overcoming existing differences. Henceforth, and before delving into the specific analysis of causation in the specific case of umbrella pricing, AG Kokott suggests the adoption of a theory of causation whereby 'the criterion of a sufficiently direct causal link is in substance intended, on the one hand, to ensure that a person who has acted unlawfully is liable only for such loss as he could reasonably have foreseen ... On the other hand, a person is liable only for loss the compensation of which is consistent with the objectives of the provision of law which he has infringed'.[107] At a closer inspection, this interpretation of the direct causal link is not rooted in CJEU's case law but rather on selected national European causal canons. This theory seemingly bundles the English concept of remoteness with the German theory of the scope of the rule.[108] In confirmation of this view, it may be observed that the European Court of Justice did not follow this approach in its judgement. On the contrary, the court joined the previous case law, stating that 'in the absence of EU rules governing the matter, it is for the domestic legal system of each Member State to lay down the detailed rules governing the exercise of the right to claim compensation for the harm resulting from an agreement or practice prohibited under Article 101 TFEU, including those on the application of the concept of "causal relationship",

---

[103] AG Kokott warns that if the legal criteria by which national courts assess civil liability for infringement of Articles 101 and 102 TFEU are different, 'there would be a risk of economic operators being treated differently'. Therefore, she observes that '[t]his would not only run counter to the fundamental objective of European competition law, which is to create framework conditions that are as uniform as possible for all undertakings active on the internal market ("level playing field"), it would also be an invitation to "forum shopping"'. Ibid., para 29.

[104] Opinion of Advocate General Kokott Case C-557/12 (n 101) para 34.

[105] Ibid.

[106] Ibid., para 35.

[107] Ibid., para 40.

[108] The CJEU predictably did not endorse this theory and enforced the principle of effectiveness in order to justify the liability of the antitrust infringer for umbrella effects. Case C-557/12 *Kone AG and Others* v *ÖBB-Infrastruktur AG*, (n 19).

68   *Causation in the European Union Competition Law and Decisions*

provided that the principles of equivalence and effectiveness are observed'.[109] The advocate general's call for convergence sheds light on an important topic that is the application of a common notion of causation in competition law. However, the analysis of national systems shows that the diversity of approaches is rooted in the legal traditions of domestic civil law that is not presently a matter of EU law – the main limit to this autonomy of national courts being the principles of effectiveness and equivalence of EU law.

---

[109] Case C-557/12 *Kone AG and Others* v *ÖBB-Infrastruktur AG* [2014] not yet published, para 24.

4

Causal Uncertainty in Competition Law Damages Claims

The thread that connects the jurisdictions analyzed, despite the different theoretical backgrounds, is that courts divide the assessment of causation in a multistage process whereby the verification of the causal link has a strong empirical base. However, at any stage, causal uncertainty may render the assessment of causation extremely difficult if not impossible to perform. While the previous chapters have mainly dealt with the definition of the different concepts of causation from a comparative perspective, this chapter presents the main situations and elements of causal uncertainty,[1] thus also introducing issues related to the proof of causation. Chapters 5 and 6 analyze in detail the proof rules of causation in competition damages actions.

In such actions, where the reparation claim is based on a pure economic loss, the judge determines the causal connection relying on economic arguments and inferences that are expressed in terms of likelihood of the damage to be caused by the defendant's action. From here, the importance of analyzing how the fact-finder utilizes probabilities in situations of causal uncertainty in antitrust damages claims. The antitrust damage consists in a loss of welfare, and the person aggrieved by the infringement has to show that the diminution of her assets, as a consequence of higher prices paid, lost chances or dead-weight losses, was caused by the antitrust infringement and not by other market factors. The particularly difficult task of ascertaining such causative link is effectively summed up by Benson, who – with reference to pure economic losses taking place on the market – observes that '[T]he fact that every individual is somewhere and is making use of some external objects, with the result that he or his property is put into relation with them and is subject to being affected by conduct that affects them, is an inevitable incident of being active

---

[1] In general, for an introduction to causal uncertainty, see Israel Gilead and Michael D Green, 'General Report – Causal Uncertainty and Proportional Liability: Analytical and Comparative Report' in Israel Gilead, Michael D Green and Bernhard A Koch (eds), *Proportional Liability: Analytical and Comparative Perspectives* (De Gruyter, 2013); Ariel Porat and Alex Stein, *Tort Liability under Uncertainty* (Oxford University Press, 2001).

70 · Causal Uncertainty in Competition Law Damages Claims

in the world ... [considered as] beings who exist in space and time and who are inescapably active and purposive, persons are necessarily and always connected in manifold ways with other things which they can affect and which in turn can affect them as part of a causal sequence'.[2] In other words, as assets are interconnected in markets and across markets, the simple use of one's property affects someone else's property, which in turn will affect a third person's property, and so on, creating causal uncertainty about the generation, contribution and responsibility for the harm.

4.1 SOURCES OF CAUSAL UNCERTAINTY

Many are the factors of causal uncertainty in competition damages actions. Generally, the uncertainty originates from a lack of complete information,[3] which precludes or makes more difficult the determination of causal relations. This evidential uncertainty affects the application of substantive laws defining causation and procedural laws on the proof of causation.

In other words, the fact-finder does not need to know all the facts but only those that fulfil the standard of proof and the definition of causation adopted in the law. The fact-finding method aims, indeed, at determining the existence of causation as it is defined by the substantive and procedural rules of the domestic law. However, it has been long debated whether, when the causal uncertainty does not depend on the failure of the claimant to produce enough evidence but on a shortcoming of general knowledge, this causal uncertainty generates an unfair situation that may justify a relaxation of rules burdening the claimant to proffer a full proof of causation.[4]

4.1.1 *Nature of the Harm and Its Source*

There are actions that typically bring about a certain effect. Once the existence of the effect and the performance of the action have been established, the causal link is inferred on the basis of the *id quod plerumque accidit*. However, this is seldom

---

[2] Peter Benson, 'The Basis for Excluding Liability for Economic Loss in Tort Law' in David G Owen (ed), *Philosophical Foundations of Tort Law* (Oxford University Press, 1997) 443; Mauro Bussani and Vernon Valentine Palmer, *Pure Economic Loss in Europe* (Cambridge University Press, 2003) 4.

[3] See Porat and Stein, who refers to 'imperfect facts' that society has to rely upon in order to take decisions, Porat and Stein (n 1) 17.

[4] See, for a debate on the topic, Chapter 6 and the following literature Ernest J Weinrib, 'Causal Uncertainty' [2015] 36 *Oxford Journal of Legal Studies* 135; Ken Oliphant, 'Causation in Cases of Evidential Uncertainty: Juridical Techniques and Fundamental Issues' [2016] 91 *Chicago-Kent Law Review* 587; Porat and Stein (n 1); Helmut Koziol, *Basic Questions of Tort Law from a Germanic Perspective* (Jan Sramek Verlag Vienna, 2012) 154.

4.1 Sources of Causal Uncertainty

true, as already observed,[5] for pure economic losses, which often generate causal uncertainty.

Firstly, it is often the case that the same economic harm has alternative or cumulative causes, including an antitrust infringement. Defendants in competition damages actions often oppose the existence of a number of alternative causes to the damage claimed. From concurrent market factors to bad management decisions, a number of different elements may determine a firm's loss of competitiveness.[6]

Secondly, uncertainty in determining causation in such actions depends on the fact that a competition law harm is rarely assessed on the basis of deterministic laws. Economic harms are unobservable phenomena, which hampers the establishment of causation in fact and in law.[7] The proof of an invisible damage will rely more on generalizations than on demonstration of a specific occurrence. But to prove wrongdoing, the causal link has to be established in the specific case. Hence, the proof of causation of economic harm is established with a certain degree of approximation whereby it is necessary to adopt probabilistic approaches or otherwise relax the proof rules.[8]

Thirdly, often antitrust causes coexist with non-antitrust causes in generating the damage. Breaches of contract, tortious interference with contracts, negligence and negligent misrepresentation,[9] unfair competition and violations of corporate laws may coexist and contribute to cause the economic loss claimed.

Fourthly, it often takes a long time to discover and punish an antitrust infringement. This means that it will be more difficult to replicate and prove the existence of required conditions in the market to generate the damage.[10]

Fifthly, competition damages actions often involve either multiple defendants or multiple claimants. Defendant and claimant indeterminacy are also factors of causal uncertainty, as it is not clear which one, among a number of defendants or claimants, has respectively caused or suffered the harm.[11]

---

[5] See Section 1.2.

[6] See, for instance, *Court of Milan, Brennercom Spa v Telecom Italia Spa* decision n 22423/2010; *Enron Coal Services Ltd (In Liquidation) v English Welsh & Scottish Railway Ltd* [2011] EWCA Civ 2.

[7] While most of our knowledge is based on the experience of the observable world – a car crash for instance – exploring the causal processes of the invisible becomes particularly burdensome, see Sandy Steel, *Proof of Causation in Tort Law* (Cambridge University Press, 2015) 8.

[8] See infra Section 4.3.

[9] See, as an example of an international case where all these demands concur, *Geneva Pharmaceuticals Tech v Barr Laboratories*, 201 F Supp 2d 236 (SDNY, 2002).

[10] On the impact of time on causal uncertainty, see Steel (n 7) 7–8.

[11] See infra Chapter 4.

4.1.2 *General or Specific Causal Uncertainty*

Causal uncertainty may regard either general or specific causation. General laws of causation, such as economic theories establishing causality, may not be able to explain with a sufficient degree of probability that two classes or types of event are causally connected (general causation). Here, expert disagreements may result from bias[12] or the generalization sets used by different expert witnesses.[13] The result is that the trier of fact receives different or even contradictory explanations of the causal connections between events.

On the other hand, due to limited knowledge of the facts and their cause–effect relationship, it may not be possible to determine – according to the information available – the causal connection between two events (specific causation).[14] Whenever there is uncertainty over general or specific causation –the scientific proof or the facts of the causal link – the law defines such situation as causal uncertainty. Sometimes, even on the balance of probabilities, the likelihood that an event has caused a specific outcome may be uncertain.

4.1.3 *Factual and Scientific Uncertainty*

It is also important to distinguish between factual and scientific uncertainty. Factual uncertainty ensues, for instance, when scarce information related to the antitrust infringement and its relation to the economic harm generates causal uncertainty. Scientific uncertainty, although related to a factual enquiry, takes place when the uncertainty regards the probative force of the scientific evidence or when there is controversy about the scientific evidence among experts.[15] Even in natural sciences, there is often disagreement as of the likelihood of the causes of a specific event – for example, the causes of a cancer or for the burning of a building. In economics, which makes the gist of the evidence of the occurrence of an anticompetitive harm, scientific uncertainty is even more recurrent. In this connection, economics has been described as a set of 'a fairly abstract, sometimes unverifiable, and largely mathematically derived conclusions about human behavior'.[16] Hence, disagreements in court about the causal connections between proven facts (such as an

---

[12] Déirdre Dwyer, *The Judicial Assessment of Expert Evidence* (Cambridge University Press, 2009) 163 ff.
[13] Ibid., 139 ff.
[14] Steel (n 7) 67 ff.
[15] Lara Khoury, *Uncertain Causation in Medical Liability* (Hart, 2006) 47–48.
[16] Herbert Hovenkamp, 'Economic Experts in Antitrust Cases' in David Faigman and others (eds), *Modern Scientific Evidence: The Law and Science of Expert Testimony*, 2nd edn, (West Group, 2002) 723.

4.1 Sources of Causal Uncertainty

anticompetitive conduct and an economic harm) are frequent.[17] Finally, the reliability of the scientific evidence, such as econometric studies in competition law litigation, and of the expert that provides it are also factors of causal uncertainty.[18]

4.1.4 Counterfactual Nature of the Proof

Anticompetitive effects and their connection to the defendant's behaviour are usually subject to a counterfactual proof. 'If not . . . then' is the logic axiom at the basis of the creation of a counterfactual. Would the damage occur without the anticompetitive behaviour? To respond to this interrogative, often the solution is to create a counterfactual world where there is no wrongdoing. This approach aims to determine if, without the wrongdoing, the economic harm did not take place. Building a proof on a hypothetical and therefore unobservable world[19] generates uncertainty of its own. The counterfactual proof in competition law has a stochastic nature, which means that it is based on the probability of occurrence of a certain event, given a specific set of conditions.[20]

Otherwise, the uncertainty may regard the proof of causation, thus concerning the facts or the evidence submitted. While many of the general rules described in Chapters 1 and 2 are based on regular causal processes, economic harms typically display a certain amount of randomness.[21] Moreover, the general proof rules of causation generally adopt an all-or-nothing approach[22] whereby it is not possible to apportion liability on the basis of the causal contribution of each defendant.[23] One may decide to solve this situation of causal uncertainty in different ways.

It may be possible to adopt a definition of causation in law which allows one to factor in randomness. For example, the principle of direct causation, if strictly interpreted, gives little leeway for accepting causal uncertainty. Adequate causation or the principle of causal regularity, on the other hand, already consider a certain amount of uncertainty, recognizing that causal processes may be to a certain extent indeterministic. The proof rules are equally important. As Chapter 5 explains, the jurisdictions analyzed greatly differ in the level of probability that they require to prove the causal connection. While, for instance, in England, it is enough to prove

---

[17] For an account on the EU, see Ioannis Lianos, '"Judging" Economists: Economic Expertise in Competition Law Litigation – A European View' in Lianos Ioannis and Ioannis Kokkoris (eds), *The Reform of EC Competition Law: New Challenges* (Kluwer, 2009).

[18] Déirdre Dwyer (n 12) 106.

[19] On unobservability and causal uncertainty, see Steel (n 7) 9.

[20] See infra Section 5.7.

[21] On the relationship between economics, finance and randomness, see Nassim Nicholas Taleb, *The Black Swan: Second Edition; The Impact of the Highly Improbable Fragility* (Random House Publishing Group, 2010).

[22] See Chapter 2.

[23] See Section 1.6.

74   *Causal Uncertainty in Competition Law Damages Claims*

on the balance of probability that the claimant's harm was caused by the defendant's action, in France, the standard adopted is not expressly stated but is usually higher.

4.2 USE OF PROBABILITIES IN NATIONAL COURTS

As Chapter 5 explains, some jurisdictions have conceptualized the use of probabilities through the 'preponderance of the evidence' rule (e.g., England), while others have opted for higher standards that rely on the 'intime conviction' of the judge, which theoretically has to be close to certainty (France), or on elaborations of this approach (Germany and Italy). However, in cases of causal uncertainty, it is not possible to establish with full certainty the chain of events that leads to the harm, leading to the adoption, in practice or simply in the language, of probabilistic approaches. Causal uncertainty imposes to find accounts of causation different from a fully deterministic approach, whereby every event is the cause of a regular or invariable pattern of causes.[24]

The regularity theories of causation evolved from the assertion of David Hume that causes are invariably followed by their effects: 'We may define a *cause* to be an object, followed by another, and where all the objects similar to the first, are followed by objects similar to the second'.[25] However, it has been noted that the limits of human knowledge make impossible to conceive a fully deterministic approach to causation in the law.[26] In this vein, Kneale defined probability as 'the substitute with which we try to make good the shortcomings of our knowledge . . . to the extent of our knowledge is less than we could wish'.[27]

The application of invariable patterns in the resolution of legal disputes are usually connected to the finding of direct and certain causation. The reliance on a direct causal link, especially in civil law jurisdictions, finds a justification in light of the principle of corrective justice, whereby 'the parties are connected solely as the doer and sufferer of the same injustice' and 'causation is the mechanism that links what this particular defendant has done to what this particular plaintiff has

---

[24] On the relationship between probability and proof of causation, see Richard W Wright, 'Proving Causation: Probability versus Belief' in Richard Goldberg (ed), *Perspectives on Causation* (Hart, 2011), available at SSRN: http://ssrn.com/abstract=1918474, accessed 20 November 2014; Ronald J Allen and Alex Stein, 'Evidence, Probability, and Burden of Proof [2013] 55 *Arizona Law Review* 557; Christopher Hitchcock, 'Probabilistic Causation' in Edward N Zalta (ed), *The Stanford Encyclopedia of Philosophy*, Fall 2018 Edition (Metaphysics Research Lab, Stanford University, 2018) https://plato.stanford.edu/archives/fall2018/entries/causation-probabilistic/, accessed 4 February 2019.

[25] David Hume, *An Inquiry Concerning Human Understanding: A Dissertation on the Passions. An Inquiry Concerning the Principles of Morals. The Natural History of Religion* (T Cadell, 1772) section VII.

[26] Porat and Stein (n 1) 121.

[27] William Kneale, *Probability and Induction* (Clarendon Press, 1966) 45.

4.2 Use of Probabilities in National Courts

suffered'.[28] However, a fully deterministic approach to causation poses limits[29] that might prevent the application of the law, as factual uncertainty requires taking decisions on the basis of what is probable rather than certain, thus generating an unfair outcome. In competition law this statement is even truer given the fact that the damage generally consists in an economic loss and no organic patterns that yields to a specific harm can be found. The limits of regularity theories have been used, in many areas of tort law, to motivate the adoption of probabilistic approaches to causation.[30]

Probability, in this book, is intended both as a semantic tool[31] and as statistical analysis of reality. Expressions such as probable, likely, possible, apparent, reasonable to think, most likely, credible, plausible and feasible, and the like, are justified by judges in order to assess the *id quod plerumque accidit* or to state a logic inference.[32] Probabilities do not just influence factual inferences but also the argument that serves as a means to substantiate the same fact. Therefore, the words 'reasonably' or 'probably', once entered into the legal jargon and accepted as a benchmark for proof, become a tool for reaching the conclusion also through their semantic structure.[33]

Probability is used to investigate singular causal claims as well as general causal claims. General causal claims are those referring to an abstract causal connection between an unlawful event and a damage – for instance, 'cartels cause damages via price effect'. Singular causal claims are instead those referring to a specific instantiation: 'the cartel X caused the overcharge, i.e. the damage via price effect'. Singular causal judgments are, however, generally framed upon generalizations, where probabilities play a significant role. These generalizations are fundamental to obviate the limitations of human knowledge in assessing life events with certainty.

Probability has to be distinguished from the concept of probabilistic causation – that is, the probability to increase the risk of the damage.[34] This chapter therefore reflects on the application of probability theories in order to gauge the likeliness that an event was caused by a specific set of causes.[35] Whereas Sections 4.3 to 4.7 discuss the application of proportional theories alternative to the all-or-nothing approach.

---

[28] Ernest J Weinrib, 'Causal Uncertainty' [2015] 36 *Oxford Journal of Legal Studies* 135, 136.

[29] See David Lewis, *Philosophical Papers, Volume II* (Oxford University Press, 1986).

[30] Porat and Stein (n 1) 16 ff, Weinrib (n 28) 141.

[31] Stephen E Toulmin, *The Uses of Argument* (Cambridge University Press, 2003) 69. The author believes that the use of the words 'probable' and 'probability' influence the assertion made to an extent that is variable, depending on the specific situation and background in which it is used.

[32] In this regard, it has to be noted that, taking into consideration the complexity of competition law damages actions, the use of common knowledge appears particularly difficult to be applied to the assessment of causation.

[33] Toulmin (n 31) 70.

[34] See infra Sections 4.2–4.6. Richard W Wright, 'Causation, Responsibility, Risk, Probability, Naked Statistics, and Proof: Pruning the Bramble Bush by Clarifying the Concepts' [1987] 73 *Iowa Law Review* 1001; Gilead and others (n 1) 23.

[35] Chapter 5 applies instead such probability theories to the proof of causation.

76   *Causal Uncertainty in Competition Law Damages Claims*

The use of probability in competition damages actions is largely needed because, in many cases, the inference that links the conditions to an event is uncertain. The probability may be relative to the statistical frequency of a conduct to cause a certain outcome. However, the generalization of causal conditions through probabilities[36] can generate several problems in the enforcement of competition law. There are actions that have very little chance to cause harm or that even decrease the probability of the damage to be produced, but, nonetheless, these actions should be accounted as causes of the harm. A well-known example is a golfer who badly slices a golf ball. The ball shoots away towards the rough, but it then bounces off a tree and then into the cup for a hole-in-one.[37] The golfer's slice lowered the probability that the ball would wind up in the cup, yet, nonetheless, it caused the desired result. The singular causation, in this case, is not explained by any generalizing theory founded on probability.[38] The same situation may be envisaged in antitrust litigation, for instance, when economic literature may define an agreement as generating efficient cooperation, but it instead resolves in an anticompetitive outcome.

In this situation, the application of the NESS account of causation leads to paradoxical results, as it presumes the certainty of the sets of conditions that are being applied.[39] In order to obviate to this problem, for some authors, probabilities should be intended as mere indicators of possible reference classes that can be used to build causal generalizations.[40] The use of probabilities, in other words, is translated into a criterion that allows a choice among different sets of conditions for the application of a NESS approach. In this vein, the NESS theory could be complemented by the definition given by Cartwright, for whom a cause is 'a factor that increases the probability of its effect in every background context'.[41] Embedding probability into the NESS theory to this extent would allow one to use the logic items of the theory of conditions without relying on deterministic approaches, above

---

[36] Christopher Hitchcock, 'Probabilistic Causation' in Edward N Zalta (ed), *The Stanford Encyclopedia of Philosophy*, Winter 2012 Edition (Metaphysics Research Lab, Stanford University, 2012), available at http://plato.stanford.edu/archives/win2012/entries/causation-probabilistic/.

[37] Ibid.

[38] The flaws of general causation theories have also being highlighted through counterexamples, divided into two categories: cases where causes fail to raise the probabilities of their effects and cases where non-causes raise the probabilities of non-effects. Peter Gärdenfors, 'Probabilistic Reasoning and Evidentiary Value' in P. Gärdenfors (ed) *The Dynamics of Thought* (Springer, 2005) 1.

[39] For discussion on this point, see John Leslie Mackie, *The Cement of the Universe: A Study of Causation* (Clarendon Press, 1980) 239–247; Richard W Wright, 'Causation, Responsibility, Risk, Probability, Naked Statistics, and Proof: Pruning the Bramble Bush by Clarifying the Concepts' [1987] 73 *Iowa Law Review* 1001, 1042–1049; Richard W Wright, 'The NESS Account of Natural Causation: A Response to Criticisms' in R. Goldberg (ed), *Perspectives on Causation* (Hart, 2011) 310; Jane Stapleton, 'Choosing What We Mean by Causation in the Law' [2008] 73 *Missouri Law Review* 433, 447 ff.

[40] David Papineau, 'Causal Asymmetry' [1985] 36 *British Journal for the Philosophy of Science* 273.

[41] Nancy Cartwright, *Hunting Causes and Using Them* (Cambridge University Press, 2007).

4.3 Causal Proportional Liability and Multiple Defendants

all when the conditions cannot be selected empirically.[42] Moreover, the use of this approach should be limited to the factual analysis of causation.[43]

On the other hand, Stapleton posits that when the law is faced with merely 'coincidental' outcomes, the concept of involvement should find application.[44] She maintains that the 'Law must be able to identify whenever a specified factor was "involved" in the existence of a particular phenomenon of interest, where the notion of "involvement" indicates that there is a contrast between the actual world and some hypothetical world from which we exclude (at least) that specified factor: this contrast being that, while in the former world the phenomenon exists, in the latter it does not'.[45] Hence, the NESS approach provides, according to Stapleton, an 'algorithm' able to accommodate the concept of 'involvement' and thus solve issues of causal uncertainty.

4.3 CAUSAL PROPORTIONAL LIABILITY AND MULTIPLE DEFENDANTS

As seen in the logic of conditions applied to legal causation,[46] a judge has to decide what conditions caused the damage. This choice often hinges on probabilistic evaluations of the event to happen as a consequence of the specific condition. The probabilistic analysis in competition law is, moreover, strictly connected to the use of econometrics in national courtrooms.[47] However, due to scientific or factual uncertainty, it might not be possible to establish causation on the requisite legal standard of proof. The legal system therefore faces a choice: whether to leave the harm uncompensated or find alternative rules under which compensation is made possible. There are two main types of rule designed for this purpose. Firstly, it is possible to relax the proof rules for causation to facilitate the claim.[48] Secondly, it is possible to adopt a causal proportional liability approach which is 'tort liability imposed on [a tortfeasor] for harm suffered by [a victim], for part of it, or for harm that [a victim] may suffer, according to the causal probability that [the tortfeasor]'s tortious conduct may have caused the harm or caused part of it or may cause harm in the future'.[49] It is therefore an ex ante assessment of the causal contribution of a

---

[42] As the authors of the theory postulates, see Richard W Wright, 'The NESS Account of Natural Causation: A Response to Criticisms' (n 39) 304.

[43] Similarly to what Stapleton states about the NESS account as elaborated by Hart and Honoré and initially developed by Wright; see Jane Stapleton, 'Unpacking Causation' in Peter Cane, Anthony M Honoré and John Gardner (eds), *Relating to Responsibility: Essays for Tony Honoré on His Eightieth Birthday* (Hart, 2001).

[44] Stapleton, 'Choosing What We Mean by Causation in the Law' (n 39) 445.

[45] Ibid., 473.

[46] See Section 2.5.

[47] See Section 6.6.

[48] See Chapters 5 and 6.

[49] Gilead and others (n 1) 2.

tortfeasor to a damage, calculated as a percentage to the total harm. Wright has rejected the validity of a probabilistic causation on the basis of the fact that it would lead to award damages also in cases where the result of the action does not happen. Wright notes that '[a] competing interpretation [of NESS approach], "probabilistic causation" has arisen from the confusion, which, despite its obvious implausibility, continues to attract a growing number of adherents at least among legal academics'.[50] And he admonishes that 'a causal law describes an invariable, non-probabilistic, causal connection between fully specified set of antecedent NESS conditions and some result'.[51] Wright looks at the probability mainly from its risk-related perspective, based on which it is the risk to cause an event to be object of the claim and not the causation of the same event. However, probabilities can be applied in order to weigh the different conditions and causes of the event.

Causal uncertainty requires, the use of reasonings which are not fully deterministic. However, there are important differences between probabilistic appreciation of causation and causal proportional liability approaches. In particular, the latter may help to overcome situations of causal uncertainty, but it also creates new problems in the enforcement of the law. With this approach, the probability would become subject to indemnification even when it is very small.[52] Hence, if the probability for a competing firm to conclude the contract 'but for' the anticompetitive behaviour are 10 per cent, the judge should grant a corresponding pro quota damage, for the firm has lost a very small chance, but still a chance. Potentially, every situation would be prone to damages claims. This approach would, therefore, contrast the general principles of causation developed in tort law traditions for which the high probability of an event to happen corresponds to a legal certainty, while a low probability corresponds to non-indemnifiability.[53] Furthermore, some scholars claim that this approach, if adopted, would open the 'floodgates of litigation'.[54]

Moreover, proportional theories go hand in hand with the observation of creation of risk. The probability of an event is indeed often reckoned by courts observing the risk added or created by the action. This risk, in competition law, takes the form of the likelihood of an impairment created on the market. For instance, in case of a claim for damages resulting from the loss of the chance to close a contract, the claimant might want to demonstrate that while without infringement, he/she would have had an 80 per cent chances to close the contract, after the infringement, due to the market distortion, the chances decreased to 30 per cent. However, proportional

---

[50] Wright, 'Causation, Responsibility, Risk, Probability, Naked Statistics, and Proof' (n 39) 1030.

[51] Ibid., 1043.

[52] Ibid., 43 ff.

[53] In this vein, the 'all-or-nothing' approach compels that, in case of causal uncertainty, the illegal behaviour of the infringer that may have caused a damage to the claimant is left uncompensated if the probability is lower than a certain threshold.

[54] Cf. Ioannis Lianos, 'Causal Uncertainty and Damages Claims for the Infringement of Competition Law in Europe' [2015] 34 *Yearbook of European Law* 170, 225.

4.3 Causal Proportional Liability and Multiple Defendants 79

liability might be used when probabilities are close to a 'turning point' but not sufficient to justify the application of the 'all-or-nothing' approach.[55]

The all-or-nothing approach to damages claims postulates that if a claimant fulfils the burden of proof, according to the requisite standard, he/she will receive full compensation. If not, the claimant will receive nothing. This is the approach that the Damages Directive seems to embrace when it refers to the right to 'full compensation'.[56] However, the same Directive potentially opens the door also to alternative approaches that will be explored in the next chapters. The burden of proof for causation may be based, as Chapter 5 shows, on probabilistic proof rules, whereby if the party wins the point, the party wins entirely. However, there are alternative approaches developed by courts and scholars – in particular loss of chance, contribution to risk and market share liability, that apportion liability on the basis of the causal contribution of the defendant to the harm. The next Chapters explore these approaches and their application in competition law litigation.

The following sections analyze the assessment of causation when competition damages actions involve multiple defendants.

4.3.1 Multiple Defendants and Defendant Indeterminacy

Causal uncertainty may also be the result of multiple defendants contributing each of them individually to the harm or the result of indeterminate defendants, where the tortfeasor is part of a group of defendants. Here, one could imagine three possible scenarios: (1) each of the defendants has contributed to an identifiable portion of the harm; (2) only the full amount of the damage is known, but it is not possible to prove the individual contributions; (3) only one of the defendants has caused the harm, but it is uncertain whom.

The first case concerns issues of contribution to the damage and causal apportionment of liability among tortfeasors. The third case is instead about establishing responsibility in the face of causal uncertainty, for instance, through assumptions or proportional approaches or denying access to compensation. The second type of cases involves multiple defendants which have all contributed to increase the risk of the damage, but not all of them are a necessary cause of it. Some scholars have called this 'alternative liability', whereby 'multiple independent Ds each may have been a cause of P's harm, but less than all (or just one D) are actually the cause'.[57]

When it is proven that each defendant has contributed to the causation of the harm but it is not possible to determine – according to the requisite legal standard – the extent of this contribution, the law usually reacts with two different systems to

---

[55] Gilead and others (n 1) 7; Helmut Koziol and others, *Principles of European Tort Law (PETL): Text and Commentary* (Springer, 2005).

[56] Article 3.

[57] Gilead and others (n 1) 12.

tackle this type of causal uncertainty. It is possible to hold all defendants 'jointly and severally' liable for the causation of the whole damage and then design systems of redress once the harm has been compensated. When multiple tortfeasors contribute to cause the harm, the claimant has to prove causation against each defendant according to the requisite legal standard.[58] However, when the proof of causal contribution of the damage is excessively difficult or even a *probatio diabolica*, general tort laws often approach issues of contribution to the damage by holding all the defendants jointly and severally liable determining their liability, to the requisite legal standard, under an all-or-nothing rule.[59] According to the principle of joint liability, all defendants are liable for the full amount of the damage, and under the principle of several liability, either and each of them has to compensate the damage in full, if requested. Each defendant usually retains a right of redress against the co-infringers, based on the portion of the damage they caused. Thus, the claimant has no obligation to prove the *quantum* of causal contribution, but only the *an*. On the other hand, a system of proportionate liability burdens the claimant with the proof of causal contribution of each defendant.[60]

When an anticompetitive harm is caused by more than one undertaking, typically in the case of cartels, a problem of imputation of cartel damages and of liability of each antirust infringer arises. The Damages Directive opted for a solution whereby all the undertakings taking part to the same breach of competition law are jointly and severally liable for the harm caused (i.e., responsibility *in solidum*, or solidary responsibility).[61] According to Article 11(1), each undertaking is 'bound to compensate for the harm in full, and the injured party has the right to require full compensation from any of them until he has been fully compensated'.[62] To this end, the Directive has shown flexibility as to the application of the corrective justice principle. Causal uncertainty may render particularly difficult the proof of the causal contribution to the harm of each of the co-infringers. By introducing the rule of joint and several liability, the Directive has shifted the risk of proving the contribution on to the defendants, thus departing from a strict application of the compensatory principle.

The solution laid down by the Directive endorses the main trend in member states tort laws, where, in order to avoid inconsistencies of the application of strict interpretation of counterfactual approaches (such as the but-for test or adequate causality) and their proof rules, they prefer to account every tortfeasor *in solidum*.[63]

---

[58] Ibid.

[59] Ibid., 3.

[60] Solution adopted, for instance, in *Barker v Corus UK Ltd* [2006] 2 AC 572.

[61] Article 11(1).

[62] Ibid.

[63] For a comparative overview of the different approaches see Koziol and others (n 55) Article 9:101; Christian von Bar, *Non-Contractual Liability Arising out of Damage Caused to Another* (De Gruyter, 2009) 945; WVH Rogers and WH van Boom, *Unification of Tort Law: Multiple*

4.3 Causal Proportional Liability and Multiple Defendants

Similarly, the PETL states that '[l]iability is solidary where the whole or a distinct part of the damage suffered by the victim is attributable to two or more persons'.[64]

In order to obviate to the shortcomings of overdetermined causation, it was suggested that in case of multiple defendants, if each action was a sufficient condition of the harm, the but-for test has to be applied to the aggregate of potential causes.[65] These rules are clearly developed in order to make possible and, in any case, ease the burden of proof of the harmed party who seeks compensation.

The apportionment of the damage among the tortfeasors takes place in a second moment, subsequent to the finding of the causal responsibility of the co-infringers. The defendant, through recourse claims, can then seek restoration. Domestic tort laws regulate this apportionment, which is generally based on comparative fault.[66] Thus, the recourse claim does not have to establish any causation issue, such as the causal contribution of each tortfeasor.

However, the Directive leaves open to the choice of each jurisdiction whether to apply an alternative system of causal proportional liability.[67] Article 11(5) of the Directive states indeed that 'the Member States shall ensure that an infringer may recover a contribution from any other infringer, the amount of which shall be determined in the light of their relative responsibility for the harm caused by the infringement of competition law'. Moreover, the Directive points out that '[t]he determination of that share as the relative responsibility of a given infringer, and the relevant criteria such as turnover, market share, or role in the cartel, is a matter for the applicable national law, while respecting the principles of effectiveness and equivalence'.[68]

It is worth noticing that the Directive makes possible the recourse claim only against co-infringers. By consequence, the infringer who pays more than his own share of the harm would not be able to obtain a contribution from subjects that did not partake to the infringement but were enriched by it. For instance, in case of umbrella pricing, the infringer is not allowed to obtain a contribution from the direct purchaser who adapted to the umbrella prices but was not part of the cartel. If the domestic tort law provides the suitable means, the cartelist might be able to ask for the restitution of that amount from the umbrella buyer.

Tortfeasors (Kluwer Law International, 2004); Luisa Antoniolli and Francesca Fiorentini, *A Factual Assessment of the Draft Common Frame of Reference* (De Gruyter, 2010).

[64] The Principles of European Tort Law Art 9:101, Koziol and others (n 55).

[65] William Lloyd Prosser, *Prosser and Keeton on the Law of Torts* (West Pub Co, 1984) 268. Where the author points out that 'When the conduct of two or more actors is so related to an event that their combined conduct, viewed as a whole, is a but-for cause of the event, and application of the but-for rule to them individually would absolve all of them, the conduct of each is a cause in fact of the event'.

[66] Gilead and others (n 1) 25.

[67] Which differs from comparative or contributory negligence where the judge holds all the tortfeasors responsible for the whole harm and, in a second stage outside the assessment of direct causation, apportions the amount of damages.

[68] Recital (37).

82 Causal Uncertainty in Competition Law Damages Claims

A different causal scenario would be, instead, the one where a number of connected infringements by different undertakings cause harms to different subjects. If the harm does not flow from a single continuous infringement of competition law, rules on joint and several liabilities are not applicable. If this is the case, it might be extremely difficult to determine which defendant caused which part of the harm.

4.3.2 Causal Contribution to the Damage

The Damages Directive apportions the contribution of other co-infringers which did not compensate the harm to the extent of their causal contribution to the damage. The first sentence of Article 11(5) establishes that the right of each infringer to recover contribution from any other infringer, in proportion to their responsibility. It is, however, not clear what is the relative responsibility for a unitary harm brought about by multiple undertakings. For instance, Lianos argues that when a network of contracts concluded by a number of different undertakings causes a foreclosure effect, 'the collective dimension of antitrust liability in this context does not avoid the necessary examination at the stage of the attribution of the damage due to the causal relation between a specific conduct by one of the multiple tortfeasors and the damage suffered'.[69] However, it is not clear how the examination of the causal contribution to the harm should take place, especially if one considers that the cumulative effects of the different contracts are considered as a unitary infringement.

The determination of that share as the relative responsibility of a given cartel member and the relevant criteria, 'such as turnover, market share, or role in the cartel', shall be a matter for the applicable national law, while respecting the principles of effectiveness and equivalence.[70] Hence, the Directive leaves to the domestic laws to determine the principles of contribution. Domestic laws may establish a principle according to which each co-infringer has to contribute equally to the payment of compensatory damages. Otherwise, the law may require one to consider the causal contribution of each infringer to the damage. However, in most cases, this may resolve in a *probatio diabolica*, as differentiating the contributions of each participant in the causation of the harm subject to claim may be excessively difficult if not impossible. Hence, it may be possible to apportion liability on the basis of the market shares of the participating undertakings.[71] Since the calculation of the market share has to be performed throughout the infringement period,

---

[69] Lianos (n 54) 185, referring to the cumulative effect doctrine in Case C-234/89, *Stergios Delimitis* v *Henninger Brau AG.* [1991] ECR I-935.

[70] Recital (33) of the Directive.

[71] When, due to overdetermined or underdetermined causation, it is not possible to establish responsibility of each tortfeasor on the requisite legal standard, some scholars have advanced the possibility of determining the responsibility of each co-infringer on the basis of his or her market share also in tort law; see Gilead and others (n 1); Steel (n 7).

4.3 Causal Proportional Liability and Multiple Defendants 83

making again the burden of proof excessively difficult, it is finally possible for the judge to establish the quantum of contribution equitatively.

It is worth noting that this approach differs from the causal proportional liability test also examined in this book. The latter examines the ex ante contribution to the causation of a portion of the present or future harm,[72] whilst the contribution rules in the Directive consider this calculation to be performed ex post. By way of derogation, Article 11(2) limits the responsibility of SMEs to the harm they caused to their direct and indirect purchasers.

4.3.3 National Legal Systems Responses

In case of overdetermined and undetermined causation, the French legal system has created solutions based on a case-by-case approach. In particular, if due to scientific uncertainty or scarce information it is not possible to determine whether who, amongst a number of defendants, caused the damage, the French legal system has either imposed compulsory insurance schemes[73] or reversed the burden of proof for causation on the defendant.[74] However, such solutions are usually justified by general reasons of fairness of the compensatory system, aimed at ensuring compensation to the harmed party on a ground of overall fairness of the proceedings, and, therefore, they rarely establish a general principle of causation or a legal presumption.

The principle of joint and several liability of the defendants established in Article 11(1) is already positive in French law.[75] On the other hand, the provisions of paragraphs 2 and 3, which limit the responsibility of SMEs, shall be expressly transposed, like those of paragraphs 4, 5 and 6, which limit those of the 'beneficiaries of immunity' – that is, in French law, the beneficiaries of a leniency program but also those of a non-grievance program. The concept of 'relative' responsibility used in paragraphs 5 and 6 may need to be clarified, although it may be thought that a clear definition will not, in practice, dispel the difficulties of assessing personal responsibility of each cartelist in the occurrence of the damage.

In *JCB Services* v *Central Parks*,[76] the court defined the extent to which the causal contribution of a legal entity part of a larger economic unit should be considered

---

[72] Gilead and Green (n 1) 2.

[73] Such as for the case of road and hunting accidents, see Olivier Moréteau, 'Causal Uncertainty and Proportional Liability in France' in Israel Gilead, Michael D Green and Bernhard A Koch (eds), *Proportional Liability: Analytical and Comparative Perspectives* (De Gruyter, 2013) 144.

[74] For instance, in the 'Des cases' (Cass civ 1, 24 September 2009, Bull I, no 187, D 2010, 49, note P B, Revue trimestrielle de droit civil (RTD Civ) 2010, 111), a woman contracted a cancer that was proven to be caused by a drug produced by either one of the two defendants. However, it was not possible to determine which one of them. Hence, 'the Court of Cassation ruled that each of the two defendants had to prove that its product had not caused the damage, thereby creating a rebuttable presumption of causation', ibid., 145.

[75] Described as an obligation *in solidum* and not *solidaire*, since the latter implies the existence of tacit mandate of representation among co-debtors.

[76] Cour de Cassation, *JCB Services et al.* v *Central Parks*, 6 October 2015, no 13-24.854.

to determine responsibility. The EC sanctioned, on 21 December 2000, JC Bamford (JCB) group for setting up an anticompetitive scheme contrary to Article 81 of the EC Treaty (now Article 101 TFEU).[77] The General Court upheld the Commission's decision on 21 September 2006.[78] A civil law action followed before the Commercial Court of Orleans, as Central Parts SA claimed damages against JCB Sales and JC Bramford Excavators for economic losses caused by the cartel. The defendants objected to the fact that the EC's decision concerned JCB Service, a different company of the group, and the claimant failed to prove any causal contribution to the damage of the defendants. The defendants sustained that the claim violated Article 1382 of the Code Civil, in the part in which it did not prove the fault of the defendant and the causation of such harm by the defendant, not by any another firm of the group. On this first plea, the Court of Cassation held that the judge of the merit has the power to determine the conduct of the defendant, regardless of whether it was part of an EC's decision. Secondly, the court observed that the judge maintains a certain discretionary power in determining the causal contribution of the defendants in the antitrust infringement; that, though, has to be motivated and proven. The Court of Appeal obtained this proof, according to the judgment of the Court of Cassation, by defining the responsibility of each company in the anticompetitive action.

In case of multiple tortfeasors, English common law has recognized the possibility to relax the burden of proof under certain conditions. Firstly, under the *Fairchild* rule, if there is scientific uncertainty over the causes of the harm and it is certain that the harm resulted from the type of risk protected by the duty of care, the trier of facts is allowed to consider 'a lesser degree of causal connection'.[79] By this standard, the judge will apportion liability on the basis of the risk that the defendant created.[80] Article 38(2) of the Competition Act[81] establishes that 'The amount of contribution that one person liable in respect of the loss or damage may recover from another must be determined in the light of their relative responsibility for the whole of the

---

[77] JCB group received a fine of 39.6 million euros.

[78] T-67/01 of 13 January 2004, Decision No C-167/04.

[79] *Fairchild* v *Glenhaven Funeral Services* [2003] 1 AC 32; see also Ken Oliphant, 'Causal Uncertainty and Proportional Liability in England and Wales' in Israel Gilead, Michael D Green and Bernhard A Koch (eds), *Proportional Liability: Analytical and Comparative Perspectives* (De Gruyter, 2013) 128.

[80] *Barker* v *Corus (UK) plc* [2006] 2 AC 572. At the same time, the Compensation Act 2006, sec. 3 has re-established the principle of joint and several liability in cases of mesothelioma involving contribution to the damage proved on the balanced of probability; see ibid. According instead to Section 1(1) of the Civil Liability (Contribution) Act 1978 any jointly and severally liable person who compensated the damage caused to another person may recover contribution from any other person liable in respect of the same damage. Pursuant to Section 2(1) 'the amount of the contribution recoverable from any person shall be such as may be found by the court to be just and equitable having regard to the extent of that person's responsibility for the damage in question'.

[81] Competition Act 1998, 'The Claims in Respect of Loss or Damage Arising from Competition Infringements' and Other Enactments (Amendment) Regulations 2017.

loss or damage caused by the infringement'. Moreover, the Civil Liability (Contribution) Act 1978 states that 'any person liable in respect of any damage suffered by another person may recover contribution from any other person liable in respect of the same damage (whether jointly with him or otherwise)'.[82] The defendant paying in full the compensation has the right to recover the difference from the other co-infringers on the basis of their individual contribution,[83] which can be determined by the court in equity.[84] Section 16 of the UK Regulation on competition law claims and damages recalls Section 1 of the Contribution Act for the contribution between participants in cartels, adding the exceptional rules on immunity recipients provided for in the Damages Directive.

German law had already envisaged joint and several liability of antitrust infringers before the enactment of the Damages Directive at Sections 830 and 840 BGB. The Federal Court of Justice, in the landmark ORWI case, had accordingly established the right of the plaintiff to claim damages against the defendant, not only for sales made by the wholesalers clients of the defendant but also by the wholesalers who purchased paper from other members of the cartel.

Similarly, Article 2055 or the Italian Civil Code establishes the principle according to which 'If the harm is attributable to more than one person, all the tortfeasors are jointly and severally liable for damages'. The second paragraph also determines that the tortfeasor who compensated the damage has regress against the others, in proportion to their contribution to the harm.[85]

4.3.4 *Causal Contributions and the Single Economic Entity Principle*

It is treat law that a wholly owned subsidiary is presumed to be under decisive control of its parent company with regard to the application of competition law rules.[86] By consequence, the judge may ascribe the infringements committed by the subsidiary to the parent company, as under a direct causal relationship. This

---

[82] Section 1(1).

[83] With a PART 20 claim under the CPR 20

[84] Section 2(1).

[85] Article 2055(3) finally establishes that, in doubt, the individual contributions are assumed to be the same.

[86] See Alison Jones, 'Drawing the Boundary between Joint and Unilateral Conduct: Parent-Subsidiary Relationships and Joint Ventures', in A Ezrachi (ed) *International Research Handbook of Competition Law* (Edward Elgar, 2012); Wouter P J Wils, 'The Undertaking as Subject of E.C. Competition Law and the Imputation of Infringements to Natural or Legal Persons' [2000] 25 *European Law Review* 99, and Cristopher Townley, 'The Concept of an "Undertaking": The Boundaries of the Corporation – A Discussion of Agency, Employees and Subsidiaries', in G Amato and CD Ehlermann (eds), *EC Competition Law: A Critical Assessment* (Hart Publishing, 2007). In the United States, see, e.g., Herbert Hovenkamp, 'American Needle and the Boundaries of the Firm in Antitrust Law' (15 August 2010), available at SSRN: http://ssrn.com/abstract=1616625, and Ernest N Reddick, 'Joint Ventures and Other Competitor Collaborations As Single Entity – "undertakings" under US Law' [2012] 8(2) *European Competition Journal* 333.

86   *Causal Uncertainty in Competition Law Damages Claims*

presumption is a corollary of the single economic unit theory developed by British courts[87] and then adopted by the CJEU in competition law.[88] The aim is to bypass the separate legal personality in groups of companies in order to pursue the parent company hiding behind a 'sham' subsidiary.

Competition law rules (Articles 101 and 102 TFEU) refer, as the subject of their provisions, to 'undertakings'. This term encompasses not only companies but also associations, cooperatives, professional regulatory bodies and any other business activity, having or not a legal personality or a corporate form.[89] However, neither the term 'undertaking' nor the concept of single economic unit is defined by European law, not even in 'soft law' provisions. The single economic entity, indeed, is semantically and practically a creation of doctrine and case law. The first definition of undertaking in the European case law hails from the *Shell* case which describes undertakings as 'economic units which consist of a unitary organization of personal, tangible and intangible elements which pursues a specific economic aim on a long-term basis and can contribute to the commission of an infringement of the kind referred to in that provision [Article 101 TFEU]'.[90] The term undertaking, therefore, refers to the economic activity carried out more than to the subject conducting it. If so, there is a plethora of definitions of 'economic activity' that could be borrowed from academia and jurisprudence.[91] As for the application of competition law, the definition given in *Shell* has been recalled by all the following decisions and is now an established principle. However, when the defendant is a conglomerate of companies,[92] it might be objected that the absence of consideration of causal contribution to the infringement within the corporate group may generate unfair outcomes. This is, for instance, the position adopted by German law whereby liability has to be personal, and, therefore, only the legal entity that caused the harm can be condemned to compensate civil damages. As parent and subsidiary companies are considered as separate legal entities (i.e., principle of *Trennungsprinzip*), under German law, their responsibility will be determined according to their causal contribution to the damage. Moreover, according to the Federal Court of Justice, companies in a conglomerate of companies are not de jure connected by an agency-principal relationship that would justify the application of §831(1) German Civil

---

[87]   *DHN Food Distributors v London Borough of Tower Hamlets* [1976] 3 All ER 852.

[88]   Case C-97/08 P *Akzo Nobel and others v Commission* [2009] ECR I-8237; see also C-293/13 P e C-294/13 P *Fresh Del Monte* ECLI:EU:C:2015:416.

[89]   See eg. Case 96/82, *IAZ International Belgium NV v Commission* [1983] ECR-3369; Case C-250/92 *Gøttrup-Klim* [1994] ECR I-564.

[90]   Case T-11/89 *Shell International Chemical Company v Commission* [1992] ECR II-757, para 311.

[91]   See, e.g., Case T-193/02, *Piau v Commission* [2005] ECR II-209, para 69.

[92]   A conglomerate can be defined as a plurality of companies that might act on different level of the supply chain or even in different markets, but where all companies are part of the same corporate group because directly or indirectly owned and directed by a parent company. Usually, it consists of a parent company and a number of subsidiaries. Moreover, it normally has an international or global presence.

4.3 Causal Proportional Liability and Multiple Defendants

Code on vicarious liability.[93] However, the Damages Directive considers the 'undertaking' as the subject of the application of EU private competition laws. In this regard, it has been wondered whether §81(3a) GWB, establishing the liability of the firm that exercise a decisive influence over another firm, contravenes the principle of *effet utile*, if interpreted restrictively.[94]

By contrast, English courts have, in more occasions, recognized the liability of subsidiaries and parent companies even without proof of direct causal contribution. In *Provimi Ltd.* v *Roche UK*,[95] the plaintiff claimed cartel damages against a UK subsidiary of the Roche group, following an EC decision sanctioning an anticompetitive agreement among vitamin producers and including Roche AG. However, the decision did not address Roche UK, and the claimant had never purchased any cartelized goods from the UK subsidiary of Roche. The claimants maintained that Roche UK had causally contributed to the damage because it implemented the pricing policy of its group. According to the claimants, had Roche UK sold at a lower price, they would have purchased directly from them or would have been able to negotiate better conditions from their supplier, Roche AG.[96] On the other hand, the defendants maintained that, within a group, individual companies almost always set prices according to group policies. And according to the *Viho* case[97] this practice does not infringe Article 101 TFEU. Therefore, the defendants concluded, the individual participation of Roche UK to the practice was not illegal and did not have any causal contribution to the economic harm of the claimant. The High Court, however, observed that since 'all companies within an "undertaking" who "implemented" the cartel are infringers of Article [101], then their action in "implementing" the cartel could cause the loss that the claimants allege', thus concluding that 'On this analysis, each infringing entity is a tortfeasor'.[98] The fact of being part of a single economic entity allowed one to presume the participation to the cartel and therefore causation. This decision concerned the establishment of jurisdiction; thus, the judge had to determine a prima facie evidence of causation.[99] In *Cooper Tire*, the court applied the *Provimi* principle to establish its jurisdiction.[100] In this case, the UK-based defendant sold some products at inflated price to the plaintiff, although for a modest amount. Dow UK, the English subsidiary of Dow Chemical

---

[93] BGH 06.11.2012, II ZR 111/12.

[94] David Ashton, *Competition Damages Actions in the EU: Law and Practice*, 2nd edn (Edward Elgar Publishing, 2018) 214–215.

[95] [2003] EWHC 961 (Comm.).

[96] Ibid., para 37.

[97] Case C-73/95 P *Viho Europe BV* v *Commission of the European Communities* [1996] ECR I-5457.

[98] *Provimi* v *Roche* (n 95) para 40.

[99] It has since become a common to find an 'anchor defendant' in the UK to establish jurisdiction there.

[100] *Cooper Tire & Rubber Co & Ors* v *Shell Chemicals UK Ltd & Ors* [2009] EWHC 2609 (Comm).

Company, was not an addressee of the previous decision of the Commission that fined some of the members of the Dow group and a total of sixteen companies forming the rubber cartel.[101] However, it can be objected that the Akzo theory of single economic entity establishes the liability of parent companies for infringements of subsidiaries, not the contrary.[102] The rationale of this principle is to ensure effective redress against the tortfeasor bypassing 'sham' entities. By contrast, this case law applies the same principle on reverse, by presuming that subsidiaries contributed to the economic harm based on the parent company's tort.[103]

The CAT has, however, adopted a different view laying somewhere in the middle between this two visions. In *Sainsbury*[104] the competition court has established that legal entities within a corporate group are liable for damages caused by other corporate entities only if they 'in some way' participated in the breach or otherwise exercised a 'decisive influence' over a company which did.[105] Moreover, In *Mersen*,[106] the Court of Appeal observed that the Commission's decision on which the follow-on action was based was not addressed to the UK subsidiary of the group.[107] The decision was not even addressed to the whole group but to specific 'undertakings' within it. Therefore, the CoA established liability to be sued for infringement only on the undertaking named in the Commission's decision, not also on the English subsidiary. This interpretation is, moreover, in line with the Recital 34 of the Damages Directive establishing the binding nature of Commission's decisions also in their 'personal' scope.[108] However, the court did not discuss the case in which the claimant submits evidence of participation of the subsidiary in the anticompetitive behaviour. While the Akzo rule has a legal significance from a causal perspective, even this rule in Sainsbury fails to fulfil this requirement of responsibility, according to the corrective justice criterion. To infer responsibility, one has to be able to establish specific causation. This would mean determining that each company acted as a single economic entity for the purpose of the antitrust infringement. Only in that case, it would be, therefore, possible to establish causation.

Under EU law, absent any causal contribution to the damage, the parent company may be held liable for damages caused by the subsidiary, under the assumption that it influenced the behaviour of its subsidiary.[109] The parent company can rebut

---

[101] European Commission Butadiene Rubber and Emulsion Styrene Butadiene Rubber Case COMP/F/38.638 29 November 2006.
[102] Case C-97/08 P *Akzo Nobel and Others v Commission* (n 88).
[103] See similarly the recent *Vattenfall AB v Prysmian SpA* [2018] EWHC 1694 (Ch).
[104] *Sainsbury's Supermarkets Ltd v Mastercard Incorporated* [2016] CAT 11.
[105] Ibid., 363.
[106] *Emerson Electric Co & Ors v Mersen UK Portslade Ltd & Anor* [2012] EWCA Civ 155.
[107] Ibid., para 80.
[108] Recital (34) 'The effect of the finding should, however, cover only the nature of the infringement and its material, personal, temporal and territorial scope as determined by the competition authority or review court in the exercise of its jurisdiction'.
[109] Of this opinion are Giorgio Afferni, 'Il Risarcimento Dei Danni per Violazioni Del Diritto Della Concorrenza: Prescrizione e Responsabilità Solidale' [2018] *Nuove leggi civili*

this presumption only by proving the absence of such 'decisive influence'; proof of lack of negligence will not suffice.[110] In other words, the decisive influence allows one to presume participation to the causation of harm. However, although the parent company is not responsible under strict liability, the proof to the contrary is not one of mere absence of negligence. It is instead a proof of absence of direct or indirect participation in the anticompetitive conduct. The theory of the decisive influence therefore seems to uphold the finding of liability when the parent causally contributed to the damage directly (by setting the anticompetitive strategy of the subsidiary) or indirectly (by facilitating it in a substantial way).

Finally, EU law does not establish a regime of contribution within the corporate group. Thus, domestic laws will determine the responsibility of each company based on their causal contribution or on other principles.[111]

4.4 CAUSAL PROPORTIONAL LIABILITY

On the basis of the Damages Directive, it is valid the apportionment of liability among the independent tortfeasors done in accordance with their causal contribution to the risk of harm.[112] Proportional liability is a general term used to refer to the apportionment of liability between defendant and plaintiffs or solely between defendants on the basis of the portion of liability they share in the illegal event.[113]

Causal proportional liability (hereinafter also CPL) systems seek to adjust liability to the extent of the tortfeasor's singular contribution to the harm. Therefore, the liability of the defendant equals the probability that he or she has caused the damage. For instance, if the company D abused of its dominant position excluding other competitors from the market and one of them claims damages deriving from loss of clientele, the judge may award damages in proportion to the probability of the loss to happen.

A second application of the proportional liability theory concerns the apportionment of liability amongst many tortfeasors. In these cases, each defendant will respond in measure of the amount of its proportional participation to the infringement. Rules of apportionment of liability such as contributory negligence and

---

commentate 171, 196; Carsten Koenig, 'An Economic Analysis of the Single Economic Entity Doctrine in EU Competition Law' [2017] 13 *Journal of Competition Law & Economics* 281, 325; Christian Kersting, 'Transposition of the Antitrust Damages Directive into German Law' 7 ff. Against, see instead J Kortmann and others, 'The Draft Directive on Antitrust Damages and Its Likely Effects on National Law' vol 81 [2014] *Serie onderneming en recht* 681; Roel Van Leuken, 'Parental Liability for Cartel Infringements Committed by Wholly Owned Subsidiaries: Is the Approach of the European Court of Justice in Akzo Nobel Also Relevant in a Private-Law Context?' [2016] 24 *European Review of Private Law* 513, 522.

[110] Afferni (n 109) 191.
[111] C-231/11 P a C-233/11 *Commission v Siemens Österreich and Others* ECLI:EU:C:2014:256.
[112] Gilead and others (n 1) 2.
[113] Ibid., 5.

comparative fault[114] differ from causal proportional liability with multiple tortfeasors. While, indeed, in the first case, factual causation is already assessed through conventional means (all-or-nothing approaches) and the apportionment is only a way to distribute the damage among the tortfeasors, in the case of CPL, the apportionment regards the assessment of causation.[115] Compared to joint and several liability, the adoption of a causal proportional liability test changes the distribution of the burden of proof. If tortfeasors are jointly and severally liable, the claimant does not need to prove the extent of contribution of each tortfeasor but will have to meet the requisite standard of proof[116] to establish causation. On the other hand, according to the causal proportional liability approach, the claimant has to provide evidence of the extent of each contribution to the damage; however, the assessment would be based on the probability of this contribution to realize in the counterfactual scenario.

Scholars also have put forward a third category comprising the uncertainty of causation of a future event.[117] In competition law actions, this could find application in actions for injunction and to deter future damages.[118] The object of this class of events is therefore an unrealized risk of a potential future harm. The retrospective application of CPL to past events, according to some scholars, fosters instead the pursuit of justice and fairness in tort law, apportioning liability on the basis of the causal contribution of each defendant, who will pay only for his or her actual responsibility.[119]

Moreover, the proportional liability test may be used to overcome the impasse created by the cumulative foreclosure effect of parallel networks. It might happen that several parallel networks are individually incapable of hindering the market. However, the aggregate effect of all such networks might foreclose other competitors, causing a restriction to the competition.[120] The application of the but-for test to each network would inevitably come to the exclusion of liability, since the single network behaviour is not a sufficient cause of the event. By contrast, the causal

---

[114] See for a comparative analysis of their usage, Cees Van Dam, *European Tort Law* (Oxford University Press, 2013) 309. In this vein, Lord Atkin confessed 'I find it impossible to divorce any theory of contributory negligence from the concept of causation', *Caswell v Powell Duffryn Associated Collieries* [1940] AC 152, 165.

[115] Gilead and others (n 1) 3.

[116] Which varies across jurisdictions, but is usually not lower than 51 per cent, see Chapter 5.

[117] Gilead and others (n 1) 16.

[118] For a comment of the recourse to injunctive relief in competition law see Richard Whish, *Competition Law* (Oxford University Press, 2012) 297 ff.; Sebastian Peyer, 'Injunctive Relief and Private Antitrust Enforcement', *CCP Working Paper No. 11-7*, 2011, available at SSRN: http://ssrn.com/abstract=1861861 or http://dx.doi.org/10.2139/ssrn.1861861; Barry J Rodger and Angus MacCulloch, 'Wielding the Blunt Sword: Interim Relief for Breaches of EC Competition Law before the UK Courts' [1996] 17 *European Competition Law Review* 17, 393–402.

[119] On the impact of CPL theories on the responsibility of tortfeasors, see Porat and Stein (n 1); Oliphant (n 79) 26.

[120] Case C-234/89, *Stergios Delimitis v Henninger Bräu AG.* [1991] ECR I-935.

4.5 LOSS OF CHANCE

The lost chances theory refers to the possibility of claiming damages for the losses that could be avoided but for the defendant's conduct. In this respect, two approaches are possible. The first establishes the lost chances according to the all-or-nothing rule.[121] Here, the claimant has to prove according to the requisite legal standard that the defendant has caused a loss of chance (e.g., loss of a chance of concluding a contract),[122] while the amount of damages will be proportionate to the probability of that chance to realize.[123] However, lost chances are formulated in probability terms that often fail to meet the requisite standard of proof, even on the balance of probability.[124]

The second approach considers the probability of avoiding a loss and allows the compensation of such portion of the damage.[125] In this vein, the creation or contribution to a risky situation can impede a particular event from being caused. The event remains in its 'potentiality', and, therefore, it is measurable only according to the probability of that event happening in a counterfactual scenario. The situation that was not realized due to the defendant's action is a lost chance.[126]

This formulation of the lost chances theory predicates that the damage consists in the probability that the claimant had (before the infringement) of avoiding the

---

[121] Porat and Stein (n 1) 117.

[122] Sandy Steel calls this, with particular reference to the English jurisprudence, the 'quantification' principle; see Steel (n 7) 300.

[123] This principle was explained by Lord Diplock in *Mallett v McMonagle*, where he observed that 'in assessing damages which depend upon its view as to what will happen in the future or would have happened in the future if something had not happened in the past, the court must make an estimate as to what are the chances that a particular thing will or would have happened and reflect those chances, whether they are more or less than even, in the amount of damages which it awards' [1970] AC 166, 176.

[124] See Section 5.3.

[125] Porat and Stein (n 1) 118.

[126] Peter Cane, *Tort Law and Economic Interests* (Clarendon Press, 1996) 137 ff; Van Dam (n 114) 337 ff; Jaap Spier and Francesco Donato Busnelli, *Unification of Tort Law: Causation* (Kluwer Law International, 2000) 141 ff; Walter Van Gerven, Jeremy Lever and Pierre Larouche, *Cases, Materials and Text on National, Supranational and International Tort Law* (Hart, 2000) 201 ff; BS Markesinis and Hannes Unberath, *The German Law of Torts: A Comparative Treatise* (Hart, 2002) 628–629.

damage. It usually finds application when the claimant is not able to prove, according to the requisite standards for causation, the factual connection between the infringement and the harm or when the harm is merely potential. The loss of chance therefore does not refer to the final damage and the probability that this might happen, as it may also consist in a different head of damage.[127]

According to this approach, in competition law damages actions, one may establish the causative link between the anticompetitive behaviour and the economic harm through the risk added by the infringement to the loss of chance.[128] Whereas this is a departure from the all-or-nothing approach underlying the right to full compensation, the Damages Directive recognizes the compensability of such kind of damages under the heading of 'loss of opportunity'.[129]

The possible cases of loss of chances causing economic damages are many – among them, the inability of the victim to develop business relationships with a customer or to enter a market, to access and exploit a particular technology, to renew a concession contract, to avoid contracting a disproportionate loan or bond,[130] to make highly risky investments[131] or, finally, to make an investment on life insurance.[132]

A further practical consequence of the application of such approach is that it affects the *quantum* of damage and not only the *an debeatur*. Indeed, if the grievance is accepted by the judge, the damage awarded will amount not to the damage but to the loss of opportunity in form of economic advantage. However, lost chances should not be confused with lost profits, although they both address a future lost income. Whereas a claim for lost chances has a probabilistic basis, the demand for lost profits follows the standard proof rules of causation. A claim for lost profits requires the proof of the existence of certain elements from which to infer, in terms of certainty or probability and not mere potentiality, the existence of an economic loss.[133]

The qualification of the damage as loss of chances or lost profits also affects the calculation of damages. For instance, let us take the case in which lost profits

---

[127] Chabas, François, 'La Perte d'une Chance En Droit Français, Colloque Sur Les Développements Récents Du Droit de La Responsabilité Civile' [1991] *Centre d'études européennes* 131 ff.

[128] Raising the risk of damage might lower the chances to avoid it. However, risks and chances should not be confused. General class-based probabilities of risk are not a proof of a loss of chances. Let us consider the example of a claimant that, in a follow-on action, claims to have lost the chance to close a contract because of the exclusionary abuse of the defendant. In this case, the judge may determine that the abuse raised the risk of such type of contract not to be concluded by competitors. However, the singular causation requires the assessment of the fact that that particular exclusionary conduct impeded the conclusion of that specific contract. Depending on the jurisdiction, it may not suffice to

The lost chance generally refers in tort law to an infringement which caused a loss to reach a rather probable outcome or objective or to avoid an undesired one.

[129] Recital 13.

[130] All hypothesis mentioned in Cour de Cassation, comm., 15 February 2011, No. 09-16.779.

[131] Cour de Cassation, comm., 15 September 2009, No. 08-14.398.

[132] Ibid.

[133] Corte di Cassazione civ. sez II, 1 December 2000, n 15385.

amount to 100 with a probability of happening of 80 per cent and to 500 for the remaining 20 per cent. If the damage is qualified as a loss of profits, the damage would be quantified in 100, since that is the amount that 'most probably' (80 per cent) the claimant was going to earn, while the 500 possible loss would remain a neglectable possibility (only 20 per cent). By contrast, if we define the damage as a loss of chances, both opportunities have to be quantified in relation to their chances to be realized. Hence, the damage would amount to 180 (that is, 100*80% e 500*20%).[134]

In general terms, while a claim for lost profits focuses on the earning which ceases to exist, the lost chances address a future income that exists as a possibility to do business.[135] In antitrust litigation, these claims are often confused by the plaintiff that, as Hovenkamp observes, 'generally claims damages for what may be loosely characterized as lost profits'.[136] The author suggests that in cases such as 'reduction in market share, a smaller markup per unit sold, an existing firm's loss of investment or business assets, or preclusion from entry into a profitable business ... the measure of damages is so imprecise that "loss of the opportunity to do business" would describe the plaintiff's loss more accurately than "lost profits," which suggests a sum that is quantifiable with a fair amount of precision'.[137]

Sometimes the theory of lost chances is formulated in the negative, meaning that the law compensates the lost chance of not being harmed.

4.6 LOST CHANCES IN DOMESTIC ANTITRUST CASE LAW

European courts have different positions over the indemnifiable nature of such hypothetical damages.[138] In some cases, the lost chances can, however, facilitate the burden of proving causation, as the claimant can move the ground for the proof from the very complex one of the causal relationship between action and damage to the more immediate one that connects the action to the loss of a chance.[139] The loss of a chance brings the judge to operate a substitution in the causal reasoning: in place of the effects of the infringement, there is the probability of that action to produce the effects.

In competition law, possible grounds for claims based on lost chances are numerous. For instance, a firm might claim the loss of the chance to conclude a

---

[134] See Laura Castelli, 'La Causalità Giuridica Nel Campo Degli Illeciti Anticoncorrenziali' [2013] 18 *Danno e responsabilità* 1049, 1059; also citing, with reference to this example, Pietro Trimarchi, *Il contratto: inadempimento e rimedi* (Giuffrè, 2010) 144.

[135] Trimarchi (n 134) 144.

[136] Herbert Hovenkamp, *Federal Antitrust Policy: The Law of Competition and Its Practice* (Thomson/West, 2005) 678.

[137] Ibid.

[138] Van Dam (n 114) 337 ff.

[139] As argued, for instance, by Jourdain and Viney observing that this is often used to avoid proof of causation; Geneviève Viney and Patrice Jourdain, *Les conditions de la responsabilité* (LGDJ, 2006).

94   *Causal Uncertainty in Competition Law Damages Claims*

contract that failed to secure because of the exclusionary infringement of the incumbent. Otherwise, a consumer might ask for the damages caused by the loss of chance to purchase a good because of its cartel-inflated price.

Modern theories tend to calculate the probability of lost chances as a quota of the final damage, if happened.[140] However, this translation of probabilities in actual damages sometimes gives the illusion that probabilities equal certainties, at least from a legal viewpoint. Moreover, the quota of lost chances has a relative weight depending on the position of the damaged party and the final damage. A 30 per cent loss, in terms of future chances of reaching a certain objective, exercises a different power whether the loss takes the chances from 90 to 60 or from 40 to 10. In the latter case, indeed, the damage is clearly more important, since the successful expectations are highly diminished almost to 0, although in both cases, the quota amounts to a 30 per cent.

4.6.1 *French Law*

In France the concept of loss of chance (*perte de chance*) is generally used in order to obviate to the shortcomings of legal causation.[141] The lost chance permits to bypass the proof of a causal connection between action and damage because, for French law, it is an independent head of damage.[142] In this vein, the *Cour de Cassation* requires the claimant to prove the lost chance as well as the causal connection between the action and the lost chance[143] also in cases of pure economic loss.[144] The probability of lost chances is calculated as a percentage, which is then compensated.

In competition law litigation, several cases have been argued on the lost chances theory before French courts. In *SAS Ajinomoto Eurolysine* v *SNC Doux Aliments*,[145] the decision of the Court of Appeal of Paris was based on a follow-on claim raised by

---

[140] Gilead and others (n 1) 40.

[141] Duncan Fairgrieve and Florence G'Sell-Macrez, 'Causation in French Law: Pragmatism and Policy' in Richard Goldberg (ed), *Perspectives on Causation* (Hart, 2011) 119.

[142] See Cour de Cassation civ., 12 November 1985, Bull. civ I, no. 298; Cour de Cassation civ., 7 February 1990, Bull. civ I, no. 39; Cour de Cassation civ., 3 November 1983, Bull. civ. I, no. 253, on which see Van Gerven, Lever and Larouche (n 126) 427, see also Viney and Jourdain (n 139); Van Dam (n 114); Gilead and others (n 1) 143.

[143] Cour de Cassation req., 17 July 1889, S. 1891. I. 399; Cour de Cassation civ. 14 December 1965, JCP 1966. II. 14753, Cour de Cassation civ. 17 November 1982, JCP 1983. II. 20056, D. 1984. 305, on which see Van Gerven, Lever and Larouche (n 126) 428; Cour de Cassation civ. 8 January 1985, D. 1986. 390, comm. Penneau; Cour de Cassation civ. 10 June 1986, Bull. civ. 1986. I. 163; see Viney-Jourdain (n 139).

[144] Cour de Cassation crim. 6 June 1990, Bull. crim. 1990. 224, on which see Van Gerven (n 126) 200–201. Cour de Cassation civ. 4 June 2007, JCP 2007. I. 185, no. 2, ETL 2007, 276.

[145] Paris Court of Appeal, *SNC Doux Aliments Bretagne etc* v *SAS Ajinomoto Eurolysine*, No 07/10478, 10 June 2009.

4.6 Lost Chances in Domestic Antitrust Case Law

Doux against a 30 per cent cartel overcharge on the price of lysine.[146] The European Commission had fined several producers of lysine for operating a global price-fixing cartel. Doux, a French poultry producer using lysine in its aliments,[147] claimed damages resulting from the cartel price increase of about 30 per cent. The claimant maintained that – as a result of the cartel operations – it suffered damages due to the price overcharge and also due to a reduction of profit margins and to a loss in competitiveness. The defendant, Ajinamoto Eurolysine, opposed the fact that Doux had passed the overcharge on to its buyers and objected also to the reliability of the expert opinion submitted by the claimant. The Court of Appeal rejected the passing-on defence and established that the claimant suffered economic harm in the form of lost chances due to reduced competitiveness, to be calculated in the amount of the 30 per cent of the amount claimed.[148]

The French *Cour de Cassation* overturned the Court of Appeal's decision, observing that the judgment failed to consider whether the claimant had totally or partially passed on to its customers the price overcharge.[149] According to the French Supreme Court, the passing-on had legal basis under Article 1382 of the French Civil Code.[150] Moreover, the Supreme Court observed that the judge must determine, according to the evidence available, the existence of a causal link between the event giving rise to liability and the loss of a chance which should not be presumed. The fact that the lysine market prices had been subject to erratic fluctuations should not bring the judge to infer the causal link between the rise in prices and the loss of competitiveness of products by Ajinomoto, as the damage remain purely hypothetical and therefore violates the principle expressed by the Article 1382 of the French Civil Code.[151]

In *Orange v Cowe*,[152] an exclusionary abuse of the dominant French Internet service provider, France Telecom, had allegedly deprived the claimant of the opportunity to enter the ADSL market. Whereas the Court of Appeal confirmed the claim granting compensation for loss of chances, the Court of Cassation reverted

---

[146] Commission Decision Case COMP/36545/F3 – Amino Acids OJ L 152, 762001, 24–72.

[147] Doux purchased the lysine from Ceva Santé Animale that, at its turn, directly purchased it from Ajinomoto.

[148] Here the Court of Appeal does not give justification of the damages calculation as it might be the result of a discretionary apportionment.

[149] Cour de Cassation *comm. Ajinomoto Eurolysine v SNC Doux Aliment Bretagne and Others* No 09/15816 (15 June 2010).

[150] See infra Chapter 7. The general rule for tortious liability in France stating that 'Any act of a person which causes damage to another makes him by whose fault the damage occurred to make reparation for the damage' (in the original version 'Tout fait quelconque de l'homme, qui cause à autrui un dommage, oblige celui par la faute duquel il est arrivé, à le réparer'). In addition, the Court of Appeal violated Article 16 of the French code of civil procedure because did not invite the parties to submit their comments when converted part of Doux's claim in an appeal for lost chances.

[151] *Ajinomoto Eurolysine v Doux* (n 149).

[152] Court de Cassation *Orange v Cowes*, 25 March 2014, n 1313839.

the decision, stating that the claimant did not provide enough evidence of the connection between the antitrust infringement and the lost chances that were claimed. Hence, in both cases, the Court of Cassation quashed the claims because of a defect in the proof of causation, which was instead presumed by the appellate judge.

In at least other three competition law damages actions, French courts have successfully granted damages for loss of chances. The first regards a judgment of the Court of Appeal of Versailles, in which a seller of electronic products claimed damages caused by a selective rebates scheme operated by the defendant, a distributor and supplier of such goods.[153] Aiwa, the supplier, applied preferential rebates policy only to some of its buyers. The damage claimed included, on the one hand, the missed rebates and, on the other hand, the loss of additional sales which the claimant could have achieved if the discount policy was applied on a non-discriminatory basis. The court observed that the claimant failed to provide enough evidence in relation to the actual loss and the lost profits claimed. However, the evidence submitted was sufficient to establish the existence of a damage in form of lost chances which was quantified in 50.000 euros.[154]

In a follow-on action, Verimedia sought relief against an exclusionary abuse in the market for media audience data. The French competition authority found that this abuse consisted in an unjustified delay in sharing the information necessary for Verimedia to provide its services. On this basis, the claimant sought damages for loss of clientele. However, the Court of Appeal of Versailles observed that whereas part of the damage was due to the defendants' anticompetitive conduct, the inexperience of the claimant in the media market also contributed to the causation of the damage. Hence, the court decided to recognize to the claimant only a right to recover the lost chances to penetrate more quickly and more effectively the market of media audit.[155]

In another case of loss of chances, a potential buyer of a newspaper stall claimed damages for exclusion from the distribution network of SNC *Société presse paris services* (SPPS), the local dominant newspaper distributor.[156] The claimant, Mr Bassam, referred that he refused to accept the standard contract proposed by SPPS, as – according to him – the clause allowing the supplier to terminate *ad nutum* the contract with 48 hours notice was abusive and therefore violated articles L. 420-1 and L. 420-2 of the French Commercial Code. The Court of Appeal granted damages to Mr Bassam in form of lost chances to open a newsstand and gain profits from it.

---

[153] Court of Appeal of Versailles, SA *Concurrence* v SA *Aiwa France*, No 01/08413, 9 December 2003.

[154] Instead of the 305,000 euros claimed by SA Concurrence.

[155] Granting in total twenty times less than the sum claimed as loss of clientele.

[156] Court of Appeal of Paris, M *Merhi Bassam* v SNC *Société Presse Paris Services – SPPS*, No 08/21750, 27 April 2011.

4.6.2 English Law

In England, the notion of loss of chances does not find the same broad application as in France. Whereas it has since long found application in contractual disputes related to financial losses,[157] in tort law, English courts have initially refused to apply the lost chances theory.[158] The application of the 'more probable than not' or '50+' rule prevents a scalar application of the lost chances. British courts therefore tend to be more reluctant to grant damages for lost chances, especially in medical negligence, where the House of Lords has twice rejected such claims, in *Hotson v East Berkshire Area Health Authority*[159] and *Gregg v Scott*.[160] However, outside the area of medical malpractice, British courts are more prone to accept such claims – in particular, in cases of pure economic losses, as, for instance, in *Allied Maples v Simmons & Simmons*,[161] related to a claim of professional responsibility and company law. With specific regard to competition law damages actions, a future economic loss has been considered too remote to be accounted as an independent head of damage. In *Crehan v Inntrepreneur Pub Company CPC* (IPC),[162] the first UK case awarding damages for breach of competition law, Mr Crehan – a pub owner – claimed damages caused by the lease contract with IPC which he maintained to be unlawful for breach of Article 81 (now Article 101 TFUE). In particular, Mr Crehan claimed to have felt consistent losses of chances to compete against pubs which were purchasing beers at more competitive prices. Moreover, he reasoned, the loss was flowing from his inability to 'shop around for best buys'.[163] The Court of Appeal considered that, under English law, the claimant grievances could not find satisfaction for a lack of breach of statutory duty.[164] The type of injury claimed, according to the court, although causally connected to the infringement, was not of the type that Article 81 (now Article 101 TFEU) was intended to protect against. Thus, the court observed that the case could not succeed in English law alone, but this would have rendered practically impossible the exercise of a right to damages conferred by EU law.[165] Thus, in application of the principle of effectiveness, such damages had to be awarded.[166]

---

[157] *Chaplin v Hicks* [1911] 2 KB 786, CA.

[158] *Hotson v East Berkshire Area Health Authority* [1988] UKHL 1.

[159] Ibid.

[160] *Gregg v Scott* [2005] UKHL 2.

[161] *Allied Maples Group Ltd v Simmons & Simmons* [1995] EWCA Civ 17.

[162] *Crehan v Inntrepreneur Pub Company CPC* [2004] EWCA Civ 637.

[163] Ibid., para 165.

[164] The Court recalls the U.S. Supreme Court in the Brunswick Corporation case, whereby a loss caused by an antitrust infringement is subject to compensation only if it is of the type that antitrust laws were intended to prevent (see supra Section 2.6.).

[165] Case C-453/99 *Courage Ltd v Bernard Crehan* and *Bernard Crehan v Courage Ltd and Others* [2001] ECR I-06297.

[166] The court mainly refers to lost profits and to hypothetical damages 'The wrong sustained by Mr. Crehan was the loss of his businesses at The Cock Inn and The Phoenix. But, for the purpose

This approach has been revised more recently by the Court of Appeal in *Enron v English Welsh & Scottish Railway*.[167] Here, the claimant sustained a loss of chances caused by the abuse of dominant position of the defendant. The infringement of competition law was fundamentally uncontested, given that the action was a follow-on type and the Office of Rail Regulation (ORR) had already established the violation of Article 102 TFEU. Moreover, the British Authority also found out that English Welsh & Scottish Railway (EWS) deliberately tried to endanger Enron's position in the relevant market through a discriminatory treatment of the claimant, which was placed at a competitive disadvantage in its contractual negotiations with Edison Mission Energy Ltd (EME). On such basis, Enron claimed that the abuse of dominant position of EWS deprived them of a real or substantial chance of winning a contract for the supply of coal to one of EME's power stations for the period 2001 to 2004.[168] The Competition Appeal Tribunal (CAT), in first instance, observed that Enron, even in absence of the anticompetitive conduct, had few (if any) chances to win the coal contract from Edison. The anticompetitive behaviour, translated in causal language, was therefore a condition of the harm but not necessary and not even probable. In this regard, the court refused to adopt the causal proportional liability method to factor in the defendant's contribution to the risk of a loss of chance, considering that the claimant failed to prove causation between the hypothetical harm (lost chances) and the antitrust infringement.

The CAT, endorsing the first instance decision, evaluated the findings of the British Authority in terms of causal connection to the harm claimed and observed that 'The finding of competitive disadvantage (which EWS accepts, as it must) means that EWS hindered the competitive position of ECSL in relation to the EME Tender. This is certainly relevant to, but not determinative of, the question of causation. It is relevant because it means that ECSL was impeded in its ability to offer EME competitive rates for coal haulage and supply. It is not determinative because the Decision does not establish that ECSL was well-placed to win a coal supply contract with EME absent the abuse'.[169] The loss of chance for not winning the contract was therefore not causally connected to the competitive impairment suffered by Enron. In this decision, the English courts argued on the right to recover lost chances, confirming that it is possible to claim such damages if adequate proof

---

of the measuring the damages recoverable, they were not actual businesses. They were hypothetical, in the sense that they had to be treated, contrary to the actuality, as having been free of tie. So they had to be treated, though for a different reason, in the same way as UYB's business. On Park J.'s approach that faces the court with the immediate difficulty that the measure of damages involves a hypothesis upon a hypothesis: the hypothetical profits of a hypothetical business', para 179.

[167] *Enron Coal Services Limited v English Welsh & Scottish Railway* [2011] EWCA Civ 2.

[168] Ibid., 74. Thus, the plaintiff claimed damages in form of lost chances for failing to close an E2E contract with Edison because of the competitive disadvantage caused by the EWS anticompetitive behaviour.

[169] Ibid., para 162.

4.6 Lost Chances in Domestic Antitrust Case Law

of causal connection is provided. However, it seems contradictory the approach positing that the court should use an all-or-nothing approach to determine whether a causal proportional liability solution should find application.

In the case 2 *Travel* v *Cardiff Bus*,[170] the CAT rejected the claims related to loss of a capital asset, loss of a commercial opportunity and the costs of 2 Travel's liquidation, on the basis of the fact that the infringement was not a necessary condition of the loss. The Office of Fair Trade (OFT)[171] found that Cardiff Bus had abused of its dominant position by seeking to force 2 Travel out of that market through a predatory conduct. 2 Travel contended that but-for the infringement its business would have grown similarly to what others did in the same sector.[172] Thus, the claimant demanded the compensation of the 'loss of capital asset' in the form of a loss of commercial opportunity.[173] To answer this demand, the CAT firstly considered 2 Travel's business plan.[174] Secondly, it analyzed the viability of this plan with reference to the characteristics of 2 Travel as a corporate entity, examining in particular: (1) management; (2) quality of service; and (3) debt and cash flow.[175] Finally, they examined the reasons for 2 Travel's insolvency and whether it could have staved off insolvency.[176] The CAT found out that the company was poorly managed and it had financial difficulties long before the abuse of dominance of the defendant started. The judges observed that 'But for extremely large injections of cash – from the flotation and from the bank ... – the company would have gone under long before May 2005'.[177] Thus, the CAT rejected the claims finding that although the infringement would have resulted in a small additional revenue to the company of £33,818.79, 'This was a drop in the ocean, and could not have saved the company.' Thus, they considered 'the Infringement to be causally irrelevant to 2 Travel's demise'.[178] 2 Travel also claimed that the infringement forced the company to mortgage and divest itself of its interest in a valuable property asset. Also on this point, the CAT argued that in the counter-factual scenario, 2 Travel would have had to divest itself anyway from the depot, and, therefore, the infringement was not causally connected to the economic loss.

---

[170] 2 *Travel Group PLC (in liquidation)* v *Cardiff City Transport Services Ltd* [2012] CAT 30.

[171] Replaced by the Competition and Markets Authority (CMA) in 2014, according to the The Enterprise and Regulatory Reform Act 2013 (c 24).

[172] As a comparator, 2 Travel used a similar company, *Rotala plc.*, ibid., para 419.

[173] Initially, 2 Travel submitted two different claims for loss of capital asset and loss of commercial opportunity, which were then united under one head of loss with its written opening; ibid., para 2.

[174] As documented by a February 2004 PwC Report submitted to the Court.

[175] Ibid., para 420(2).

[176] Ibid., para 420.

[177] Ibid., 432.

[178] Ibid., 433.

4.6.3 *German Law*

German tort law generally rejects the application of loss of chances theory, on the basis of the fact that 'If the chance has no economic value, redefining the damage encounters difficulties because the loss of this chance cannot be qualified as recognisable damage which can be compensated'.[179]

German law predicates an all-or-nothing approach that, for the prevalent doctrine, cannot be reconciled with the application of lost chances theory.[180] In competition law damages actions, claimants generally qualify the head of damage as a loss of profits,[181] when possible. According to Section 252 of the German Civil Code, lost profits are those that the claimant would have earned in the normal course of events. The claim for lost profits benefits from a lower standard of proof, as it is sufficient for the claimant to prove the loss 'with probability according to the ordinary course of things, or according to the particular circumstances, in particular, according to the preparation and provisions made'.[182] Some cases, however, concern future harms which are not strictly lost profits flowing from an actual loss suffered. For instance, a private lottery agent sought damages against the German lotteries for being excluded from the market of distribution of lottery tickets.[183] This private distributor set up a national distribution system alternative to the one owned and utilized by the state lotteries. At the time, 16 regional lottery networks existed and agreed to sell tickets only within the respective regions.[184] Moreover, barriers to entry to the regional markets of lottery tickets were very high due to licensing requirements for gambling games.[185] The German antitrust authority (Bundeskartellamt) proved the anticompetitive agreement and fined the state lotteries.[186] With a follow-on action, the claimant maintained that the exclusionary practice of the state lotteries caused 'lost profits' to his future business. The company documented these future losses by submitting to the regional court an internal business plan, one market study provided by an investment bank and a second study commissioned to a research company. Both studies were performed before the exclusion from the market. The first instance court rejected the claimant's grievances on the basis of the court's expert's testimony, which raised doubts over causation of lost profits. The appellate judge overturned this decision on the basis of a substantive revision of the

---

[179] Helmut Koziol, 'Loss of a Chance: Comparative Report' in Winiger, Bénédict and others (eds), *Digest of European Tort Law. Vol. 1: Essential Cases on Natural Causation* (Springer, 2007).

[180] Marc Stauch, *The Law of Medical Negligence in England and Germany: A Comparative Analysis* (Bloomsbury Publishing, 2008).

[181] Recoverable under Section 33 GWB and Section 252 of the German Civil Code. See BGH, 28/6/2011, KZR 75/10, BGHZ 190, 145, 162 ff.

[182] Section 252 German Civil Code, see also Koziol (n 179) 19, 215.

[183] Higher Regional Court of Düsseldorf, 9 April 2014, VI-U (Kart) 10/12.

[184] *Bundeskartellamt*, B10–148/05, 8.

[185] Ibid., 9.

[186] Ibid.

claimant's business plan. Given its commercial feasibility and the proof of antitrust behaviour, the judge established a presumption of causation of loss of future profits.[187] The economic harm consisted, therefore, in a future opportunity of making new profits rather than a loss of actual earnings.

4.6.4 *Italian Law*

Italian judges may accept claims based on lost chances, relying on probabilistic theories of adequate causation.[188] In Italy, the lost chance became a compensable head of damage through the interpretative revision of tort rules by the Supreme Court, which has declared the lost possibility to realize a positive outcome in the future as protected by law also.[189] As Article 1223 of the Civil Code allows only the compensation of actual loss and lost profits, the Supreme Court has qualified the lost chances sometimes as lost profits and sometimes as an actual loss. The loss of opportunity has to be a certain result that the claimant would have achieved but for the defendant's tort.[190] It has been observed that this entails a *probatio diabolica* of the causal requirement, as a future loss can never be certain.[191] For this reason, the Court of Cassation has preferred to adhere to the doctrinal approach that qualifies the loss of chance as an actual loss.[192] The chance, according to this approach, does not concern a future earning but is an asset already existing and belonging to the injured person.[193] Preventing this chance from happening causes an actual loss to be understood as 'a concrete and actual damage ... [which] should not be commensurate with the loss of profits, but with the mere possibility of achieving it'.[194] The injured party has the burden of proving that the tort was the *conditio sine qua non* of the lost chance; it also has the burden of proving all the circumstances making probable the realization of the chance.[195] As for the quantification of the damage, if uncertain, the court can determine its amount in equity. On

---

[187] On the standard and burden of proofs adopted, see Chapter 5. While on the use of causal presumptions as relaxation rules, see Chapter 6.

[188] Roberto Pucella and Giovanni De Santis, *Il nesso di causalità. Profili giuridici e scientifici* (Wolters Kluwer Italia, 2007); Roberto Pucella, *La causalità 'incerta'* (Giappichelli, 2007) 82.

[189] Corte di Cassazione, *Montani et al* v Lloyd *Adriatico*, 25 September 1998, no 9598, in Studium Juris 1999, 81 Danno e resp. 1999, 534; see also Corte di Cassazione civ., 25 May 2007, n 12243, in Giust. civ. Mass., 2007, 5; Corte di Cassazione civ., 21 July 2003, n 11322, in Danno e resp., 2004, 567.

[190] See Fulvio Mastropaolo, *Risarcimento Del Danno* (Jovene, 1983) 12; Giovanna Visintini, *Trattato Breve Della Responsabilità Civile: Fatti Illeciti, Inadempimento, Danno Risarcibile* (CEDAM, 1996) 545.

[191] C Severi, 'Perdita Di Chance e Danno Patrimoniale Risarcibile' [2003] *Resp. civ. e prev* 296, 302.

[192] Corte di Cassazione sez. III, 4 March 2004, n 4400.

[193] Corte dei Conti (Italian Court of Audit), Sez. Lombardia, 13 marzo 1998, n 436.

[194] Corte di Cassazione sez. III, 4 marzo 2004, n 4400.

[195] Severi (n 191) 305.

102 *Causal Uncertainty in Competition Law Damages Claims*

the other hand, the defendant has the burden to identify the causes that could have compromised the achievement of the result.[196]

In a competition law case concerning an insurance contract, the insurance company Fondiaria SAI S.p.A. was found to be part of a cartel by the Italian antitrust authority.[197] An insured client filed a lawsuit for compensation of the damage due to the overcharge paid on insurance premiums and for the loss of a chance of obtaining better policy conditions if the insurance market had not been altered by the anticompetitive conduct. The Court of Cassation qualified this opportunity as a loss of chance, which had to be proven 'according to a probabilistic calculation or for presumptions'.[198]

The probability of the positive event of happening does not necessarily have to be more than 50 per cent, as the Italian case law, differently from common law traditions, requires a 'reasonable certainty of a positive probability'.[199]

The Tribunal of Milan has dealt with the issue of loss of chances also in two recent competition law damages actions filed by the same firm.[200] The Italian Antitrust Authority (ICA) ascertained an abuse of dominant position of Telecom Italia S.p.A (Telecom) with a decision confirmed by the Supreme Administrative Court.[201] Brennercom, a telecom company, claimed damages with two different actions against Telecom, the former national telecommunications incumbent. Although Brennercom was not mentioned in the ICA's decision, the judge deemed it reasonable to define both actions as follow-on type. Brennercom was operating in the same market interested by the ICA's decision, although its business activity was mainly (if not solely) performed in the Region of Trentino and Alto Adige. Brennercom claimed to have lost reasonable chances to close contracts with potential clients due to Telecom's abuse of dominant position. The claimant therefore observed that, in absence of Telecom's infringement, it would have had the opportunity to acquire more clients and reckoned the damage as a percentage corresponding to the probability of this positive outcome. The Italian court acknowledged that the loss of chances is potentially subject to compensation in competition law actions.[202] However, the court quashed the claim in the part related to the loss of chances on the ground that the claimant had failed to substantiate the possible

---

[196] According to Article 1226 Civil Code.

[197] Decision n. 8546 of 28 July 2000.

[198] Corte di Cassazione, 28 May 2014, no 11904/2014, in Foro it, 2014, I, 1729, the court here refers to those precedents regarding the deprivation of the possibility of winning a competition for violation by the employer of the obligation to observe the criteria of correctness and good faith in the relative procedures, in particular to the Cassation's decision of 18 January 2006, No 852.

[199] Corte di Cassazione, *Blasi v Az. cons. trasp. pubbl.* Napoli, 22 April 1993, no. 4725, in Giust. civ. Mass. 1993, 720.

[200] Tribunale di Milano, *Brennercom Spa v Telecom Italia Spa*, 3 March 2014 no 14802/2011 and Tribunale di Milano, *Brennercom Spa v Telecom Italia Spa*, 27 December 2013 no 22423/2010.

[201] Italian Competition Authority (ICA), 16 November 2004, decision A351 n 13752.

[202] The court lists the compensable damages as actual loss;, loss of profits, lost chances and damage to the company's image.

4.7 Claimant Indeterminacy and Collective Redress

future chance and its causal connection to the antitrust infringement. In particular, Brennercom did not submit sufficient evidence of the fact that potential clients were redirected to Telecom Italia due to the antitrust infringement, therefore depriving Brennercom of the chance to gain new clients.[203] Without this evidence, the court argued, it was not possible to establish if the claimant had any chance at all to win new clients, had the antitrust infringement not been committed.[204]

4.7 CLAIMANT INDETERMINACY AND COLLECTIVE REDRESS

There are cases in which the defendant has wrongfully injured a number of claimants, but it is uncertain whom or the type of injury caused to each claimant. Steel observes that, in such cases, the liability reflects the following conditions:

> (1) each defendant has wrongfully caused injury to someone, (2) there is some probability that each defendant may have wrongfully caused each claimant's injury, (3) at least some of those for whom there is a probability that the defendant caused their injury have in fact been caused injury by the defendants' wrongdoing (4) if no liability is imposed upon any defendant, a defendant which is liable to a claimant will not be required to pay compensation; (5) if each defendant is held liable in full to each claimant, each defendant will pay more compensation than it ought to pay.[205]

Hence, given the proof of wrongful causation of an injury, it would not be unfair to impose on the defendant to compensate the damage divided by the number of claimants and apportioned according to the causal probability of the injury to be caused to each person.[206] However, the claimants which are members of a group may decide to collectively claim the total amount of damages as a class. The EC Recommendation on class actions defines as a 'mass harm situation' 'a situation where two or more natural or legal persons claim to have suffered harm causing damage resulting from the same illegal activity of one or more natural or legal persons'.[207] If a collective redress mechanism exists in a member state, it therefore would be possible for the class of claimants to exercise the action for damages jointly or through a representative entity.[208] Some scholars pointed out how collective actions obliterate the meaning of causal responsibility, justifying the action as a

---

[203] Tribunale di Milano, *Brennercom Spa* v *Telecom Italia Spa* decision n 14802/2011.

[204] To similar conclusions attain the decisions, Tribunale di Milano, OK Com Spa c. Telecom Italia SpA, 13 February 2013, R.G. 76568/2008 and Corte di Cassazione civ., *Telecom* v *Sign and Others*, 16 May 2007, n 11312; although both refer to loss of profits rather than to a lost chance.

[205] Here Steel combines defendant and claimant liability; see Steel (n 7) 356.

[206] Ibid., 357.

[207] Section II.3(b) of the Commission Recommendation of 11 June 2013 on common principles for injunctive and compensatory collective redress mechanisms in the member states concerning violations of rights granted under Union Law OJ L 201, 26.7.2013, p. 60–65.

[208] Section III.4.

104 *Causal Uncertainty in Competition Law Damages Claims*

matter of moral responsibility.[209] In such cases, the class of claimants has to be homogenous because of the causal responsibility connecting the tortfeasor to the claimant. Otherwise, the class would include claimants filing compensation for different injuries caused by the same infringement – for instance, actual losses and lost chances – thus bringing actions with different legal causal requirements.[210] Hence, lead plaintiffs in a class action have to be able to prove that all members of the class will be able to equally substantiate all the elements of the tort, including causation.[211] This is true both in jurisdictions having special collective redress mechanisms – such as Italy,[212] France[213] and England[214] – and for jurisdictions such as Germany, relying on general civil procedural laws and other general provisions.[215]

4.8 PREEMPTION AND DUPLICATIVE CAUSES

The but-for test may fail to find causation in cases of causal redundancy or duplicative causes. When there are multiple potential causes of an event, but one of them pre-empts the other from producing an effect, the former is the only cause of the event. Consider the situation in which an exclusionary abuse precedes a decision of the excluded company that would have caused anyway their exclusion from the market. The actual cause of the event pre-empted the hypothetical cause, thus making it unnecessary.

Differently from pre-emption, there are cases in which multiple causes contribute to bring about an event, but some of them are overdetermined. In standard tort law, a typical example is the medical malpractice that contributes to exacerbate an injury, although the pre-existing situation was alone sufficient to bring about the

---

[209] Marion Smiley, 'Collective Responsibility' [2017] *The Stanford Encyclopedia of Philosophy*, https://plato.stanford.edu/archives/sum2017/entries/collective-responsibility/, accessed 15 March 2019; Jan Narveson, 'Collective Responsibility' [2002] 6 *The Journal of Ethics* 179.

[210] See, for instance, Afferni discussing a class action filed to the Rome Tribunal (first instance, court) in which 'The class included both mothers and infants that were infected by tuberculosis as well as mothers and infants that were not infected by this disease but simply feared for a certain period that they had been infected'. The Tribunal decided to admit this class action, although, Afferni observes, 'It is clear that in this case the issue of damages (as the issue of causation) is not common to all members of the class. Therefore, the Tribunal is expected to run separate trials for each member of the class (lead plaintiffs and consumers opting-in)'. Giorgio Afferni, '"Opt-In" Class Actions in Italy: Why Are They Failing?' [2016] 7 *Journal of European Tort Law* 82, 87.

[211] Ibid., 91; G Afferni, 'Azione Di Classe e Danno Antitrust' [2010] 3 *Mercato concorrenza e regole* 491, 506.

[212] Article 140-bis of the Italian Consumers Code as amended by Law 23 July 2009, no 99.

[213] Law no 2014-344 of 17 March 2014 'Loi Hamon', which was enacted by the decree no 2014-1081 of 24 September 2014.

[214] Where Section 47B of the Competition Act 1998 allows to bring opt-in representative actions, and the Schedule 8 of the Consumer Rights Act 2015, which came into force on 1 October 2015, allowing instead opt-out class actions.

[215] Section 33(a) GWB.

4.8 Preemption and Duplicative Causes

same injury. Similarly, in company law, is often used the case in which three directors of a company negligently vote to launch a defective and dangerous product. Since the decision is taken on a simple majority vote, each of them is unnecessary and insufficient.[216]

In competition law, the same could be said, for instance, of a situation in which a dominant firm anticompetitively excludes a competitor, which was already losing market shares due to bad management.

Theory of causation also has to solve another problem: the injured party cannot be exempted from risks that would, in any case, bear.[217] Some authors pointed out that this is connected to the 'theory of the aim'.[218] That is to say that liability of the antitrust infringer covers only the consequences that the specific rule protects, but this protection finds no application when the damage would have, in any case, happened.

For instance, if a cartel fixes an overcharge to the market price of a good, some consumers might renounce the purchase. However, not all of them may have renounced it because of the increased price, as it also involved external causes such as loss of interest in that good.[219] In these cases, judges have to gauge the likeliness or probability of the events in order to infer the causative link. Most cases of preemption and overdetermination are solved by judges on a case-by-case basis. Where a strict application of causal laws, especially of the but-for test, would lead to paradoxical results, judges have adopted alternative approaches focusing on the material contribution to the damage or referring to the doctrinal theory of double causation.[220] While the former considers even a unnecessary and insufficient contribution to the damage, the latter recognizes that, in some cases, damages caused by multiple tortfeasors, none of them a conditio sine qua non of the harm, can be ascribed to all tortfeasors at the same time. Such case law is, however, inconsistent in its application[221] as it seems to be based more on common-sense decisions then on the application of specific causal theories.

---

[216] Steel (n 7) 20
[217] Castelli (n 134) 1052.
[218] Trimarchi (n 134) 69; HLA Hart and Tony Honoré, *Causation in the Law* (Oxford University Press, 1985) 477.
[219] Luigi Prosperetti, Eleonora Pani and Ines Tomasi, *Il danno antitrust: Una prospettiva economica* (Il Mulino, 2009) 225.
[220] See Steel (n 7) 21.
[221] See Ibid.

5

Proof Rules of Causation

Causation, as any other element of an actionable tort, has to be proven in the proceedings. Having described the substantive aspects of causation (Chapters 1 and 2) and the kinds of causal uncertainty in competition litigation (Chapter 4), this chapter explains the general rules of evidence regarding the burdens and the standards of proof in the four selected jurisdictions and in the EU.

As pointed out in Chapter 1, the causal link is not a fact; it is, indeed, a connection between two known facts,[1] also defined as 'an empirical relation between concrete conditions'.[2] It follows that it is not subject to the same burden of proof as any other evidence submitted to the court. The causal link needs a demonstration through logic, statistic and common sense that is supported by general scientific theories and, simultaneously, by specific justification of the singular causation. Proof of singular causation therefore needs (1) scientific validity of causal generalizations that control the condition and (2) complete instantiation of the empirical relation.

Often, proof of causation hinges upon inferences and legal presumptions. These logic tools are used in competition law to draw conclusions about statistical and econometric evidence, which has an important role in the array of means of proofs available. Generally, the plaintiff can prove its claim by submitting documentary evidences or gathering them through inspections, proof by witnesses or by interrogations and, finally, expert reports that form evidences of the existence of a causal link. When an expert's evidence hinging on a well-acclaimed theory (such as passing-on or umbrella effects) is laid out, this evidence may constitute a

---

[1] See Patti, Salvatore, 'La Responsabilità Degli Amministratori: Il Nesso Causale' (2002) 3 *Responsabilità civile e previdenziale* 106.

[2] Richard W Wright, 'Proving Causation: Probability versus Belief' in Richard Goldberg (ed), *Perspectives on Causation* (Hart, 2011) 205. This means that, from this point of view, causation does not correspond to the probability of an event to happen but, rather, to a law of nature that describes the relation between a set of conditions (NESS set of conditions) and a consequence.

Proof Rules of Causation

presumption of damages, which may be particularly difficult to rebut.[3] In some cases, therefore, causal generalizations can form presumptions that revert the burden of proof on to the claimant.[4]

In competition damages actions, the victim must prove to the satisfaction of the court the antitrust infringement (in the case of stand-alone actions), the economic injury (in form of an actual loss, loss of profits or lost chances) and the causal link between the unlawful behaviour and the damage. Indeed, the claimant has to show that the diminution of her assets – as a consequence of a higher price paid, lost chances or dead-weight loss – was caused by the antitrust infringement and not by other market factors. Here, the law of evidence defines the rules of adjudicative fact-finding. It does so by establishing what elements the trier of fact must consider, who has to submit this evidence and what level of certainty the trier has to reach to establish that the evidence presented is proof of the claim. Based on any of the tests described in Chapters 1 and 2, the claimant has the burden to substantiate the claim and therefore that, for instance, the supra-competitive price caused economic losses that are causally linked to the antitrust infringement and meet the requisite legal requirements.[5] The different legal requirements analyzed in Chapters 1–4 have an important bearing on the outcome of the litigation. This is a fundamental aspect of the proof, especially for substantiating an indirect harm. For instance, proving the passing-on or a damage by 'umbrella pricing' under the rule of causal regularity is different from substantiating the same damage using the concept of remoteness.[6] In other words, the concept of causal connection defines the object of the proof and

---

[3] See Chapter 6.

[4] Patti observes that the causal link, being it a connection between two facts, may not be presumed, as it is applicable only to facts and events: 'There is therefore no presumption, which can only be used for the demonstration of a fact. The existence of a causal link can not be so "presumed" but it has to be proven as any other element required by law to set up the responsibility'. Patti, Salvatore (n 1) 601. The presumption of an etiologic relationship between damage and action can be drawn instead from the regular outcome of the typical set of events repeating in the specific case. Hence, the proof of damage through presumption does not imply causation that, differently, corresponds to a 'regular' set (or chain) of conditions that repeat in those cases. In other cases, while the presumption would rebut the burden of proving the infringement, the causation would be assessed only by scientific laws. Moreover, the judge faces the choice of balancing different, overlapping and sometimes opposing assumptions, on the basis of policy reasons.

[5] Depending on the applicable law, the claimant has to prove that the damage is direct, falls within the scope of the rule, is a regular consequence, is probable or is not remote.

[6] Although the Directive 2014/104/EU of 26 November 2014 on Certain Rules Governing Actions for Damages under National Law for Infringements of the Competition Law Provisions of the Member States and of the European Union, [2014] OJ L349/1, (the 'Damages Directive') has introduced rebuttable presumptions which have partially harmonized the requirements for the proof of causation in case of passing-on in Europe, see Claudio Lombardi, 'The Passing-On of Price Overcharges in European Competition Damages Actions: A Matter of Causation and an Issue of Policy' [2015] Discussion Paper, Europa-Kolleg Hamburg, Institute for European Integration, available at https://ssrn.com/abstract=2700042 or http://dx.doi.org/10.2139/ssrn.2700042.

therefore also the difficulty of discharging the burden of proof. The level of certainty required by the substantive rule of causation is, therefore, a relevant factor of the proof.

Rules of evidence can establish causation on an all-or-nothing basis or on a proportional basis. According to the all-or-nothing approach to causation, if the applicant in the proceedings meets the requisites standard of proof, the damage is compensated in full, regardless of the probability establishing causation. In this vein, the CAT established in *Allied Maples Group Ltd v Simmons & Simmons* that 'on the balance of probability, that fact is taken as true and the plaintiff recovers his damage in full. There is no discount because the judge considers that the balance is only just tipped in favour of the plaintiff; and the plaintiff gets nothing if he fails to establish that it is more likely than not that the accident resulted in the injury'.[7] The judge will then determine the amount of damages on the basis of different procedural rules, allowing also for estimation.[8] On the other hand, causal proportional liability theories propose to determine the causal contribution of the agent to the harm on the basis of the probability of causation.[9]

Besides establishing the burden of proof of the parties, rules of evidence have at least other three functions. Firstly, they aim at minimizing the litigation costs for fact-finding.[10] Secondly, they apportion the risk of error between the parties.[11] The standard of proof, therefore, also determines to what extent a legal regime is willing to accept type I or type II errors. Thirdly, they aim at achieving a fair decision through fair proceedings.

However, the different requirements for the burden of proof and the different standards adopted by national courts vary the uncertainty related to its assessment. The standard of proof that a legal system adopts is also an important factor in determining the outcome of the claim. As parties in competition law actions can rarely substantiate causation with full certainty, courts generally decide on the basis of probabilities. But the standards of proof and persuasion[12] vary across Europe as to the degree of probability required for the proof of causation. Chapters 1–4 analyzed the different causal tests utilized by courts, observing their differences, similarities and fallacies. The but-for test, for instance, may make it excessively difficult to reconstruct the chain of events that leads to the damage when overdetermined causation or multiple causes occur. On the other hand, scarce scientific information may prevent generalizing theories from finding adequate causes of certain events.

This chapter analyzes the general rules on the burdens and standards of proof in competition damages actions. Chapter 6 will instead clarify in what cases is possible

---

[7] *Allied Maples Group Ltd v Simmons & Simmons* [1995] 1 WLR 1602, para 191.
[8] See Article 17 Directive 2014/104/EU.
[9] See Chapter 6.
[10] Alex Stein, *Foundations of Evidence Law* (Oxford University Press, 2008) 1.
[11] Ibid.
[12] This is the level of proof demanded in a certain type of cases.

5.1 THE BURDEN OF PROOF

to depart from these general rules, relaxing the standard of proof or reversing the burden of proof on the defendant (or, more rarely, imposing higher standards).

The Latins used to say that 'the necessity of proof always lies with the person who lays charges' (*semper necessitas probandi incumbit ei qui agit*). As a general rule, the claimant has the 'legal' or 'objective' burden of proving the facts of the claim, and failing to do so would deny any right to compensation.[13] On the other hand, the defendant has the right to give proof of the contrary and the burden to prove such facts rests with them. This is a general rule of justice, fairness[14] and common sense,[15] as well as a rule of efficiency, as the claimant and the defendant are deemed to be better situated to prove, respectively, the facts in favour and against the existence of the elements of a tort, including causation.[16] More generally, one can define the burden of proof as a 'a set of decision rules to instruct judges and jurors how to decide cases in the face of uncertainty'.[17]

Thus, the legal requirements that put the risk of proving a factual issue on a party form the legal or objective burden of proof. This burden of proof is therefore identified with the burden of persuading the fact-finder about the formation of a fact.[18] According to this, the party bearing the burden of proof has to produce evidence and plead certain facts according to the requisite legal standards in order to persuade the judge about the truth of the claim.[19]

The burden of proof should not be confused with the evidential burden – i.e., the burden of producing evidence. In German law, this has been referred to as *Beweisführungslast*, in France as *charge de la preuve*[20] and in Italy as *onere di allegazione*. While the burden of proof obliges a party to demonstrate his or her claim, according to the requisite standard, the evidential burden refers to specific facts and may be

---

[13] Richard Glover, *Murphy on Evidence* (Oxford University Press, 2013) 72 ff.; Sandy Steel, *Proof of Causation in Tort Law* (Cambridge University Press, 2015) 48.

[14] For example, in *Joseph Constantine Steamship Line Ltd v Imperial Smelting Corporation Ltd* [1942] AC 154, 174 (Viscount Maugham), the court pointed out that 'It is an ancient rule founded on considerations of good sense, and it should not be departed from without strong reasons'; Similarly, *Cassazione civile sez III, 22/03/2013, n 7269*; Ernst Karner, 'The Function of the Burden of Proof in Tort Law' [2009] 2008 *European Tort Law* 68, 70.

[15] Lara Khoury, *Uncertain Causation in Medical Liability* (Hart, 2006) 31.

[16] Proof-proximity principle in competition law; see Cristina Volpin, 'The Ball Is in Your Court: Evidential Burden of Proof and the Proof-Proximity Principle in EU Competition Law' [2014] 51 *Common Market Law Review* 1159.

[17] Ronald J Allen and Alex Stein, 'Evidence, Probability, and the Burden of Proof [2013] 55 *Arizona Law Review* 557, 559.

[18] John T McNaughton, 'Burden of Production of Evidence: A Function of a Burden of Persuasion' [1955] 68 *Harvard Law Review* 1382.

[19] Karner (n 14) 71.

[20] However, see Steel, observing that many scholars do not recognize the difference between the two concepts Steel (n 13) 49.

held by any of the parties. If they fail to produce the evidence, they will have to face adverse ruling on the issue related to that proof.[21] Hence, the evidential burden does not necessarily remain confined to one party. In this vein, it has been observed that the evidential burden may shift from one party to the other according to his or her proximity to the evidence that has to be adduced.[22] This approach has been long used in litigation under the 1980 Vienna Sales Convention[23] and, in some member states, jurisprudence as well.[24] In EU law, this shifting burden has been also called a 'tactical burden' which 'depends on ordinary common sense rather than the force of law'.[25]

5.2 THE STANDARDS OF PROOF

The standard of proof (or standard of persuasion) is the level of belief that the fact-finder has to reach to establish that some evidence has probative value.[26] What the law generally asks is for the judge to establish the truth of the case by determining the relevant facts and giving them probative value.[27] Once the standard of proof has been satisfied, the facts are considered true. The level of the standard of proof varies according to the type of claim and to the jurisdiction. For instance, in criminal proceedings, most jurisdictions require the fact-finder to determine liability 'beyond any reasonable doubt'. This standard is often mitigated in civil cases, whereby probabilistic approaches find application. However, the level of probability required differs across jurisdictions. These differences will be analyzed in this chapter.

Issues of evidence are generally covered by rules of procedure[28], subject to the principle of procedural autonomy of EU member states. EU competition law and

---

[21] David Bailey, 'Presumptions in EU Competition Law' [2010] *European Competition Law Review* 20.

[22] Volpin (n 16); Andriani Kalintiri, 'The Allocation of the Legal Burden of Proof in Article 101 TFEU Cases: A "Clear" Rule with Not-So-Clear Implications' [2015] 34 *Yearbook of European Law* 232.

[23] Franco Ferrari, 'Burden of Proof under the United Nations Convention on Contracts for International Sale of Goods (CISG)' [2000] Spring *International Business Law Journal* 665.

[24] Chiara Besso Marcheis, 'La Vicinanza Della Prova' 16 Revista Eletrônica de Direito Processual – Procedural Law Electronic Review; Italian Court of Cassation, 10 October 2001, no 13533.

[25] Mark Brealey, 'The Burden of Proof before the European Court' vol 10 [1985] *European Law Review* 254.

[26] For a general overview, see Glover (n 13) 74.

[27] The goals of adjudication are multiple; among the others, Judge Weinstein finds out: 'economizing of resources, inspiring confidence, supporting independent social policies, permitting ease in prediction and application, adding to the efficiency of the entire legal system, and tranquilizing disputants. Jack B Weinstein, 'Some Difficulties in Devising Rules for Determining Truth in Judicial Trials' [1966] 66 *Columbia Law Review* 223, 241.

[28] However, it is still debated whether the burden of proof is a matter of substance or procedure; see Khoury (n 15) 31, noticing that 'the incidence of the burden of proof is a question of substantive law'.

5.2 The Standards of Proof

the CJEU have developed unique principles on how to prove facts in Article 101 and 102 TFEU proceedings.[29] However, these principles regard the proof of facts determining the liability of undertakings for the public enforcement of competition law which – given its punitive nature[30] – can only indirectly influence the proof of causation in competition damages actions. Moreover, according to Recital (5) of Regulation No 1/2003, the rules on the burden of proof should be limited to infringements of Articles 101 and 102 and should not affect national rules on the standard of proof.[31] However, it also has been observed that the standard applied to damages claims 'may be the same or lower, but certainly not higher than that normally applied in competition cases by EU Courts'.[32]

Therefore, in competition law cases, national courts apply the standards of proof provided by their domestic laws of procedure with some adaptations, on a lower threshold than the one used in public antitrust enforcement. This book argues that – to a certain extent – domestic courts are developing tailored rules on standards and burdens of proof for competition law litigation. The CJEU case law on public antitrust enforcement shows that when the EU courts have to review a Commission's decision in the part related to the finding of liability for an infringement, they require a high standard of proof.[33] Presumptions of facts and legal inferences are rarely accepted to ease the burden of proof. So, for instance, parallel behaviours alone do not create a presumption of existence of a concerted practice, unless the concertation constitutes 'the only plausible explanation for such conduct'.[34] By contrast, once the infringement has been proven, the proof of causation often benefits from a relaxation of the standard of proof. The ECJ has admitted the use

---

[29] Fernando Castillo de la Torre and Eric Gippini Fournier, *Evidence, Proof and Judicial Review in EU Competition Law* (Edward Elgar Publishing, 2017) chapter 2.

[30] Ibid., 2.001.

[31] Recital (5) states:

> In order to ensure an effective enforcement of the Community competition rules and at the same time the respect of fundamental rights of defence, this Regulation should regulate the burden of proof under Articles 81 and 82 of the Treaty. It should be for the party or the authority alleging an infringement of Article 81(1) and Article 82 of the Treaty to prove the existence thereof to the required legal standard. It should be for the undertaking or association of undertakings invoking the benefit of a defence against a finding of an infringement to demonstrate to the required legal standard that the conditions for applying such defence are satisfied. This Regulation affects neither national rules on the standard of proof nor obligations of competition authorities and courts of the Member States to ascertain the relevant facts of a case, provided that such rules and obligations are compatible with general principles of Community law.

[32] Castillo de la Torre and Gippini Fournier (n 29), 2.112, referring to two pronouncements of the ECHR in *Ringvold v Norway*, no. 34964/97, ECHR 2003-II, § 38 and *Lundkvist v Sweden* (dec), no. 48518/99, ECHR 2003-XI, where the court considered that albeit the defendant had been acquitted in a criminal case, the insurer could be condemned to pay compensation for the civil damages caused by the same wrongful action on the basis of a lower standard of proof.

[33] Castillo de la Torre and Gippini Fournier (n 29), 2.046.

[34] Ibid.

of inferences from mere indicia and has even allowed the creation of specific presumptions – for example, regarding price effects.[35] However, as already noted, the standards adopted for the public enforcement of competition law usually differ from those in private enforcement in nature and scope. Moreover, the assessment of a violation of Articles 101 and 102 aims at establishing an infringement that has distorting or restricting effects in the market.[36] Private damages actions, instead, ought to determine the existence and magnitude of losses caused to a specific person, the claimant, in connection with an infringement of competition law. This chapter considers the rules developed by the European courts and then analyzes comparatively the different approaches adopted by the four countries under scrutiny.

5.3 PROOF OF CAUSATION IN EU LAW

The EU law offers little guidance on the standard of proof in competition law enforcement. Article 2 Regulation 1/2003 establishes that the party or authority alleging the infringement shall have the burden of proving it.[37] However, it has been recognized that this principle does, anyway, allow for the evidentiary burden to be moved from one party to the other, once it discharges the initial evidentiary requirement.[38] As the ECJ has observed in the *Telefónica* case, once the Commission has discharged the *onus probandi*, it is not sufficient for the defendant to 'raise the possibility that a circumstance arose which might affect the probative value of that evidence in order for the Commission to bear the burden of proving that that circumstance was not capable of affecting the probative value of the evidence'.[39] On the contrary, the evidentiary burden has shifted on to the defendant that has to proffer counterproof according to the requisite legal standard.[40]

---

[35] Ibid., 2.047.

[36] The OECD also observed that 'the need for simple rules may be less pressing in the context of administrative enforcement, since competition agencies will have more resources and powers to engage in detailed market analyses than private parties or courts, or of established regimes, because they will have the knowledge and experience required to minimize errors and regulation costs'. Organisation for Economic Co-Operation and Development (OECD), 'Safe Harbours and Legal Presumptions in Competition Law, Background Note by the Secretariat' (2017) DAF/COMP (2017) 9 12. DAF/COMP (2017) 9, 12.

[37] Article 2: 'In any national or [EU] proceedings for the application of Articles [101 and 102] of the Treaty, the burden of proving an infringement of Article [101(1)] or of Article [102] of the Treaty shall rest on the party or the authority alleging the infringement'. In this sense, see also Joined Cases C-204/00 P, C-205/00 P, C-211/00 P, C-213/00 P, C-217/00 P and C-219/00 P *Aalborg Portland and Others* v *Commission*, ECLI:EU:C:2004:6 para 78.

[38] Anne-Lise Sibony and Eric Barbier de La Serre, 'Charge de La Preuve et Théorie Du Contrôle En Droit Communautaire de La Concurrence: Pour Un Changement de Perspective' vol 43 [2007] *Revue Trimestrielle de Droit Européen* 205.

[39] Case T-216/13 *Telefónica* v *Commission*, ECLI:EU:T:2016:369 para 130.

[40] Similarly, AG Kokott observed that 'if in its decision the Commission draws conclusions as to the conditions prevailing in a particular market on the basis of objectively verifiable evidence

5.3 *Proof of Causation in EU Law*

The European Treaties omit rules on standards of proof or submission of evidence and the Regulation 1/2003 clearly excludes regulating the standards of proof.[41] The Directive n 104/2014 considers that the effectiveness and consistency of the application of Articles 101 and 102 TFEU requires a convergence of the approaches across the Union on the disclosure of evidences in order to ease homogeneously the burden of proof across the EU.[42] Moreover, the Directive notes that 'Actions for damages for infringements of Union or national competition law typically require a complex factual and economic analysis" and, since "The evidence necessary to prove a claim for damages is often held exclusively by the opposing party or by third parties ... strict legal requirements for claimants to assert in detail all the facts of their case at the beginning of an action and to proffer precisely specified items of supporting evidence can unduly impede the effective exercise of the right to compensation guaranteed by the TFEU'.[43] Whereas the Damages Directive avoids setting a legal standard of proof for causation, it provides some guidance to the national legislator and to the fact-finder on shaping and enforcing such rules. In particular, the Directive is concerned with the information asymmetry often characterizing antitrust litigation, which may impair the possibility for the harmed party to prove their claim. Recital (14) of the Directive observes that the opposing or third parties often have the evidence necessary to prove a claim and, for this reason, national legislation should refrain from imposing strict legal requirements for claimants for proving their claim. One of the solutions offered by the Directive is that, once the case has started, the claimant has the possibility to obtain the disclosure of the evidence to prove the elements of the tortious damage.[44] In the pursuit of this objective, the Directive states that 'Member States shall ensure that national courts are able, upon request of the defendant, to order the claimant or a third party to disclose relevant evidence'.[45] With regard to the level of proof required to discharge the burden, the Directive remains silent. Although the definition of the term 'standard of proof' remains rather vague and is not defined by EU law, it appeared in many of the court's competition law cases, which will be analyzed in the next chapter.

---

from stated sources, the undertakings concerned cannot refute the Commission's findings simply by unsubstantiatedly disputing them. Rather, it falls to them to show in detail why the information used by the Commission is inaccurate, why it has no probative value, if that is the case, or why the conclusions drawn by the Commission are unsound. This requirement does not represent the reversal of the burden of proof assumed by the FEG but the normal operation of the respective burdens of adducing evidence', Opinion of AG Kokott, Case C-105/04 P *Nederlandse Federatieve Vereniging voor de Groothandel op Elektrotechnisch Gebied (FEG) v Commission*, ECLI:EU:C:2005:751 74.

[41] Council Regulation (EC) No 1/2003 of 16 December 2002 on the Implementation of the Rules on Competition Laid Down in Articles 81 and 82 of the Treaty OJ L 001, 04/01/2003 2003 Recital (5). See supra.

[42] Recital (21).

[43] Directive 2014/104/EU, Recital (14).

[44] Recital (15).

[45] Article 5, Directive 2014/104/EU.

5.4 STANDARDS OF PROOF, JUDGES' PERSUASION AND CAUSAL UNCERTAINTY IN COMPETITION LAW

The reluctance of EU courts to conceptualize issues of standards of proof is only understood if one considers the nature of EU law, which is the result of the amalgamation and compromise between different legal systems. Despite being an independent legal order,[46] the EU pursues the legal integration of the member states' legal regimes. It is therefore not surprising that the EU courts avoided conceptualizing issues of proof and evidence, given the existing differences in the national approaches.[47] With regard to the distinction to be maintained between burden of proof and standard of proof, Advocate General Kokott, in her opinion to *Akzo Nobel and Others* v *Commission*, pointed out that 'The standard of proof determines the requirements which must be satisfied for facts to be regarded as proven. It must be distinguished from the burden of proof. The burden of proof determines, first, which party must put forward the facts and, where necessary, adduce the related evidence [*subjektive* or *formelle Beweislast*, also known as the evidential burden]; second, the allocation of that burden determines which party bears the risk of facts remaining unresolved or allegations unproven [*objektive* or *materielle Beweislast*]'.[48]

The expression 'standard of proof' has been used with increasing frequency in recent years[49] in a number of judgments without reference to a specific standard.[50] In competition law, the European courts have not provided any detailed specification of the level of the standard of proof,[51] limiting often the definition of the

---

[46] *Costa* v *ENEL/*Case 6/64/.

[47] Torre and Fournier (n 29) para 1.005.

[48] Opinion of Advocate General Kokott Case C-557/12 Kone AG and Others v ÖBB-Infrastruktur AG ECLI:EU:C:2014:45. Similarly, in a state aid case, Advocate General Jääskinen considered in the case *French Republic* v *Commission* that 'in the case of an implied guarantee inferred from a body of evidence, the standard of proof must be based on serious probability and sufficiency of evidence. The requisite standard is thus more than mere probability, whilst falling short of a requirement of being beyond all reasonable doubt'. Opinion of Advocate General Jääskinen in Case C-559/12 P, *French Republic* v *Commission*, 21 November 2013, para 35.

[49] See, for example, Case C-260/09 P *Activision Blizzard Germany GmbH* v *European Commission*, on the standard of proof necessary to establish the existence of a vertical agreement; Case C-413/06 P *Bertelsmann AG and Sony Corporation of America* v *Independent Music Publishers and Labels Association (Impala)*, on the standard of proof for clearance of concentrations by the Commission.

[50] Joined Cases C-12/03 P-DEP and C-13/03 P-DEP Tetra Laval [2010] ECR I-00067; Joined Cases C-403/04 P and C-405/04 P *Sumitomo Metal Industries and Nippon Steel* v *Commission* [2007] ECR I-729; C-413/06P *Bertelsmann and Sony Corporation of America* v *Impala* [2008] ECR I-4951 and C-501/06 P, C-513/06 P, C-515/06 P and C-519/06 P, *GlaxoSmithKline Services and Others* v *Commission and Others* [2009] ECR I-9291, para 87.

[51] For a general overview, see Sibony and Barbier de La Serre (n 38) 205, and the Opinion of Mr Advocate General Jääskinen Case C-559/12 P *French Republic* v *Commission* ECLI:EU: C:2013:764.

5.4 Standards of Proof, Judges' Persuasion and Causal Uncertainty 115

requirement to the 'requisite legal standard' (*à suffisance de droit*).[52] While in the UBC case, the ECJ seemed to apply an approach leaning toward the interests of the defendant, saying that 'the benefit of any doubt must be given to the undertaking accused of the infringement',[53] this approach has been revised. The ECJ has ruled that there is an infringement of competition law if 'it is possible to foresee with a sufficient degree of probability' that the conduct negatively affects, directly or indirectly, the trade between member states.[54] Moreover, in *Tetra Laval*, the ECJ also noted with reference to the proof of causation, that it is 'necessary to envisage various chains of cause and effect with a view to ascertaining which of them are the most likely'.[55]

The court has also sketched the evidential burden required to prove the infringement, stating that the Commission's decision has to be 'sufficiently proved in law',[56] supported by a 'sufficiently precise and coherent proof',[57] and, finally, the court also applied the method of 'a firm, precise and consistent body of evidence' where there is no documentary evidence of concertation between producers.[58] Finally, the General Court (GC) has maintained that 'the Commission must produce precise and consistent evidence to support the firm conviction that the infringement took place, since the burden of proof concerning the existence of the infringement and, therefore, its duration, falls upon it'.[59]

However, this case law regards the burden of proof in public antitrust enforcement. The proof of causation in competition law damages action mixes the requirements of national tort law with the limits established by EU rules and the typical causal uncertainty surrounding antitrust damages actions. It has been pointed out that the civil law standard may be the same but not higher than the administrative standards applied in EU competition cases.[60] Thus, it seems that national courts should apply a standard of proof establishing the causal link 'with a sufficient degree of probability' or a lower standard that does not make it impossible or excessively difficult to exercise the right to compensation of damages.

---

[52] Case T-303/02 *Westfalen Gassen Nederland BV* v *Commission of the European Communities* [2006] ECR II-4567; Case C-185/95 P *Baustahlgewebe* v *Commission* [1998] ECR I 8417, para 58; *Schneider Electric SA* v *Commission*, Case T-310/01, [2002] E.C.R. 11-4071, 4182, 402, [2003] 4 C.M.L.R. 17, 832.

[53] Case 27/76 *United Brands Co* v *Commission* ECLI:EU:C:1978:22 para 265.

[54] Case 61/80 *Coöperatieve Stremsel- en Kleurselfabriek* v *Commission* ECLI:EU:C:1981:75 para 14.

[55] Case C-12/03 P *Commission of the European Communities* v *Tetra Laval BV ECR* [2005] ECR I-987.

[56] Case 107/82 *AEG-Telefunken* v *Commission* [1983] ECR 3151, para 136.

[57] Case 29/83 and 30/83 *Compagnie Royale Asturienne des Mines and Rheinzink* v *Commission* [1984] ECR 1679, para 20.

[58] Joined Cases C-89/85, C-104/85, C-114/85, C-116/85, C-117/85 and C-125/85 to C-129/85 *Ahlström Osakeyhtiö and Others* v *Commission* [1993] ECR I-1307, para 70 and 127.

[59] Case T-67/00 *JFE Engineering* v *Commission* ECLI:EU:T:2004:221 para 341.

[60] See n 32.

Below this threshold, national courts have ample room to exercise their discretionary power and accommodate the different standards of proof adopted by European national legal systems, although it requires some flexibility and a convergence toward a probability-based standard. But there are some discrepancies as to the general standards of proof adopted by each system. In general, civil law countries showed to be more prone to accept false acquittals rather than false condemnations adopting a higher standard of proof. Moreover, most civil law jurisdictions deal with questions of evidence and standards of proof in a more fragmented way. On the other hand, common law jurisdictions have traditionally elevated the law of evidence and the study of the standard of proof to a unitary topic and adopted a balance of probability rule whereby the claimant should not be overly burdened with a proof that goes beyond the mere 'preponderance of the evidence',[61] otherwise any claim would be too difficult and expensive to prove.[62]

However, even under these probability-based rules, it often seems excessively difficult for many classes of claimants to prove causation in competition damages actions. Testament to this is the scarcity of damages claim,[63] especially for 'indirect damages',[64] such as harms to counterfactual buyers and umbrella buyers.[65]

The difficulty of proving causation in competition damages actions may explain, to a certain extent, the problems in launching private antitrust enforcement in Europe, where, indeed, the main hurdle seems to be the proof of the harm and its causal connection to the antitrust infringement.[66] On the other hand, the

---

[61] Kevin M Clermont and Emily Sherwin, 'A Comparative View of Standards of Proof' [2002] 50(2) *The American Journal of Comparative Law* 243; Kevin M Clermont, 'Standards of Proof Revisited' [2008] 33 *Vermont Law Review* 469.

[62] Richard A Posner, 'An Economic Approach to the Law of Evidence' [1999] University of Chicago Law School, John M. Olin Law & Economics Working Paper No. 66, available at SSRN: http://papers.ssrn.com/abstract=165176, accessed 21 January 2015.

[63] Lianos identifies only a handful of cases in the UK initiated by indirect purchasers, one in Germany, and none in France and Italy see table 4.1 in Ioannis Lianos, Peter Davis and Paolisa Nebbia, *Damages Claims for the Infringement of Competition Law* (Oxford University Press, 2015).

[64] We will call 'indirect loss' the harm consequence of an infliction of damage upon a third party. When the harm inflicted upon a third person in turn causes harm to the claimant, we will instead refer to it as 'secondary harms'. For instance, umbrella effects do not cause damages to the third party that transfers the harm on the claimant and are, therefore, indirect losses. On the other hand, in the pass-on situation, the third party (direct purchaser) is the first victim of the harm, which passes on to the claimant. This classification helps one to apply rules on remoteness, foreseeability, mitigation and intervening causation, as well as to understand what it takes to prove them under the different national regimes. This expansion mainly regards what the paper defines as 'indirect damages', which are further divided in two types: (1) indirect loss and (2) secondary harm. On the analysis of the case law, see also, Ioannis Lianos, 'Causal Uncertainty and Damages Claims for the Infringement of Competition Law in Europe' [2015] 34 *Yearbook of European Law* 170, 179.

[65] See Chapter 7.

[66] In this sense, see also Lianos (n 64) 177.

European legislator and the national courts are trying to relax this burden by introducing factual inferences and 'bespoke presumptions' that reverse the burden of proof on to the subject that has, assumingly, more information to provide the counter-proof – i.e., the defendant.[67]

Knowledge of causal laws is limited; hence, nothing is certain. For this reason, proponents of the probability approach maintain that the only way to objectivize and render a predictable judgment is to rely on laws of probability rather than on obscure subjective conviction.[68] Some other authors object that mere class-based aggregate probability cannot say what happened in the specific case.[69]

In this dispute, two remarks are central for the analysis of the standard of proof in competition law damages actions. As already pointed out, the majority of the European legal traditions avoided designing a general and comprehensive theory of evidence that included the different standards of persuasions.[70] But the objective of harmonizing the private enforcement of European competition law before national courts is posing the problem, calling for a major confrontation.

However, all these differences between the different European legal traditions tend to lose significance when causal uncertainty is particularly high. As an example, after a thorough probabilistically based analysis of the case, the English judge in *Arkin v Borchard Lines Limited* considered that the assessment of causation between damages and the antitrust infringement was a matter of 'common sense'[71] – that is, a way to solve with the use of a 'broad axe'[72] and ample discretionary power, a complex situation that class-based probabilities and economic reasoning have brought to a dead end. Causal uncertainty creates therefore incentives to alleviate the burden of proof, through presumptions or by relaxing the standard of proof, that though are inherently based on the evaluation of the specific case and on the judge's common sense. As such, it is not always possible to conceptualize such decisions and distil rules from judgments that are very fact specific.

---

[67] See Chapter 6.

[68] Clermont and Sherwin (n 61) 271.

[69] On the issue of the formation of the conviction of the judge about the issue at stake, the author translate the dispute in other terms, saying that 'the holding of a belief regarding what actually happened in a particular situation is very different from being willing to place a bet on what happened, and that while class-based statistics are very useful for the placing of the bet, they are insufficient and generally unhelpful for the formation of the belief, for which instead particularistic evidence is essential because only it is capable of converting possibly applicable causal generalizations (with their associated statistical frequencies) into actually instantiated causal laws', Wright, 'Proving Causation' (n 2) 197.

[70] Eric Gippini-Fournier, 'The Elusive Standard of Proof in EU Competition Cases' [2009] World Competition.

[71] *Arkin v Borchard Lines Ltd. & Ors* [2003] EWHC 687 (Comm).

[72] Concept effectively explained by Lord Shaw in *Watson Laidlaw & Co Ltd v Pott, Cassells and Williamson* (1914) 31 RPC 104 at 117–118: '[t]he restoration by way of compensation is therefore accomplished to a large extent by the exercise of a sound imagination and the practice of the broad axe'.

5.5 PROVING CAUSATION IN EU COMPETITION LAW

As Section 5.1 has shown, national legal regimes combine domestic rules of procedure and substance to EU law and jurisprudence, which has influenced also the application of evidence rules.[73] According to Article 2, Regulation 1/2003, the party or authority alleging an infringement has the burden to prove it. This general principle, supported by the EU courts,[74] has been transposed in by the Damages Directive.[75] However, the Directive recognizes departures to this principle through the procedural autonomy of domestic laws within the limits of the principles of equivalence and effectiveness[76] and, at the same time, applies special relaxation rules.[77]

Hence, while member states are independent in establishing their evidence rules, 'it is apparent from the case-law that the Member States must ensure that evidential rules and, in particular, the rules on the allocation of the burden of proof applicable to actions relating to a breach of EU law do not make it impossible in practice or excessively difficult for individuals to exercise rights conferred by EU law'.[78] As observed in Chapter 3, the principles of equivalence and effectiveness operate as positive limits to the application of national rules of procedure, whereby they disallow outcomes detrimental to the rights of the parties established by EU law and therefore indirectly shaping the application of the domestic rules of procedure. However, questions of proof often blur the line between substance and procedure, and the principle of procedural autonomy concerns only the latter. For example, the ECJ has maintained that the presumption of existence of causation between 'concertation' and 'practice' – established to prove the existence of a concerted practice – is a matter of substance – i.e., interpretation of article 101 TFEU – and not an issue of

---

[73] For a broader discussion on such limits, especially for the public enforcement of competition law, see Andriani Kalintiri, *Evidence Standards in EU Competition Enforcement: The EU Approach* (Hart, 2019).

[74] See C 362-95 P *Blackspur DIY Ltd, Steven Kellar, J.M.A. Glancy and Ronald Cohen v Council of the European Union and Commission of the European Communities* [1997] ECR I-04775, observing that 'it is first and foremost for the party seeking to establish the Community's liability to adduce conclusive proof as to the existence or extent of the damage he alleges and to establish the causal link between that damage and the conduct complained of on the part of the Community institutions'. para 31, citing Case 26/74 *Roquette Frères v Commission* [1976] ECR 677, para 22 and 23.

[75] Recital (45).

[76] See Chapter 3.

[77] See Chapter 6.

[78] Opinion of Advocate General Jääskinen in Case C-536/11 *Bundeswettbewerbsbehörde v Donau Chemie AG and others* ECLI:EU:C:2013:67, 49; also Case C-228/98 Dounias [2000] ECR I-577, para 69 and case law cited; Case C-224/02 Pusa [2004] ECR I-5763, para 44; Case C-55/06 Arcor [2008] ECR I-2931, para 191 and case law cited. With respect to rules of evidence, see also Case C-526/04 Laboratoires Boiron [2006] ECR I-7259, para 52–57; Case C-35/09 Speranza [2010] ECR I-6581, para 47.

procedure.[79] By contrast, the opinion of the Advocate General Kokott, in the same case, concluded that a presumption of causation has to be regarded as an issue of proof.[80]

The principle of procedural autonomy is consequence of the fact that the EU Treaties omit rules of procedure and, according to established case law, 'in the absence of community rules on this subject, it is for the domestic legal system of each Member State to designate the courts having jurisdiction and to determine the procedural conditions governing actions at law intended to ensure the protection of the rights which citizens have from the direct effect of community law'.[81] The EU lacks clear competence for the adoption of procedural laws applying in member states, since there is no specific legal bases in the EU Treaties for this. However, this has not impeded the adoption of specific provisions – in particular, within the Damages Directive – affecting the evidence rules for responsibility and causation in competition damages actions. As Chapter 6 will show, these provisions, rather than pave the way to full harmonization, propose the adoption of common relaxation rules to the general proof rules. In other words, there is not a clearly defined standard of proof for EU competition law damages actions; nor do we find general evidence rules for the proof of causation but only the exceptions that have been made to it.

5.6 PROVING CAUSATION IN NATIONAL COURTS

Judges exercise a certain degree of discretion in evaluating the proof of causation. This is true in both civil law and common law jurisdictions, although with some differences. The standards of persuasion of the judge can be lax or constrained by formal limits, but they are generally funded on the principle of 'free evaluation' of the proof. Recent scholarship has ignited a debate around the efficiency and accurateness of the different standards, with the result that most common lawyers have maintained that the common law preponderance standard is able to produce more accurate results.[82] On the other hand, civil lawyers firstly have observed the diversity of approaches in civil law jurisdictions, also attenuating the claim that their standards are unpredictable and obscure.[83] However, civil law jurisdictions generally share the fact that are less accustomed to conceptualize issues of evidence.

---

[79] Case C-8/08 T-Mobile v Raad van bestuur van de Nederlandse Mededingingsautoriteit [2009] ECR I-4529, 17, and Torre and Fournier (n 29) 1.019.

[80] Opinion of Advocate General Kokott, Case C-8/08 T-Mobile v Raad van bestuur van de Nederlandse Mededingingsautoriteit ECLI:EU:C:2009:110, 77.

[81] Case 33-76 Rewe-Zentralfinanz eG and ReweZentral AG v Landwirtschaftskammer für das Saarland ECR 1976-1989.

[82] Clermont and Sherwin (n 61) 248, defining the civil law standards as 'obscure'. See, also, for a more balanced approach, Steel (n 13) 382, suggesting that 'the common law's general rule that the claimant bears the burden of proving causation on the balance of probability is generally justified'.

[83] See, among the others, Michele Taruffo, 'Rethinking the Standards of Proof [2003] The American Journal of Comparative Law 659; Christoph Engel, 'Preponderance of the Evidence versus Intime Conviction: A Behavior Perspective on a Conflict between American and

Class-based statistical probability forms full proof of causation in common law countries[84] and an evidence in most of the civil law jurisdictions.[85] Competition law damages actions have followed generally in the wake of these domestic traditions.

In civil litigation, European national courts apply standards that are diversely formulated but that generally converge toward the intime conviction of the judge in civil law countries and to the balance of probabilities in common law countries. Common law jurisdictions generally apply instead the 'preponderance of the evidence' rule or the balance of probabilities. In competition law cases, the free appreciation of the proof by the judge is even more significant if we think that rarely national courts possess full documentary evidence of both damage and infringement.[86] However, treating 'civil law jurisdictions' as applying homogenous standards of proof would be a mistake, as they have developed different standards for the assessment of the causal link. It is therefore a useful exercise – but not a resolving one – to observe the different standards adopted in civil and common law countries in order to understand how the degree of the proof of causation in competition law varies depending on the court where the case is heard.

Understanding the level of proof required in claims for infringement of competition law is of fundamental importance, as the proof usually consists in a stochastic (probabilistic) measurement of causality.[87] If the domestic tort law adopts a deterministic approach to establishing causation – i.e., the causal link has to be established with (almost) full certainty – this creates an irreconcilable contrast with the type of evidence that in most cases the claimant will be able to provide. Hence, the degree of proof required in each jurisdiction has a fundamental role in determining the litigation outcome.

Continental European Law' [2008] 33 *Vermont Law Review* 435; Richard W Wright, 'Proving Causation' (n 2). In particular, Taruffo asserted that Clermont and Sherwin have fallen prey to a 'reductivist fallacy', due to a shallow comparative overview (at 659).

[84] Robert Cooter, 'Torts as the Union of Liberty and Efficiency: An Essay on Causation' (1987) 63 *Chicago-Kent Law Review* 523; Guido Calabresi, The Cost of Accidents: A Legal and Economic Analysis (Yale University Press, 2008); Alan Schwartz, 'Causation in Private Tort Law: A Comment on Kelman' (1987) 63 *Chicago-Kent Law Review* 639; Mario J Rizzo, 'The Imputation Theory of Proximate Cause: An Economic Framework' [1980] 15 *Georgia Law Review* 1007; William M Landes and Richard A Posner, 'Causation in Tort Law: An Economic Approach' [1983] *The Journal of Legal Studies* 109.

[85] Luigi P Comoglio, Le prove civili (Utet Giuridica, 2010), 345 ff.; Juliane Kokott, The Burden of Proof in Comparative and International Human Rights Law: Civil and Common Law Approaches with Special Reference to the American and German Legal Systems (Martinus Nijhoff Publishers, 1998), 18 ff.; Joachim Schulz, Sachverhaltsfeststellung und Beweistheorie: Elemente einer Theorie strafprozessualer Sachverhaltsfeststellung (Heymann, 1992) 168.

[86] Ioannis Lianos, '"Judging" Economists: Economic Expertise in Competition Law Litigation – A European View', in Lianos Ioannis and Kokkoris (ed), Ioannis The Reform of EC Competition Law: New Challenges (Kluwer, 2009), available at SSRN: http://ssrn.com/abstract=1468502 or http://dx.doi.org/10.2139/ssrn.1468502, 90–91.

[87] See infra Section 5.6.

5.6.1 *Probability versus Belief*

In civil law countries, the degree of proof varies, but it is generally acknowledged that the proof submitted has to be at least 'sufficient' in order to convince the judge about the claim or defence. These jurisdictions usually refer to the intime conviction of the judge,[88] as a standard of proof, meaning that the judge has to be personally persuaded, but this is developed in different ways across Europe.[89] The definition of intime conviction clearly differs from the standard 'beyond reasonable doubts' that should characterize the criminal procedure, although in some civil law systems, such requirements are not differentiated by law.[90] However, the civil law standards – although not formalized – tend to be higher than the common law balance of probabilities, which requires the event to be 'more probable than not'. But even under this standard, causal uncertainty due to lacking or asymmetric information may make impossible or excessively difficult the formation of the proof. German antitrust courts have to abide to the same standards of proof designed for tort cases. Therefore, the judge has to reach a personal conviction that the claim has a 'high level of plausibility'.[91] Similar standards are adopted by other Continental jurisdictions. For instance, the Italian Court of Cassation conceded that, while applying the usual standard of intime conviction, the judge can infer the existence of a causal link between the agreement and the alleged damage also 'through criteria of high logic probability or through presumptions'.[92] In other words, the standard of 'probabilistic certainty' in some civil law jurisdictions should not be exclusively based on the quantitative determination of statistical frequency of classes of events, which could also be missing or ineffective, but should be verified by the judge, who has to determine whether the elements of the case at hand confirm the assumption based general probabilities and – at the same time – has to exclude other possible alternative causes.[93]

Whereas limited information often impedes the plaintiff from proving the facts of the claim, the standard of proof, being on the balance of probabilities or based on the intime conviction of the judge, would not change the outcome of the decision, which has to be based on the facts presented to the judge. In such cases, courts and

---

[88] See French Code de Procédure Pénale, Art. 3531; German Zivilprozessordnung, § 286 I 1; German Strafprozessordnung, § 261, Art. 116 Italian Codice di procedura civile.

[89] Taruffo (n 83) 660.

[90] Ibid.

[91] Barry E Hawk, *International Antitrust Law & Policy: Fordham Corporate Law 2005* (Juris Publishing Inc, 2006) 224.

[92] Corte di Cassazione, *Fonsai v Nigriello*, 2 February 2007, n 2305, In 'Foro it.', vol. I, 2007, 1097, commentary by A Palmieri, Cartello fra compagnie assicuratrici, aumento dei premi e prova del pregiudizio: Il disagevole cammino dell'azione risarcitoria per danno da illecito antitrust; and R Pardolesi, Il danno antitrust in cerca di disciplina (e di identità?); S Bastianon, Tutela risarcitoria antitrust, nesso causale e danni 'lungolatenti', in Danno e resp., 2007, 764.

[93] Ibid.

statutes have challenged both standards, introducing presumptions of facts and legal inferences and sometimes reversing the burden of proof on to the defendant (see infra Chapter 6). The Damages Directive adopted a very similar approach, recurring to these legal tools to facilitate the claim and relax the standard of proof of causation.

Moreover, one has to consider that the standard of proof refers to a causal link which is not necessarily certain. Establishing the existence of adequate causation is not the same as proving certain (deterministic) causation. Thus, adopting a very high standard of proof does not necessarily mean that the proof of causation will be more difficult than with a lower standard. It is, indeed, fundamental to determine what kind of causation one has to prove. In other words, proving with 90 per cent certainty that an event is 51 per cent probable, is not necessarily more complicated than proving with 51 per cent probability that an event is 90 per cent probable.

5.6.2 *English Law*

Common law jurisdictions distinguish the criminal standard of 'beyond reasonable doubt' to the civil procedural standards of preponderance of the evidence (chiefly American definition) and balance of probabilities (generally preferred in English evidence law).[94] These two definitions traditionally attest that the subject burdened has to prove that the event was 'more probable than not' – that is to say that the event had more than a 50 per cent chance of happening.[95]

In the case of *Miller* v *Minister of Pensions*, Lord Denning pointed out in this regard that 'The ... [standard of proof] ... is well settled. It must carry a reasonable degree of probability ... if the evidence is such that the tribunal can say: "We think it more probable than not" the burden is discharged, but, if the probabilities are equal, it is not'.[96] The balance of probability rule therefore predicates that a fact is true – for the law – if it is more probable than not.[97] This approach also finds application in competition law litigation as the Competition Appeal Tribunal and the High Court have consistently applied it, stating that 'under domestic law the standard of proof we must apply in deciding whether infringements of the Chapter

---

[94] The standard of 'clear and convincing evidence' is rarely required in civil law cases; see Engel (n 83) 3.

[95] Richard Glover (n 13) 104.Clermont and Sherwin (n 61); Dominique Demougin and Claude Fluet, 'Preponderance of Evidence' [2006] 50 *European Economic Review* 963; Juliane Kokott, *The Burden of Proof in Comparative and International Human Rights Law: Civil and Common Law Approaches with Special Reference to the American and German Legal Systems* (Martinus Nijhoff Publishers, 1998).

[96] *Miller v Minister of Pensions* [1947] 2 ALL ER, 372. See also *Mallett v McMonagle* AC 166 (1970), where the English court notoriously stated that 'Anything that is more probable than not is treated as certainty', 176.

[97] Steel (n 13) 50; *Bonnington Castings v Wardlaw* [1956] AC 613, 625; *Snell v Farrell* [1990] 2 SCR 311, 321; *Chappel v Hart* [1998] 195 CLR 232, 273; D Dobbs, R Keeton and D Owen, *Prosser & Keeton on Torts*, 5th edn, 243; K Barker, P Cane, M Lunney, and F Trindade, *The Law of Torts in Australia*, 5th edn, 532; Khoury (n 15) 31.

5.6 Proving Causation in National Courts

I or Chapter II prohibitions are proved is the civil standard, commonly known as the preponderance or balance of probabilities, notwithstanding that the civil penalties imposed may be intended by the Director to have a deterrent effect'.[98]

Once the defendant has persuaded the judge that the fact is more probable than not, he or she will have right to full compensation of the damages claimed. Whether the probability is close to full certainty or is just a little more than 50 per cent is irrelevant indeed for the amount of damages that have to be recognized in full in either case. For this reason, this is also called an all-or-nothing rule.[99] Moreover, the balance of probability rule considers only past events and past losses. Any possible future harm has to be established, instead, on the basis of a 'proportional liability test'.[100] Claims regarding losses caused by the defendant that will take place in the future will be therefore compensated on the basis of the causal contribution of the defendant, reckoned as a higher chance of the claimant to be worse off.

In England, the antitrust courts have clarified that, in competition law also, litigation parties have to substantiate their claim under the standard of the balance of probabilities (i.e., more likely than not).[101] With regard to the standard of evidence in competition law proceedings, the CAT has observed that 'There is no requirement, under the ECHR, of proof beyond reasonable doubt'[102] and that 'The balance of probabilities is a sufficiently flexible standard to require that the Tribunal (or Director) should be more sure before finding serious allegations proved than when deciding less serious matters'.[103]

The English courts believe, therefore, that the standard of balance of probabilities meets the requirements of the type of proceeding involved in competition law damages actions and that, moreover, it is in line with the European courts' jurisprudence.[104] As an exceptional measure, the seriousness of an infringement of the competition rules justifies, in the opinion of the *High Court in Attheraces v British Horseracing Board*,[105] the adoption of a standard where the proof has to be 'commensurately cogent and convincing'.[106] This is usually defined as a 'heightened civil standard'.[107] However, this standard is generally required for the proof of the antitrust

---

[98] *Napp Pharmaceuticals Holdings Ltd v Director General of Fair Trading* [2002] CAT 1, 105; see also, more recently, *JJB Sports Plc v Office of Fair Trading* [2004] CAT 17, [2005] Comp. A.R. 29,195 and *Bookmakers Afternoon Greyhound Services Ltd v Amalgamated Racing Ltd* [2009] EWCA Civ 750, 392.

[99] Khoury (n 15) 66.

[100] See Section 4.3. See also *Doyle v Wallace* [1998] PIQR Q146, and Steel (n 13) 290 ff.

[101] *JJB Sports Plc v Office of Fair Trading* (n 98) 195; *Greyhound Services Ltd v Amalgamated Racing Ltd* (n 98) 392.

[102] Making reference here to Richard Buxton, 'The Human Rights Act and the Substantive Criminal Law' [2000] *Criminal Law Review* 331.

[103] *Napp Pharmaceuticals v Office of Fair Trading* (n 98) 96.

[104] Ibid., 112.

[105] [2005] EWHC 3015.

[106] Ibid., para 126.

[107] See Glover (n 13) 114.

124 *Proof Rules of Causation*

infringement. By contrast, the proof of causation may benefit from a lower standard, especially when prima facie evidence is available.[108]

This approach is often described as 'more objective' as compared to the continental European traditions, as it focuses on class-based probabilities and specific probability of an event to take place, not the intime conviction of the trier of facts. The preponderance of the evidence standard based on the use of probability would therefore suffice alone for discharging the burden of proof.[109] However, a number of judicial decisions in England, United States and Australia have seen judges explicitly declaring that they do not solely rely on statistical probability to deliver the judgment, but, rather, they require 'the formation of a minimal belief regarding the truth of the fact(s) at issue'.[110] Hence, the trier of fact will find that an event is true when he or she is persuaded that the event is more probable than not.[111] The inclusion of judges' persuasion in the assessment of facts is almost unavoidable in cases of causal uncertainty, especially due to scientific or economic uncertainty. Treating statistical probability as an exact science would indeed be a mistake,[112] as a judge is, in most cases, presented with contrasting evidences pointing in different directions.[113] Their evidential value, moreover, will have to be determined on the basis of all the other evidences shown. Hence, reducing the proof of causation to a merely scientific exercise of mechanistic connections is often not desirable or even possible. For the same reason, common law judges have often inferred causation based on common sense when there was no evidence to the contrary.[114]

5.6.3 *German Law*

German law has established a regime of 'free evaluation of the evidence' (*freie beweiswürdigung*) in its Code of Civil Procedure. According to §286 ZPO, the judge shall form an intime conviction about the truth of the case, taking into account all the information provided in the proceedings and the circumstances of the case.[115]

---

[108] Chapter 6.

[109] Clermont and Sherwin (n 61); Dominique Demougin and Claude Fluet, 'Preponderance of Evidence' [2006] 50 European Economic Review 963; Kokott (n 95).

[110] Wright, 'Proving Causation' (n 2) 199–200.

[111] However, there are differences in common law jurisdictions. 'The difference in the formulations is that, under the English law view, the "probability" in the BPR is part of the content of what the factfinder must be persuaded. In the Australian formulation, the "probability" in the BPR is a measure of the strength of the factfinder's being persuaded that p'. Steel (n 13) 51, n 15.

[112] Anne-Lise Sibony, Le juge et le raisonnement économique en droit de la concurrence (LGDJ, 2008).

[113] Lianos (n 86) 190.

[114] Khoury (n 15) 66.

[115] 'Paying due regard to the entirety of the proceedings, including the evidence presented, if any, it is for the court to decide, based on its personal conviction, whether a factual claim is indeed true or not', translation taken from Engel (n 83) 5.

5.6 Proving Causation in National Courts

However, the civil procedural code does not clarify the level of conviction that the judge has to reach for the ruling. The jurisprudence has interpreted the requirements of §286 ZPO in light of the civil code explaining that the judge may harbour some doubts about the proof of the claim but has to overcome these doubts before the decision is taken.[116] This is not to say that the judge has to reach full certainty about all the elements of the proof but that the decision has to be formed on the basis of a high level of conviction.

Further judicial interpretation of the standard of proof has clarified that even a very high probability may not suffice if the judge did not reach a personal conviction about the case at hand.[117] For more than a discretionary decision, some authors explain, the judge is asked to adopt an empirical standard[118] resting on 'ethos, experience and intuition'.[119] The judge's conviction builds on a rational interpretation of the facts of the case and on a sound use of deductions.[120] In this vein, some authors contend that the intime conviction refers to a rational, not a merely personal belief.[121]

But one may reformulate this standard in probability terms as requiring the judge to be convinced when there is a very high probability of a claim to be true.[122] Although, according to many scholars, the level of probability has to be 'close to certainty',[123] it has been observed that while in some cases, judges accepted a level of certainty not lower 90 per cent, in others, they have been content with as low as 70 per cent.[124] This reason alone would justify the rejection of the claim that German law ignores probabilities in establishing the standards of proof for causation.[125] Moreover, it should be observed that jurisdictions requiring a higher

---

[116] BGH, 17 February 1970 ('Anastasia Decision'), 53 BGHZ 245, 256 (German Federal Court of Justice), interpreting s 286 of the German Code of Civil Procedure as requiring 'full judicial conviction in the form of a degree of certainty that silences doubt for practical purposes, even if it does not eliminate them entirely'.

[117] Ibid.

[118] Engel (n 83) 440.

[119] Ibid.; Joachim Schulz, Sachverhaltsfeststellung und Beweistheorie: Elemente einer Theorie strafprozessualer Sachverhaltsfeststellung (Heymann, 1992) 168; SL Goren, The Code of Civil Procedure Rules of the Federal Republic of Germany of January 30, 1877 and the Introductory Act for the Code of Civil Procedure Rules of January 30, 1877 (Littleton, Fred B Rothman & Co, 1990) 73; Wright, Proving Causation (n 2) 194.

[120] Steel (n 13) 54; also citing C Katzenmeier, 'Beweismaßreduzierung und probabilistische Proportionalhaftung', 195; G. Mäsch, Chance und Schaden, 373.

[121] Steel (n 13) 54.

[122] Ibid.; referring to C. Katzenmeier, 'Beweismaßreduzierung und probabilistische Proportionalhaftung', 194, citing H Musielak, Die Grundlagen der Beweislast im Zivilprozeß, 105–119.'

[123] Steel (n 13) 54.

[124] Ibid.

[125] Clermont and Sherwin (n 61).

126 *Proof Rules of Causation*

standard of proof often recur to other expedients to ease the burden of proof of the claimant – in particular, by shifting the evidential burden according to the proximity of the proof.[126]

According to §33a(3) GWB, the assessment and quantification of damages in competition law claims are subject to the lower standard of §287 ZPO.[127] This norm establishes that the court decides 'whether a damage exists and the extent of the damage … at its free discretion taking into account all the circumstances'. The standard of proof is therefore lower than the one applied by §286 ZPO, requiring a very high degree of probability. In a decision dating before the entry into force of the introduction of §33a GWB, the German Federal Court of Justice (BGH), established that §287 ZPO, determines not only the proof standard for the *quantum* of damages but also for the *an* debeatur. Here the court applied a fine distinction between the assessment of causation of specific damages and proof of causation of an anticompetitive harm. The BGH maintained that the claimant has to prove whether he or she was affected by the antitrust violation, according to standard set out in §286 ZPO.[128] On the other hand, a prima facie evidence of the existence of a concerted practice is enough to establish causation of harm under the lower standard of §287 ZPO.[129] It remains to be seen what will be the impact of this decision on the following cases based on the reformed § 33 GWB, applying a clearer distinction of the standards of proof required for causation.

Competition damages claims are based on a breach of a statutory duty, but the mere breach of the duty does not give rise to liability. On the contrary, § 33 (3) GWB requires the finding of intention or negligence to establish liability.

---

[126] In this sense, for a comparative perspective, see Taruffo (n 83) 672.

[127] The law establishes that '§ 287 of the German Code of Civil Procedure [*Zivilprozessordnung*] shall apply to quantify the harm caused by the infringement. In quantifying the harm, account may, in particular, be taken of the proportion of the profit which the infringer has derived from the infringement under paragraph 1', English translation available at www.gesetze-im-internet.de/englisch_gwb/englisch_gwb.html#p0229. Moreover, German courts have often used § 287 ZPO, dealing with the compensation of damages, to relax the standard for proving causation – for example, in case of consequential losses, observing that the standard of more probable than not (50 plus 1 per cent) would be acceptable. However, this standard has been deemed insufficient for proving the causal link between the claimant's harm and the defendant's conduct, if the claim is based on the infringement of § 823 I BGB, regarding liability for damages to the body, property, freedom or other rights, except pure economic losses. On the other hand, for damages caused by infringements of a statutory duty (§ 823 II BGB), German courts assess liability under the lighter § 287 ZPO standard; see Steel (n 13) 57.

[128] Ibid., para 57.

[129] Ibid., para 56 and 59. See, in more detail, Chapter 6.

5.6 Proving Causation in National Courts

Thus, in Germany it is required a minimum standard of persuasion of the judge based on her free conviction,[130] but courts, in the evaluation of the proof, generally apply a standard closer to the 'preponderance of the evidence' rule.[131]

5.6.4 *French Law*

As a general rule, French law of civil procedure puts the *onus probandi* of causation on the claimant.[132] As for other systems, this is a risk allocation mechanism as well as a basic rule of fairness, although there exists a number of exceptions to this rule, which are analyzed in Chapter 6. But the required level of proof is a more complex question that needs further analysis.

French law of civil procedure does not set an explicit standard of proof. While the code of civil procedure remains silent on the issue of the standard of proof, the Article 353 of the French Code of Criminal Procedure establishes that the standard of proof is the intime conviction of the judge. Scholars have therefore observed that there is no clear separation between the criminal and civil law standards of proof.[133] However, this should not bring to the conclusion that judges necessarily adopt the same standard in criminal and civil procedural laws.[134] The jurisprudence has established a civil standard for the proof of causation, which – according to the literature – requires the evidence of causation to be 'certain',[135] although some leeway of discretion should be left to the judge.[136] Some scholars indeed prefer to formulate their approach to the proof of causation in the negative, observing that if the judge is uncertain about the existence of a causal link, he or she has to reject the claim.[137] Considering that French law requires the proof of a direct causal link established on an empirical basis, the standard of proof usually relies on the application of common sense by the judge.[138] This considered, it is difficult to find a single, unique way to determine the standard of proof of causation, as some French courts have even accepted the proof based on a

---

[130] Subsection 1 of section 286 of the Code of Civil Procedure states: 'The court shall decide at its free discretion, by taking into account the whole substance of the proceedings and the results of any evidence taking, whether a factual allegation should be regarded as true or untrue. The grounds which prompted the court's conviction shall be stated in the judgment'.

[131] Peter L Murray and Rolf Stürner, *German Civil Justice* (Carolina Academic Press, 2004) 310–311; Peter Gottwald, 'Civil Procedure Reform in Germany' [1997] *The American Journal of Comparative Law* 753.

[132] See Article 9 of the Code of Civil Procedure (*Code de procédure civile*), and Henri Lévy-Bruhl, *La preuve judiciaire: Étude de sociologie juridique* (M Rivière, 1964) 39 ff.

[133] Ibid.

[134] Taruffo (n 83) 665.

[135] Christophe Quézel-Ambrunaz, *Essai sur la causalité en droit de la responsabilité civile* (Dalloz, 2010) 1066.

[136] Ibid.

[137] René Savatier, 'La Responsabilité Médicale En France (Aspects de Droit Privé)' [1976] 28 *Revue internationale de droit comparé* 493, 501; Khoury (n 15) 92.

[138] Boris Starck, Henri Roland and Laurent Boyer, *Droit civil – Les Obligations, tome 1: Responsabilité délictuelle* (Litec, 1996) 1066.

'sufficient degree of probability'.[139] Thus, the judge has to reach a firm, subjective belief in the truth of the facts of the proceeding.[140]

The code of commerce and the civil code admit the compensation of a wide array of damages in competition law litigation, provided that they respect the principle of 'full compensation'. However, the judge has ample discretionary power in establishing damages,[141] and their motivations may often take the form of obiter dicta on the issue of causation – so much so that, for instance, the Commercial Court of Paris has once recognized only loss of profits, observing that 'actual loss and loss of profit are concepts that overlap, . . . so there is a redundancy' and only allowed the "loss of profit" damage corresponding to "the non profitable investments because of the difficulty of attracting new customers and / or loss of former clients"'.[142]

The adoption of strict requirements for the proof of causation has brought some scholars to observe that if the defendant can make a sufficiently significant argument questioning the existence of the causal link, the plaintiff may be denied compensation. The defendant will put forward the fact of a third party or of the victim which has contributed to the damage and is the determining factor in its occurrence.

On the other hand, while Continental civil law traditions similarly apply a standard recalling the subjective conviction of the judge on the specific case at hand, some of them have also sided this analysis with a probabilistic approach.

5.6.5 *Italian Law*

The general principle placing the burden of proof on the claimant applies also in Italian law. Despite the law of evidence being generally regarded as a matter of procedure,[143] the provisions on the burden and standards of proof are divided between the Italian Civil Code CC and the Code of Civil Procedure. Article 2697 CC establishes the general principles according to which 'who wants to assert a right in court must prove the facts that constitute its foundation', and 'whoever objects to the ineffectiveness of such facts or claims that the right has been modified

---

[139] Khoury (n 15) 38; P Jourdain, 'Imputablité d'une contamination virale à une transfusion sanguine: la preuve par exclusion du lien de causalité érigée en présomption du droit [2001] Revue trimestrielle de droit civil 889 14; Starck, et al (n 138) para 1441; Raymond Legeais, *Les regles de preuve en droit civil: Permanences et transformations* (Libr Generale de Droit Et de Jurisprudence, 1955) 174.

[140] Wright, 'Proving Causation' (n 2) 205, according to whom this conviction has to be 'personal'.

[141] Muriel Chagny and Jean-Louis Fourgoux, Competition Law, *Private Enforcement and Collective Redress in France, in AHRC Project on Competition Law: Comparative Private Enforcement and Consumer Redress*, led by Prof. Barry Rodger, available at www.clcpecreu.co.uk/, 15.

[142] French commercial court, 30 March 2011, SA *Numericable et al.* v SA *France Telecom Orange*, Communication Commerce Electronique, No 9, Sept. 2011, comm. 76, M. Chagny.

[143] However, for a long and never-silenced debate on the nature of the law of evidence, see Proto Pisani, 405 ff.

5.6 Proving Causation in National Courts

or extinguished must prove the facts on which the exception is based'.[144] With specific reference to the proof of causation, the Italian Court of Cassation has confirmed that, according to Article 2697 CC, the plaintiff has the burden to prove the causal link between the behaviour of the defendant and the harm for which he or she is seeking restoration.[145]

As for the civil standard of proof for causation, the law does not establish a precise level of certainty that the judge has to achieve. The Italian system recognizes three types of evidences: 'legal proof', 'free evidence' and secondary evidence.[146] While the 'legal proof' is direct evidence of the *probandum*, the 'free evidence' has to be evaluated by the judge also on the basis of the secondary evidence available. Article 116 CCP predicates the principle of 'cautious evaluation' of the proof, an attenuated version of the standard of intime conviction; whereas Article 115 CCP states that the judge has to base his or her decision on the evidence submitted by the parties.[147] Hence, the decision, which is always motivated, hinges on the proof lodged by the parties during the proceedings, but the evaluation of this proof remains discretionary to a large extent, as the judge has the power to establish the details of the level of certainty that has to be achieved. With legislative decree 19 January 2017, n 3[148], the Damages Directive was transposed in the Italian law, however, bringing no substantial addition to the text of the Directive nor to the general laws of evidence.

However, where the law leaves a lacuna, the judiciary often intervenes to fill it. So, after years of debate, the Court of Cassation expressly stated that it pursues the application of the standard of 'more probable than not' in civil cases and 'beyond reasonable doubt' in criminal proceedings: 'As this Court has previously stated, the main difference [between the penal and civil processes] is in the standards of proof that each system requires (. . .). The Penal Code requires proof "beyond a reasonable doubt" while the Civil Code merely requires "more probable than not." The different standards correspond to the different values at stake in each system'.[149] In this decision, the Italian Supreme Court recalls the ECJ's decision in *Manfredi* – in particular, where it observes that the court has to determine with a 'sufficient degree of probability'[150] the existence of a causal connection between the infringement of EU competition law and the damage. In the same decision, the judges of the Italian Court of Cassation continue in their analysis of the standard of proof for causation observing that the probabilistic standard is not met by merely providing quantitative

---

[144] For a general description, see Michele Taruffo, Onere della prova, in Dig. disc. priv., sez. civ., XIII, Turin 1995, 65 ff.

[145] See Italian Court of Cassation, Division III, no. 7026, 2001.

[146] Crisanto Mandrioli and Antonio Carratta, *Diritto processuale civile* (Giappichelli, 2016) 176 ff.

[147] Salvatore Patti, *Delle prove: Art. 2697–2739* (Zanichelli, 2015); Mandrioli and Carratta (n 146) 276; Luigi P Comoglio, *Le prove civili* (UTET, 2010).

[148] GU 15 19-1-2017

[149] *Corte di Cassazione SU*, 11 January 2008, no 581, in *Danno e resp*, 2009, 667. s 3.9. The translation is taken from Wright, 'Proving Causation' (n 2) 198.

[150] Joined Cases C-295/04 to C-298/04, para 47.

or statistical evidence of general causation (8.10).[151] But it is fundamental to verify the credibility of this assessment with the level of validity of the evidence produced in court. In other words, the general probabilities can be used as a hypothesis of which the trier of facts has to verify the soundness and validity. Hence, contrary to what is often believed,[152] the Italian law has developed an approach whereby causation has to be proved according to a standard of 'reasonable probability' which can be assessed on the basis of statistical evidence, if exhaustive.[153]

In the *Comi/Cargest* case,[154] the Italian Court of Cassation stated that – in appraising the evidence – the judge has to take into account the information asymmetry existing between the parties and has to adopt an interpretation of the procedural rules functional to the objective of a correct implementation of competition law. This can be achieved, the Court observed, by an extensive interpretation of the conditions established in the civil procedural code regarding the submission of documents, the request for information[155] and, above all, the expert witness, which can be also ordered ex officio, if it is necessary to acquire and evaluate information useful for reconstructing the anticompetitive case reported and its causal connection to the damage.

However, this standard of reasonable probability is not the same as the 'more probable than not' adopted in England, as it leaves more leeway to the judge to determine the level or reasonableness. Moreover, for the civil standard of proof to be fulfilled, it is necessary to reach the judge's conviction that the general statistical probability finds application in the case at hand.[156]

For instance, the Italian Court of Cassation in the case *Fondiaria SAI*[157] stated that, in competition damages action, the judge can proceed to the assessment of causation using probability, but also logic, presumptions and the yardstick of 'more probable than not'[158] to reach conviction about the 'truth' of the case.[159] This last

---

[151] The court here explicitly refers to the aleatory or Pascalian principles as opposed to the Baconian probability.

[152] Clermont (n 61).

[153] Court of Cassation n 7997/2005; Court of Cassation n 11755/2006.

[154] Court of Cassation n 11564/2015.

[155] See also Article 15 of EC Reg. No. 1/2003.

[156] Luigi P Comoglio, *Le prove civili* (Wolters Kluwer Italia, 2010) 124.

[157] Corte di Cassazione, *Fonsai v Nigriello*, 2 February 2007, n 2305, In 'Foro it.', vol. I, 2007, 1097, commentary by A Palmieri, Cartello fra compagnie assicuratrici, aumento dei premi e prova del pregiudizio: Il disagevole cammino dell'azione risarcitoria per danno da illecito antitrust; and R Pardolesi, Il danno antitrust in cerca di disciplina (e di identità?); S Bastianon, Tutela risarcitoria antitrust, nesso causale e danni 'lungolatenti', in Danno e resp., 2007, 764. In this decision, the Court of Cassation deployed a flexible approach to causation in antitrust. However, in the final decision, the court rejected the approach of the appellate judge for which the assessment of causation was 'in re ipsa' and demonstrated by the verification of the antitrust infringement already purported by the National Authority.

[158] See also Tribunale di Milano, *Brennercom Spa v Telecom Italia Spa* 27.12.2013 no 22423/2010.

[159] See *Fonsai v Nigriello* (n 157) 1104.

method is often used in antitrust, above all, when the claim is based on lost chances and passing-on of overcharges.[160]

5.7 ECONOMETRICS AND THE 'CALCULATION' OF CAUSATION IN EU COMPETITION LAW

Economic theories and econometric techniques have a central role in the assessment of both material and legal causal links in competition damages actions. Economic testimony may become evidence in the proceedings. Usually experts provide this testimony which the trier of facts has the power to admit.[161] The rules of admissibility and evaluation of scientific expert evidence may vary across jurisdictions, but they usually have to be based on scientific analysis and aid the resolution of the dispute.[162] However, what should be considered 'scientific' is subject to debate. Certainty is not required for it, but the evidence has to meet a falsification standard, which means that it should not be refutable.[163] This falsification standard considers all the causal evidence that is not only deterministic but also statistically probable.

The tangled nature of business activities renders particularly difficult, if not impossible, the application of deterministic approaches to causation in antitrust actions,[164] also recurring to discretionary powers in the assessment of the proof. Judges firstly started to depart from a deterministic approach when they endorsed the theory of stochastic causality[165] in the area of medical responsibility[166] and asbestos-related illnesses.[167] The same probabilistic approach found fortune for the assessment of the loss of chance in tort liability.[168] Similarly, competition law frequently deals with cases where it is impossible to state with certainty the direct cause of the

---

[160] Chapter 7.

[161] For a complete analysis of admissibility of evidence in common law jurisdictions, see Déirdre Dwyer, *The Judicial Assessment of Expert Evidence* (Cambridge University Press, 2009).

[162] *Daubert v Merrell Dow Pharmaceuticals, Inc,* 509 US 579 (1993).

[163] Karl R Popper, *Conjectures and Refutations: The Growth of Scientific Knowledgee.* (Routledge & Kegan Paul, 1972).

[164] Hanns A Abele, Georg F Kodek and Guido K Schaefer, 'Proving Causation in Private Antitrust Cases' (2011) 7 *Journal of Competition Law and Economics* 847, 852.

[165] For an introductory description, see James Robins and Sander Greenland, 'The Probability of Causation under a Stochastic Model for Individual Risk' *Biometrics*, 1989, 1125–1138.

[166] *Sienkiewicz v Greif (UK) Ltd* [2009] EWCA Civ 1159 (EWCA (Civ)); *AB & Ors v British Coal Corporation & Anor* [2004] EWHC 1372 (QB) (EWHC (QB)); Richard Goldberg, 'The Role of Scientific Evidence in the Assessment of Causation in Medicinal Product Liability Litigation: A Probabilistic and Economic Analysis' [1998] 1 *Current Legal Issues* 55.

[167] See *Rothwell v Chemical and Insulating Co Ltd and Another, Topping v Benchtown Ltd* (formerly Jones Bros Preston Ltd), *Johnston v NEI International Combustion Ltd, Grieves v F T Everard & Sons Ltd and Another* [2007] UKHL 39, [2008] 1 AC 281; *Cartledge v E Jopling & Sons Ltd* [1963] AC 758 (HL); Cassazione penale, sez. IV, sentenza 12.03.2012 n° 9479; Cass. pen. Sez. IV, 10-06-2010, n 38991 (rv. 248851), CED Cassazione, 2010.

[168] Wesley C Salmon, *Causality and Explanation* (Oxford University Press, 1997); Wesley C Salmon, *Scientific Explanation and the Causal Structure of the World* (Princeton University Press, 1984); DH Mellor, *The Facts of Causation* (Routledge, 2002); Robert Young, Michael

132 *Proof Rules of Causation*

damage.[169] In these cases, courts are able to depart from the analysis of each single transaction that was affected by the antitrust infringement to take into account statistical data from which they can obtain average patterns to establish a stochastic causation.[170] This is not a causal proportional liability test, as analyzed in Chapter 2, as it still relies on an all-or-nothing approach based on a counterfactual scenario. This test is, instead, mostly based on an evaluation of general causation through economic expertise whereby the judge is able to infer specific causation.

Many scholars have observed the important use of economics in antitrust litigation to establish counterfactual scenarios.[171] This is not surprising, considering that the antitrust harm is a pure economic loss and its relation to the anticompetitive behaviour can be understood mainly through the study of economic causality. The objective of this reconstruction is to understand if the different concepts of causation in law might correspond to the one of causality in econometrics.

Econometrics is defined as 'statistics that is centrally conditioned by economic theory'.[172] The objective of econometrics is, therefore, 'the quantitative analysis of actual economic phenomena based on the concurrent development of theory and observation, related by appropriate methods of inference'.[173] Hence, this method consists of the interpretation of data through economic theories, in order to infer effects from selected causes. Econometrics, indeed, contrary to law, is mainly forward looking, since it aims at foreseeing future events.[174] In order to do this, econometrics uses economics, mathematics and statistics. The result is a probability addressing average quantitative data gathered in order to confirm or disprove the underlying economic theory.

A first approach to the interrelation drawn in this 'triangle' (formed by statistics, economics and mathematics) wants economics to provide the underling theory that makes statistics economically interpretable.[175] This view is openly criticized by

---

Faure and Paul Fenn, 'Causality and Causation in Tort Law' [2004] 24 *International Review of Law and Economics* 4, 507–523.

[169] Abele, Kodek and Schaefer (n 164) 468.

[170] Ibid., 470.

[171] Lianos and Genakos, 'Econometric Evidence in EU Competition Law' 85; Cento Veljanovski, 'Counterfactual Tests in Competition Law' [2010] 4 *Competition Law Journal*; Damien Geradin and Ianis Girgenson, 'The Counterfactual Method in EU Competition Law: The Cornerstone of the Effects-Based Approach' (December 11, 2011) available at SSRN: http://papers.ssrn.com/sol3/papers.cfm?abstract_id=1970917.

[172] Kevin D Hoover, 'The Methodology of Econometrics' [2006] 1 *New Palgrave Handbook of Econometrics* 61, as cited by Ioannis Lianos and Christos Genakos, 'Econometric Evidence in EU Competition Law: An Empirical and Theoretical Analysis' [2012] CLES Research Paper series 06/12 87, available at http://papers.ssrn.com/abstract=2184563, accessed 26 August 2014.

[173] Paul A Samuelson, Tjalling C Koopmans and J Richard Stone, 'Report of the Evaluative Committee for Econometrica' [1954] 22 *Econometrica* 2, 141.

[174] Lianos and Genakos, (n 171) 84.

[175] Nancy Cartwright, 'Causal Structures in Econometrics' in *On the Reliability of Economic Models* (Springer, 1995) 63–89; Nancy Cartwright, 'Counterfactuals in Economics: A Commentary' [2007] 4 *Causation and Explanation*, 191.

5.7 *Econometrics and the 'Calculation' of Causation in EU Competition Law* 133

Hoover, who remarks that 'if the inferential direction runs only from theory to data, how could we ever use empirical evidence to determine which theory is right?'[176]

A second and contrasting position explains that econometrics differs from statistics because, while the former seeks causality, the latter simply finds correlations.[177] As maintained by Stigum, indeed, the aim of econometrics is nothing but 'to obtain knowledge concerning relations that exist in the social reality' through a theory-data confrontation.[178]

Econometrics has been approached by economist in three different ways. The first (also chronologically) is a structural approach[179] used by Haavelmo[180] and the Cowles Commission[181] in the 1940s, where the effects are inferred by theories that are stated as underlying assumptions. Here the aim of Haavelmo was to bridge theory and empirical research in a logically rigorous manner.[182] This type of a priori approach has been opposed in the following years by different types of inferential approaches[183] such as the VAR method[184] and the LSE approach.[185]

Finally, a third model of econometric evaluation of causal inference found place with the name of 'counterfactual (test)'.[186] Only this last approach found application in competition law enforcement; hence, we will focus exclusively on that.

Lianos and Genakos divide the relevant factors for determining if and how legal causation borrows from economic causality in competition law, finding out that this happens, in particular, in two cases.[187] Firstly, they observe that causation in the law is often determined by reference to the general concept of economic causality.[188]

---

[176] Hoover, 'The Methodology of Econometrics', 66.

[177] James J Heckman, 'Causal Parameters and Policy Analysis in Economics: A Twentieth Century Retrospective' [2002] 115 *The Quarterly Journal of Economics* 1, 85.

[178] Bernt P Stigum, *Econometrics and the Philosophy of Economics: Theory-Data Confrontations in Economics* (Princeton University Press, 2003) 3, also cited by Ioannis Lianos and Christos Genakos (n 171).

[179] See Ragnar Frisch, 'Autonomy of Economic Relations: Statistical versus Theoretical Relations in Economic Macrodynamics' (reproduced by University of Oslo in 1948 with Tinbergen's Comments), Memorandum, Oslo; published in Hendry and Morgan (eds.) 1995, *The Foundations of Econometric Analysis*, 1938.

[180] Trygve Haavelmo, 'The Probability Approach in Econometrics' *Econometrica: Journal of the Econometric Society*, 1944, iii–115, also cited by Ioannis Lianos and Christos Genakos (n 172).

[181] TC Koopmans and WC Hood, 'The Estimation of Simultaneous Linear Economic Relationships', in WC Hood and T Koopmans (eds), *Studies in Econometric Method, Cowles Commission Monograph 14*. 112–199 (Yale University Press, 1953).

[182] Duo Qin, *A History of Econometrics: The Reformation from the 1970s* (Oxford University Press, 2013).

[183] Hoover (n 172) 69.

[184] The VAR method focuses on the detection of appropriate theoretical models for specific set of data; see Qin (n 182) 41 ff; Badi Baltagi, *Econometrics* (Springer Science & Business Media, 2011).

[185] Christopher L Gilbert, 'LSE and the British Approach to Time Series Econometrics' [1989] *Oxford Economic Papers*, 108–128.

[186] James J Heckman, 'Econometric Causality' [2008] 76 *International Statistical Review* 1, 28–42.

[187] Lianos and Genakos (n 171).

[188] Ibid., 85.

134 *Proof Rules of Causation*

In this case, causation in law uses the result of the verification of causality outside law[189] (as in the case of economic counterfactual explanation of the causes of damages). Secondly, there are cases, especially in administrative procedures, in which the judge establishes causation on the basis of the legal policy question of distribution of social risk and relies on theories of causality outside the law, especially economics, to find the answer.[190]

The concept of causality advanced by econometrics is, however, largely different from the legal concept of causation. Firstly, econometric does not select causes on their legal significance. Indeed, the aim of economic theories is not to determine responsibility of agents in the market but, rather, to establish connections between causes and effects. Hence, the econometric analysis will not consider the legal characteristics of the causal conditions – for instance, necessary, sufficient or adequate.[191] By the same token, econometrics does not distinguish between types of responsibility (e.g., negligence based or strict liability) in order to determine the elements of causation.

Moreover, in the law, any assumption that is not imposed by the law itself is part of a procedural debate that can disprove the truthfulness of its underlying theory. Therefore, the theoretical basis for material and legal causation are questioned before the judge by parties, to the extent that their reliability lies mostly on the method of assessment rather than the 'direction' of it, marking another difference with causality.

5.7.1 *When 'But-For' Becomes 'If-Then': The Counterfactuals*

The last decades have seen arising academic and judicial interest around the problem of the assessment of counterfactuals.[192] Counterfactuals scenarios are generally used to prove causation when it is not possible to infer a sufficient (or necessary) connection between agency and effects, based on the mere reasonableness of the assumptions.[193] In this vein, for counterfactuals here, we refer to a but-for

---

[189] As argued by HLA Hart and Tony Honoré in *Causation in the Law* (Oxford University Press, 1985) 141.

[190] Lianos and Genakos (n 171) 86.

[191] See Chapter 1.

[192] Although the first analysis of counterfactuals is attributable to John Stuart Mill, *A System of Logic, Ratiocinative and Inductive: Being a Connected View of the Principles of Evidence and the Methods of Scientific Investigation* (John W Parker, 1843), it is only from the 1960s that the theory had been thoroughly developed, mainly thanks to Ardon Lyon, 'Causality, [1967] 18 *British Journal for the Philosophy of Science* 1, 1–20; John Leslie Mackie, *The Cement of the Universe: A Study of Causation* (Clarendon Press, 1980); David Lewis, 'Causation' [1973]. *The Journal of Philosophy*, 556–567.

[193] Hart and Honoré (n 189) 495.

test applied in antitrust through economic theories. These counterfactuals aim at describing a hypothetical situation through econometric explanations. In other words, the decision maker compares the actual situation with a counterfactual (or theoretical) one created through economic theories and aggregate data.[194]

In public competition law enforcement the causal link between the infringement and the damage to the market is sometimes presumed as an effect automatically brought about by a specific conduct. For this reason, the research of a causal connection generally shifts to the link between the behaviour and the infringement.[195] However, the Court of Justice opened at the use of counterfactuals with the *Société Technique Minière* v *Maschinenbau Ulm GmbH* decision[196] where a case of infringement was analyzed by effect. In the recent cases *Visa* and *MasterCard*, the European courts have adopted a broad counterfactual approach stating that 'irrespective of the context or aim in relation to which a counterfactual hypothesis is used, it is important that that hypothesis is appropriate to the issue it is supposed to clarify and that the assumption on which it is based is not unrealistic'.[197] Public enforcement of competition law generally applies a wide number of different counterfactuals, based on the antitrust rule infringed or on their being purported ex ante (for the assessment of future conditions) or ex post (to find out a breach of competition law).[198]

Merger control and self-assessment of Article 101 violations use ex ante counterfactuals.[199] The standard counterfactual for merger control assumes that the situation changes only if the merger takes place. Thus, in the hypothetical scenario, the concentration level may vary only if the merger is cleared.[200]

---

[194] Geradin and Girgenson, (n 171); Veljanovski (n 171).

[195] See, for instance, Commission decision of 14 December 1993, Case IV/M.308, Kali and Salz/MdK/Treuhand, 1994 OJ L 316/1.

[196] Case C-56/65 [1966] ECR 235, where the court stated that 'The competition in question must be understood within the actual context in which it would occur in the absence of the agreement in dispute. In particular it may be doubted whether there is an interference with competition if the said agreement seems really necessary for the penetration of a new area by an undertaking'; see also *Deere (John) Ltd* v *Commission* (Case C-7/95 P) [1998] ECR I-3111, at para 76.

[197] T-461/07 – *Visa Europe and Visa International Service* v *Commission* [2013] ECR II-01729 para 108.

[198] Geradin and Girgenson (n 171) 12 ff; Veljanovski (n 171).

[199] See Geradin and Girgenson (n 171) 3 ff.

[200] At first, the EC determines the Herfindahl-Hirschman Index (HHI) before the merger and after the merger to analyze the increase in market concentration: see 'Guidelines on the Assessment of Horizontal Mergers under the Council Regulation on the Control of Concentrations between Undertakings' ('Horizontal Merger Guidelines'), 2004 OJ C 31/5, para 16. See also Damien Geradin and Ianis Girgenson, 'The Counterfactual Method in EU Competition Law: The Cornerstone of the Effects-Based Approach' [2011] (11 December 2011) 3 ff, available at SSRN: http://papers.ssrn.com/sol3/papers.cfm?abstract_id=1970917, accessed 25 August 2014.

Causation can be also inferred relying on the *id quod plerumque accidit* but only when the infringement is 'by object'.[201]

The Commission enjoys a broad discretion in the assessment of 'complex economic and technical assessment', which can be overturned only on the base of a manifest error.[202] Finally, the use of counterfactuals also impacts the phase of quantification of damages.[203]

The EC has extended the concept of restrictions by object to reduce the use of counterfactuals for determining causation between the antitrust infringement and market distortions.[204] When causation cannot be so inferred, it is necessary to rely on the use of counterfactuals in order to confront the present scenario with a hypothetical one where no antitrust infringement is committed. In the words of the CJEU, this approach consists in 'taking into account of the competition situation that would exist in the absence of the agreement'.[205]

In competition law damages actions, the assessment is done ex post, and the counterfactual scenario aims at presenting an alternative situation where there are no market distortions due to the antitrust infringement.[206] This method mainly consists in the assessment of stochastic causation that implies the analysis of the probability of effects across a set of data corresponding to a group of transactions. In other terms, this method generates a probability that the damage would not have occurred in absence of the infringement.[207] In this case, the probability is used as a tool to substantiate an event. In the case of a loss of chance, instead, the probability is the object of compensation. The but-for (or in counterfactual terms, the if-then) test for causation is particularly difficult to prove on a case-by-case basis.[208]

---

[201] Case T-286/09 *Intel v Commission* [2014] not yet published (Court Reports – general), publication in extract form, para 141 ff. See also 'Guidelines on the Applicability of Article 101 of the Treaty on the Functioning of the European Union to Horizontal Co-Operation Agreements', 2011 OJ C 11/1 ('Guidelines on Horizontal Agreements').

[202] Case 42/84, Remia [1985] ECR 2545, para 34; Joined Cases 142/84 and 156/84, BAT and Reynolds v Commission [1987] ECR 4487, para 62; Case C-7/95, John Deere v Commission [1998] ECR I-3111, para 41, noting that '(d)etermination of the effects of an agreement on competition constitutes a complex economic appraisal'.

[203] Cento Veljanovski, 'Market Power and Counterfactuals in New Zealand Competition Law' (2013) Journal of Competition Law and Economics, available at SSRN: http://ssrn.com/abstract=1908088 or http://dx.doi.org/10.2139/ssrn.1908088; Geradin and Girgenson (n 171) 42.

[204] Case T-286/09 *Intel v Commission* [2014] not yet published ECLI:EU:T:2014:547, para 1576 ff.

[205] Case T-328/03, O2 (Germany) *GbmH & Co. OHG v Commission* [2006] ECR II-1231, para 69, 71.

[206] Geradin and Girgenson (n 171); Veljanovski (n 171).

[207] Nancy Cartwright, 'Counterfactuals in Economics: A Commentary' (2007) 4 *Causation and Explanation* 191.

[208] *Arkin v Borchard Lines Ltd* (No 4) [2003] EWHC 687 (Comm), [2003] 2 Lloyd's Rep 225, *Crehan v Inntrepreneur Pub Co (CPC) (Office of Fair Trade Intervening)* [2003] EWHC 1510 (Ch), [2003] LLR 573, and *Enron v EWS* [2009] CAT 36 are all unsuccessful damages actions which failed to establish 'but-for' causation.

5.7 Econometrics and the 'Calculation' of Causation in EU Competition Law 137

Probabilities may be used to determine classes of events based on the fewer chances that a risk would take place, which becomes element of proof, in substitution of the specific causation.[209] For instance, the *Kone* case[210] introduced a new class of causative events where the damage is inferred from the main stochastic evaluation that markets are generally behaving in a way that prices tend to follow the 'umbrella price'. However, it has to be observed that probabilities in similar categories of events should not displace the objective or even stochastic analysis of the specific causative event.

The detection of a causal connection implies a qualification and not a mere description of the event.[211] Indeed, causation in law does not totally depend on factual determinants. Legal causation is, in fact, product of a judgment over the type of consequences that are connected by law to the unlawful behaviour. In this legal reasoning, scientific and economic concepts also have to be turned in juridical truth.[212]

5.7.2 Economic Models to Establish Causation

As previously discussed, there are cases in antitrust where it is not possible to determine with certainty which transactions were affected by the antitrust violation. For this reason, courts and authorities endorsed quantitative approaches that provide only an estimation of the probable damages over a set of transactions. This application of stochastic causality echoes the risk-liability theory developed in tort law. Here, indeed, the ex ante analysis of a risk to happen legitimizes a court to award damages for antitrust infringement. In the *Microsoft* case, the CJEU stated that in order to give application to Article 102 TFEU, it suffices that the agency has a 'high probability of eliminating effective competition'.[213] This approach, if reproduced in private enforcement, would burden the claimant with the proof of a general probability of a harm to be caused. This would reverse the risk of substantiating the tort on the defendant that is assumed as the party that can – in a most efficient, cost-effective way   bear this burden in order to reduce negative externalities due to

---

[209] Roberto Pucella, *La causalità 'incerta'* (Giappichelli, 2007); Richard W Wright, 'Causation, Responsibility, Risk, Probability, Naked Statistics, and Proof: Pruning the Bramble Bush by Clarifying the Concepts' [1987] 73 *Iowa Law Review* 1001; Guido Calabresi, 'Concerning Cause and the Law of Torts: An Essay for Harry Kalven, Jr.' [1975] *The University of Chicago Law Review* 69.

[210] Case C-557/12 *Kone AG and Others v ÖBB-Infrastruktur AG* [2014] ECLI:EU:C:2014:1317.

[211] Pucella (n 209) 68.

[212] Vaughn C Ball, 'The Moment of Truth: Probability Theory and Standards of Proof' [1960] 14 *Vanderbilt Law Review* 807, 905.

[213] Case T-201/04, *Microsoft Corp. v Commission*, ECR [2007] II-3601, para 439. In the US parallel case, the FTC requested the assessment of causation in order to infer a reasonable connection between the conduct and the injury suffered, *United States v Microsoft* 253 F.3d 34 [D.C. Cir. 2001].

informational asymmetries.[214] However, when an ex post examination of the activity is required, judges normally resort to two different techniques for reconstructing a hypothetical situation as if the infringement was not committed.

On the one hand, it is possible to use a comparator-based model[215] where the anticompetitive prices are compared with a non-infringement scenario. This empirical study can be operated on the same market before or after the infringement, on a similar geographic market or on similar product markets.[216]

On the other hand, when it is not possible to utilize the comparator model because of evident differences between geographical or product markets, authorities usually recur to a simulation model. This second technique consists in the simulation of market outcomes on the basis of economic models.[217] Here econometrics finds wide application since the proof of causation consists in finding average patterns through the analysis of set of data interpreted on the basis of economic theories.

Other approaches can also be distinguished on the basis of the benchmark of evaluation adopted. For instance, it is possible to analyze the differences in prices on a case-by-case basis or through average patterns gained from statistical data.[218] The case-by-case analysis may become excessively difficult to perform as damages claim comprises a vast number of transactions. In such cases, a statistical study is needed in order to infer effects from the general market patterns.[219] This demonstration implies a comparison between different versions of reality in order to ascertain which of them is the most likely.[220] Through these techniques, substantiating causation implies to prove that, for instance, the price overcharge was due to the antitrust infringement and not to other price determinants.

5.7.3 The Use of Counterfactuals in the Case law

Factual causation in competition damages actions is therefore established either through counterfactuals or on the basis of inferences and presumptions. When the

---

[214] Landes and Posner, (n 84), 112.
[215] Commission's Practical Guide Quantifying Harm in Actions for Damages Based on Breaches of Article 101 or 102 of the Treaty on the Functioning of the European Union, SWD (2013) 205, available at http://ec.europa.eu/competition/antitrust/actionsdamages/quantification_en.html. The Commission explains the usage of these methods in order to quantify damages. However, they are based on the counterfactual method that, in the same words of the Commission, 'is based on comparing the actual position of claimants with the position they would find themselves in had the infringement not occurred. In any hypothetical assessment of how market conditions and the interactions of market participants would have evolved without the infringement, complex and specific economic and competition law issues often arise. Courts and parties are increasingly confronted with these matters and with considering the methods and techniques available to address them'.
[216] Ibid., para 33.
[217] Commission's Practical Guide, para 96.
[218] Abele, Kodek and Schaefer (n 164) 857.
[219] Ibid.
[220] Case C-12/03 P, *Commission v Tetra Laval* [2005] ECR I-987, para 42.

5.7 Econometrics and the 'Calculation' of Causation in EU Competition Law 139

economic harm can be presumed, as in the case of cartels,[221] this introduces a rebuttable presumption of harm, without ruling out the onus of the claimant to substantiate causation between the type of harm that is not immediate in its connection to the cartel. However, while proving causation is a fundamental step for the recognition of damages, the quantification is not subject to similarly strict requirements, as the judge can estimate uncertain damages.

In *Healthcare at Home*, the CAT used a counterfactual to determine causation in a margin squeeze case.[222] Genzyme Limited was a drug producer manufacturing Cerezyme, used for treating Gaucher disease. Between 1999 and 2001, Healthcare at Home Limited provided the drug to patients, thanks to an exclusive contract with Genzyme. At termination of the contract, Genzyme started an independent home care service to administer autonomously the drug to patients. From this moment on, other companies, such as Healthcare, had to purchase the Cerezyme at the 'NHS list price', which also included the home service costs. In 2003, the Office of Fair Trading (OFT) noted that Genzyme had abused its dominant position, imposing a margin squeeze on the upstream market for home care delivery.[223]

In a follow-on action initiated by *Healthcare at Home*, the CAT awarded damages, with an interim decision, based on the percentage discount that should have been applied in order to avoid margin squeeze.[224] In other words, the CAT's experts reckoned the pricing that would have ensured a reasonable profit margin to the defendant and, from that amount, obtained the percentage discount. The damages, therefore, were awarded to the claimant in form of loss of revenues.[225]

The use of economic counterfactuals in order to prove lost profits is also well described by the case 2 *Travel Group PLC* v *Cardiff City Transport*,[226] where the Tribunal adopted a 'but-for' approach in order to establish the cause in fact connecting the loss to the infringement.[227] Here the CAT compared the market condition with the situation of a hypothetical market in absence of the infringement. Through this counterfactual, the CAT observed that without the infringement, the claimant would have made further profits.

Similarly, the Commercial Court of Milan in the case *Brennercom*[228] assessed legal causation relying on the economic experts' report which construed the counterfactual. The counterfactual reasoning proceeded through a three-step assessment.

---

[221] See Article 17(2) Directive 2014/104/EU.
[222] *Healthcare at Home* v *Genzyme Ltd* [2006] CAT 29.
[223] Ibid.
[224] Ibid., 110 ff.
[225] Ibid., 148.
[226] 2 *Travel Group PLC (in liquidation)* v *Cardiff City Transport Services Ltd* [2012] CAT 19.
[227] Explicitly recalling also *Enron Coal Services Limited* v *English Welsh & Scottish Railway Limited* [2009] CAT 36 (at para 85(a)) and the assessment reported by *Colman J in Arkin* v *Borchard Lines Ltd* [2003] EWHC 687 (Comm), [2004] 2 CLC 242.
[228] Tribunale di Milano, *Brennercom Spa* v *Telecom Italia Spa*, 3.3.2014 no 14802/2011.

140 *Proof Rules of Causation*

Firstly, the experts studied the difference between the prices that the antitrust infringer, Telecom Italia (TI), provided to its internal divisions and the ones fixed for the same services (LLs) to competitors. Hence, secondly, they determined the raise in price of TI's services. Finally, they established the price effect on the claimant (Brennercom).

The experts used different theories and standard economic models for the creation of different counterfactual scenarios. There was indeed no evidence of the LLs prices and, therefore, of real differences of LLs prices over time and between the competitors. However, the experts presented different models reckoning the market price in a situation of oligopoly.[229] On the basis of the different models, the judge was able to determine causation as a probability of such price differentials to have caused an economic harm, observing that in absence of TI's infringement, Brennercom would have had more clients.[230] In connection to this case law, this section has maintained that while the assessment of causation is generally left to the evaluation of the judge, the evidence provided by economic experts has naturally gained a fundamental importance in gauging economic data submitted to the court.[231] Through econometrics, economists infer causal links between causes and effects using average quantitative data. However, these results should not be confused with causation in law which stands outside the realm of economic theory.[232] In competition law, it is very easy to confuse these two notions, reducing causation to a quantitative substantiation of causality.

---

[229] Based on the two theories of Martin Shubik and Richard Levitan, *Market Structure and Behavior* (Harvard University Press, 1980); and Nirvikar Singh and Xavier Vives, 'Price and Quantity Competition in a Differentiated Duopoly' [1984] *The RAND Journal of Economics*, 546–554.

[230] Tribunale di Milano, *Brennercom* (n 228) 9.

[231] Lianos (n 86) 206 ff.

[232] The Italian Supreme Court has noted in two recent cases that the insured party has the right to presume that the premium paid to the insurance company was higher than the market price due to the effect of the collusive behaviour of the defendant, in an amount corresponding to the increase in premiums as compared to the European average. The defendant may provide contrary evidence concerning both the existence of the causal link between the anticompetitive behaviour and the damage, and the amount of such damages. However, the court further stated that if that company has participated in the proceedings before the antitrust authority, the burden of proof cannot be limited to general considerations relating to the interpretation of economic data on the formation of premiums in the market of insurance policies, as already taken into account by the antitrust authority, but must provide precise indications of situations and behaviours specifically attaining the undertaking concerned and the insured subject, capable of demonstrating that the level of the premium has not been determined by participation in an the illegal conduct, but by other factors. Corte di Cassazione, Allianz v Tagliaferro, 26 May 2011, n 11610, in Giust. civ. Mass. 2011, 5, 808 (2011); Corte di Cassazione Sara Assicurazioni v GV, 30 May 2013, n 13667, not yet published.

6

Proving the Uncertain Causation

The previous chapter has presented the general proof rules of causation in competition damages actions. These standard rules burden the claimant with the proof of the essential elements of a tort, including causation. However, the claimant may find it very difficult if not impossible to prove causation, especially when information is limited or not accessible. As observed in Chapter 5, the standard proof rules place the risk for the proof of the claim and the risk of error due to evidential uncertainty on the claimant.[1] The rules allocating this risk are mainly the result of policy-based decisions aiming at distributing the risk fairly between the parties based on a moral statement.[2] However, on the basis of equally justifiable policy and moral choices, it is possible to create exceptions to this rule in two cases: (1) when the information is readily available to the other party and (2) when it is fair, according to the type of responsibility, to allocate the risk differently.

Uncertainty and the Burden of Proof

Scientific or economic uncertainty, scarce information, and informational asymmetries may render the claimant's burden of proof too onerous or even impossible to discharge. In such cases, the legal system poses questions related to the justice and fairness of the allocation of the burden of proof of causation and therefore the risk connected to it entirely on the claimant.

---

[1] In this sense, see also Lara Khoury, *Uncertain Causation in Medical Liability* (Hart, 2006) 38; Raymond N Emson, *Evidence* (Palgrave Macmillan, 2008) 419.

[2] Ariel Porat and Alex Stein, *Tort Liability under Uncertainty* (Oxford University Press, 2001) 17. They argue that there are two frameworks of analysis that characterize this doctrine of 'political morality': (1) fairness and (2) utility. While fairness explains the civil proof rules from the perspective of corrective justice, the utility framework takes the point of view of deterrence (ibid., 17).

142 *Proving the Uncertain Causation*

The law has sometimes answered by relaxing the standard of proof or by creating special rules reversing the burden of proof or the evidential burden on to the defendant.[3] Moreover, questions of fairness sometimes affect the allocation of the burden of proof. Causal uncertainty lays the basis for the creation of exceptions to the standard *onus probandi* with the aim of rendering the procedure fair.

It is possible to identify four types of departures from the general burden-of-proof rules.[4] Firstly, it is possible to reverse the burden of proof by obliging the defendant to provide contrary proof.[5] Secondly, the court may only shift the evidential burden of certain facts on the defendant when the claimant establishes a prima facie case.[6] Thirdly, the judge may be allowed to reduce the standard of proof to a level that makes it possible to demonstrate uncertain causation.[7] Fourthly, it may be possible to shift from an all-or-nothing approach to a system based on causal proportional liability.[8]

Competition law damages actions show a marked causal uncertainty due to a number of factors, including limited information – especially on the side of the claimant – and multiplicity of causal conditions typical of pure economic losses.[9] When this lack of evidence is the consequence of the limits of scientific knowledge about causal processes, little can be done without lowering the standard of proof required. Sometimes, instead, the evidence is available but not to the party that has to provide it. In this case, as this chapter explains, the legal system usually prefers to relax the burden of proof by creating rebuttable presumptions.

6.1 RELAXATION OF PROOF RULES

The recurrence of causal uncertainty in competition damages actions has created incentives to relax the evidential requirements, use rebuttable presumptions or relax the standards of proof for causation. This section analyzes how rebuttable presumptions and the shifting of the evidentiary burden operate in order to relax the burden of proof in competition damages actions. Section 6.4 examines instead the ways in which courts and legal systems relax the standards of proof to discharge the claim. Exceptional rules, departing from the general tort law rule whereby the claimant should offer full proof of the claim, may take different forms. Rules pertaining to the disclosure of evidence, whereby the defendant or other parties have to grant access

---

[3] See Section 6.1.
[4] For a thorough analysis of such departures in general tort law, see Sandy Steel, Proof of Causation in Tort Law (Cambridge University Press, 2015).
[5] Section 6.1.2.
[6] Section 6.1.
[7] Section 6.4.
[8] Chapter 4.
[9] Chapter 1.

6.1 *Relaxation of Proof Rules*

to evidentiary materials, also contribute to levelling the informational asymmetry that underlies the difficulties in proving causation.

When it is excessively difficult for the claimant to access and obtain information about the causation of the harm, the relaxation of the proof rules may be justified for at least two reasons. Firstly, when it is highly probable – also according to common sense – that a certain fact or set of facts usually brings about a specific outcome. A rule presuming this result – when the underlying facts are proven – is justified, as it is a probabilistic approximation coherent with the general laws justifying the basic proof rules, which are equally based on probabilities. Secondly, when information about causation is available or easily obtainable only to the defendant, a rebuttable presumption maximizes the efficiency of the proceedings. Rules allocating the risk of proving causation on the party that is better placed often accelerate the decision-making process and reduce the overall costs of the proceedings.[10] However, it is important to differentiate between causal inferences, presumptions, and inversions of the evidential burden, as they entail different outcomes for the proceedings.

6.1.1 *Causal Inferences*

Causal conclusions are inferential by definition[11] as they imply extrapolating information from generalizations and facts to draw conclusions about their effects. Inferences are therefore instruments of logical thinking and part of the proof of causation. As such, they can be of three types: deductive, inductive and abductive.[12] A deductive inference derives a conclusion from known facts or general assumptions that are universally true (i.e., a major premise).[13] For example, if one adopts as a general assumption that all cartels generate an economic harm, and it is known that the claimant has purchased goods from cartel members, then the claimant has been harmed by that cartel, unless a further exception or a proof to the contrary is submitted.

Inductive reasoning instead uses specific facts to infer general conclusions – for example, if it has been observed that the same type of exclusionary conduct in the past caused different harms to competitors of the infringer, and one concludes that the same harm has been caused to the claimant. Abductive reasoning involves a similar logic pattern, whereby – starting from an observation of facts – one reaches a conclusion that is the most probable. In other words, abductive reasoning accepts as

---

[10] For a study on presumptions, costs and efficiency of the antitrust proceedings, see Organisation for Economic Co-Operation and Development (OECD), 'Safe Harbours and Legal Presumptions in Competition Law, Background Note by the Secretariat' (2017) DAF/COMP (2017) 9.

[11] Steel (n 4) 66.

[12] As developed by Charles Sanders Peirce, see Terence Anderson, David Schum and William Twining, *Analysis of Evidence* (Cambridge University Press, 2005) 55.

[13] Ibid., 55–56.

true what is possible or plausibly true.[14] Both inductive and abductive reasoning accept the possibility of error in the inferential conclusion.

Inferences are generally used when all that is available is indirect evidence. Whereas direct evidence demonstrates the relevant fact and is therefore called 'inculpatory',[15] indirect evidence proves a fact which is the logical antecedent of the fact that needs to be proven. If there are no clear physical forces that can be observed, causation cannot be directly observed either.[16] For this reason, especially in claims for the infringement of competition law in which no observable physical forces intervene in the causation of the damage, causation will be often proven through logic inferences relying on indirect evidence. For the public enforcement of competition law, the ECJ has established that – according to the principle of effectiveness – 'objective and consistent' indicia are also indirect evidence of a fact[17] so that a prima facie evidence can be established when a 'set of indicia relied on … meets that requirement'.[18]

Inductive and abductive reasoning usually rely on a set of facts to infer a conclusion. Hence, access to as much evidence as possible is fundamental to prove causation. Especially for antitrust infringements affecting more than one country, this evidence may be sparse and difficult to reach for the claimant. Here, the Evidence Regulation,[19] as recalled by Recital (17) of the Damages Directive, may help the claimant to obtain the relevant information constituting evidence.[20] In addition to this, the parties will be able to obtain evidence also through alternative procedural tools since, the regulation 'does not restrict the options to take evidence situated in other Member States, but aims to increase those options by encouraging cooperation between the courts in that area … [I]n certain circumstances, it may be simpler, more effective and quicker for the court ordering such an investigation, to take such evidence without having recourse to the regulation'.[21]

A first type of causal inference relies on generalizations finding that a certain event causes another with a certain frequency.[22] Assume, for instance, that a judge has to determine whether a claimant would have purchased the cartelized products

---

[14] Ibid., 57.

[15] Fernando Castillo de la Torre and Eric Gippini Fournier, *Evidence, Proof and Judicial Review in EU Competition Law* (Edward Elgar Publishing, 2017) 4.007.

[16] Steel (n 4) 67.

[17] Case C-74/14 *Eturas and Others* ECLI:EU:C:2016:42 para 37.

[18] Case T-44/02 *Dresdner Bank AG and Others v Commission of the European Communities* ECR II-3567, para 63; Case T-110/07, *Siemens AG v Commission*, [2011] ECR II-477, para 47.

[19] Council Regulation (EC) No 1206/2001 of 28 May 2001 on cooperation between the courts of the member states in the taking of evidence in civil or commercial matters. OJ L 174, 27.6.2001.

[20] David Ashton, *Competition Damages Actions in the EU: Law and Practice*, 2nd edn (Edward Elgar Publishing, 2018) 95.

[21] Case C-332/11 *ProRail BV v Xpedys NV and Others* EU:C:2013:87, paras 44 and 45.

[22] HLA Hart and Tony Honoré, *Causation in the Law* (Oxford University Press, 1985) 16; Richard W Wright, 'Causation in Tort Law' [1985] *California Law Review* 1735, 1807; Steel (n 4) 68.

6.1 Relaxation of Proof Rules

if they were sold at market price. The production of an internal document showing that the company lamented the scarce availability of inputs of production (cartelized goods) would have probative value of the counterfactual scenario.

However, often the standard of proof demands demonstration of the process that causes the damage. In this second type of causal inference, the mere evidence of the occurrence of an event is insufficient. What the claimant has to prove is the causal mechanism that brings about the damage.[23] This means that the claimant has to explain how the antitrust infringement has generated the injury. But, the mechanics of market processes are often unpredictable and difficult to prove. For this reason, causal inferences in competition damages actions often consider generalizations based on associations observed through statistical experiments. For example, judges often recur to the before-and-after method, which is 'is based on the simple idea that once all other relevant supply and demand side factors are accounted for and to the extent that cartel prices differ in a statistically significant way from the prices prior to the implementation of the cartel agreement and the prices once the cartel ceased to operate, the difference could be attributed to the cartel'.[24] By comparing statistical data before and after the cartel implementation, the judge deduces the cartel effect on prices, in absence of other more likely causes.

6.1.2 Presumptions

In general, a presumption is an inference of facts (the presumed facts) from another set of facts (the primary facts) which has to be proven according to the standard of proof.[25] Hence, presumptions require the proof of a basic fact to arise. Some presumptions may regard specific facts of the case or the causal link between them (factual presumptions), without the law imposing on the parties or on the judge to consider them. By contrast, legal presumptions introduce a rebuttable or an irrebuttable inference between two facts, which – as a matter of law – directly follows the proof of a specific fact. Some studies on competition law enforcement, also classified presumptions, focusing on the their evidential burdens.[26] Hence, they

---

[23] Steel (n 4) 69.

[24] Ashton (n 20) 432.

[25] For a general introduction to presumption in the civil proceedings, see Emson (n 1) 456 ff; Richard Glover, *Murphy on Evidence* (Oxford University Press, 2013) 684 ff; Alex Stein, *Foundations of Evidence Law* (Oxford University Press, 2008); Julius Stone, 'Burden of Proof and the Judicial Process' [1944] *Law Quarterly Review* 262; Sir Richard Eggleston, *Evidence, Proof, and Probability* (Weidenfeld and Nicolson, 1983) 92; John Henry Wigmore, *A Students' Textbook of the Law of Evidence* (Foundation Press, 1935) 454; Simon Deakin, Angus Johnston and Basil Markesinis, *Markesinis and Deakin's Tort Law* (Oxford University Press, 2012) 234; Terence Anderson, David Schum and William Twining, *Analysis of Evidence* (Cambridge University Press, 2005); James Franklin, *The Science of Conjecture: Evidence and Probability before Pascal* (Taylor & Francis, 2002) 6.

[26] David Bailey, 'Presumptions in EU Competition Law' [2010] *European Competition Law Review* 20; Andriani Kalintiri, *Evidence Standards in EU Competition Enforcement: The EU*

146 *Proving the Uncertain Causation*

have been divided into provisional presumptions, evidential presumptions, persuasive presumptions and conclusive presumptions.[27]

Factual presumptions, or provisional presumptions, also called *praesumptiones hominis*, state a matter of fact but do not need to be rebutted, as they are left to the free evaluation of the judge.[28] These are presumptions based on circumstantial evidence of a fact that, according to common sense, usually causes a certain harm. They are often used to shift the evidentiary burden, asking the defendant to adduce evidence to the contrary. For example, in the *Fondiaria Sai Assicurazioni* case, the Italian Court of Cassation stated that the judge can infer a causal link between the anticompetitive conduct and the damage through presumptions based on the probability – also based on common knowledge – that a certain anticompetitive behaviour has specific effects at the consumer level.[29]

Legal presumptions are instead generally divided into two categories: rebuttable and conclusive.[30] Rebuttable presumptions (also known as *praesumptiones iuris tantum*) are instead divided in common law countries into evidential presumptions and persuasive presumptions,[31] while they are generally left as a unitary class in civil law jurisdictions.[32] These presumptions shift the burden of proving the existence of certain facts on the party which is assumed to have more information or, anyway, on the party that should bear the risk of proving the existence or the absence of certain facts.[33]

A conclusive presumption (*presumptio iuris et de jure*), instead, is a presumption of law that cannot be rebutted by evidence and must be taken as true whatever the evidence to the contrary.[34] For instance, the 'per se' rule applied in the United States is a substantive non-rebuttable presumption.[35] In EU competition law, neither

---

Approach (Hart, 2019) 193 ff; Cristina Volpin, 'The Ball Is in Your Court: Evidential Burden of Proof and the Proof-Proximity Principle in EU Competition Law' [2014] 51 *Common Market Law Review* 1159, 1159–1185.

[27] Bailey (n 26) 20 ff.

[28] Glover (n 25).

[29] *Court of Cassation, Fonsai v Nigriello*, 2 February 2007, n 2305, In 'Foro it', vol I, 2007, 1097, commentary by A Palmieri, *Cartello fra compagnie assicuratrici, aumento dei premi e prova del pregiudizio: Il disagevole cammino dell'azione risarcitoria per danno da illecito antitrust*, and R Pardolesi, *Il danno antitrust in cerca di disciplina (e di identità?)*; S Bastianon, Tutela risarcitoria antitrust, nesso causale e danni 'lungolatenti', in Danno e resp, 2007, 764 para 3.2.

[30] Julius Stone (n 25) 262; Eggleston (n 25) 92; Wigmore (n 25) 454; Deakin, Johnston and Markesinis (n 25) 234.

[31] Ian Dennis, *The Law of Evidence* (Sweet & Maxwell, 2013) 525.

[32] For a historical perspective on the evolution of these presumptions in civil law jurisdictions in comparison with common law jurisdictions, see Richard H Helmholz and W David H Sellar, 'Presumptions in Comparative Legal History' in Richard H Helmholz and W David H Sellar (eds), *The Law of Presumptions: Essays in Comparative Legal History*, vol 9 (Duncker & Humblot, 2009).

[33] On rebuttable presumptions as a risk-allocation mechanism, see Emson (n 1) 461.

[34] Ibid.

[35] David Bailey (n 26) 22.

6.2 Use of Causal Presumptions by EU Courts

national domestic legislation nor European law have established any such presumptions with regard to causation of damages to private subjects. Some scholars object that this is a not presumption but a substantive law formulated as a rule of evidence.[36]

Rather, EU competition law damages actions often utilize evidential presumptions, substantive presumptions and procedural presumptions to presume facts allowing one to facilitate the proof of causation. In competition law, substantive causal presumptions 'are invariably an expression of mainstream economic theory',[37] as they presume specific causation on the observation of general causation through economic theories. In competition law litigation, one can also find several procedural presumptions that can be divided into rebuttable and conclusive categories as well.[38]

6.2 USE OF CAUSAL PRESUMPTIONS BY EU COURTS

EU courts tend to discern the probative value of a fact judging on the body of evidence gathered for the case.[39] Logical inferences are often used in order to reconstruct the relevant circumstances[40] from the scarce evidence gleaned.

In the *T-Mobile* case, the ECJ responded to the question regarding the application of a presumption indicating the causal link between a concerted practice and the market conduct of the operators. The question regarded, in particular, the relevance of the presumption established in the cases *Commission v Anic Partecipazioni*[41] and *Hüls v Commission*,[42] 'according to which, subject to proof to the contrary, which it is for the economic operators concerned to produce, undertakings participating in concerting arrangements and remaining active on the market are presumed to take account of the information exchanged with their competitors when determining their conduct on that market, particularly when they concert together on a regular basis over a long period'.[43] The ECJ observed that the presumption used by the court in the mentioned decisions stems from the interpretation of Article 101 TFEU and therefore forms an integral part of community law.[44]

---

[36] Emson (n 1) 457; Glover (n 25) 686.

[37] David Bailey (n 26) 22.

[38] Ibid., 24 ff.

[39] Case T-44/02 *Dresdner Bank AG and Others* v *Commission of the European Communities* [2006] ECR II-3567, para 60–61.

[40] T-112/07 *Hitachi Ltd, Hitachi Europe Ltd and Japan AE Power Systems Corp.* v *European Commission* [2011] ECR II-03871.

[41] C-49/92 P *Commission v Anic Partecipazioni* [1999] ECR I-4125.

[42] C-199/92 P *Hüls v Commission* [1999] ECR I-4287.

[43] C-8/08 *T-Mobile* v *Raad van bestuur van de Nederlandse Mededingingsautoriteit* [2009] ECR I-04529, para 21.

[44] Ibid., para 52: 'In those circumstances, it must be held that the presumption of a causal connection stems from Article 81(1) EC, as interpreted by the Court, and it consequently forms an integral part of applicable Community law'.

148 *Proving the Uncertain Causation*

Consequently, the presumption has to be applied as it is, and there is no room for the national procedural laws to overcome its application. The principle of procedural autonomy of national judges has therefore been cracked also in the realm of competition law. Lianos observes that by permitting the Commission to operate by inferences, the courts eased the burden on the Commission; however, legal presumptions limit that discretion within the boundaries of a 'ready-made causal inference'.[45]

While the courts have dealt, even if for a limited extent, with the use logical inferences in order to form evidence out of a set of 'coincidences' and 'indicia' for finding an infringement of competition law,[46] no such guidance is provided in order to infer damages to private subjects. The Damages Directive makes extensive use of such causal presumptions to remedy to the informational asymmetry of parties.[47]

6.3 CAUSAL PRESUMPTIONS IN THE DAMAGES DIRECTIVE

Chapter 2 has observed the absence of a clear definition of causation in the Damages Directive. However, the same directive acknowledges the difficulty in proving causation, especially for certain types of claimants and has accordingly introduced a number of causal presumptions.

A first causal presumption concerns cartel harms. The Directive presumes that a cartel causes harm via price effect.[48] Recital (47) explains that this rule has the aim of remedying the information asymmetry between claimant and defendant and the difficulties in reckoning the amount of damages. This Recital argues that 'Depending on the facts of the case, cartels result in a rise in prices, or prevent a lowering of prices which would otherwise have occurred but for the cartel'.[49] This is

---

[45] Ioannis Lianos and Christos Genakos, 'Econometric Evidence in EU Competition Law: An Empirical and Theoretical Analysis' [2012] CLES Research Paper series 06/12 76, available at http://papers.ssrn.com/abstract=2184563, accessed 26 August 2014.

[46] Case T-112/07 *Hitachi Ltd, Hitachi Europe Ltd and Japan AE Power Systems Corp.* v *European Commission* [2011] ECR II-03871.

[47] See Chapter 7 for the presumptions used in passing-on actions.

[48] Article 17(2) Directive 2014/104/EU of the European Parliament and of the Council of 26 November 2014 on Certain Rules Governing Actions for Damages under National Law for Infringements of the Competition Law Provisions of the Member States and of the European Union, OJ L 349.

[49] Recital (47) establishes that

> To remedy the information asymmetry and some of the difficulties associated with quantifying harm in competition law cases, and to ensure the effectiveness of claims for damages, it is appropriate to presume that cartel infringements result in harm, in particular via an effect on prices. Depending on the facts of the case, cartels result in a rise in prices, or prevent a lowering of prices which would otherwise have occurred but for the cartel. This presumption should not cover the concrete amount of harm. Infringers should be allowed to rebut the presumption. It is appropriate to limit this rebuttable presumption to cartels, given their secret nature, which increases the information asymmetry and makes it more difficult for claimants to obtain the evidence necessary to prove the harm.

6.3 Causal Presumptions in the Damages Directive 149

a rebuttable presumption, although some authors pointed out that such inversion of the burden of proof brings an 'erosion' of the defendant's right of defence 'so that in this type of actions it seems that the defendant is prevented from proving the lack of "causal link" between the infringement and the alleged harm'.[50] This presumption[51] is based on a study commissioned by the EC finding out that 93 per cent of the cartels lead to an overcharge.[52] The Directive limits this rebuttable presumption to cartels, arguing that their 'secret nature' increases the information asymmetry and makes it more difficult for claimants to obtain the evidence necessary to prove the harm.[53] Although the damage is presumed, it can be argued that the claimant has to show at least a prima facie evidence of causation of harm when it is not possible to determine this connection on the basis of the *id quod plerumque accidit*.[54]

Secondly, the purchaser of a good, being it direct or indirect, can claim damages on the basis of the price overcharge. According to Article 12.2, 'Member States shall ... ensure that compensation for actual loss at any level of the supply chain does not exceed the overcharge harm suffered at that level' – meaning that the actual loss equals the overcharge, which in turn is defined as 'the difference between the price actually paid and the price that would otherwise have prevailed in the absence of an infringement of competition law'.[55] In this regard, Lianos argues that this is, in fact, a rebuttable presumption of the amount of the economic harm to equal the overcharge, as the actual loss could be lower.[56] If so, the defendant will have to rebut this presumption by proving the passing-on of at least part of this overcharge.[57]

Thirdly, the Directive relaxes the burden of proof for indirect purchasers using both provisional presumptions and rebuttable presumptions. These presumptions, as Chapter 7 argues, are based more on policy reasoning than on general economic theories of causation. In this case, the Directive mostly intends to tackle the informational asymmetries impairing the possibility of the indirect purchaser to prove causation. In that vein, this approach seems to pursue distributive justice and fairness-based concerns besides corrective justice objectives.

---

[50] Aldo Frignani, 'La Difesa Disarmata Nelle Cause Follow on per Danno Antitrust. La Cassazione in Guerra Con Se Stessa' [2015] Mercato Concorrenza Regole 429, 447.

[51] See Practical Guide on Quantifying Harm in Actions for Damages Based on Breaches of Article 101 or 102 of the Treaty on the Functioning of the European Union, SWD (2013) 205, available at http://ec.europa.eu/competition/antitrust/actionsdamages/quantification_guide_en.pdf, 44,

[52] See External Study Prepared for the Commission 'Quantifying Antitrust Damages' (2009) 88 ff, available at http://ec.europa.eu/competition/antitrust/actionsdamages/index.html.

[53] Recital (47).

[54] For instance, in case of cartel price fixing for the direct buyers of cartelized products.

[55] Article 2(20).

[56] Ioannis Lianos, 'Causal Uncertainty and Damages Claims for the Infringement of Competition Law in Europe' [2015] 34 *Yearbook of European Law* 170, 213–214.

[57] Ibid., 214. See also Chapter 6.

150   *Proving the Uncertain Causation*

Moreover, the Directive has also regulated the legal value of decisions of antitrust authorities in the civil proceedings. Article 9(1) establishes that when a final decision is taken by the national competition authority or by a review court, it constitutes a conclusive proof of the infringement in the following action for damages. When, instead, the decision comes from an antitrust authority of another member state, it is 'at least prima facie evidence that an infringement of competition law has occurred'.[58] These procedural rules have an important bearing on the assessment of causation. In cases of follow-on claims based on infringements of Article 101 TFEU, the clamant benefits from two rules facilitating the proof of causation. Firstly, the claimant does not need to prove the infringement of competition law and submit the NA's decision.[59] On the basis of this decision, moreover, the parties have to presume that a damage was caused to either direct or indirect purchasers.[60]

With these rules, the EU law allegedly intends to ensure effectiveness to the right to compensation for harm caused by an antitrust infringement. These rules tend not only to ease the burden of proof of the claimant but also to slightly reconcile the different approaches adopted by national systems of law.[61] However, the use of these presumptions can be misleading for claimants who might be tempted to skip the proof of causation, which is only indirectly involved in this process. The claimant has, in any case, the burden of proving that the presumed damage was caused to his or her business due to specific market operations connected to the infringer. For example, if an undertaking claims damages caused by a cartel that fixed higher prices, the claimant needs to submit evidences that the overcharge was applied to him or her. Similarly, if a firm that assumes to be injured by an abuse of dominant position, which effected a price squeeze, has to substantiate the specific damage consequence of the exclusionary abuse.

6.3.1 *The Presumption of Innocence and the Presumptions of Causation of Harm*

It is sometimes recalled in the literature that the law embodies a presumption of innocence that justifies the allocation of the burden of proof of causation of the harm on the claimant.[62] This presumption finds its legal basis in the civil procedures of most member states and in Article 6(2) of the Charter of Fundamental Human

---

[58] Article 9(2).

[59] Article 9.

[60] Article 17(2).

[61] For a comparative overview of the different approaches, see Joaquín Almunia and others, *Private Enforcement of Competition Law* (Lex Nova, 2011) 158 ff.

[62] Stein (n 25) 17; Glover (n 25) 11–12; Steel (n 4) 126. According to some, the presumption of innocence is not even technically a presumption. Paul Roberts and AAS Zuckerman, *Principles of Criminal Evidence* (Oxford University Press, 2003) 110; Colin Tapper, *Cross and Tapper on Evidence* (Butterworths, 1995) 120; RA Duff, *Strict Liability, Legal Presumptions, and the Presumption of Innocence* (Oxford University Press, 2005) 130.

6.4 Lowering the Standard of Proof for Causation

Rights of the EU. In the same vein, the presumption of innocence would contrast with the presumption of cartel damages and other equivalent presumptions, as the latter presume that the defendant committed a wrong before knowing whether that wrong was committed. The procedural norm stating the centrality of the presumption of innocence is a basic rule of fairness and a policy-based principle allocating the risk of error in the proceedings on the claimant.[63] This means that the law generally prefers false negatives to false positives, as it recognizes the asymmetry between these two errors as 'producers of harm'.[64] And this asymmetry has 'moral roots' whereby the law justifies their application.[65] However, a sound legal justification can be found also for the presumptions and relaxation rules that seem to contrast with this principle.

Firstly, a presumption of harm usually requires the substantiation of a set of facts that allows one to infer the existence of a causal link between the infringement of the law and a damage that needs to be quantified. Hence, the claimant still has to substantiate the facts triggering the application of the presumption. The proof of the underlying facts, moreover, demonstrates the high probability of the event to happen. The law presumes causation only when a set of facts is known to bring about a specific effect. This high probability of the two events to be causally connected, together with the difficulties in proving causation for the claimant, justify the rebuttable presumption as a fairness-based mechanism.

Secondly, some scholars maintain that many of the competition law presumptions are only evidential presumptions whereby the burden of providing evidence shifts from one party to the other, while the legal burden of proof remains on the claimant.[66] In this vein, it is often recounted that in competition law, as in any other civil proceedings, these rules generally allocate the burden of proof 'on the party to whom the evidence is available or who is better situated to furnish it easily and promptly'.[67]

6.4 LOWERING THE STANDARD OF PROOF FOR CAUSATION

Legal systems can facilitate the proof of causation not only by relieving the burden of proof from the claimant but also by lowering the standard of proof of causation that needs to be met. It has been observed that while factual uncertainty may allow for the use of common sense to infer causation, scientific uncertainty calls for a 'special approach to causation'.[68] This is because often common sense cannot replace scientific findings for reaching a motivated verdict.

---

[63] Stein (n 25) 17.
[64] Ibid., 18.
[65] Steel (n 11) 126.
[66] Volpin (n 26) 1177; Torre and Fournier (n 15) 2.005–2.011.
[67] Volpin (n 26) 1; Lianos (n 56).
[68] Khoury (n 1) 46 ff.

152   *Proving the Uncertain Causation*

The European courts have established two main standards that they apply to competition law procedures. A first, higher standard is used to determine the anticompetitive behaviour. In this case, the CJEU generally requires direct evidence.[69] A second, lighter standard of proof is instead adopted to determine the causative link between the anticompetitive conduct and its effects on the market.[70] In this case, the CJEU has repeatedly accepted circumstantial evidence and secondary facts to infer causation. In this connection, it has been observed that 'the substantive test for "effect on trade" is itself a relatively low standard formulated in lenient, probabilistic terms, by the case law'.[71] In this vein, the CJEU has stated that 'it must be possible to foresee with a sufficient degree of probability on the basis of a set of objective factors of law or fact that it may have an influence, direct or indirect, actual or potential, on the pattern of trade between Member States'.[72] However, assessing causation for a damage to trade between member states is not the same as determining causation in a claim for compensation of damages. The overall objective of these two types of litigation differs,[73] for while public enforcement of competition law tends to protect the public interest to a fair competition in the marketplace, private antitrust enforcement is said to pursue corrective justice. But, despite the importance that the corrective justice principle puts on causation as an essential element of responsibility, there are incentives to relax the standard of proof or create causal presumptions to the benefit of the claimant. Moreover, as observed in Chapter 5, the standard applied to damages claims may be the same or lower than that normally applied in competition cases by EU courts,[74] thereby providing a benchmark to national courts to establish their standards and their relaxation rules. The following section analyzes the relaxation rules adopted in this sense by national regulatory systems. Chapter 7 considers instead the relaxation rules created for indirect damages and secondary damages.

The following sections analyze the rules whereby EU and national laws relax evidentiary standards of causation.

6.4.1 *English Law*

Causal uncertainty allows departures from the general proof rules of causation. However, English law does not offer any specific conceptualization of these

---

[69] C-89/85 *Ahlström Osakeyhtiö and Others* v *Commission* [1994] ECR I-99, 71, 72, 126; Torre and Fournier (n 15) 2.046.

[70] Ibid., 2.047 ff.

[71] Ibid., 2.048.

[72] T-24/93 *Compagnie Maritime Belge Transports and Others* v *Commission*, para 201; Case C-250/92 DLG [1994] ECR 1-5641, para 54.

[73] As discussed in Chapter 3.4.

[74] Torre and Fournier (n 15) 2.112, referring to two pronouncements of the ECHR in *Ringvold* v *Norway*, no. 34964/97, ECHR 2003-II, § 38, and *Lundkvist* v *Sweden* (dec.), no. 48518/99, ECHR 2003-XI.

6.4 Lowering the Standard of Proof for Causation

exceptional proof rules.[75] In general, English common law has created exceptions to the general proof rules of causation in case of defendant indeterminacy and scientific uncertainty.

Causation can be inferred on the basis of common sense when causal uncertainty would generate an unfair outcome. According to general evidence law, when the claimant successfully establishes a prima facie claim with regard to each essential element of the action,[76] including causation, the judge has the power (though not the obligation) to declare that the claimant has discharged the evidential burden.[77] In *Jayasena v R*, Lord Devlin argued that 'such evidence as, if believed and left uncontradicted and unexplained, could be accepted by the jury as proof'.[78] Hence, if the defendant does not offer contrary evidence, the fact claimed will be successfully proven.

In case of scientific uncertainty, English common law has created causal presumptions subject to the proof that the defendant has 'materially contributed' to the injury.[79] In *Holtby v Brigham & Cowan (Hull) Ltd.* [2000],[80] the court held that the defendants are liable for the whole or a part of the damage if it is proven on the balance of probability that they materially contributed to the injury. In evaluating the evidence, and in absence of scientific certainty, the judge has to determine the causal contributions using common sense.[81] In a subsequent case,[82] however, the court of appeal maintained that when scientific knowledge fails to explain whether one of the cumulative causes is a but-for condition of the harm, it is enough for the claimant to prove that the contribution was sufficiently material.[83]

In competition damages actions, the UK regulation on competition law claims and damages transposing the Damages Directive presumes that cartels cause harm.[84] This presumption has been at the centre of a long debate that brought to its rejection in the consultation for the Consumer Rights Bill because it was

---

[75] Steel (n 4) 220.

[76] *Jayasena v R* [1970] AC 618, 623

[77] Glover (n 25) 74.

[78] [1970] AC 618, 624.

[79] SH Bailey, 'Causation in Negligence. What Is a Material Contribution?' [2010] 30 *Legal Studies* 167. Other presumptions apply for cases of mesothelioma; see Khoury (n 1) 158; Steel (n 4) 231.

[80] 3 All ER 421.

[81] Ibid., 429.

[82] *Bailey v Ministry of Defence* [2008] EWCA Civ 883.

[83] Ibid., 1068. Steel is critical of this decision, observing that 'in Bailey there is uncertainty as to whether the injury may have been overdetermined entirely by non-tortious conditions. Since a burden of proof rule determines which party succeeds where the facts are impossible to establish, the effect of Bailey is to reverse the burden of proof on the issue of whether the injury would have happened anyway'. Steel (n 4) 246.

[84] Section 13, establishing that 'For the purposes of competition proceedings, it is to be presumed, unless the contrary is proved, that a cartel causes loss or damage'.

deemed to contrast with the general principles of allocation of the burden of proof.[85] Another doubt harboured during the consultation was that this presumption might have lead to the creation of additional hurdles in proving causation in case of multiple claims by claimants from different levels of the supply chain.[86] In cases of defendant indeterminacy, which is when the claimant cannot prove according to the requisite legal standard which of the several wrongful defendants caused the damage, English courts have sometimes lowered the standard of proof.[87]

In such cases of multiple defendants in which the claimant is able to prove the wrongdoing and the harm but is unable to prove who among the defendants caused the injury, English law establishes that if the wrongdoing has been proven on the balance of probabilities, the co-infringers are jointly liable for the whole harm.[88] As already observed, this is also a policy-based rule preferring to do justice to the victim of an injury (the claimant), as the possibility of injustice would be directed toward a defendant that has already been shown to have infringed the law.

Moreover, English courts have adopted a lower standard of proof for causation under special circumstances. The creation of a higher risk of causing a damage has been used to lower the evidential standard to prove causation.[89] The creation of the higher risk was deemed as enough to morally and legally blame the defendant, even when causation was not proven on the balance of probability but according to a lower standard. Similar reduction of proof standard was granted in cases concerning torts that deprive claimants of evidence of causation.[90]

Finally, English common law generally disallows a wrongful defendant to rely on the wrongful behaviour of another subject when they are both but-for factors of the harm. For example, assume that an undertaking took part to an anticompetitive agreement. But before doing that, they consulted their lawyers who failed to warn them about the illegality of their behaviour. Here, English common law argues that

---

[85] Florian Wagner-von Papp, 'Implementation of the Damages Directive in England & Wales' [2015] 2 *Concurrences* 29.

[86] Ibid.

[87] *Fairchild v Glenhaven Funeral Services Ltd.* [2003] 1 AC 32.

[88] Section 38(2) of the Competition Act 1998 and Other Enactments (Amendment) Regulations 2017 establishes, in relation to the contribution of each co-infringer, that 'The amount of contribution that one person liable in respect of the loss or damage may recover from another must be determined in the light of their relative responsibility for the whole of the loss or damage caused by the infringement'.

[89] Cf *Vaile v Havering LBC* [2011] EWCA Civ 246.

[90] *Roadrunner Properties Ltd v Dean* [2003] EWCA Civ 1816.

6.4 Lowering the Standard of Proof for Causation

the undertaking is prevented from using the negligent conduct of their lawyers as a shield to avoid liability.[91]

6.4.2 German Law

Under § 292 ZPO, rebuttable presumptions are allowed if the law assumes the existence of certain facts.[92] Competition law damages actions benefit from a sector specific regulation, which has been recently updated[93] with the introduction of Section 33 of the Ninth Amendment, which transposes the Directive 104/2014. In line with the Damages Directive, this law introduces a presumption of cartel harm.[94] This presumption is not new to the German competition law, as there was already established a prima facie evidence of causation of damages in cartel cases.[95] However, to rebut this presumption, 'the defendant only needed to show that the circumstances of the case were considerably different from a normal cartel case so that damages to claimants could not be seen as the normal and typical consequence of the defendant's behaviour'.[96] On the contrary, according to § 33a (2), the defendant has to prove the absence of any harm or the lack of a causative link. The standard of the contrary proof is set by §287 ZPO. According to this norm, the judge has to decide according to the lighter standard analyzed in Chapter 5 and has the power to order the parties the submission of new evidence, if needed.[97] The

---

[91] This is in line with the ECJ's decision in Case C-681/11 *Bundeswettbewerbsbehörde, Bundes-kartellanwalt* v *Schenker & Co. and Others* ECLI:EU:C:2013:404. Steel – in this vein – observes that 'The extended principle is that each defendant who has wrongfully risked injury to the claimant is precluded from pointing to the wrongful conduct of another defendant, where, if that same argument were open to the other defendant, the victim of an injury which would not have occurred but-for wrongful conduct, would have no legal entitlement to compensation in relation to that injury'. Steel (n 4) 191.

[92] See Bacher in Vorwerk and Wolf (eds), Beck'scher Online-Kommentar zur ZPO, 15. Ed., 2015, § 292 Rz. 1

[93] For an overview on the impact on the general rules of causation, see supra Chapter 2.

[94] § 33a (2) states that 'It shall be rebuttably presumed that a cartel results in harm'.

[95] See BGH, 28/6/2005, KRB 2/05, NJW 2006, 163, 164 et seq. – Berliner Transportbeton I; BGH, 19/6/2007, KRB 12/07, NJW 2007, 3792, 3794, para 18 – SD-Papier.

[96] Christian Kersting, 'Transposition of the Antitrust Damages Directive into German Law' in Barry Rodger, Miguel Sousa Ferro and Francisco Marcos (eds), *The EU Antitrust Damages Directive* (Oxford University Press, 2018) 10, available at SSRN: https://ssrn.com/abstract=2998586.

[97] §287 ZPO recites, 'Should the issue of whether or not damages have occurred, and the amount of the damage or of the equivalent in money to be reimbursed, be in dispute among the parties, the court shall rule on this issue at its discretion and conviction, based on its evaluation of all circumstances. The court may decide at its discretion whether or not – and if so, in which scope – any taking of evidence should be ordered as applied for, or whether or not any experts should be involved to prepare a report. The court may examine the party tendering evidence on the damage or the equivalent in money thereof; the stipulations of section 452 (1), first sentence, subsections (2) to (4) shall apply mutatis mutandis'. English translation available at www.gesetze-im-internet.de/englisch_zpo/englisch_zpo.html.

156 *Proving the Uncertain Causation*

judge therefore has ample discretionary power to modify the evidential burden of the parties in order to reach the intime conviction proof standard to establish causation. However, this assumption only concerns the causation of a damage, not its amount.[98] It follows that the claimant has to prove the full amount of the economic damage. Since, under §287 ZPO, the judge is not allowed to estimate the damages, the failure to prove the extent of the loss would jeopardize the damages action. Especially in those antitrust cases in which there is not enough information to establish a 'usual course of events', the proof of the extent of the loss through counterfactuals can be particularly thorny. However, recently, the Federal Court of Justice[99] admonished that when the proof of the counterfactual scenario virtually impedes discharging the burden of proving the extent of the loss, the legal system should lower the evidential standard[100] and allow the estimation of a minimum damage.[101] This decision was taken before the entry into force of the new law transposing the Damages Directive. Thus, it has to be seen how German courts will use it in the future. To a certain extent, however, it has been observed that dismissing a case for a lack of proof of the amount of damages would negate the application of the presumption of damages and infringe the principle of effectiveness of EU law.[102]

In 2006, the Bundeskartellamt fined the German lotteries for hindering local commercial lottery agents from selling lottery tickets through local retailers, dividing the market among themselves and allocating the stakes to the *land* of residence of the lottery through a complex information mechanism.[103] The plaintiff, a commercial lottery agent, sued the lottery company of North Rhine-Westphalia for loss of profits in the period 2006–2008, as the lottery companies refused to cooperate on the basis of their anticompetitive conduct, which continued after the Bundeskartellamt decision.[104] The Federal Court observed that the antitrust authority's decision had a

---

[98] This approach is in line with Recital (47) of the Damages Directive, whereby the presumption of cartel harm 'should not cover the concrete amount of harm. Infringers should be allowed to rebut the presumption. It is appropriate to limit this rebuttable presumption to cartels, given their secret nature, which increases the information asymmetry and makes it more difficult for claimants to obtain the evidence necessary to prove the harm'.

[99] BGH, 12/7/2016, KZR 25/14, NZKart 2016, Lottoblock II.

[100] See BGH, judgment of 6 July 1993 – VI ZR 228/92, NJW 1993, 2673.

[101] BGH, 12/7/2016, KZR 25/14, NZKart 2016, Lottoblock II, para 81, cf with cf BGH, judgment of 17 June 1998 – XII ZR 206/95, WM 1998, 1787.

[102] Kersting (n 96) 10.

[103] In particular, the Bundeskartellamt sanctioned a resolution of the Committee of the German lottery (DLTB) whereby it was decided that 'The Legal Affairs Committee calls on the companies of the German Lotto and Totoblock to refuse to accept any revenue that has been generated through distribution of commercial goods at local retailers, which in its opinion is unlawful' (translation of the author). Bundeskartellamt, B10–148/05.

[104] *Lottoblock II*, para 15, stating that the continuation is assumed as the defendant did not refute the claimant's allegation.

6.4 Lowering the Standard of Proof for Causation

binding effect only with regard to the facts that it reported until 2005. Although the defendant terminated the contract with the claimant in 2006, the Federal Court established that the presumption of participation to the concerted practice[105] could be reasonably inferred from the fact that the conditions remained the same. In accordance with the ECJ's decision in Eturas,[106] the Federal Court therefore established that the presumption of causal connection between a concertation and the market conduct of the undertakings participating in the concerted practice was justified in light of the principle of effectiveness of EU law, whereby the law of procedure should not render excessively difficult or impossible the implementation of EU laws, including the right of victim of antitrust damages to claim for compensation.

However, the assessment of the existence of the damage and of its extent should not prescind from the finding of causation. In this vein, the Federal Court also observed that while §287 ZPO applies to determine 'whether a damage exists and the extent of the damage or of a compensable interest', §286 ZPO finds application in assessing causation.[107] In other words, to establish causation, the trier of fact needed to assess whether but for the antitrust violation cooperation between the applicant and the lottery companies would have taken place and whether the claimant would have lost profits. Although the collaboration with the claimant was deemed by the Federal Court as a commercially reasonable behaviour, due to the commercial and economic advantages that would have produced, the court retained that the plausibility of the sales and profit expectations derived from the applicant's business concept, which gave the lottery companies economic incentives to cooperate with the plaintiff, was not sufficient.[108] In the assessment of causation for loss of profits, the decisive factor for the German judge was whether, on the basis of the market circumstances, it was to be expected after the ordinary course of events that the defendant or other lottery companies would have entered into brokerage agreements with the applicant and paid commissions to them if the anticompetitive conduct had not taken place.[109]

In other general tort law cases, German courts have reduced the standard of proof when the claimant has provided proof of negligence and of increased risk, if evidence over causation is not available due to a defendant's breach of duty to maintain evidence.[110]

---

[105] As established in Case C_74/14 Eturas and Others ECLI:EU:C:2016:42, 144 and C-8/08 T-Mobile v Raad van bestuur van de Nederlandse Mededingingsautoriteit [2009] ECR I-4529.
[106] Ibid.
[107] Lottoblock II, para 52.
[108] Ibid., para 61.
[109] Ibid., para 82.
[110] See Steel (n 4) 209 ff.

158   *Proving the Uncertain Causation*

6.4.3 *French law*

French tort law recognizes both factual presumptions (*présomptions du fait de l'homme*) and legal presumptions (*présomptions légales*). According to Article 1353 of the Code Civile, the judge can infer the existence of certain facts (the presumed facts), if the primary facts are 'serious, precise and convergent' (*graves, précises et concordantes*).[111] Legal presumptions can be found in the law, as in the case of law transposing the Damages Directive. Some others, instead, are the result of legal interpretation of the Court of Cassation, which – thanks to its authoritative powers – has established that under certain circumstances a set of primary facts infer the certain presumed facts with high probability.[112] In competition law, the Court of Appeal of Paris[113] established that the claimant had to prove that an anticompetitive agreement restricting passive sales caused economic harm, but that in absence of clear evidence about the damage, the court can presume cartel harm and order an expert testimony to quantify the damage. In the same case, the Commercial Division of the Court of Cassation dismissed a plea alleging that the trial judges did not characterize 'the causal link between the damage alleged and the facts imputed to each of the entities'. The court introduced a presumption of damage caused by cartel, observing that 'the anticompetitive practices denounced by the company [claimant] ... necessarily caused a commercial disturbance', on the ground that the anticompetitive agreement created a difficult commercial situation for the claimant who had to bear extra costs to purchase.[114]

The 2017 Ordonnance transposing the Damages Directive has been clear and far-reaching in establishing a presumption of harm. According to Article L 481-7 of the French Code of Commerce (FCC), victims of cartel infringements benefit from a rebuttable presumption of harm. The rule, transposing Article 17(2) of the Damages Directive, states that there is a presumption of harm caused by cartels, unless the claimant provides evidence to the contrary.[115]

---

[111] See also Steel (n 4) 262.
[112] Ibid., 261. P Jourdain, 'Imputablité d'une contamination virale à une transfusion sanguine: la preuve par exclusion du lien de causalité érigée en présomption du droit' [2001] Revue trimestrielle de droit civil 889; G. Julia, 'La réception juridique de l'incertitude médicale' [2009] 2009 Médecine & Droit 131, 132.
[113] Paris Court of Appeal, *JCB Ltd* v *Central Parts*, 26 June 2013, no 1204441.
[114] Cour de Cassation, *JCB Services et al.* v *Central Parks*, 6 October 2015, no 13-24.854.
[115] Article L 481-7 FCC establishes that 'Il est présumé jusqu'à preuve contraire qu'une entente entre concurrents cause un préjudice'.

6.4.4 *Italian Law*

The Italian law of evidence has developed a number of mechanisms to cope with the proof of uncertain causation. While Article 2697 of the Civil Code is unequivocal in putting the onus on the claimant, it is possible to shift the evidential burden on the defendant or to reverse the burden of proof under special circumstances.

According to the principle of proof proximity, the evidential burden encumbers the party for whom it is easier to find or offer evidence to the court.[116] It is generally submitted that this principle has constitutional nature, as the right to a fair process, enshrined in Articles 24 and 111 of the Italian Constitution, prohibits an interpretation of the law that make it impossible or too difficult to exercise a procedural right.[117] Once the claimant has offered a prima facie evidence of causation, the judge can shift the evidential burden on the defendant. This is even truer, according to the jurisprudence, when the lack of information of causal processes is due to the wrongdoing of the defendant.[118]

In the case *Fondiaria Sai*,[119] the Corte di Cassazione stated that – in follow-on actions – the claimant discharges the burden of proof with the production of the sanctioning measure of the antitrust authority and of the insurance policy. In fact, the Italian judge established that the decision of the Italian antitrust authority is an evidence of the anticompetitive conduct. Furthermore, it considered the 'abstract suitability' of the anticompetitive conduct to cause damage to consumers, which allowed one to presume, without violation of the principle *praesumptum de praesumpto non admittitur* (a presumption of a presumption is not admitted), that the anticompetitive effect had caused an economic harm to the customers of the insurance companies concerned by the decision. Since the claimant was part of this group, the judge could presume the causation of the damage, while the defendant had the burden, under the principle of proof proximity,[120] to offer contrary evidence showing that, according to the relevant standard of proof, the 'interruption of the causal link between the antitrust offense and the damage suffered both by the consumers and by the individual'.[121] Since the claimant was part of a class of consumers that was damaged by an antitrust infringement and was able to submit evidence of it, the judge presumed causation of the damage, therefore shifting the burden of proof to the defendant. The Court of Cassation also considered that the proof proximity principle

---

[116] Chiara Besso, 'La Vicinanza Della Prova' [2015] 70 *Rivista di diritto processuale* 1383, 1383; Michele Taruffo, 'La Valutazione Delle Prove' [2012] La prova nel processo civile 207, 255.
[117] Corte Cost. 21 aprile 2000 n 114; and Corte di Cassazione, sez. un., No 141/2006.
[118] See Corte di Cassazione No 10060/2010.
[119] Corte di Cassazione, *Fonsai v Nigriello* (n 29).
[120] Corte di Cassazione, civil section, No. 11904/2014 in Foro it., 2014, I, 1729 ss commented by Pardolesi, and Resp. civ. e prev., 2015, 129, commentary by Di Peio, 1741.
[121] Ibid.

would, anyway, justify the inversion of the evidential burden, given the fact that the defendant is better placed to discharge the *onus probandi*.

A later decision of the Italian Court of Cassation[122] has then clarified the extent and requirements of the evidence to the contrary. Firstly, the court established that a previous decision of the ICA finding an infringement of competition law as a privileged proof in relation to the existence of the established behaviour and the position held on the market and its possible abuse.[123] However, the court also observed that this was a rebuttable presumption, and, therefore, the defendant had the right to offer evidence to the contrary. But, the court maintained, the defendant's proof – here again an insurance company – cannot be limited to the production of circumstantial evidence of lack of information about causation. The defendant tried to discharge the evidential burden by submitting the opinion of the ISVAP (Italian authority for the supervision of the insurance sector), which documented that, on average, car insurance companies were registering heavy losses. The Court of Cassation, by contrast, ruled that an inference of specific causation from general statistical evidence was not justified – specifically in this case because the defendant could provide direct information about its financial performance and because the higher premium charged resulted from this financial situation and not from the anticompetitive conduct.[124] While, indeed, the defendant retained that the claimant had the burden of proving such causal circumstances, by contrast, the Court of Cassation established that the instauration of a rebuttable presumption of harm implies that the defendant has to prove the exculpatory elements of his or her conduct. This approach of the Court of Cassation is also consistent with the principle of proof proximity generally followed by Italian courts, as it burdened the insurance companies to provide evidence that was mostly, if not only, in their possession.

6.5 THE MORAL JUSTIFICATION OF THE STANDARDS OF PROOF FOR CAUSATION

Although Article 23(2)(a) of Regulation 1/2003 states that competition law violations 'shall not be of a criminal law nature', EU competition law has acquired a quasi-criminal structure determined by the extent and function of administrative fines.[125] Moreover, some national competition law regimes have criminalized specific

---

[122] Corte di Cassazione, 22 September 2011 n 19262.
[123] Ibid.
[124] Ibid.
[125] Wouter PJ Wils, 'Is Criminalization of EU Competition Law the Answer' (2005) 28 *World Competition* 117; Peter Whelan, 'Competition Law and Criminal Justice' [2018] in Galloway (ed.), *The Intersections of Antitrust* (Oxford University Press, in press); Peter Whelan, 'A Principled Argument for Personal Criminal Sanctions as Punishment under EC Cartel Law' [2007] 4 *Competition Law Review* 7.

6.5 The Moral Justification of the Standards of Proof for Causation 161

infringements of competition law, clarifying the nature of this legal instrument in specific cases.[126] However, competition law damages actions have tortious nature, and, since they have no legal bearing on the criminal decision (depending on the laws of procedure of the forum the facts of the case may be accepted in the criminal procedure as evidence), the proof standards are those established for civil liability, with the adaptations examined throughout this book.

The analysis of case law shows an aspect of the assessment of the standard of persuasion of the judge with relation to causation partly different from the theoretical background of the different systems that is usually acknowledged. Judges, both in civil law and common law jurisdictions, often tend to assess the causal link in cases of uncertainty relying on the persuasiveness of the evidence rather than on the general probability of the outcome. As seen, in all jurisdictions examined, the more the causal uncertainty, the more judges rely on common sense to establish causation. Hart and Honoré pointed out that common law courts 'often insist that the causal questions which they have to face must be determined on common-sense principles'.[127] However, they note that common sense is a concept that can be technically delineated for its judicial use, as it does not depend on a mere impression or intuition of the judge.[128] As Chapter 1 explained, common sense includes prescriptive and descriptive knowledge subject to simultaneous interpretation.[129] While Chapter 4 examined the civil law standards based on the principle of the intime conviction of the judge, observing that the decision is not funded on ethos alone but on a compound evaluation of prescriptive and normal value of the norm. Common sense, in this vein, also determines the use of prima facie evidence and inferences. Common sense is often used by the European courts to justify inferential reasoning and shift the evidential burden from one party to the other.[130] As Allen and Stein find in their research, 'the factfinders decide cases predominantly by applying the relative plausibility criterion guided by inference to the best explanation, rather than by using mathematical probability'.[131]

The claims quashed for lack of proof of causation, such as in the English *Enron* and Italian *Brennercom* cases, demonstrate that the attention of the judge is focused on the value of the proof submitted as able, in the specific case, to yield the supposed effect. In this context, causal generalizations, such as that in the x per

---

[126] Such as the UK and Germany.
[127] Hart and Honoré (n 22) 108.
[128] Ibid.
[129] Adam Bear and Joshua Knobe, 'Normality: Part Descriptive, Part Prescriptive' [2017] 167 *Cognition* 25, 25–26; Christopher Hitchcock and Joshua Knobe, 'Cause and Norm' (2009) 106 *The Journal of Philosophy* 587, 598; Andrew Summers, 'Common-Sense Causation in the Law' [2018] 38 *Oxford Journal of Legal Studies* 793, 811.
[130] Mark Brealey, 'The Burden of Proof before the European Court' [1985] *European Law Review* 254.
[131] Ronald J Allen and Alex Stein, 'Evidence, Probability, and the Burden of Proof' [2013] 55 *Arizona Law Review* 557, 560.

cent of cases a cartel causes a damage via price effect to customers, certainly play a fundamental role in determining the judge's persuasion, but they are only an element of the proof. This evaluation is influenced by the judge's perception of 'normality'[132] and by his or her intuition of standard patterns drawn by experience and common sense.

For this reason, using class-based probabilities in order to build presumptions that revert the burden of proof can be a useful solution to offset a possible imbalance in the competition between the opposite explanations of the facts and the issues at stake. However, to accept class-based probabilities as proof of a causal link would be not only a logical mistake but also an empirical one.

Finally, the analysis of case law shows that, in all jurisdictions, the judge's persuasion is shaped by two competing narratives, the ones brought by the parties into the proceeding. Claimant, defendant and other intervening subjects, such as expert witnesses, present a narrative construction of reality on which the decision of the judge is based.[133] The level of persuasion of the judge is indeed determined by the evidences submitted and by the interpretation of their value. That applies in particular to the proof of causation, which – as already noted – is not a fact and therefore cannot be simply submitted as – for instance – a documentary evidence but needs to be 'explained'. This approach to the evaluation of the proof recalls the application of those theories[134] based on the 'comparative plausibility of the parties' explanations offered at trial'.[135] Allen and Leiter believe that the fact-finder, in civil cases, identifies the most plausible of the competing explanations rather than merely applying pre-confectioned probabilities.[136] The relative plausibility theory was formulated by Allen,[137] who opposed the idea of absolute probability benchmarks of the burden of proof.[138] Allen therefore posited that the trier of fact generally deduces facts and connections not necessarily on the basis of objective general standards,

---

[132] Anne-Lise Sibony, *Le juge et le raisonnement économique en droit de la concurrence* (LGDJ, 2008) 746.

[133] Jerome Bruner, 'The Narrative Construction of Reality', *Critical Inquiry*, 1991, 1–21; Joshua A. Newberg, 'The Narrative Construction of Antitrust', [2002] *Southern California Interdisciplinary Law Journal* 12, 181.

[134] Hock Lai Ho, *A Philosophy of Evidence Law: Justice in the Search for Truth* (Oxford University Press, 2008) 154.

[135] Ronald J Allen and Brian Leiter, 'Naturalized Epistemology and the Law of Evidence' [2001] *Virginia Law Review*, 1527.

[136] Ibid., 1528.

[137] Ronald J Allen, 'A Reconceptualization of Civil Trials' [1986] 66 *Boston University Law Review* 401; Ronald J Allen, 'The Nature of Juridicial Proof' [1991] 13 *Cardazo Law Review* 373; Ronald J Allen, 'Factual Ambiguity and a Theory of Evidence' [1993] 88 *Northwestern University Law Review* 604; Ronald J Allen and Brian Leiter, 'Naturalized Epistemology and the Law of Evidence' [2001] *Virginia Law Review* 1491.

[138] For a general contextualization and analysis of the relative plausibility theory, see Ho (n 134) 155 ff. Louis Kaplow, 'Burden of Proof,' [2011] 121 *Yale Law Journal*, 738; Edward K. Cheng, 'Reconceptualizing the Burden of Proof' [2012] 122 *Yale Law Journal* 1254.

6.5 The Moral Justification of the Standards of Proof for Causation

such as the preponderance-of-the-evidence rule, but relatively to the explanations provided by the parties.[139] This narrative-based approach would be coherent with the application of the proof – proximity principle, whereby the trier of fact shifts the evidential burden any time the narrative unfolds to the advantage of one of the parties. At the same time, the relative-plausibility theory entails the phasing-out of factual inferences that are equally reasonable to the one submitted by the claimant. As Ho observes, this is not new to civil procedures.[140] For instance, in *Sweeney* v *Coote*,[141] the House of Lords had early established the principle whereby while causation can be established by way of inference. By the same token, this inference requires the absence of any other inference which can be drawn from the same facts.[142]

Causal uncertainty creates therefore incentives to relax proof rules, when the judge is persuaded by the plausibility of a narration. Here, the judge can use a number of procedural tools, including presumptions and inferences, to facilitate the proof of causation and render a fair judgement.

---

[139] In the end, what indeed is asked to the decision maker is not to establish the absolute truth but, rather, to seek the 'truth of the decision'.

[140] Ho (n 134) 157.

[141] [1907] UKHL 1004, 44 SLR 1004.

[142] Ibid., 1005.

7

Causation in Indirect and Secondary Antitrust Damages

A competition law infringement is capable of damaging different subjects at the same time – virtually all the market players that are directly or even indirectly connected with the business of the competition law infringer.[1] Economic activities are indeed structured on value chains,[2] which are interconnected networks of contracts and hierarchies operating in a market. Here, the action or decision of a market player may impact many of the other market participants –both their future strategies and their actual assets. For instance, the abuse of a dominant position causing the foreclosure of a competitor may equally impact the business partners of that competitor, its employees and the consumers of both markets. We will call 'indirect economic losses' all those damages that are a consequence of an infliction of damage upon a third party. When the harm is inflicted upon a third person which, in turn, causes harm to the claimant, we will instead refer to it as 'secondary harms'. For instance, umbrella effects do not cause damages to the third party that transfers the harm on the claimant and are, therefore, indirect losses. On the other hand, in the passing-on situation, the third party (the direct purchaser) is the first victim of the harm which passes on to the claimant.

A harm caused by an antitrust infringement is a pure economic loss, recoverable on the basis of a statutorily protected interest and of a subjective right, under EU law. In addition to this, indirect damages include the action of a third party, which intervenes without 'breaking the causal chain'[3] – for instance, passing on a price

---

[1] Green Paper – Damages Actions for Breach of the EC Antitrust Rules SEC (2005) 1732 COM/2005, 672 2005 678; Laura Castelli, 'La Causalità Giuridica Nel Campo Degli Illeciti Anticoncorrenziali' (2013) 18 *Danno e responsabilità* 1049, 1050.

[2] Michael E Porter, *Competitive Advantage: Creating and Sustaining Superior Performance* (Free Press, 1985) 36 ff.

[3] That is to introduce an independent and sufficient cause of the damage.

Causation in Indirect and Secondary Antitrust Damages 165

overcharge or adapting selling prices to the 'price umbrella'. Pure economic losses have historically generated contrasting views about their recoverability.[4]

Since the decisions *Courage*[5] and *Manfredi*,[6] 'any individual can claim compensation for the harm suffered where there is a causal relationship between that harm and an agreement or practice prohibited'.[7] However, it is uncertain how to determine those 'individuals' whose harm is causally connected to the antitrust infringement, what is the harm subject to compensation and how the claimants can fulfil their burden of proof, especially in relation to causation. The aim of this chapter is to present the vast array of potential indirect damages that an antitrust infringement may cause, with a particular focus on indirect purchasers and umbrella buyers. In each of these cases, as we will see, the key aspect is the one of causation or, rather, resolving the problem of causal uncertainty due to the remoteness of the damage. Moreover, this chapter analyzes the substantive and procedural hurdles that indirectly damaged parties need to overcome in order to substantiate their claim and prove the causal nexus. As it will be shown, despite the efforts of the EU judges and legislation, the actions for damages still heavily rely on domestic principles of procedure and evidence, especially for the proof of causation.

Anticompetitive agreements and abuses of dominance bring about different types of damages to a potentially vast array of subjects. In particular, exploitative abuses and cartels may cause damages to (1) direct purchasers of the goods or services, (2) indirect purchasers to whom the overcharge was passed on, (3) customers of goods affected by umbrella prices, (4) buyers harmed by waterbed effects, (5) potential customers who renounced to the purchase due to the rise in prices (counterfactual customers), (6) producers of complementary goods and (7) providers of services and goods to direct and indirect purchasers.

On the other hand, exclusionary abuses tend to damage (1) undertakings excluded from the relevant market, (2) suppliers of undertakings excluded from the market, (3) future customers of excluded undertakings and (4) employees dismissed because of market foreclosure. One can formulate additional hypotheses with regard to subjects that may be damaged by a breach of competition law, since, as already noted, it potentially reaches all market players. According to the ECJ's jurisprudence, all these indirect parties may potentially bring a claim for compensation of competition damages. The Damages Directive has clinched to this principle, according the right

---

[4] Efstathios K Banakas, *Tortious Liability for Pure Economic Loss: A Comparative Study* (Hellenic Institute of International and Foreign Law, 1989); Efstathios K Banakas (ed), *Civil Liability for Pure Economic Loss* (Kluwer Law International, 1996).

[5] Case C-453/99 *Courage Ltd v Bernard Crehan* and *Bernard Crehan v Courage Ltd and Others* ECR I-6297.

[6] Joined Cases C-295/04 to C-298/04 *Vincenzo Manfredi v Lloyd Adriatico Assicurazioni SpA* (2006) ECR I-6619.

[7] Ibid., para 61.

to claim for full compensation to anyone who suffered harm caused by an antitrust infringement.[8] For obtaining the compensation of the damage, the claimant has to substantiate the infringement, the prejudice suffered and the causal connection between the two. Moreover, the damages that the court may award in competition law damages actions fulfil a compensatory function; thus, they should put the claimant in the position in which it would have been had the wrong not occurred.[9] Therefore, overcompensation, as a matter of principle, should be avoided. Even where the claimant can well substantiate the infringement and the harm, the causative link between the two remains extremely difficult to disentangle, especially in the case of indirect damages. Meaningfully, the impact study ordered by the Commission in 2007 pointed out that 'it seems that the success of a claim in the EU would be dependent on whether the plaintiff is actually able to prove causation'.[10]

European courts are generally accustomed to relational or consequential damages, rather than indirect or secondary (as defined here). Commonwealth jurists define relational economic losses as a pure economic harm caused by a physical injury to the person or property of a third party.[11] Indirect losses for infringement of competition laws are not consequences of a harm to persons or property, because they originate from an economic tort. Currently, the most discussed case of such losses is the passing-on of a price overcharge.

---

[8] Article 3.

[9] However, this is not the only aim of European private enforcement, as the discussion is still open; see Ioannis Lianos, 'Competition Law Remedies in Europe: Which Limits for Remedial Discretion?' [2013] CLES Research Paper No. 2/2013, available at http://papers.ssrn.com/abstract=2235817, accessed 12 May 2014; Ioannis Lianos, 'Causal Uncertainty and Damages Claims for Infringement of Competition Law in Europe', available at http://papers.ssrn.com/sol3/Papers.cfm?abstract_id=2564329, accessed 26 July 2015; Renato Nazzini, 'The Objective of Private Remedies in EU Competition Law' [2011] *Global Competition Litigation Review* 131. The principle was stated in Joined Cases C-295/04 to C-298/04 *Vincenzo Manfredi v Lloyd Adriatico Assicurazioni SpA*; Case C-453/99 *Courage Ltd v Bernard Crehan* and *Bernard Crehan v Courage Ltd and Others* ECR I-06297, and subsequently adopted by the Directive 2014/104/EU of the European Parliament and of the Council of 26 November 2014 on Certain Rules Governing Actions for Damages under National Law for Infringements of the Competition Law Provisions of the Member States and of the European Union, OJ L 349. For an historical reconstruction of the right to damages in competition law, see Veljko Milutinović, *The 'Right to Damages' under EU Competition Law: From Courage v. Crehan to the White Paper and Beyond* (Kluwer Law International, 2010).

[10] Meaningfully, in this vein, the impact study ordered by the Commission in 2007 pointed out that 'it seems that the success of a claim in the EU would be dependent on whether the plaintiff is actually able to prove causation'. Centre for European Policy Studies (CEPS), Erasmus University Rotterdam (EUR) and Luiss Guido Carli (LUISS), 'Making Antitrust Damages Actions More Effective in the EU: Welfare Impact and Potential Scenarios', http://ec.europa.eu/competition/antitrust/actionsdamages/files_white_paper/impact_study.pdf, accessed 8 May 2014, 36.

[11] Bruce P Feldthusen, *Economic Negligence: The Recovery of Pure Economic Loss* (Carswell Legal Publications, 1984) 199; Peter Cane, *The Anatomy of Tort Law* (Hart, 1997) 164; Robby Bernstein, *Economic Loss* (Longman, 1993) 163.

7.1 INDIRECT PURCHASERS' CLAIMS

An antitrust infringement often results in harm via price effects.[12] This means that the cartel, or the dominant undertaking, fixes a supra-competitive price that it charges to its customers. However, these buyers might not be the end consumers of those goods or services but, rather, the first juncture of a supply chain that can be more or less complex.[13] The direct purchaser, therefore, may choose from a number of options. Firstly, he or she may internalize the overcharge and charge on his or her clients the same as before the infringement. Alternatively, he or she may pass on the full overcharge, raising prices by the same amount as the overcharge, burdening the indirect purchaser with the corresponding cost. The direct purchaser may also pass on only part of the overcharge, internalizing the remainder of it. Finally, he or she may reduce the firm's expenditures or save on firm's costs.

In case of the passing-on of the overcharge, the direct purchaser is generally depicted as a median between the antitrust infringer and the subject harmed by the infringement. The scenario is even more complicated if we think that, in the downstream market, after the direct purchaser, there may be a long chain of subjects buying, implementing or reselling the good or service and the other derived products. In addition, we should think of the market chain as a network of relationships, which springs both vertically and horizontally; and so does the damage that is transmitted through the price adaptations that follow a cost change.[14]

However, the passing-on is at present conceptualized as taking place only vertically, upstream or downstream in the supply chain. This is the approach adopted by the European Directive 2014/104, which envisions the damage as a token overcharge that can be passed on in whole or in part through price adaptations of the same or derived good or services.

In this account, the passing-on is due to trade relations that bind the production to the distribution process so that what happens at a certain level of the supply chain

---

[12] This is particularly true about cartels: a study from Boyer and Kotchoni, for instance, shows that 95 per cent of the cartels analyzed caused an overcharge harm; see also Siragusa, Mario, 'Private Damages Claims: Questions Relating to the Passing-on Defence' [2011] Oxera, www.oxera.com/Oxera/media/Oxera/downloads/Agenda/Private-damages-claims-%28Mario-Sir agusa%29_1.pdf?ext=.pdf. They also quantify the mean overcharge in all cartel cases as 17.5 per cent and the median 14 per cent. In contrast, the EC 'Quantification Study' observed that the average overcharge amounts to 20 per cent, while the study conducted by Connor and Lande quantified it as 23 per cent; see 'Quantifying Antitrust Damages – Towards Non-binding Guidance for Courts' ('the Quantification Study'), available at http://ec.europa.eu/competi tion/antitrust/actionsdamages/quantification_study.pdf, 91; and JM Connor and RH Lande, 'Cartel Overcharges and Optimal Cartel Fines', in SW Waller (ed.), *Issues in Competition Law and Policy*, volume 3, ABA Section of Antitrust Law.

[13] Hence, for price overcharge, we mean the difference between the supra-competitive price fixed by the antitrust infringer and the market price of the same goods or services.

[14] See, inter alia, Keith Cowling and Michael Waterson, 'Price-Cost Margins and Market Structure' [1976] 43 *Economica* 267; Jochen Meyer and Stephan Cramon-Taubadel, 'Asymmetric Price Transmission: A Survey' [2004] 55 *Journal of Agricultural Economics* 581.

168   *Causation in Indirect and Secondary Antitrust Damages*

tends to be passed on to the next level.[15] Even this restricted view of the passing-on raises questions of 'proximity' of the causal connection between the damage and the infringement, because at each step of the supply chain, a new action will be implemented, resulting in an additional possibility to introduce an independent and sufficient cause of damage.

7.1.1 *Cause-in-Fact and the Passing-On*

The position of the indirect purchaser in passing-on actions is generally analyzed as a matter of standing rather than of causation.[16] However, as related to the passing-on of price overcharges in EU competition damages actions, the CJEU and the Directive 2014/104 have clearly stated that any natural or legal person who has suffered harm caused by an infringement of competition law is able to claim full compensation for that harm,[17] irrespective of whether he or she is a direct or indirect purchaser.[18] Therefore, no room remained for speculations about the right to claim for damages by indirect purchasers.[19] The general question regarding causation in passing-on cases, instead, is whether and to what extent a competition law

---

[15] For an introduction to the problem of passing-on of price overcharges in competition law, see David Ashton and David Henry, *Competition Damages Actions in the EU: Law and Practice* (Edward Elgar Publishing, 2013) 40 ff.; Magnus Strand, 'Indirect Purchasers, Passing-on and the New Directive on Competition Law Damages' [2014] 10 *European Competition Journal* 361, Ivo Van Bael, *Due Process in EU Competition Proceedings* (Kluwer Law International, 2011) 86 ff; Damien Geradin, Anne Layne-Farrar and Nicolas Petit, *EU Competition Law and Economics* (Oxford University Press, 2012); Richard Craswell, 'Passing on the Costs of Legal Rules: Efficiency and Distribution in Buyer-Seller Relationships' [1991] 43 *Stanford Law Review* 361; Frank Verboven and Theon Van Dijk, 'Cartel Damages Claims and the Passing-on Defense' [2009] 57 *The Journal of Industrial Economics* 457; Robert G Harris and Lawrence A Sullivan, 'Passing on the Monopoly Overcharge: A Comprehensive Policy Analysis' [1979] 128 *University of Pennsylvania Law Review* 269; Earl E Pollock, 'Standing to Sue, Remoteness of Injury, and the Passing-On Doctrine' [1966] *Antitrust Law Journal* 5.

[16] Süleyman Parlak, 'Passing-on Defence and Indirect Purchaser Standing: Should the Passing-on Defence Be Rejected Now the Indirect Purchaser Has Standing after Manfredi and the White Paper of the European Commission?' [2010] 33 *World Competition* 31; Ashton and Henry (n 15) 36; Firat Cengiz, 'Passing-On Defense and Indirect Purchaser Standing in Actions for Damages against the Violations of Competition Law: What Can the EC Learn from the US?' [2007] University of East Anglia Centre for Competition Policy, Working Paper 07; Assimakis P Komninos, *EC Private Antitrust Enforcement: Decentralised Application of EC Competition Law by National Courts* (Hart, 2008).

[17] Article 2 Directive 2014/104/EU of the European Parliament and of the Council of 26 November 2014 on Certain Rules Governing Actions for Damages under National Law for Infringements of the Competition Law Provisions of the Member States and of the European Union, OJ L 349.

[18] Article 12, ibid.

[19] It remains certainly still vivid in terms of the policy-based discussion about the opposite choice made by the US Supreme Court and the most efficient system, confronting the aim it pursues.

7.1 Indirect Purchasers' Claims

infringement harmed the different market actors, including direct and indirect purchasers.[20] Causation determines the factual link between the infringement and the damage (material or factual causation) and delimits the compensable damages (legal causation).[21] The factual causal nexus links the antitrust infringement to the damage – thus, the anticompetitive behaviour to the specific damage claimed, be it an actual loss or lost profit. Nonetheless, the different market actors transacting the good may interfere with the transmission of the damage, contributing to it or absorbing it.[22]

In particular, regarding the actual loss caused by the overcharge, it has to be assessed if buyers and sellers transacting the good after the infringer contributed to the magnitude of the damage passed through, reduced it or interrupted the causal connection. The causal link is, therefore, a structural element of the infringement, which generally responds to an objective reconstruction of a syllogistic type, between an action abstractly considered (not yet classified as *damnum injuria datum*)[23] and the harmful event. In order to identify the primary relationship between conduct and event, the judge in the first instance determines the factual connection, therefore excluding any assessment of foreseeability, both subjective and objective, that is an analytic element placed at the second stage of the reconstruction of the causal nexus.

The questions related to material causation are different and specifically related to the factual situation. On this basis, a general subdivision of causal questions can be framed as follows. The material causation demands that the claimant (indirect purchaser) gives sufficient proof that the cartel overcharge was passed on to him or her. The question would then be whether or not the damage would have

---

[20] For an analysis of causation in competition damages actions, see Ioannis Lianos, 'Causal Uncertainty and Damages Claims for the Infringement of Competition Law in Europe' [2015] 34 *Yearbook of European Law* 170.

[21] The doctrine on causation in the law is particularly rich. However, an important contribution was made by HLA Hart and Tony Honoré, *Causation in the Law* (Oxford University Press, 1985); moreover, see Richard W Wright, 'Causation, Responsibility, Risk, Probability, Naked Statistics, and Proof: Pruning the Bramble Bush by Clarifying the Concepts' [1987] 73 *Iowa Law Review* 1001; Jane Stapleton, 'Unpacking Causation' in Peter Cane, Anthony M Honoré and John Gardner (eds), *Relating to Responsibility: Essays for Tony Honoré on His Eightieth Birthday* (Hart, 2001); Richard Goldberg, *Perspectives on Causation* (Hart, 2011); Anthony M Honoré, 'Causation and Remoteness of Damage' in A Tunc (ed), *International Encyclopedia of Comparative Law*, vol 6 (Mohr Siebeck, 1983); Michael S Moore, *Causation and Responsibility: An Essay in Law, Morals, and Metaphysics* (Oxford University Press, 2010).

[22] The causal contribution of market actors may be interpreted in the light of quantitative or scalar approaches to causation, which allow the evaluation of the multiple causes of the damage apportioning the damage on the basis of the causal contribution, although this is not subject of scrutiny of the present text. See Jane Stapleton, 'The Two Explosive Proof-of-Causation Doctrines Central to Asbestos Claims' [2008] 74 *Brooklyn Law Review* 1011; Moore (n 21).

[23] The damage unlawfully inflicted to the property of another.

170 *Causation in Indirect and Secondary Antitrust Damages*

happened but for the antitrust infringement.[24] On the other hand, the defendant (the antitrust infringer) has to prove that the steps taken after the first purchase reduced or eliminated the damage. When instead the direct purchaser is to claim for damages, the evidential burden related to causation varies according to the specific characteristics of the domestic system.[25]

When the overcharge is the result of an antitrust infringement that inflates the prices of goods or services, the material causation determines whether indirect purchasers can claim compensation for the relative damages or not. At this point, the material causal link between the conduct and the event finds correspondents in each antecedent (near, intermediate and remote) that has generated or even contributed to this objective relation to the fact and, therefore, should be considered a cause of the event. The second stage requires instead the analysis of legal causation in order to ascertain that the damage claimed falls within the scope of competition regulation and therein is attributable to the antitrust infringer.

7.1.2 *Legal Causation*

The illegal overcharge passed through the market chain may cause different types of damages to both direct and indirect purchasers. Firstly, there is the actual loss of the purchaser who did not pass on the overcharge, which amounts to the level of the overcharge multiplied by the number of items purchased.[26] As for intermediate buyers of the goods or services under infringement, when they succeed to pass on the overcharge paid, they can claim for lost profits caused by the decline in demand

---

[24] In a more sophisticated way, the judge can ask whether the overcharge passed-on was a necessary element of a set of conditions jointly sufficient for causing the damage claimed. For an analysis of the NESS theory and its application in tort law, see supra, para 2.6; Wright, (n 21); Hart and Honoré (n 21); Richard W Wright, 'Causation in Tort Law' [1985] 73 *California Law Review* 1735; Richard W Wright, 'The NESS Account of Natural Causation: A Response to Criticisms' in R. Goldberg (ed), *Perspectives on Causation* (Hart, 2011).

[25] See Chapter 3; Damien Geradin and Ianis Girgenson, 'The Counterfactual Method in EU Competition Law: The Cornerstone of the Effects-Based Approach' [2011] (11 December 2011), available at SSRN: http://papers.ssrn.com/sol3/papers.cfm?abstract_id=1970917, accessed 25 August 2014; Cento Veljanovski, 'Counterfactual Tests in Competition Law' [2010] 4 *Competition Law Journal*. Although the first analysis of counterfactuals is attributable to John Stuart Mill, *A System of Logic, Ratiocinative and Inductive: Being a Connected View of the Principles of Evidence and the Methods of Scientific Investigation* (John W Parker, 1843), it is only from the 1960s that the theory had been thoroughly developed, mainly thanks to the work of Ardon Lyon, 'Causality' [1967] 18 *British Journal for the Philosophy of Science*, 1, 1–20; John Leslie Mackie, *The Cement of the Universe: A Study of Causation* (Clarendon Press, 1980); David Lewis, Causation' [1973] 70(17) *The Journal of Philosophy*, 556–567.

[26] This actually happens only in perfectly competitive markets where the pass-on rate is 100 per cent; see Commission Staff Working Document – Practical Guide on Quantifying Harm in Actions for Damages Based on Breaches of Article 101 or 102 of the Treaty on the Functioning of the European Union SWD (2013) 205 2013, para 170.

7.1 Indirect Purchasers' Claims

due to higher prices.[27] However, the passing-on of the overcharge may cause other types of damages – for instance, the raise in prices by the cartel may generate umbrella effects[28] – or may bring a counterfactual purchaser to renounce the purchase.

The evaluation of legal causation – both in terms of the dependence of the event on its factual antecedents and with regard to the scope of the rule infringed – is done according to criteria of scientific probability or relying on logical inferences[29] determined by domestic tort laws. Legal causation delimits the compensation, identifying which damages are ruled out from the compensation to the claimant materially injured by the infringement.[30] Some of the principles developed by European jurisdictions to assess legal causation are remoteness, directness, scope of the rule, causal regularity and probability.[31] Hence, based on these or any other tests adopted by the domestic law of a member state, the claimant has to substantiate that the supra-competitive price caused damages that are causally linked to the antitrust infringement and meet the legal requirements.[32] As Section 7.2 clarifies, the Damages Directive includes specific norms on the passing on of the overcharge. On the other hand, the same directive does not clearly address other types of damages that may be caused through the passing-on to, for instance, counterfactual purchasers or other buyers in the form of loss of profits or lost chances. Neither does the Directive address the harm inflicted upon the direct and indirect purchasers of the supplier of a buyers' cartel,[33] thereby raising doubts about their compensation.[34]

---

[27] Ibid., para 175 ff.

[28] Roman Inderst, Frank P Maier-Rigaud and Ulrich Schwalbe, 'Umbrella Effects' (2014) 10 *Journal of Competition Law and Economics* 739.

[29] Hart and Honoré (n 21) 85 ff.

[30] The determination of the compensable damages should not be confused with the quantification of damages and the calculation of the share of the overcharge that was passed on, which, according to Article 12(5) of the Directive, the judge has the power estimate.

[31] For an analysis of some national European approaches to the legal causation, see Chapter 3.

[32] Therefore, for instance, the claimant will have to prove, depending on the applicable law, that the damage is direct, falls within the scope of the rule, is a regular consequence, is probable or is not remote.

[33] This is the so-called waterbed effect that may apply if we define the overprice applied to the buyers, as a pass-on of the disutility due to the price conditions imposed by the buying cartel. For a general overview of the waterbed effect, see Roman Inderst and Tommaso M Valletti, 'Buyer Power and the "Waterbed Effect"' (2011) 59 *The Journal of Industrial Economics* 1; Adrian N Majumdar, 'Waterbed Effects and Buyer Mergers' [2005] CCP Working Paper No 05-7. Available at http://papers.ssrn.com/sol3/papers.cfm?abstract_id=911574, accessed 15 July 2015; Zhiqi Chen, 'Dominant Retailers and the Countervailing-Power Hypothesis' [2003] 34(4) *RAND Journal of Economics* 612.

[34] See infra at Section 7.2.

172   *Causation in Indirect and Secondary Antitrust Damages*

The time is not yet ripe to base a response on national and European case laws that – so far – have not dealt with such cases.[35] National and European courts have dealt with a limited number of cases regarding the application of passing on in competition law cases. However, courts have long discussed the concept and dynamic of passing on in other areas. The following section offers an analysis of the case law of the European courts dealing with passing on in competition law.

7.1.3 *Passing On in National Courts: A Comparative Overview*

National courts have long been dealing with the passing-on of price overcharges in competition damages actions, preceding in time the choices made with the Damages Directive. Generally, national courts have accepted passing-on considerations, granting indirect purchasers the right to claim damages and ensuring, at the same time, the defendants' right to exercise the passing-on defence. However, the degree and extent of these rights are slightly different in modulation.

German Law

The German Act against Restrictions of Competition (ARC) provides in Section 33 that 'Whoever intentionally or negligently commits an infringement pursuant to § 33(1) shall be liable for any damages arising from the infringement'. According to the wording of this paragraph, the antitrust infringer is liable for damages to direct purchasers and to indirect purchasers, indifferently. In 2005, the German legislator amended the law and specified that 'if a product or a service has been purchased at an excessive price, the damage is not excluded because the good or service has been resold'.[36] Therefore, the fact that the direct purchaser passed on the price overcharge does not exclude his or her right to claim compensation for damages. But the provision fails to indicate what type of damages are subject to compensation, paving the way to a predictable fracture in the case law, which was recently resolved with a seminal decision of the Federal Court of Justice.[37]

Two opposite positions, indeed, were adopted by German courts on the admissibility of passing-on actions and defences. As German laws initially granted standing only to subjects in the 'protective scope' of the law, courts accordingly restricted the claims for damages to direct purchasers.[38] Moreover, courts tended to deny the

---

[35] See Section 2.1.
[36] Section 33, subsection 3, sentence 2 ARC. This provision is applicable only to cartels taking place from 2005 on. However, the Supreme Court considered the amended text in order to interpret and decide previous cases.
[37] *Bundesgerichtshof* [BGH] [Federal Court of Justice] KZR 75/10 (FRG).
[38] See, for instance, Mainz District Court, 15 January 2004, Cases 12 HK.O 52/02, 12 HK O 55/02 and 12 HK O 56/02, in NJW-RR 2004, 478; Mannheim District Court, 11 July 2003, Case 7 O 326/02, in GRUR 2004, 182; Karlsruhe Court of Appeal, 28 January 2004, Case 6 U 183/03, in WuW DE- R 1229.

7.1 Indirect Purchasers' Claims

availability of the passing on defence, on the basis of the formulation of Section 33 (3) and considering that, otherwise, the defendant could avoid liability for damages.[39]

In order to avoid multiple compensations and unjust enrichment on the side of the direct purchaser passing-on the damage, these courts held that the defendant could not raise the passing-on defence. In the *Readymix* case, the Higher Regional Court of Berlin[40] disallowed the cartelist to object the passing-on of the overcharge. When the defendant objected that this approach would lead to multiple compensations, the court observed that the payment, either to a direct or indirect purchaser, extinguishes the infringer's obligation to pay damages caused by the same cartel.[41] By contrast, the Appellate Court of Berlin held that both the direct and indirect purchasers could claim the entire amount of damages, but only when the distribution of the compensation is an internal matter, as claimants are joint creditors of the damages payment obligation.[42] However, the Berlin Court disallowed the passing-on defence.[43]

In a later case, related to the carbonless paper cartel (the ORWI case), the Federal Court of Justice finally granted the indirect purchaser the right to stand and, at the same time, allowed the direct purchaser to raise the passing-on defence.[44] The proceedings involved three parties, a savings bank (claimant), a printing firm (injured party) and the cartelist (defendant), a carbonless paper producer.

The damaged party, an insolvent printing firm, transferred its own right to compensation to the savings bank through an assignment of claims. The defendant, on the other hand, was part of a cartel fined by the European Commission.[45] The claimant purchased carbonless paper from a wholesaler of the defendant at an inflated price. By consequence, when it learned about the existence of the cartel, it claimed for compensation of the damages due to the price overcharge.

The court of first instance (District Court of Mannheim) dismissed the claim, stating that only direct purchasers of cartel members had the right to claim compensation.[46] Moreover, the judge of the merit clung to the motivation, observing that the claimant – by its turn – might have passed the overcharge on to their clients. The

---

[39] *Regional Court of Dortmund* WuW/E DE-R 1352.
[40] Higher Regional Court Berlin, judgment of 1 October 2009, 2 U 17/03 – Readymix Concrete. The proceeding is a follow-on action of the cement cartel. The claim was first rejected by the Regional Court of Berlin in 2003 because the claimant was not a specific target of the cartel. The Appellate Court of Berlin reversed this decision and established that the claimant does not necessarily have to be targeted by the cartel. The court also stated that the existence of a cartel constitutes a rebuttable presumption of a cartel overcharge.
[41] Higher Regional Court Berlin 2 U 17/03.
[42] KG, 2 U 10/03 Kart, 01.10.2009. The case was appealed before the Supreme Court but was quashed on procedural grounds and confirmed by the court, BGH, 08/06/2010 – KZR 45/09.
[43] KG, 2 U 10/03 Kart, 24.
[44] *Bundesgerichtshof* [BGH] [Federal Court of Justice] KZR 75/10 (F.R.G.).
[45] *Commission Decision Carbonless Paper Cartel* (2001) OJ L 115, 21.04.2004.
[46] *Landgericht Mannheim* (District Court of Mannheim) (2005) 22 O 74/04 Kart EWiR 659.

174 *Causation in Indirect and Secondary Antitrust Damages*

claimant appealed the judgment to the Court of Appeal of Karlsruhe – which, however, endorsed the position of the first grade judge with regard to the passing-on issue.[47] The Appellate Court, however, found that, in the specific case, the claimant was entitled to claim for damages. The claimant purchased the paper from a wholesaler, who was fully owned by the cartelist. On this basis, the judge reasoned that – since the direct purchaser, being a subsidiary, would have never recovered the damage against the parent company – the judge had to grant the indirect purchaser the right to claim compensation in order to avoid unjust enrichment of the cartelist.[48] On the other hand, both courts agreed that the passing-on defence should not be allowed. For, in that case, the cartel member would be exempted from any sort of compensatory liability. By consequence, the appellate court granted ordered the compensation of damages, calculating only the sales from the wholly owned subsidiary of the cartel member and excluded the passing-on exception by denying any possible reduction of damages based on the pass-on of the overcharge.

By contrast, and finally, the Supreme Court also held that indirect purchasers should be able to bring damages claims against the members of a cartel.[49] In addition, the court determined the admissibility of the passing-on defence, hence dismissing the argument of the Court of Appeal.[50] As a result, the Supreme Court stated that every damaged party is entitled to claim compensatory damages from any of the antitrust infringers.[51] Consequently, each cartelist is jointly and severally liable for the whole damage caused to a purchaser, be it direct or indirect. On the other hand, the defendant has the right to object the fact that the direct purchaser had passed the damage through the market chain. The court, moreover, reasserted the power of the trial judge to estimate damages caused by a cartel.[52] The court also based its interpretation on Section 33(3), Sentence 2 GWB (even though it was not applicable to the case at hand), making it more difficult to object the passing-on defence. The court stated that the defendant can invoke the passing-on defence, pleading an adjustment of profits. In order to do this, the defendant has to substantiate the simultaneous fulfilment of three conditions. Firstly, the defendant has to support with plausible proof or evidence that the passing-on was economically possible. Secondly, he or she has to show that there was a causal link between the infringement and the damage

---

[47] *Oberlandesgericht Karlsruhe* (Higher Regional Court of Karlsruhe) (2010) June 11, 2010, 6-U 118/05 (Kart) (F.R.G).

[48] Here the reasoning appears to be fallacious, since it recognizes the right to compensation only as a counterbalance to avoid unjust enrichment of the cartelist.

[49] *Bundesgerichtshof* [BGH] [Federal Court of Justice] KZR 75/10 (F.R.G.).

[50] Ibid.

[51] Ibid.

[52] Ibid. The estimation has to be conducted within the specific framework that the Supreme Court draws. Firstly, the judge has to base the estimation on the prices of goods actually paid by the claimant. Secondly, the prices can be adjusted by decreasing or increasing factors. Finally, there are lingering effects that the judge can use in taking the decision for adapting the rule to the specific case.

passed on. Finally, the defendant's burden of proof also compels him to give evidence for the fact that no other economic disadvantages injured the direct purchaser. In particular, the court refers to the loss of profit resulting from the decrease in demand that is a normal market response to the increase in prices.

The Bundesgerichtshof (BGH) made clear that the burden of proof of the passing-on of the overcharge lies with the defendant. Therefore, when the direct purchaser claims compensation from the antitrust infringer, it is up to the cartelist to show evidence of the passing-on. On this point, commentators already noticed that the proof in many cases may become a *probatio diabolica*, given that access to information needed to substantiate the passing-on may be particularly difficult if not impossible.[53] Some scholars pointed out that the obstacle could be overcome by courts accepting the so-called secondary burden of allegation.[54] This is a special procedural instrument used in some jurisdictions to oblige claimants to disclose the relevant information for providing rebuttal evidence.[55] Hence, the claimant has to demonstrate and to prove that his damage is based on the prohibited cartel. If the victim did not purchase directly from the cartel members, he must also prove that the overcharge was passed on to him as an indirect purchaser. Given the complexity of pricing, the BGH held that there is no presumption that an increase in prices during the period of cartelization results from such a cartel. According to this approach, the BGH requires evidence of specific causation in every individual case.

French Law

Under French law, there was no specific statutory basis for actions proposed by indirect purchasers before the entry into force of the Ordonnance transposing the Damages Directive.[56] Hence, all claims were based on the general rule set by Article 1382 French Civil Code, for which 'Any act of a person which causes damage to another makes him by whose fault the damage occurred to make reparation for the damage'.[57] Given the broadness of the rule, French judges facing indirect purchasing actions for the first time had enough room to interpret the law as they deemed reasonable. This discretion created conflicting judgments that ended in the Court of Cassation decision of 2010.[58]

---

[53] Johannes Zöttl and Lisa Schleppe, 'Die Private Durchsetzung von Kartellrechtlichen Schadensersatzansprüchen – Status Quo in Deutschland' [2012] 23 *European Journal of Business Law Europäische Zeitschrift für Wirtschaftsrecht* 573.

[54] Kai Hüschelrath and Heike Schweitzer, *Public and Private Enforcement of Competition Law in Europe: Legal and Economic Perspectives* (Springer, 2014) 274.

[55] Although, at the moment, the burden of proof of the claimant appears to be rather heavy, it seems to be that the possibility of actions from indirect purchasers are rare, given the difficulties related to substantiating the claim and given that the German procedural law does not give the possibility of using class actions.

[56] Ordonnance no 2017-303, 9 March 2017.

[57] In the original version, 'Tout fait quelconque de l'homme, qui cause à autrui un dommage, oblige celui par la faute duquel il est arrivé, à le réparer'.

[58] Cour de Cassation, Doux Aliments v Ajinomoto Eurolyne 09-15816.

176   *Causation in Indirect and Secondary Antitrust Damages*

This case takes place as a follow-on action of the lysine cartel decision of the European Commission.[59] The claimant, Doux aliments Bretagne (Doux), a poultry farmer group, purchased lysine from Ceva santé animale (Ceva), which did not take part in the cartel. However, Ceva purchased lysine from cartel members – in particular, Ajinomoto Eurolyne (Ajinomoto) – at an inflated price and supplied Doux. Doux decided to bring an action for damages directly against Ajinomoto before the French courts, arguing that the overcharge of the cartel had been passed on.

The court of first instance, the Commercial Court of Paris,[60] rejected the claim because the claimant failed to prove that it was unable to pass the overcharge on. Moreover, the judge observed that the claimant failed to calculate the amount of damages. However, Doux appealed the decision before the Court of Appeals of Paris that reversed the judgment on both points.[61] The appellate judge observed that Doux was entitled to damages since it suffered a loss of profits due to a diminution of competitiveness of its products for which it should be compensated up to 30 per cent of its demanded sum and, by consequence, was awarded damages amounting to €380,000.[62] Finally, the Court of Cassation heard the dispute and stated that the Court of Appeal failed to explain the underlying reasons for accepting Doux's claim. The appellate judge, indeed, erred when considering the passing-on as insignificant in the assessment of the damage and its quantification.[63] Although the Cassation concluded that indirect purchasers are allowed to bring claims against cartelists, the decision has been criticized for taking a rather defensive approach with regard to the pass-on of the cartel overcharge.[64]

In a following case,[65] the French Supreme Court specified that, as a matter of usual market dynamics, there is a presumption that purchasers tend to pass on the price overcharge paid for the good or service. Hence, the claimant has the burden to

---

[59]   Commission Decision Choline Chloride, 9.12.2004, Case COMP/E-2/37533.

[60]   Commercial Court of Paris, Laboratoires JUVA c/ Hoffmann La Roche.

[61]   Paris Court of Appeal, *SNC Doux Aliments Bretagne Etc v SAS Ajinamoto Eurolysine*, No 07/10478.

[62]   This ruling clearly admits that indirect purchasers have standing under French law to bring a damages action against a competition law infringer. Not only is this ruling in line with the recommendations of the Commission in the White Paper, but it also complies with the ruling rendered on July 13, 2006, by the ECJ in *Manfredi*, 14, in which the court stated that '[A]ny individual can claim compensation for the harm suffered where there is a causal relationship between that harm and an agreement or practice prohibited under Article 81 EC'.

[63]   Cour de cassation, civile, Chambre commerciale, 15 juin 2010, 09-15816, Inédit [2010] Cour de cassation 09-15.816, Inédit. '[A]warding damages without assessing whether Doux aliments had fully or partly passed on to its clients the overcharge resulting from AE's infringement could have resulted in an unjust enrichment'.

[64]   Hugues Parmentier and Mathilde Descôte, 'The French Commercial Supreme Court Validates the Passing-on Defence in a Follow-on Action Based on the Lysine Cartel (Doux Aliments/Ajinomoto Eurolyne)' [2010] e-Competitions.

[65]   Cour de Cassation, Gouessant, arrêt no 540, pourvoi no 11-18495.

7.1 Indirect Purchasers' Claims

prove that he or she internalized the damage and avoided to pass the overcharge on to the next level of the market chain.

In both cases, the court ruled that the claimant has the burden to substantiate the claim and also to prove that he or she internalized the overcharge, avoiding the passing-on.

The Commercial Court of Nanterre, in 2006, adopted a similar approach[66] that, however, brought the judge to draw different conclusions. In this case, the judge burdened the plaintiff to prove why she could not have passed on the price increase to consumers. The court ruling its decision on the Commission's decision in the vitamin cartel, presuming that price increases were likely to be passed on to consumers.[67] Ultimately, the court held that the cartel was implemented worldwide, and, consequently, every competitor of the plaintiff was subject to the same conditions. Therefore, the plaintiff had the possibility of passing on the increase, and the choice not to do so was part of the plaintiff's pricing policy. In view of this, the court concluded that the plaintiff had not established the causal link between the fault and the damage.

However, by recognizing the standing to indirect purchasers, the Court of Cassation's decision should bring about a new wave of antitrust damages actions and could have a deterrent effect on potential infringers. However, it must be underlined that, under French tort law, only damages amounting to the actual loss are awarded to the claimant, since no punitive damages are admitted. Therefore, given the costs of proceedings, only indirect purchasers left with a significant damage should, in practice, seek compensation in court.

Italian Law

Some of the earliest cases regarding the passing-on in antitrust damages actions have taken place in Italy – in particular, with the proceedings *Indaba v Juventus*[68] and *Unimare v Geasar*.[69]

In the former case, Indaba, a travel agency, agreed with Juventus Football Club to sell tickets for the 1997 Champions League final match in Munich, offering the tickets along with extra services such as transportation, excursions and the like. The 'travel package' had no success among supporters, and Indaba sued Juventus, claiming that the football club abused its dominant position, infringing Article 102 TFEU, by imposing an unreasonable surcharge on the ticket prices. The Court of Appeal ruled that the parties entered an agreement that restricted competition and that Juventus imposed excessive prices. Moreover, the practice of tying the sales of the tickets to the sale of travel packages amounted to a second infringement of

---

[66] Commercial Court of Nanterre (Arkopharma).

[67] Commission Decision (Case COMP/E-2/37.533 – Choline Chloride n 1060).

[68] Court of Appeal of Turin, judgment of 6 July 2000, *Indaba Incentive Co v società Juventus FC S.pA*.

[69] Court of Appeal of Cagliari, judgment of 23 January 1999, *Unimare S.r.l v Geasar S.p.a.*

competition law, as it illegally restricted the relevant market, ultimately damaging consumers.

However, the Court observed that Indaba entered into the agreement with the intention to pass on the overcharge to its customers. The Turin Court reasoned about the effects of the passing-on in the specific case, applying Article 1227 of the Italian Civil Code, according to which the causal contribution of the damaged party to the event reduces or even annuls the damage subject to compensation. For this reason, the court rejected the claim, noting that Indaba passed on the full amount of the costs with which it was illegally burdened. In this vein, the court stated that only the indirect customers 'would be the ones entitled to claim damages for the overcharges they did not want'.[70] In a second case, the plaintiff Unimare, the former provider of handling services to the airport Olbia, argued that Geasar, the management body of the airport, had abused its dominant position causing economic harm to them. According to Unimare, the defendant had abused its dominance imposing of excessive tariffs requested for handling services. Moreover, Geasar had took Unimare's main client, the US Naval Service Order (UNSO), claiming to be the only qualified handling service provider at the Olbia Airport. The Court of Appeal of Cagliari rejected both claims, asserting that there was no abuse of dominance. The fact that Geasar was the exclusive provider of services to the Olbia airport was in itself an obstacle to the performance of this activity by Unimare. Moreover, the fact that Geasar presented itself as the sole supplier of the ground services covered by the contract could not constitute abuse, as the alleged exclusion from the market was not proved. Finally, the Court assumed that there had been a pass-on of the overcharge from Unimare to the UNSO. The latter covered the tariff increase and this did not cause it to switch to another supplier. Hence, the court concluded that the harmed party was the final customer of such services, who had no alternative suppliers to pass the overcharge to.

English Law

English courts have long been reluctant to deal with the problem of passing on in competition damages actions. The admissibility of passing on has been accepted with a few *obiter dicta*[71] but never became the object of judicial interpretation. In *Devenish Nutrition Ltd v Sanofi-Aventis SA*, for instance, Tuckey LJ considered that 'Devenish is claiming the overcharge as if it were the defendants' net profit so as to avoid having to take into account the fact (if true) that it passed on the whole of the

---

[70] Siragusa, Mario, 'Private Damages Claims: Questions Relating to the Passing-on Defence' [2011] *Oxera*, available at www.oxera.com/Oxera/media/Oxera/downloads/Agenda/Private-damages-claims-%28Mario-Siragusa%29_1.pdf?ext=.pdf.

[71] *Emerald Supplies Ltd & Anor v British Airways Plc* [2010] EWCA Civ 1284; *WH Newson Holding Ltd & Ors v IMI Plc & Ors* [2013] EWCA Civ 1377; *Devenish Nutrition Ltd v Sanofi-Aventis SA (France) & Ors (Rev 1)* EWCA Civ 1086.

overcharge to its customers. I can see no way in which it could avoid taking this "pass on" into account in any compensatory claim for damages'.[72]

Moreover, in *Emerald Supplies v British Airways*, Mummery LJ stated in this regard that 'The potential conflicts arising from the defences that could be raised by [British Airways] to different claimants, such as direct purchasers who have "passed on" the inflated price and would not want BA to run that passing on defence to their claims and those indirect purchasers to whom the inflated price has been passed on and who would want BA to raise the pass on defence to claims by direct purchasers, reinforce the fact that they do not have the same interest and that the proceedings are not equally beneficial to all those to be represented'.[73]

Following, in *Cooper Tire*, the parties settled the case and agreed that the availability of the passing-on defence should depend on normal English principles of causation and mitigation.[74]

The ostensible reluctance to treat the problem of passing on in depth might be explained by the factual approach that English judges have with regard to the pass-on issue. As explained by Mr Justice Popplewell in *Fulton Shipping Inc v Globalia Business Travel SAU*: 'In order for a benefit to be taken into account in reducing the loss recoverable by the innocent party for a breach of contract, it is generally speaking a necessary condition that the benefit is caused by the breach ... The test is whether the breach has caused the benefit; it is not sufficient if the breach has merely provided the occasion or context for the innocent party to obtain the benefit, or merely triggered his doing so ... Nor is it sufficient merely that the benefit would not have been obtained but for the breach'.[75] Hence, the court should adopt a case-by-case approach, verifying whether the cartel 'has caused the benefit' or 'provided the occasion or context for the innocent party to obtain the benefit', and it is part of the claimant's burden of proof to demonstrate how the cartel influenced prices.

However, as a matter of principle, the English system is in line with the other European jurisdictions that accept both claims from indirect purchasers and the defence of passing on. The new Part 2 of the Competition Law Act 1998[76] introduced with the Act implementing the Damages Directive, is devoted to the passing on. The law recognizes the right of indirect purchasers to claim damages and the right of respondents to oppose the passing-on defence.

---

[72] *Devenish Nutrition Ltd v Sanofi-Aventis SA (France) & Ors (Rev 1)* (n 71).

[73] *Emerald Supplies Ltd & Anor v British Airways Plc* [2010] EWCA Civ 1284 (n 71).

[74] *Court of Appeal (Civil Division) Cooper Tire & Rubber Co Europe Ltd v Shell Chemicals UK Ltd 23 July 2010* [2010] EWCA Civ 864; [2010] Bus LR 1697; [2011] CP Rep 1; [2010] 2 CLC 104; [2010] UKCLR 1277; (2010) 160 NLJ 1116; Official Transcript.

[75] *Fulton Shipping Inc of Panama v Globalia Business Travel SAU (formerly Travelplan SAU) of Spain* (2014) EWHC 1547 (Comm).

[76] The Claims in respect of Loss or Damage arising from Competition Infringements (Competition Act 1998 and Other Enactments (Amendment) Regulations 2017 No. 385.

180 *Causation in Indirect and Secondary Antitrust Damages*

Meanwhile, in the United States, the Supreme Court, with the *Hanover Shoe*[77] and *Illinois Brick*[78] cases, rejected the defence of passing on and barred indirect purchaser claims under federal antitrust law.[79] Defendants are not allowed to invoke the defence of passing on against the claims of direct purchasers, and indirect purchasers cannot claim damages on the basis that an overcharge has been passed on to them.[80]

These two opposite views show dogmatic, legal and economic differences that are worth analyzing, but their enforcement is mainly based on considerations connected to the specific legal, economic and geographical drawbacks. The US approach, however, is deeply complicated by the fact that state courts have generally disregarded this case law. In many states, the indirect purchaser has the right to claim antitrust damages, and the antitrust infringer can use the passing-on argument as a defence. It is reported that 'thirty-six states and the District of Columbia, representing over 70 per cent of the nation's population, now provide for some sort of right of action on behalf of some or all indirect purchasers'.[81] This situation has generated paradoxical litigation where indirect purchasers are claiming for damages before state courts, and direct purchasers sue the infringers before the federal courts.

7.2 THE REGULATORY FRAMEWORK IN THE EU

The choice of the EU Commission, expounded in White Paper 2008 and confirmed in Directive 104/2014, has been to grant indirect purchasers with the right to claim for damages due to the passing on of the overcharge and, simultaneously, to allow respondents to oppose the passing-on defence. This choice is justified by the aim of ensuring the effective exercise of the victims' right to full compensation. However, the actual formulation of the Directive is the result of a process that counts at least 10 years of different drafts. During the same period of time, the priorities of the European legislator changed and with them also the formulation of the relative rules on the passing on, some of whose were hardly uncomplicated by a cryptic formulation.[82] The following two paragraphs lay down a critical description of such evolution.

---

[77] *Hanover Shoe, Inc v United Shoe Machinery Corp*, 392 US 481 (1968).
[78] *Illinois Brick Co v Illinois*, 431 US 720.
[79] Phillip Areeda, Herbert Hovenkamp and John L Solow, *Antitrust Law* (Aspen Publishers, 2001); Phillip Areeda and Herbert Hovenkamp, *Fundamentals of Antitrust Law* (Aspen Publishers Online, 2011).
[80] See Timothy F Bresnahan, 'Antitrust Modernization Commission' (New York University, 2006), available at http://govinfo.library.unt.edu/amc/commission_hearings/pdf/Roundtable_Participant_List.pdf, accessed 12 May 2014.
[81] Kevin J O'Connor, 'Is the Illinois Brick Wall Crumbling' [2000] 15 *Antitrust* 34, 34. See also 'Antitrust Modernization Commission Report and Recommendations VI' (2007).
[82] See, for instance, Article 12(3) of the Directive Proposal.

7.2.1 *The Green Paper and the White Paper*

In the Green Paper,[83] the Commission left open the question whether or not a defendant should be able to invoke the passing-on defence. The Green Paper proposed four different alternatives to the passing on of to the passing-on defence issue and indirect purchaser standing.[84] The Ashurst study laid down, instead, a highly skeptical position in this regard, noting that 'The existence of the passing on defence itself is an obstacle to the extent it complicates claims. Moreover, to the extent it reduces the money paid to the plaintiff it clearly also reduces the latter's incentive to bring a claim. Lack of clarity as concerns the possibility for the indirect purchaser to claim and the difficulties of proof (in particular as regards causation and damages) both constitute obstacles to the indirect purchaser's claim. The combination of the passing on defence (in particular where this is readily accepted) and the difficulties faced by indirect purchasers will seriously restrict private claims'.[85]

This advice remained however largely unheard.[86] Basing their assumption on the evolution of the CJEU case law, the Commission argued in the White Paper[87] that it was time to introduce a common European rule about passing on in private antitrust enforcement. With the *Courage* and *Manfredi* cases,[88] the CJEU stated that anyone should be able to claim for damages caused by an illegal conduct, agreement or practice, where there is a causal link between the infringement and the harm, and that the compensation is limited to the *damnum emergens* and *lucrum cessans*, plus interests.

The aim of the White Paper was to ensure a consistent application of this principle, through a twofold action. Firstly, it intended to deny that the application

---

[83] Green Paper – Damages Actions for Breach of the EC Antitrust Rules SEC (2005) 1732 COM/2005, 672 at 2.4.

[84] Ibid., para 2.4.

[85] Denis Waelbroeck, Donald Slater and Gil Even-Shoshan, 'Study on the Conditions of Claims for Damages in Case of Infringement of EC Competition Rules (Ashurst Study)' (2004) 6, available at http://ec.europa.eu/competition/antitrust/actionsdamages/comparative_report_clean en.pdf.

[86] Some of the US scholars share a similar view commenting on the point that 'We, however, address a more fundamental question: assuming the procedural details could be worked out, would the objectives of the antitrust laws be advanced or retarded by allowing indirect purchasers to sue? This question, we believe, can be fruitfully addressed with the assistance of economic analysis. That analysis leads us to conclude that allowing indirect purchasers to sue would probably retard rather than advance antitrust enforcement. The basis for this conclusion lies in the detrimental impact that allowing a passing-on defense would have on enforcement by direct purchasers'. William M. Landes and Richard A. Posner, 'Should Indirect Purchasers Have Standing to Sue Under the Antitrust Laws? An Economic Analysis of the Rule of Illinois Brick' [1979] 46 *The University of Chicago Law Review* 602, 620.

[87] White Paper on Damages Actions for Breach of the EC Antitrust Rules SEC (2008) 404–406.

[88] Joined Cases C-295/04 to C-298/04 *Vincenzo Manfredi v Lloyd Adriatico Assicurazioni SpA* [2006] ECR I-6619; Case C-453/99 *Courage Ltd v Bernard Crehan and Bernard Crehan v Courage Ltd and Others* ECR I-06297.

182   *Causation in Indirect and Secondary Antitrust Damages*

of the right to compensation could lead to multiple compensation and artificial multiplication of lawsuits.[89] Secondly, the White Paper sought to avoid unjust enrichment of the claimant who actually passed on the overcharge.[90]

Therefore, the Commission proposed to make available both a passing–on defence for the defendant and the right for the indirect purchaser to claim for damages connected to the cartel. Regarding the standard of proof, the White Paper also pointed out that for the defendant it should not be lower than the burden imposed on the claimant to prove the damage. For indirect purchasers, instead, the Commission suggested the integration of the normative text with a rebuttable presumption that the illegal overcharge was passed on to them.[91]

7.2.2 *The Directive Proposal and Its Amendments*

In the wake of the previously mentioned CJEU case law and the White Paper, the Draft Directive[92] stated that injured parties are entitled to compensation for actual loss (overcharge harm) and loss of profit. The direct purchaser who passes the overcharge on is entitled, therefore, to claim the loss of profit due to the reduction of the volume sold consequent to the increase of price.

The Commission then pointed out the situation – before neglected – that the pass-on can take place also in an upward direction on the supply chain (for instance, in cases of buying cartels).[93]

With Article 12, the Commission then introduced the main innovation to the previous formulations. In particular, Article 12(2) states that 'Insofar as the overcharge has been passed on to persons at the next level of the supply chain for whom it is legally impossible to claim compensation for their harm, the defendant shall not be able to invoke the defence referred to in the preceding paragraph'.

This article changed with a norm stating more simply that the defendant in an action for damages can invoke the passing on as a defence if the claimant passed on the whole or part of the overcharge resulting from the infringement. Moreover, it provided that the burden of proving that the overcharge was passed on rested with the defendant.

Article 13 determined that the passing-on of the overcharge is presumed unless the infringement is proven. The defendant is entitled to give proof that the overcharge has not been passed on or has been only partially passed on to the indirect purchaser.

---

[89]   Ibid., para 2.6.
[90]   Ibid., para 2.6.
[91]   Ibid., para 2.6.
[92]   Proposal for a Directive of the European Parliament and of the Council on Certain Rules Governing Actions for Damages under National Law for Infringements of the Competition Law Provisions of the Member States and of the European Union COM (2013) 404.
[93]   Ibid., para 4.4.

7.2.3 *The Directive 104/2014*

Article 12(1) of the Damages Directive lays down the general principle establishing both the indirect purchaser claims and the passing-on defence. With regard to passing on, the compensatory and unjust enrichment principles are further developed in Article 12(2), for which 'compensation for actual loss at any level of the supply chain does not exceed the overcharge harm suffered at that level'. Firstly, Article 12(1) applies the judgments *Manfredi*[94] and *Courage*, stating that compensation of harm can be claimed by anyone who suffered a damage, including indirect purchasers.[95] Moreover, it clarifies that, as for all the other claims based on infringement of competition law, the compensation consists of actual loss and loss of profits.

As a general rule, the indirect purchaser claiming for damages bears the burden of proving the passing-on.[96] The indirect purchaser, however, benefits from a sum of presumptions (provisional and rebuttable), which (at least at first glance) should simplify the claim.

Firstly, the Directive instructs the national judge that the passing-on has to be assessed, 'taking into account the commercial practice that price increases are passed on down the supply chain'.[97] This statement is partly disproven by part of the economic literature[98] and by the same Commission's Practical Guide on Quantifying Harm, which states that 'Where the direct customer of the infringing undertakings uses the cartelised goods to compete in a downstream market, it is likely that the direct customer will normally not be able to pass on this increase in cost (or only to a very limited degree) if their own competitors in that downstream market are not subject to the same or a similar overcharge (for example, where they receive their input from a market that is not subject to the cartel)'.[99] This apparent inconsistency may be justified by the objective of simplifying the burden of proof for indirect purchasers. However, this statement accounts to a provisional presumption, as it simply states a matter of fact but does not need to be rebutted, since it is left to the free evaluation of the judge. Moreover, it is apparently limited to benefit the indirect purchaser, and it should not operate in support of a passing-on defence.

At Article 14(2), the Directive lays out instead a rebuttable presumption of damage dependent on the realization of three conditions: (1) that the defendant infringed the competition law; (2) that it applied an overcharge to the direct purchaser, causally linked to the infringement and (3) that the claimant purchased those or derived

---

[94] Joined Cases C-295/04 to C-298/04 *Vincenzo Manfredi v Lloyd Adriatico Assicurazioni SpA* [2006] ECR I-6619.

[95] Article 12(1).

[96] Article 14.

[97] Ibid.

[98] Frank P Maier-Rigaud, 'Toward a European Directive on Damages Actions' [2014] 10 *Journal of Competition Law and Economics* 341.

[99] Commission Staff Working Document – Practical Guide on Quantifying Harm in Actions for Damages Based on Breaches of Article 101 or 102 of the Treaty on the Functioning of the European Union SWD (2013) 205.

184 Causation in Indirect and Secondary Antitrust Damages

goods or services. The broad formulation of the third condition placed by Article 14 (2) also simplifies the burden of proof of the claimant but creates interpretative issues. What does the norm mean by 'goods or services derived from or containing the goods or services that were the subject of the infringement'? This is open to question. For instance, firms generally deliver services relying on their assets (facilities and other goods). A sensitive increase in the price of a specific asset may predictably cause a relative increase of firm's costs and therefore may affect the price of the service offered.[100] However, it is not clear whether the service can be defined as being derived from the goods subject to antitrust infringement. We may replicate the same reasoning for goods containing or derived from other goods – for instance, by processing. In both cases, a causative link must exist between the price overcharge and the increase passed on. This may happen when the direct purchaser sets the price of the goods or services on a cost-plus basis and the price increase is directly determined by the overcharge. This reasoning can be extended to all cases where the good or service passed through the supply chain is somehow related but not yet part of the good or service subject to the infringement. Otherwise, we should admit damages actions from any indirect purchaser related to any of the goods or services of subjects that purchased cartel products. The link of causation would be definitely lost, and the function of the antitrust compensation would be distorted. On the other hand, limiting the compensation to those market actors that purchased goods derived from the ones subject to infringement may bring substantial inequalities in treatment.

In a recent case, the Tribunale di Milano (the Italian first instance court)[101] assumed that the overcharge imposed by SEA, an undertaking managing the airports of Milan, to Swiss International Air Lines was passed on by the airliner, as the ticket price included the airport fees.[102] Hence, the court seemed to maintain that, when a cost item is part of the good resold by the direct purchaser, one has to presume that the price included the overcharge which was therefore passed on.

---

[100] Take, for instance, the following example. The international law firm 'X' purchases a number of printers from the undertaking 'Y'. After few years, it comes out that the seller took part to a printers' cartel. In the meantime, the law firm decides to raise its fees. Are the clients of the law firm entitled to claim compensation as indirect purchasers? Can we say that the service offered by the law firm is derived by the use of the printers and therefore its cost reflects also the cartel overcharge? See Robin Noble, 'Passing Game: The Ongoing Debate about Pass-on in Damages Actions' (*Oxera*, January 2014), available at www.oxera.com/agenda/passing-game-the-ongoing-debate-about-pass-on-in-damages-actions/, accessed 5 April 2019.

[101] Tribunale di Milano, *SEA v Swiss International Air Lines*, n 7970/2016, 27.06.2016.

[102] Here the judge granted the passing-on defence, dismissing, therefore, the claim for damages of Swiss Airlines.

7.2.4 Indirect Purchasers of Buyers' Cartels

Recital (43) of the Directive argues that 'Infringements of competition law often concern the conditions and the price under which goods or services are sold, and lead to an overcharge and other harm for the customers of the infringers. The infringement may also concern supplies to the infringer (for example in the case of a buyers' cartel). In such cases, the actual loss could result from a lower price paid by infringers to their suppliers. This Directive and in particular the rules on passing-on should apply accordingly to those cases'. In other words, the Directive maintains that the price reduction obtained by the cartelists should be treated as an overcharge. Generally, a buyers' cartel either reduces prices downstream or leaves them unchanged, depending on the level of competition in the downstream market. Economic theory explains that when the buying cartel does not face enough competition in the downstream market, it is likely that the cartel or, similarly, the monopsony will not pass on the price reduction downstream.[103] The cartel or monopsony will, rather, reduce the level of inputs, thus generating a welfare loss.[104] The quantity of inputs purchased by a company is determined at the point of intersection between the marginal costs and the purchase price; thus, lower prices generally correspond to a reduction of inputs. However, in the case of a buyers' cartel this brings also a reduction of outputs and, therefore, to a distortion in the downstream market.

Recital (43) of the Directive qualifies the lower price paid by the buying cartel as an actual loss – that is, the harm to the supplier corresponding to the difference between the competitive price and the price actually paid by the cartelists. Therefore, the lower price obtained by buyers' cartels and monopsonists, and paid by suppliers, qualifies as anticompetitive harm, which is subject inter alia to the rules on passing-on established by the Directive. The indirect buyers of the cartel's supplier will benefit from Article 14(2), as it is presumed that the price reduction will be passed on upstream if the three conditions specified are fulfilled. This presumption, though, does not take into consideration that upstream price adaptation is possible only if the supplier has a relevant buyer's power. In all the other cases, the supplier will more likely adapt prices of its other outputs, especially to competitors of the infringers that are not able to impose similar discounts (i.e., the waterbed effect).[105] Moreover, according to a strict interpretation of the Directive, some of these subjects will not be entitled to damages based on passing on, as they

---

[103] Organisation for Economic Co-Operation and Development, *Monopsony and Buyer Power [Roundtable on Monopsony and Buyer Power Held in October 2008]* (OECD, 2008).

[104] Jean Tirole, *The Theory of Industrial Organization* (MIT Press, 1988) 66–92; Ariel Ezrachi, 'Buying Alliances and Input Price Fixing: In Search of a European Enforcement Standard' [2012] 8 *Journal of Competition Law and Economics* 47.

[105] Roman Inderst and Tommaso M Valletti, 'Buyer Power and the "Waterbed Effect"' (2011) 59 *The Journal of Industrial Economics* 1; Adrian N Majumdar, 'Waterbed Effects and Buyer Mergers' [2005] CCP Working Paper No. 05-7, available at http://papers.ssrn.com/sol3/papers.cfm?

have not purchased goods or services derived from the ones subject to infringement. However, they may try to claim damages under the general rules of compensation.[106] Furthermore, the application of the passing-on presumption to upstream cartels may create incongruent judgments if the cartelists pass downstream at least part of the price reduction, assuming that this pass-on does not fulfil the requirement of Article 101(3) TFEU. Although the unjust enrichment of the infringers is not a criterion for determining compensation for the Directive,[107] the passing-on of at least part of the price reduction downstream may prove that that part of the reduction may have benefited the downstream market and did not distort it. In consequence, there would be a mitigated enrichment on the side of the cartelists.

7.2.5 Cost Savings and Reduced Expenditures

The identification of the damage with a token overcharge, which can be passed on only vertically, fails to show that price changes are transmitted throughout the supply chain, rippling both horizontally and vertically. In other words, the victim of the antitrust infringement, instead of simply passing on the overcharge to the next stage, may, for instance, adapt prices of goods and services that he or she sells or buys, depending on the market structure and the bargaining power he or she can exert in that market. More in detail, the purchaser may, instead of passing on the token overcharge, try to reduce its expenditures or cut costs. While the former may bring about a loss of profits because the firm cuts back on the scope of production, the latter may cause damages to third parties connected to the firm. These damaged parties may well bring a claim for compensation of damages, provided that they can substantiate a causal relationship between the harm suffered and the prohibited arrangement. However, it seems that they will not be able to rely on the special provisions regulating the passing-on of the overcharge.[108]

As already observed, when the direct purchaser reacts to the illegal overcharge adapting the firm's costs, these adaptations may not fulfil the definition of passing on. For instance, a car producer affected by a cartel on car glasses may decide, instead of increasing the price of its cars, to reduce its marketing budget. Here it is clear that the marketing services are not derived from the upstream (car glass) market. The CAT has investigated an equivalent hypothesis in the *Sainsbury's* case. Sainsbury's claimed losses due to the credit card payment cartel, which inflated the interchange fees.

---

abstract_id=911574, accessed 15 July 2015; Zhiqi Chen, 'Dominant Retailers and the Countervailing-Power Hypothesis' [2003] 34(4) *RAND Journal of Economics* 612.

[106] As established in Article 3.

[107] The Damages Directive does not mention the unjust enrichment or any other provision on restitution, therefore leaving the regulatory power to domestic laws.

[108] Ibid.

7.2 The Regulatory Framework in the EU

The cartel was based on the so-called MasterCard scheme, which consisted in a network of contracts adopted by MasterCard to regulate the terms of the use of the payment service and connect shops to consumers.[109] MasterCard licensed a number of institutes ('Acquiring Banks') that, at their turn, stipulated contracts with the merchants for the acceptance of a MasterCard card. The holder of a credit or debit card, on the other hand, was enabled to swap his or her card at the merchant cash register, thanks to the agreement concluded with an 'Issuing Bank' that participated to the MasterCard network. This scheme was governed by the 'MasterCard Scheme Rules'. When a card transaction is required, the acquiring bank transmits the information of the transaction to the issuing bank. The latter, authorizes the payment and retains an 'interchange fee' before sending the rest of the amount to the acquiring bank, which forwards this amount minus a charge to for the service to the merchant.

Sainsbury's contended that this network of contracts essentially was an anticompetitive agreement, thus violating Article 101 TFEU and chapter I of the Competition Act 1998, and that the damage corresponded to the overcharge fee reckoned as the difference between the UK MIF applied to the merchants and the interchange fee that would have been applied but for the anticompetitive agreement.[110]

MasterCard objected that there was no infringement of competition law, that the fee was objectively necessary and that, in any case, the claimant passed on the fee.[111] On this latter point, the CAT wondered whether reducing the expenditures or the running costs accounts to a passing on. It concluded that, while for an economist this may be a pass-on case, legally it is not.[112] If we think of the overcharge damages as a token that can be passed on in whole or in part, cost savings and reduced expenditures would not account to a pass-on. We have a pass-on only when there is an increase in retail price, which is causally connected to the price overcharge. For this reason, the CAT observed that the claimant has to show that the defendant has raised prices and that this raise is causally connected to the overcharge paid.[113] The CAT established that the passing-on defence can be used only if two conditions are met: (1) there is an identifiable increases in prices by a firm to its customers and (2) the increase in price must be causally connected with the overcharge, and demonstrably so.[114]

---

[109] *Sainsbury's Supermarkets Ltd v MasterCard Incorporated and Others* [2016] CAT 11.

[110] Ibid., para 12 ff.

[111] Ibid., para 17 ff.

[112] Ibid., para 95.

[113] See para 485, where the CAT states that 'It follows that MasterCard's pass-on defence must fail. No identifiable increase in retail price has been established, still less one that is causally connected with the UK MIF. Nor can MasterCard identify any purchaser or class of purchasers of Sainsbury's to whom the overcharge has been passed who would be in a position to claim damages'.

[114] Para 484.

188   *Causation in Indirect and Secondary Antitrust Damages*

This opinion seems to be consistent with the Directive 104/2014, describing the damage more as a token overcharge, which can be passed on only vertically, rather than a costs-price adaptation. However, this would not impede possible claims from market actors harmed by reduced expenditures or costs savings. These subjects may, for instance, claim damages for lost profits or lost chances however without relying on the special norms on the passing-on.

7.3 INDIRECT PURCHASERS AGGRIEVED BY UMBRELLA EFFECTS

A cartel exerts, by definition, a monopolist-like power on the market,[115] even when it does not control the whole relevant market. This situation makes it possible for the cartel to impose prices higher than the market value of the goods or services.[116] However, some competitors may remain in the market, or the market itself may maintain a certain degree of elasticity as to redirect buyers to substitute goods.[117]

In order to determine the price of the good or service, the seller does not consider solely elements internal to the firm such as turnover, production costs and the units sold but also examines the price choices of competitors. For doing so, the firm adopts as a benchmark for setting its own prices the market price of the same goods. Hence, if, due to an illicit collusion, this market price is artificially inflated, the non-cartelist will likely follow the price trend and raise its selling prices, causing a damage to its buyers. In a nutshell, this is what the ECJ stated in the case *Kone AG and Others* v *ÖBB-Infrastruktur AG*.[118] ÖBB, a subsidiary of the Austrian Federal Railways, the national railway company purchased a number of elevators and installed a considerable amount of supplies of escalators and lifts from suppliers which were not connected to the cartel.[119] ÖBB claimed, therefore, damages against

---

[115] ECJ, Case C-13/60 'Geitling', ECR 1962/00083; Luis Ortiz Blanco, *Market Power in EU Antitrust Law* (Hart, 2011) 128.

[116] Jonathan B Baker and Timothy F Bresnahan, 'Empirical Methods of Identifying and Measuring Market Power' [1997] 27 *Journal of Reprints for Antitrust Law and Economics* 743; *Market Power Handbook: Competition Law and Economic Foundations* (American Bar Association, 2005) 142.

[117] Roman Inderst, Frank P Maier-Rigaud and Ulrich Schwalbe, 'Umbrella Effects' [2014] 10 *Journal of Competition Law and Economics* 739. The American doctrine began to include umbrella damages into the 'net harm to others' long ago. See John M Connor and Robert H Lande, nde, Connor and Robert H n to include umbrella damages into the Effectsfectsa da, 461; Phillip Areeda and Herbert Hovenkamp, *Fundamentals of Antitrust Law* (Aspen Publishers Online, 2011) 337.3. However, the US courts reject the idea that the umbrella effects can give right to claim damages; see US District Court of Columbia, *In Re: Vitamins Antitrust Litigation* (2001) Lexis 12114; 2001-2 Trade Cas. (CCH) P73, 339 and U.S. District Court, S.D. New York, *Gross c. New Balance Athletic Shoe*, 11 February 1997, Inc. n 96 CIV. 4921 (RWS), MDL-1154.

[118] Case C-557/12 *Kone AG and Others* v *ÖBB-Infrastruktur AG*, 5 June 2014 ECLI:EU: C:2014:1317.

[119] The claim included three heads of damages: the first for purchases done directly from cartel members; the second for the overcharge passed-on by suppliers of ÖBB that purchased supplies

7.3 Indirect Purchasers Aggrieved by Umbrella Effects

the cartel members, maintaining that in absence of the cartel, the price charged by non-cartel members would have been lower.

The *Kone* decision considers only this possibility. However, a second scenario also can be advanced. The non-cartelist may decide to raise prices not by imitation but consequently to the increase in demand of its substitute goods.[120] Those who can no longer purchase the goods subject to cartel will turn, in fact, to the producers of alternative goods with a consequent increase in demand for them. This second possibility seems more likely, moreover, in markets where information about the prices charged by competitors is difficult to access. From the point of view of the causal relationship, it does not matter, though, if the issue at hand falls in one case or the other. Both dynamics are anticompetitive effects of the offense that has distorted the market, resulting in fixing supra-competitive prices. The problem is to determine whether there is an adequate causal link between the first and the second.

7.3.1 *Causation and Umbrella Effects*

According to the Austrian Supreme court, the 'umbrella' seller had freely established the selling price of the goods, thus interrupting the causal link between the anticompetitive conduct and the harm suffered by the plaintiff. To reach this conclusion, the Austrian judge relied on the domestic principle of causation.[121]

For the purpose of solving the case, the ECJ considered that, in spite of the doubts harboured by the national court, the domestic theories of causation, as applied in the specific case, violate the principle of effectiveness of European law.[122] If the national judge denies the right to compensation for lack of adequate legal causation under domestic law, the effectiveness of the prohibition of anticompetitive agreements would inevitably be compromised. The wrongfulness of the conduct occurs, therefore, not only, as claimed by the *Oberster Gerichtshof*, with respect to damages caused to the direct buyers of the cartel but also to other subjects, provided that the damage is causally linked to the behaviour and is foreseeable.[123]

---

from cartelists; and, finally, part of the action concerned the umbrella prices. ÖBB claimed reparation of damages felt as a consequence of price overcharges caused by the cartel, for a total amount of 8.134.344,54 euros. Only a third of it (precisely 1.839.239,74 euros) has become subject of the plea that induced the Austrian Supreme Court to submit a request for preliminary ruling to the CJEU.

[120] Inderst, Maier-Rigaud and Schwalbe (n 117) 742, where the authors comment also on the umbrella effects caused by the overcharge passed through the market chain.

[121] Case C-557/12 *Kone AG* (n 118) para 28.

[122] For which the domestic legal system should not render practically impossible or excessively difficult the exercise of rights conferred by community law, CJEU, C-453/99 *Courage Ltd v Bernard Crehan* and *Bernard Crehan v Courage Ltd and Others*, 20 September 2001, in ECR I-06297.

[123] Case C-557/12 *Kone AG* (n 118) para 28.

190 *Causation in Indirect and Secondary Antitrust Damages*

The ECJ observed that the causal chain is not interrupted by a decision taken *ad nutum* by the non-cartelist, for the direct purchaser has determined the selling price based on the market price altered by the cartel.[124] The court also stated that the increase in the prices of alternative goods is a phenomenon that must certainly be foreseen by the cartelists.[125] It follows that the buyer of the distributor, unrelated to the illegal agreement, has the right to seek compensation for the damage caused by the overcharge, just as the direct or indirect purchasers of the cartelists do.

7.3.2 *Legal Causation and the Burden of Proof*

The Court of Justice also requires the application of a principle of direct causality that, in spite of what is said, was never detailed by the court's case law.[126] The European legislator admits, in the Directive on damages claim, the lack of a common concept of legal causation and refers to the judgment *Manfredi* for a provisional solution.[127]

The Court of Justice in its judgment considers necessary for the award of damages a prior verification that, given the peculiarities of the specific market, the agreement is likely to create a price umbrella in the market. Additionally, the CJEU argues that this effect shall be expected by all cartelists.[128] However, the court avoids detailing the burden to prove such circumstances in future similar cases.

The attempt to harmonize the various positions adopted by domestic laws with respect to damages resulting from the umbrella effects was then arrested on the ground of the burden of proof. It will be, therefore, up to the national courts to identify the rules applicable to it. According to a generally accepted principle amongst European jurisdictions in the field of non-contractual liability, the claimant bears the burden of proving whether the injury has been caused by the defendant's behaviour.

The victim must then prove the existence of a cartel (in the case of stand-alone actions), the suitability of this cartel to create an umbrella effect on the market and the presence of a causal link between the unlawful behaviour and the damage.

It might be objected that it is necessary for the claimant also to substantiate the causative link between the fact of the cartel and the increase in prices by the non-colluding seller. This must be ruled out, first of all, based on what the court says, since the judgment limits the burden of proof only on the suitability of the collusion

---

[124] Ibid., para 33.

[125] Case C-557/12 *Kone AG* (n 118) para 29.

[126] See supra para 4.2.

[127] Directive 2014/104/EU of the European Parliament and of the Council of 26 November 2014 on Certain Rules Governing Actions for Damages under National Law for Infringements of the Competition Law Provisions of the Member States and of the European Union, OJ L 349 Recital (11).

[128] Para 37.

7.3 Indirect Purchasers Aggrieved by Umbrella Effects

to create an umbrella price and not also to its inflating effect on seller's prices. Moreover, a careful examination of the causal link within the principles of national law reveals that the damage (i.e., the overcharge paid by the buyer) must be a probable consequence of the wrongful act, which is the anticompetitive agreement and not the sale made by the independent undertaking. Therefore, the claimant should not be asked to prove the behaviour of the seller in relation to the cartel or that he or she had increased prices as a result of the anticompetitive agreement. In this regard, the claimant shall only prove the presence of a (potential) 'price umbrella' created by the cartel, together with the circumstance that the prices imposed by the non-colluding seller are higher than the market standard price. The decision requires that the umbrella purchaser, in order to claim for damages, has to establish that 'the cartel at issue was, in the circumstances of the case and, in particular, the specific aspects of the relevant market, liable to have the effect of umbrella pricing being applied by third parties acting independently, and that those circumstances and specific aspects could not be ignored by the members of that cartel'.[129]

In this perspective, it is also useful to refer to the presumption of cartel damage laid down in the Directive.[130] However, the rule does not define or otherwise delimit such damages. With this presumption, therefore, the buyer of goods or services of colluding undertakings would have to prove only the extent of the injury and not the damage itself. In the case of umbrella pricing, however, the damage is induced and not directly caused by the cartel overcharge. Indeed, even the Court of Justice provides that it must first be established that the characteristics of the market concerned has made possible the application of a price umbrella. Therefore, it must be the claimant to prove these market conditions. He or she will benefit from the presumption of cartel damage when it is given sufficient justification of the adequacy of the cartel to influence market prices. At this point, based on the interpretation of the Directive in conformity with the law in question, the presumption will play its role.

A further aspect of the test, not clarified by the court, is the quantification of the damage caused by umbrella pricing. The independent undertaking, in fact, does not necessarily apply an overcharge equal to the one imposed by the cartel. The proof of the quantum of damages appears, therefore, entrusted in such cases to complex economic arguments which will have to determine to what extent the non-colluding firm increased prices with reference to the market price.

---

[129] Case C-557/12 *Kone* (n 118) para 34.
[130] Article 17(2).

Conclusion

Causation in competition law damages actions shows peculiarities that distinguish it from any other tort in civil law and common law countries. An antitrust infringement causes a pure economic loss that the victim is entitled to recover – depending on the jurisdiction – on the basis of a statutorily protected interest or a subjective right, under EU law. The wide range of subjects and heads of damages involved in this process makes the identification of the causal link a particularly difficult task for parties and judges. In confirmation of this, the analysis of national case law suggests that claimants are often discouraged from bringing damages claims characterized by high causal uncertainty. Moreover, causation is closely related to other legal concepts, especially the right to stand, responsibility for tortious damages, and the wrongful harm. The confusion in the case law and jurisprudence, which often use these terms interchangeably, fuels the uncertainty in the assessment of causation.

This book has therefore examined the concept of causation, identifying its essential elements in EU competition law litigation. Whereas each jurisdiction has developed a different concept of causal nexus, they have started a slow process of harmonization in competition law. This is bringing about a certain degree of convergence, through successive judgements of the CJEU and the implementation of the Damages Directive. However, as this book explains, the diversities in the approaches to the reconstruction of the causal link in the jurisdictions analyzed still exist and are evident.

The European Union courts have dealt with the issue of the causal link in different cases. Notwithstanding this, it is not possible to find in this case law the formulation of an independent principle of causation. By consequence, it is necessary to resort to the domestic antitrust laws and laws of obligations. On a theoretical level, the solutions laid down by national courts differ in many aspects. They differ from a substantive as well as a procedural perspective. As Chapters 1 and 2 examined, each jurisdiction adopts different visions and theories of causation, both factual and legal.

Conclusion

The book has then analyzed also the proof rules for causation. In this regard it concluded that they also tend to differ as to the standards they impose and with regard to the exceptions to the standard burden of proof. From a practical viewpoint, these differences are more important for parties that need to know how to substantiate and pose a question of fact or a question of law, rather than for the results they bring with the judicial decisions.

CAUSAL UNCERTAINTY

The assessment of causation generally takes place according to a multistage process. The but-for test for material or factual causation poses interpretative issues especially in cases of overdetermined causes and preemption. Here, judges generally analyze the contribution of each event to determine if they are causes of the harm or not. From a theoretical perspective, in such cases, it is therefore better to utilize scalar theories of causation considering the 'involvement' or the 'contribution' of a cause to the harm, rather than their necessary nature to the causation of the same harm.

Moreover, the book has considered the causal uncertainty due to defendant indeterminacy. In case of cartels and other joint infringements of competition law, Article 11 of the Damages Directive establishes the joint and several liability of each infringer. Here, the breach of law of each potential defendant is established, while their specific causal contribution to the claimant's harm may be uncertain. In such cases, the claimant has the burden to prove causation only between the joint infringement and his or her harm. This system, in other words, puts on the defendant the burden to prove the causal contribution of its co-infringers through special redress mechanisms.

In all other cases of uncertain causation due to multiple defendants, the domestic laws of causation apply. Some jurisdictions potentially accept causal proportional liability approaches in place of the traditional all-or-nothing. Compared to joint and several liability, the adoption of a causal proportional liability test changes the distribution of the burden of proof. If antitrust infringers are jointly and severally liable, the claimant does not need to prove the extent of contribution of each tortfeasor but will have to meet the requisite standard of proof to establish causation. On the other hand, according to the causal proportional liability approach, the claimant has to provide evidence of the extent of each contribution to the damage; however, the assessment would be based on the probability of this contribution to realize in the counterfactual scenario.

Defendant indeterminacy may be due also to the establishment of liability within corporate conglomerates. Under EU law, the parent company is liable for the harm caused by the subsidiary, even when there was no direct causal contribution to the harm of the former. There is indeed a rebuttable presumption that the parent influenced the behaviour of its subsidiary, by exercising 'decisive influence'. The parent can rebut this presumption by proving lack of control. It is, in other words, a

194 *Conclusion*

proof of absence of direct or indirect participation in the anticompetitive conduct. EU law does not establish a regime of contribution within the corporate group. Thus, domestic laws may opt for causal proportional liability or traditional all-or-nothing approaches to determine the responsibility of each company in the group or of the single economic entity as a whole. Here, the causal proportional liability approach may find application for the apportionment of liability among multiple tortfeasors and in conglomerates of companies not deemed responsible altogether as a single economic entity, when the circumstances would bring to a rejection of the claim. In particular, once established that each company causally contributed to the damage, the extent of their contribution, when too difficult to prove otherwise, may be determined on the basis of the market share rule.

The same system of causal proportional liability may find application in determining responsibility and damages for loss of opportunities. While causal proportional liability systems should not become the rule, they have a role in the proof of causation in claims for lost chances. An exploitative abuse brings about an actual loss in form of a diminution of value of a firm's assets. By the same token, the loss of chance is an actual loss caused in form of a heightened risk. Both are economic-immaterial injuries, but the latter justifies departures from the general proof rules of causation due to its special characteristics, in particular the uncertainty of the causal connection. However, the book has also observed that not all lost chances should be treated the same in competition litigation. A 30 per cent loss, in terms of future chances of reaching a certain objective, exercises a different power whether the loss takes the chances from 90 to 60 or from 40 to 10. In the latter case, indeed, the damage is clearly more important, since the successful expectations are highly diminished almost to 0, although in both cases, the quota amounts to 30 per cent. Here, the judge could exercise its discretionary power at the stage of calculation of damages, which can also be estimated in the amount deemed fair.

Finally, the adoption of an all-or-nothing approach shows its limits when the likeliness of a damage is close to a 'turning point'. In other words, when the probability of a damage is close to 50 per cent, the judge has to decide whether to award damages or leave the possible harm without compensation. In these cases, the application of a causal proportional liability approach may be introduced, although none of the analyzed jurisdictions adopts a similar approach for the time being.

THE SCOPE OF CAUSATION AND THE PROOF RULES

The book has also argued that the second stage of the causal assessment, generally called 'legal causation', needs a deeper analysis of the goals of competition law as they shape the scope of the protected interests in private enforcement. However, while EU law has established the right to full compensation of damages, the definition of the scope of this right is, to a large extent, left to the national judge. In absence of an overarching definition of the scope of this right, the EU courts are advancing a piecemeal harmonization of national rules. According to this jurisprudence it seems that restrictive interpretations of the principles of causation, especially with relation to the scope of the competition law rules, would hardly fulfil the requirements of the new rules of antitrust responsibility.

The second part of the book has explored the general proof rules for causation and the departures to these rules that have been established in each jurisdiction in cases of causal uncertainty. All these proof rules have been analyzed in connection to the causal theories that they operationalize. The legal requirements for factual and legal causation have an important bearing on the outcome of the litigation. Proving the anticompetitive harm under the rule of causal regularity is different from using the concept of remoteness. In other words, the concept of causal connection defines the object of the proof and therefore also the difficulty of discharging the burden of proof. The level of certainty required by the substantive rule of causation is, therefore, a relevant factor of the proof.

General proof rules relying on probabilities are usually more efficient, predictable, and fair than rules requiring a quasi-certainty standard, such as the finding of a direct causation. Moreover, they are generally consistent with the procedural rule establishing the 'presumption' of innocence of the defendant. The procedural norm stating the centrality of the presumption of innocence is a basic rule of fairness and a policy-based principle allocating the risk of error in the proceedings on the claimant. However, causal uncertainty in competition damages actions has created incentives to relax the evidential requirements, use rebuttable presumptions, or relax the standards of proof for causation.

A similar legal justification can be found for the adoption of presumptions benefitting the claimant under special circumstances. In cases of causal uncertainty, courts are often allowed to use rebuttable presumptions if the harm and the infringement have been already proven. Moreover, the claimant has to provide a prima facie evidence of causation between the two events. Here, the law may presume the existence of causation due to the high probability of such events to be connected, thanks to the evidence provided by the claimant. Given the likeliness of causation and the uncertainty due to informational asymmetries, the law deems fairer to burden the defendant with the proof of the absence of causation. In some other cases, courts use evidential presumptions whereby the burden of proof stays with the claimant, while the burden of providing evidence shifts to the defendant.

With regard to the use of presumptions in competition law litigation, the main risk is to conflate the proof of general with specific causation through economic presumptions. Economic expertise is a fundamental aspect of most if not every antitrust damages action. However, the concept of causality advanced by econometrics is largely different from the legal concept of causation. Econometric does not select causes on their legal significance. The aim of economic theories is not to determine responsibility of agents in the market but, rather, to establish connections between causes and effects. Moreover, econometric finds connections between

196 *Conclusion*

classes of events. This means that, at best, econometrics can determine the general causation. On the other hand, specific causation requires the establishment of objective or stochastic analysis of the specific causative event. Frequently, most of the evidence is based on expert witness testimonies. When courts presume causation based on the econometric study submitted by one of them, the risk is that the proof to the contrary may be impossible or too difficult to discharge, if the other party has not much more than a competing testimony. Thus, causation will be decided at the level of general class-based probabilities, rather specific probabilities of causation.

INDIRECT DAMAGES AND THE LIMITS OF HARMONIZATION

The use of causal presumptions is even higher for 'indirect' and 'secondary' antitrust damages, given their high causal uncertainty. Passing-on of overcharges and umbrella effects have now a unified approach under the Damages Directive and the ECJ's jurisprudence. While it remains uncertain the treatment of other damages of the same nature. It seems that courts will have to rely on the creation of causal presumptions based on the provision of prima facie evidence by the claimant. Moreover, courts may relax the standards of proof, especially in those jurisdictions having requirements higher than the balance of probability.

The case law on the passing-on of the overcharge has shown that the diversity of approaches to the causal link does not impede the achievement of the common aims established by EU law and the uniform interpretation of the function of competition law damages actions. The CJEU appears to be still reluctant to conceptualize such aspects of the private antitrust enforcement, and the recent legislative interventions have put forward the same cautious approach. The European Commission and the Parliament while aiming at the convergence of domestic laws of obligations, offered a similar piecemeal harmonization of liability standards. It seems therefore that the principles of effectiveness and equivalence put the main curbs on the interpretation of national rules of causation. Within these limits, there is still room for regulatory competition among domestic laws of obligations and procedure. Here, the EU law will have to solve the tension that will inevitably arise between the different member states' approaches to causation and the unfairness of having the same infringement of EU law treated differently across the union.

Bibliography

BOOKS

ABA, *Market Power Handbook: Competition Law and Economic Foundations* (ABA Publishing, 2005).

ABA Antitrust, *Proving Antitrust Damages* (ABA Publishing, 2010).

Almunia J and others, *Private Enforcement of Competition Law* (Lex Nova, 2011).

Alpa G, *La responsabilità civile: Parte generale* (Wolters Kluwer Italia, 2010).

Diritto privato comparato: Istituti e problemi (Laterza, 2012).

Alpa G and Bessone M, *La Responsabilità Civile*, vol 2 (Giuffrè, 1980).

Anderson T, Schum D and Twining W, *Analysis of Evidence* (Cambridge University Press, 2005).

Andersson H and Winiger B, *Digest of European Tort Law*, vol 1 (Springer, 2007).

Areeda P and Hovenkamp H, *Fundamentals of Antitrust Law* (Aspen Publishers, 2011).

Areeda P, Hovenkamp H and Solow JL, *Antitrust Law* (Aspen Publishers, 2001).

Ashton D, *Competition Damages Actions in the EU: Law and Practice*, 2nd edn. (Edward Elgar Publishing, 2018).

Ashton D and Henry D, *Competition Damages Actions in the EU: Law and Practice* (Edward Elgar Publishing, 2013).

Baltagi B, *Econometrics* (Springer Science & Business Media, 2011).

Banakas EK, *Tortious Liability for Pure Economic Loss: A Comparative Study* (Hellenic Institute of International and Foreign Law, 1989).

Banakas EK, (eds), *Civil Liability for Pure Economic Loss. Proceedings of the Annual International Colloquium of the United Kingdom National Committee of Comparative Law Held in Norwich, September 1994* (Kluwer Law International, 1996).

Barcellona M, *Inattuazione dello scambio e sviluppo capitalistico: formazione storica e funzione della disciplina del danno contrattuale* (Giuffrè, 1980).

Trattato della responsabilità civile (UTET Giuridica, 2011).

Barnard C and Odudu O, *The Outer Limits of European Union Law* (Hart, 2009).

Basedow J, *Private Enforcement of EC Competition Law* (Kluwer Law International, 2007).

Basedow J and Wurmnest W, *Structure and Effects in EU Competition Law: Studies on Exclusionary Conduct and State Aid* (Kluwer Law International, 2011).

Bastianon S, *L'abuso di posizione dominante* (Giuffrè, 2001).

198   *Bibliography*

Diritto antitrust dell'Unione europea (Giuffrè, 2011).

Beebee H, Hitchcock C and Menzies P, *The Oxford Handbook of Causation* (Oxford University Press, 2009).

Beever A, *Rediscovering the Law of Negligence* (Hart, 2009).

Benacchio GA and Carpagnano M, *Il private enforcement del diritto comunitario della concorrenza: ruolo e competenze dei giudici nazionali: Atti del II Convegno di studio tenuto presso la Facoltà di giurisprudenza di Trento, 8-9 maggio 2009* (Wolters Kluwer Italia, 2009).

I rimedi civilistici agli illeciti anticoncorrenziali. Private Enforcement of Competition Law (CEDAM, 2012).

Bonvicini E, *La responsabilità civile: Responsabilità da accadimento tipico. Parte speciale: Il danno a persona* (Giuffrè, 1971).

Boyer M, Kotchoni R and CIRANO, *The econometrics of cartel overcharges* (CIRANO, 2011)

Breccia U, *Le obbligazioni* (Giuffrè, 1991).

Burrows AS, *Remedies for Torts and Breach of Contract* (Oxford University Press, 2004)

Busnelli FD, *La Lesione Del Credito Da Parte Di Terzi* (1963).

Busnelli FD and Patti S, *Danno e responsabilità civile* (G Giappichelli Editore, 2013).

Bussani M and Palmer VV, *Pure Economic Loss in Europe* (Cambridge University Press, 2003).

Buttigieg E, *Competition Law: Safeguarding the Consumer Interest: A Comparative Analysis of US Antitrust Law and EC Competition Law* (Kluwer Law International, 2009).

Cafaggi F, *Contractual Networks, Inter-Firm Cooperation and Economic Growth* (Edward Elgar Publishing, 2011).

Cafaggi F and Iamiceli P, *Reti di imprese tra crescita e innovazione organizzativa. Riflessioni da una ricerca sul campo* (Il Mulino, 2007).

Calabresi G, *The Costs of Accidents: A Legal and Economic Analysis* (Yale University Press, 1970).

Campbell D, Collins H and Wightman J, *Implicit Dimensions of Contract: Discrete, Relational and Network Contracts* (Hart, 2003).

Campbell JK, O'Rourke M and Silverstein H, *Causation and Explanation* (MIT Press, 2007).

Cane P, *Tort Law and Economic Interests* (Clarendon Press, 1996).

Responsibility in Law and Morality (Hart, 2002).

Cane P, Honoré T and Gardner J, *Relating to Responsibility: Essays for Tony Honoré on His Eightieth Birthday* (Hart, 2001).

Capecchi M, *Il Nesso Di Causalità: Dalla Condicio Sine qua Non Alla Responsabilità Proporzionale* (CEDAM, 2012).

Carbone V, *Il fatto dannoso nella responsabilità civile* (Jovene, 1969).

Cartwright N, *Hunting Causes and Using Them* (Cambridge University Press, 2007).

Hunting Causes and Using Them (Cambridge University Press, 2007).

Nature's Capacities and Their Measurement (Clarendon Press, 2010).

Castelli L, *Disciplina antitrust e illecito civile* (Giuffrè, 2012).

Catricalà A, *I contratti nella concorrenza* (UTET Giuridica, 2011).

Chalmers D, Davies G and Monti G, *European Union Law: Cases and Materials* (Cambridge University Press, 2010).

Collins JD, Hall EJ and Paul LA, *Causation and Counterfactuals* (MIT Press, 2004).

Causation and Counterfactuals (MIT Press, 2004).

Comoglio LP, *Le prove civili* (UTET, 2010).

Bibliography

Cooter R and others, *Il mercato delle regole: analisi economica del diritto civile* (Il Mulino, 2006).

Cooter R and Ulen T, *Law and Economics* (Pearson, 2013).

Craig P and Búrca GD, *EU Law: Text, Cases, and Materials* (Oxford University Press, 2011).
  The Evolution of EU Law (Oxford University Press, 2011).

Cseres KJ, *Competition Law and Consumer Protection* (Kluwer Law International, 2005).
  and others, *Criminalization of Competition Law Enforcement: Economic and Legal Implications for the EU Member States* (Edward Elgar Publishing, 2006).

Daintith T and Teubner G, *Contract and Organisation: Legal Analysis in the Light of Economic and Social Theory* (Walter de Gruyter, 1986).
  Contract and Organisation: Legal Analysis in the Light of Economic and Social Theory (Walter de Gruyter, 1986).

David R, *International Encyclopedia of Comparative Law* (Brill Archive, 1986).

Davidson D, *Essays on Actions and Events* (Clarendon Press; Oxford University Press, 1980).

De Cupis A, *Il danno: Teoria generale della responsabilità civile* (Giuffrè, 1979).

Deakin S, Johnston A and Markesinis B, *Markesinis and Deakin's Tort Law* (Oxford University Press, 2012).

de la Torre FC and Fournier EG, *Evidence, Proof and Judicial Review in EU Competition Law* (Edward Elgar Publishing, 2017).

Dennis I, *The Law of Evidence* (Sweet & Maxwell, 2013).

Denozza F, *Norme efficienti: L'analisi economica delle regole giuridiche* (Giuffrè, 2002).

Deringer A and Armengaud A, *The Competition Law of the European Economic Community: A Commentary on the EEC Rules of Competition (Articles 85 to 90) Including the Implementing Regulations and Directives* (Commerce Clearing House, 1968).

Dine J and Koutsias M, *Company Law* (Palgrave Macmillan, 2014).

Dougan M, *National Remedies before the Court of Justice: Issues of Harmonisation and Differentiation* (Hart, 2004).

Drahos M, *Convergence of Competition Laws and Policies in the European Community: Germany, Austria, and the Netherlands* (Kluwer Law International, 2001).

Duff RA, *Strict Liability, Legal Presumptions, and the Presumption of Innocence* (Oxford University Press, 2005).

Dwyer D, *The Judicial Assessment of Expert Evidence* (Cambridge University Press, 2009).

Eggleston SR, *Evidence, Proof, and Probability* (Weidenfeld and Nicolson, 1983).

Elhauge E, *Research Handbook on the Economics of Antitrust Law* (Edward Elgar Publishing, 2012).

Emson RN, *Evidence* (Palgrave Macmillan, 2008).

Epstein RJ, *A History of Econometrics* (North-Holland Amsterdam, 1987).

Etro F and Kokkoris I, *Competition Law and the Enforcement of Article 102* (Oxford University Press, 2010).

Ezrachi A, *Research Handbook on International Competition Law* (Edward Elgar Publishing, 2012).

Fagnart J-L, *La responsabilité civile: Chronique de jurisprudence 1985-1995* (Larcier, 1997).

Faure M, *Tort Law and Economics* (Edward Elgar Publishing, 2009).

Feldstein M and Auerbach AJ, *Handbook of Public Economics* (Elsevier, 2002).

Foer AA and Cuneo JW, *The International Handbook on Private Enforcement of Competition Law* (Edward Elgar Publishing, 2010).

Forchielli P, *Il rapporto di causalità nell'illecito civile* (CEDAM, 1960).
  Responsabilità civile (CEDAM, 1983).

Franklin J, *The Science of Conjecture: Evidence and Probability before Pascal* (Taylor & Francis, 2002).

Frei MA, *Der Rechtlich Relevante Kausalzusammenhang Im Strafrecht Im Vergleich Mit Dem Zivilrecht* (Schulthess Juristische Medien AG, 2010).

Galgano F, *Trattato di diritto civile* (Wolters Kluwer Italia, 2010).

Gardenfors P, *The Dynamics of Thought* (Springer Netherlands, 2005).

and others, *Evidentiary Value: Philosophical, Judicial, and Psychological Aspects of a Theory: Essays Dedicated to Sören Halldén on His Sixtieth Birthday* (CWK Gleerups, 1983).

Genovese A, *Il risarcimento del danno da illecito concorrenziale* (Edizioni scientifiche italiane, 2005).

Geradin D, Layne-Farrar A and Petit N, *EU Competition Law and Economics* (Oxford University Press, 2012).

Gerber D, *Global Competition: Law, Markets, and Globalization* (Oxford University Press, 2010).

Gerven W, Lever J and Larouche P, *Tort Law* (Hart, 2000).

Ghestin J and others, *Traité de droit civil: Les conditions de la responsabilité* (LGDJ, 1998).

Ghezzi F, Polo M and Preite D, *L'attuazione delle politiche di tutela della concorrenza e l'esperienza italiana di attività antitrust* (Università Bocconi, 1994).

Gilead I and others, *Proportional Liability: Analytical and Comparative Perspectives* (De Gruyter, 2013).

Glover R, *Murphy on Evidence* (Oxford University Press, 2013).

Goldberg JCP, Sebok AJ and Zipursky BC, *Tort Law: Responsibilities and Redress* (Wolters Kluwer Law & Business, 2016).

Goldberg JCP and Zipursky BC, *The Oxford Introductions to U.S. Law: Torts* (Oxford University Press, 2010).

Goldberg R, *Perspectives on Causation* (Hart, 2011).

Goldstein WM and Hogarth RM, *Research on Judgment and Decision Making: Currents, Connections, and Controversies* (Cambridge University Press, 1997).

Goudkamp J, Winfield SPH and Jolowicz JA, *Winfield and Jolowicz on Tort* (Sweet & Maxwell, 2014).

Green L, *Rationale of Proximate Cause* (Rothman Reprints, 1927).

Rationale of Proximate Cause (Rothman Reprints, 1927).

Judge and Jury (Vernon Law Book Company, 1930).

Green S, *Causation in Negligence* (Hart, 2015).

Harper FV, James F and Gray OS, *The Law of Torts* (Little, Brown, 1986).

Hart HLA and Honoré T, *Causation in the Law* (Oxford University Press, 1985).

Hawk BE, *International Antitrust Law & Policy: Fordham Corporate Law 2005* (Juris Publishing, Inc, 2006).

Ho HL, *A Philosophy of Evidence Law: Justice in the Search for Truth* (Oxford University Press, 2008).

Hodgson D, *The Law of Intervening Causation* (Ashgate Publishing, Ltd, 2008).

Holmes OW, *The Common Law* (Barnes & Noble Publishing, 2004).

Hovenkamp H, *Federal Antitrust Policy: The Law of Competition and Its Practice* (Thomson/West, 2005).

Hovenkamp H and Lemley MA, *IP and Antitrust: An Analysis of Antitrust Principles Applied to Intellectual Property Law* (Aspen Publishers Online, 2009).

Bibliography

Hume D, *An Inquiry Concerning Human Understanding. A Dissertation on the Passions: An Inquiry Concerning the Principles of Morals. The Natural History of Religion* (T Cadell, 1772).

— *A Treatise of Human Nature* (Clarendon Press, 1817).

Hüschelrath K and Schweitzer H, *Public and Private Enforcement of Competition Law in Europe: Legal and Economic Perspectives* (Springer, 2014).

— *Public and Private Enforcement of Competition Law in Europe: Legal and Economic Perspectives* (Springer, 2014).

Indirect Purchaser Litigation Handbook (American Bar Association, 2007).

Infantino M and Zervogianni E, *Causation in European Tort Law* (Cambridge University Press, 2017).

Ioannidou M, *Consumer Involvement in Private EU Competition Law Enforcement* (Oxford University Press, 2016) http://oxcat.ouplaw.com/view/10.1093/law:ocl/9780198726432.001.0001/law-ocl-9780198726432, accessed 6 March 2019.

Jones A and Sufrin BE, *EC Competition Law: Text, Cases, and Materials* (Oxford University Press, 2008).

Kalintiri A, *Evidence Standards in EU Competition Enforcement: The EU Approach* (Hart, 2019).

Keeton RE, *Legal Cause in the Law of Torts* (Ohio State University Press, 1963).

Khoury L, *Uncertain Causation in Medical Liability* (Hart, 2006).

Kneale W, *Probability and Induction* (Clarendon Press, 1966).

Kokott J, *The Burden of Proof in Comparative and International Human Rights Law: Civil and Common Law Approaches with Special Reference to the American and German Legal Systems* (Martinus Nijhoff Publishers, 1998).

Komninos A, *EC Private Antitrust Enforcement: Decentralised Application of EC Competition Law by National Courts* (Hart, 2008).

Koopmans TC and Marschak J, *Statistical Inference in Dynamic Economic Models*, vol 10 (Wiley New York, 1950).

Koziol H, *Basic Questions of Tort Law from a Germanic Perspective* (Jan Sramek Verlag Vienna, 2012).

— *Principles of European Tort Law (PETL): Text and Commentary* (Springer, 2005).

Koziol H and Busnelli FD, *Unification of Tort Law: Wrongfulness* (Kluwer Law International, 1998).

Koziol H and Schulze R, *Tort Law of the European Community* (Springer Vienna, 2012).

Koziol H and Steininger BC, *European Tort Law 2009* (Walter de Gruyter, 2010).

Landes WM and Posner RA, *The Economic Structure of Tort Law* (Harvard University Press, 1987).

Larouche P, *Competition Law and Regulation in European Telecommunications* (Hart, 2000).

Lasok KPE, *The European Court of Justice: Practice and Procedure* (Butterworths, 1994).

Legeais R, *Les regles de preuve en droit civil permanences et transformations* (Libr. Génerale de Droit Et de Jurisprudence, 1955).

Lévy-Bruhl H, *La preuve judiciaire: Étude de sociologie juridique* (M Rivière, 1964).

Lewis D, *Philosophical Papers, Volume II* (Oxford University Press, 1986).

Lianos I, Davis P and Nebbia P, *Damages Claims for the Infringement of Competition Law* (Oxford University Press, 2015).

Lianos I and Geradin D, *Handbook on European Competition Law: Enforcement and Procedure* (Edward Elgar Publishing, 2013).

— *Handbook on European Competition Law: Substantive Aspects* (Edward Elgar Publishing, 2013).

Bibliography

Lipari N and others, *Diritto civile* (Giuffrè, 2009).
  and others, *Diritto civile* (Giuffrè, 2009).
Losee J, *Theories of Causality: From Antiquity to the Present* (Transaction Publishers, 2012).
Lucy W, *Philosophy of Private Law* (Oxford University Press, 2007).
Lunney M and Oliphant K, *Tort Law: Text and Materials*, 5th edn, Oxford University Press, 2013).
Mackie JL, *Truth, Probability and Paradox: Studies in Philosophical Logic* (Oxford University Press, 1973).
  The Cement of the Universe: A Study of Causation (Clarendon Press, 1980).
Macneil IR, *The Relational Theory of Contract: Selected Works of Ian MacNeil* (Sweet & Maxwell, 2001).
Macneil IR and Gudel PJ, *Contracts: Exchange Transactions and Relations: Cases and Materials* (Foundation Press, 2001).
Mandrioli C and Carratta A, *Diritto processuale civile* (Giappichelli, 2016).
Marchetti GG, Clarich M, Di Porto e Piergaetano F, *Concorrenza e mercato: Rassegna degli orientamenti dell'autorità garante* (Giuffrè, 2010).
Markesinis BS and Unberath H, *The German Law of Torts: A Comparative Treatise* (Hart, 2002).
Marshall KS, *The Economics of Antitrust Injury and Firm-Specific Damages* (Lawyers & Judges Publishing Company, 2008).
Mastropaolo F, *Risarcimento Del Danno* (Jovene, 1983).
Mellor DH, *The Facts of Causation* (Routledge, 2002).
Mill JS, *A System of Logic, Ratiocinative and Inductive: Being a Connected View of the Principles of Evidence and the Methods of Scientific Investigation* (John W Parker, 1843).
Milutinović V, *The 'Right to Damages' Under EU Competition Law: From Courage V. Crehan to the White Paper and Beyond* (Kluwer Law International, 2010).
Monateri PG, Gianti D and Cinelli LS, *Danno e risarimento* (G Giappichelli Editore, 2013).
Monti G, *EC Competition Law* (Cambridge University Press, 2007).
Moore MS, *Causation and Responsibility: An Essay in Law, Morals, and Metaphysics* (Oxford University Press, 2010).
Murray PL and Stürner R, *German Civil Justice* (Carolina Academic Press, 2004).
Navarretta E, *Diritti inviolabili e risarcimento del danno* (Giappichelli, 1996).
Neyers JW, Chamberlain E and Pitel SGA, *Emerging Issues in Tort Law* (Bloomsbury Publishing, 2007).
Odudu O, *The Boundaries of EC Competition Law: The Scope of Article 81* (Oxford University Press, 2006).
Owen DG, *Philosophical Foundations of Tort Law* (Oxford University Press, 1997).
Özer Ö and Phillips R, *The Oxford Handbook of Pricing Management* (Oxford University Press, 2012).
Palmer VV and Bussani M, *Pure Economic Loss: New Horizons in Comparative Law* (Taylor & Francis, 2009).
Parcu PL, Monti G and Botta M, *Private Enforcement of EU Competition Law: The Impact of the Damages Directive* (Edward Elgar Publishing, 2018).
Patti S, *Le prove: Parte generale* (Giuffrè, 2010).
  Delle prove: Art. 2697-2739 (Zanichelli, 2015).
Peczenik A, *Causes and Damages* (Juridiska fören, 1979).
Pitofsky R, *How the Chicago School Overshot the Mark: The Effect of Conservative Economic Analysis on U.S. Antitrust* (Oxford University Press, 2008).

Popper KR, *Conjectures and Refutations: The Growth of Scientific Knowledge* (Routledge & Kegan Paul, 1972).

Porat A and Stein A, *Tort Liability under Uncertainty* (Oxford University Press, 2001).

Posner RA, *Economic Analysis of Law* (Wolters Kluwer Law and Business, 2014).

Pothier RJ, *Traité des obligations, selon les règles, tant du for de la conscience que du for extérieur* (Letellier, 1805).

Prosperetti L, Pani E and Tomasi I, *Il danno antitrust: una prospettiva economica* (Il Mulino, 2009).

Prosser WL, *Handbook of the Law of Torts* (West Pub Co, 1971).

Prosser and Keeton on the Law of Torts (West Pub Co, 1984).

Pucella R, *La causalità 'incerta'* (Giappichelli, 2007).

Pucella R and Santis GD, *Il nesso di causalità: profili giuridici e scientifici* (Wolters Kluwer Italia, 2007).

Qin D, *A History of Econometrics: The Reformation from the 1970s* (Oxford University Press, 2013).

Quézel-Ambrunaz C, *Essai sur la causalité en droit de la responsabilité civile* (Dalloz, 2010).

Realmonte F, *Il problema del rapporto di causalità nel risarcimento del danno* (Giuffrè, 1967).

Roberts P and Zuckerman AAS, *Principles of Criminal Evidence* (Oxford University Press, 2003).

Rodger B, *Competition Law, Comparative Private Enforcement and Collective Redress Across the EU* (Kluwer Law International, 2014).

Rodger B, Ferro MS and Marcos F, *The EU Antitrust Damages Directive: Transposition in the Member States* (Oxford University Press, 2018).

Rodger B and MacCulloch A, *Competition Law* (Cavendish Publishing, 2001).

Rogers WVH and van Boom WH, *Unification of Tort Law: Multiple Tortfeasors*, vol 9 (Kluwer Law International, 2004).

Salmon WC, *Scientific Explanation and the Causal Structure of the World* (Princeton University Press, 1984).

Schulz J, *Sachverhaltsfeststellung und Beweistheorie: Elemente einer Theorie strafprozessualer Sachverhaltsfeststellung* (Heymann, 1992).

Seuring S and Goldbach M, *Cost Management in Supply Chains* (Springer Science & Business Media, 2002).

Shavell S, *Foundations of Economic Analysis of Law* (Harvard University Press, 2009).

Shubik M and Levitan R, *Market Structure and Behavior* (Harvard University Press, 1980).

Sibony A-L, *Le juge et le raisonnement économique en droit de la concurrence* (LGDJ, 2008).

Simon H and others, *Price management. I: Strategia, analisi e determinazione del prezzo* (FrancoAngeli, 2013)

Skyrms B, *Causal Necessity: A Pragmatic Investigation of the Necessity of Laws* (Yale University Press, 1980).

Spier J and Busnelli FD, *Unification of Tort Law: Causation* (Kluwer Law International, 2000).

Starck B, Roland H and Boyer L, *Droit civil – Les Obligations, tome 1: Responsabilité délictuelle* (Litec, 1996).

Droit civil – Les Obligations, tome 1: Responsabilité délictuelle (Litec, 1996).

Stauch M, *The Law of Medical Negligence in England and Germany: A Comparative Analysis* (Bloomsbury Publishing, 2008).

Steel S, *Proof of Causation in Tort Law* (Cambridge University Press, 2015).

Stein A, *Foundations of Evidence Law* (Oxford University Press, 2008).

204 *Bibliography*

Stigum BP, *Econometrics and the Philosophy of Economics: Theory-Data Confrontations in Economics* (Princeton University Press, 2003).

Stix C, *Gerichtliche und außergerichtliche Durchsetzung ziviler Rechtsansprüche: Rechtlicher Vergleich und ökonomische Analyse* (Springer-Verlag, 2013).

Storskrubb E, *Civil Procedure and EU Law: A Policy Area Uncovered* (Oxford University Press, 2008).

Suppes P, *A Probabilistic Theory of Causality* (North-Holland Pub Co, 1970).

Taleb NN, *The Black Swan: The Impact of the Highly Improbable Fragility* (Random House Publishing Group, 2010).

Tapper C, *Cross and Tapper on Evidence* (Butterworths, 1995).

Terré F (ed), *Pour une réforme du droit de la responsabilité civile* (Dalloz, 2011).

Terré F, *Simler P and Lequette Y, Droit civil: Les obligations* (Dalloz, 1999).

Teubner G, *Networks as Connected Contracts*. Edited with an Introduction by Hugh Collins (Bloomsbury Publishing, 2011).

Tirole J, *The Theory of Industrial Organization* (MIT Press, 1988).

Toulmin SE, *The Uses of Argument* (Cambridge University Press, 2003).

Townley C, *Article 81 EC and Public Policy* (Bloomsbury Publishing, 2009).

Traeger L, *Der Kausalbegriff Im Straf-Und Zivilrecht: Zugleich Ein Beitrag Zur Auslegung Des BGB* (Keip, 1904).

Tridimas T, *The General Principles of EU Law* (Oxford University Press, 2013).

Trimarchi P, *Causalità e danno* (Giuffrè, 1967).

Il contratto: inadempimento e rimedi (Giuffrè, 2010).

Turton G, *Evidential Uncertainty in Causation in Negligence* (Hart, 2016).

Twining W, *Rethinking Evidence: Exploratory Essays* (Northwestern University Press, 1994).

Van Bael I, *Due Process in EU Competition Proceedings* (Kluwer Law International, 2011).

Van Bael I and Bellis J-F, *Competition Law of the European Community* (Kluwer Law International, 2005).

Van Dam C, *European Tort Law* (Oxford University Press, 2013).

Van Gerven W, Lever J and Larouche P, *Cases, Materials and Text on National, Supranational and International Tort Law* (Hart, 2000).

Vande Walle S, *Private Antitrust Litigation in the European Union and Japan: A Comparative Perspective* (Maklu, 2013).

Vineis P, *Modelli di rischio: epidemiologia e causalità* (Einaudi, 1990).

Viney G and Jourdain P, *Les conditions de la responsabilité* (LGDJ, 2006).

Visintini G, *Trattato Breve Della Responsabilità Civile: Fatti Illeciti, Inadempimento, Danno Risarcibile* (CEDAM, 1996).

Vogel L, *Les Actions Civiles de Concurrence: Union Européenne, France, Allemagne, Royaume-Uni, Italie, Suisse, États-Unis* (EPA, 2013).

von Bar C, *The Common European Law of Torts*, vol II (Oxford University Press, 2000).

Non-Contractual Liability Arising Out of Damage Caused to Another (De Gruyter, 2009).

Principles, Definitions and Model Rules of European Private Law: Draft Common Frame of Reference (DCFR) (Sellier European Law Publishers, 2009).

von Bar CL, *Zur Lehre von Versuch und Theilnahme am Verbrechen* (Hahn, 1859).

Von Kries J, *Die Principien Der Wahrscheinlichkeitsrechnung: Eine Logische Untersuchung* (JCB Mohr-Siebeck, 1886).

von Wright GH, *A Treatise on Induction and Probability* (Routledge, 1951).

Weinrib EJ, *Corrective Justice* (Oxford University Press, 2012).

Wesley CS, *Causality and Explanation* (Oxford University Press, 1998).

Bibliography

Whish R, *Competition Law* (Oxford University Press, 2012).

Wigmore JH, *A Students' Textbook of the Law of Evidence* (Foundation Press, 1935).

Williamson OE, *Markets and Hierarchies, Analysis and Antitrust Implications: A Study in the Economics of Internal Organization* (Free Press, 1975).

The Mechanisms of Governance (Oxford University Press, 1996).

Wils WPJ, *The Optimal Enforcement of EC Antitrust Law: Essays in Law & Economics* (Kluwer Law International, 2002).

Winiger B and others, *Essential Cases on Natural Causation* (Springer, 2010).

Wittman DA, *Economic Analysis of the Law: Selected Readings* (Blackwell, 2003).

Wolf JG, *Der Normzweck im Deliktsrecht: ein Diskussionsbeitrag* (Schwartz, 1962).

Wright GH, *Explanation and Understanding* (Cornell University Press, 2004).

Wurmnest W, *Grundzüge eines europäischen Haftungsrecht: eine vergleichende Untersuchung des Gemeinschaftsrechts* (Mohr Siebeck, 2003).

Zimmer D, *The Goals of Competition Law* (Edward Elgar Publishing, 2012).

BOOK SECTIONS

Alpa G, Bessone M and Zencovich Z, 'I Fatti Illeciti' in Pietro Rescigno (ed), *Trattato di Diritto Privato* (Utet, 1995).

Benson P, 'The Basis for Excluding Liability for Economic Loss in Tort Law' in David G Owen (ed), *Philosophical Foundations of Tort Law* (Oxford University Press, 1997).

Brown JP, 'Economic Theory of Liability Rules' in Donald A Wittman (ed), *Economic Analysis of Law: Selected Readings* (Blackwell, 2003).

Carbone SM, 'Il Rapporto Di Causalità', in Guido Alpa and Mario Bessone (eds), *La responsabilità civile* (Giuffrè, 2001).

Cartwright N, 'Causal Structures in Econometrics', in D Little (eds), *On the Reliability of Economic Models* (Springer, 1995).

Coleman J, Hershovitz S and Mendlow G, 'Theories of the Common Law of Torts' in Edward N Zalta (ed), *The Stanford Encyclopedia of Philosophy*. Winter 2015 Edition, Metaphysics Research Lab, Stanford University, 2015) https://plato.stanford.edu/archives/win2015/entriesort-theories/, accessed 1 February 2019.

Craufurd Smith R, 'Culture and European Union Law', *The Evolution of EU Law* (Oxford University Press, 1999)

De Mot J, 'Pure Economic Loss' in Michael Faure (ed), *Tort Law and Economics* (Edward Elgar Publishing, 2009).

Duff RA, 'Strict Liability, Legal Presumptions, and the Presumption of Innocence' in Andrew Simester (ed), *Appraising Strict Liability* (Oxford University Press, 2005).

Durant IC, 'Causation' in Helmut Koziol and Reiner Schulze (ed), *Tort Law of the European Community* (Springer, 2010).

Fairgrieve D and G'Sell-Macrez F, 'Causation in French Law: Pragmatism and Policy' in Richard Goldberg (ed), *Perspectives on Causation* (Hart, 2011).

Frisch R, 'Autonomy of Economic Relations: Statistical versus Theoretical Relations in Economic Macrodynamics' in Hendry and Morgan (eds.), *The Foundations of Econometric Analysis* (Cambridge University Press, 1995).

Fumagalli C, Padilla J and Polo M, 'Damages for Exclusionary Practices: A Primer' in Kokkonis I. and Etro F. (eds.), *Competition Law and the Enforcement of Article 82* (Oxford University Press 2010), 203–220.

Bibliography

Gärdenfors P, 'Probabilistic Reasoning and Evidentiary Value' in P. Gärdenfors (ed) *The Dynamics of Thought* (Springer, 2005) 1.

Gilead I and Green MD, 'General Report – Causal Uncertainty and Proportional Liability: Analytical and Comparative Report' in Israel Gilead, Michael D Green and Bernhard A Koch (eds), *Proportional Liability: Analytical and Comparative Perspectives* (De Gruyter, 2013).

Helmholz RH and Sellar WDH, 'Presumptions in Comparative Legal History' in Richard H Helmholz and W David H Sellar (eds), *The Law of Presumptions: Essays in Comparative Legal History*, vol 9 (Duncker & Humblot, 2009).

Hitchcock C, 'Probabilistic Causation' in Edward N Zalta (ed), *The Stanford Encyclopedia of Philosophy*, Winter 2012 Edition (Stanford University Press, 2012) available at http://plato .stanford.edu/archives/win2012/entries/causation-probabilistic/.

Hoefer C, 'Causal Determinism' in Edward N Zalta (ed), *The Stanford Encyclopedia of Philosophy* (2016 Edition) (Stanford University Press, 2016) available at https://plato .stanford.edu/entries/determinism-causal/.

Honoré A, 'Causation in the Law' in Edward N Zalta (ed), *The Stanford Encyclopedia of Philosophy*, Winter 2010 Edition (Stanford University Press, 2010) available at http:// plato.stanford.edu/archives/win2010/entries/causation-law/, accessed 30 August 2014.

Honoré AM, 'Causation and Remoteness of Damage' in A Tunc (ed), *International Encyclopedia of Comparative Law*, vol 6 (Mohr Siebeck, 1983).

Hovenkamp H, 'Economic Experts in Antitrust Cases' in David Faigman and others (eds), *Modern Scientific Evidence: The Law and Science of Expert Testimony* (West Group, 2002).

Iezzi MC, 'La Chance: Nella Morsa Del Danno Emergente e Del Lucro Cessante. Il Danno Da Perdita Di Chance Quale Tecnica Risarcitoria Applicabile Alla Responsabilità Contrattuale, Alla Luce Delle Più Recenti Elaborazioni Giurisprudenziali e Dottrinali' in R Garofoli, P Bortone and R Vaccaro (eds), *Tracce di civile*, (Neldiritto, 2008).

Irti N, 'Legge e Caso: Diagnosi Giuridica e Diagnosi Medica' in Natalino Irti (ed), *Il salvagente della riforma* (Editori Laterza, 2007).

Jones A, 'Drawing the Boundary between Joint and Unilateral Conduct: Parent–Subsidiary Relationships and Joint Ventures' in Ariel Ezrachi (ed), *Research Handbook on International Competition Law* (Edward Elgar, 2012).

Kersting C, 'Transposition of the Antitrust Damages Directive into German Law' in Barry Rodger, Miguel Sousa Ferro and Francisco Marcos (eds), *The EU Antitrust Damages Directive* (Oxford University Press, 2018).

Koopmans TC and Hood WC, 'The Estimation of Simultaneous Linear Economic Relationships' in WC Hood and T Koopmans (eds), *Studies In Econometric Method, Cowles Commission Monograph 14.*, pp. 112–199 (Yale University Press, 1953).

Koziol H, 'Loss of a Chance: Comparative Report' in Bénédict Winiger and others (eds), *Digest of European Tort Law. Vol.: Essential Cases on Natural Causation* (Springer, 2007).

Lianos,I, '"Judging" Economists: Economic Expertise in Competition Law Litigation – A European View' in Lianos Ioannis,and Kokkoris Ioannis,(eds), *The Reform of EC Competition Law: New Challenges* (Kluwer Law International, 2009).

Magnus U, 'Causal Uncertainty and Proportional Liability in Germany' in Israel Gilead and Michael D Green (eds), *Proportional Liability: Analytical and Comparative Perspectives, De Gruyter* (De Gruyter, 2013).

Markesinis B, 'Tort Law', *Encyclopædia Britannica*, available at www.britannica.com/topic/ tort, accessed 1 February 2019.

Miller D, 'Justice' in Edward N Zalta (ed), *The Stanford Encyclopedia of Philosophy*, Fall 2017 Edition (Metaphysics Research Lab, Stanford University, 2017) https://plato.stanford.edu/archives/fall2017/entries/justice/, accessed 1 February 2019.

Bibliography

Moréteau O, 'Causal Uncertainty and Proportional Liability in France' in Israel Gilead, Michael D Green and Bernhard A Koch (eds), *Proportional Liability: Analytical and Comparative Perspectives* (De Gruyter, 2013).

Nazzini R, 'Potency and Act of the Principle of Effectiveness: The Development of Competition Law Remedies and Procedures in Community Law' in Catherine Barnard and Okeoghene Odudu (eds), *The Outer Limits of European Union Law* (Hart, 2009).

Oliphant K, 'Causal Uncertainty and Proportional Liability in England and Wales' in Israel Gilead, Michael D Green and Bernhard A Koch (eds), *Proportional Liability: Analytical and Comparative Perspectives* (De Gruyter, 2013).

Pinori A, 'Il Criterio Legislativo Delle Conseguenze Immediate e Dirette' in Giovanna Visintini (ed), *Il risarcimento del danno contrattuale ed extracontrattuale* (Giuffrè, 1984).

Stapleton J, 'Unpacking Causation' in Peter Cane, Anthony M Honoré and John Gardner (eds), *Relating to Responsibility: Essays for Tony Honoré on His Eightieth Birthday* (Hart, 2001).

'Causation in the Law' in Helen Beebee, Christopher Hitchcock and Peter Menzies (eds), *The Oxford Handbook of Causation* (Oxford University Press, 2009).

'Reflections on Common Sense Causation in Australia' in Simone Degeling and James Edelman (eds), *Torts in Commercial Law* (Thomson Reuters, 2011).

Spickhoff A, 'Folgenzurechnung Im Schadensersatzrecht: Gründe Und Grenzen', in E Lorenz (ed), *Karlsruher Forum 2007* (VVW, 2008).

Taruffo M, 'Onere Della Prova', in *Dig. disc. priv., sez. civ.*, XIII (1995).

Taruffo M, 'La Valutazione delle Prove' in Taruffo M (ed.), *La Prova nel Processo Civile* (Giuffré, 2012) 207.

Teubner G, 'Coincidentia Oppositorum: Hybrid Networks Beyond Contract and Organization' in Marc Amstutz and Gunther Teubner (eds), *Networks: Legal Issues of Multilateral Co-operation* (Hart, 2009).

Townley C, 'The Concept of an "Undertaking": The Boundaries of the Corporation-A Discussion of Agency, Employees and Subsidiaries', in G Amato & C Ehlermann (eds) *EC Competition Law: A Critical Assessment* (Hart, 2007) available at http://papers.ssrn.com/sol3/papers.cfm?abstract_id=1358649, accessed 18 February 2015.

von Bar C, *The Common European Law of Torts: Damage and Damages, Liability for and without Personal Misconduct, Causality, and Defences* (Clarendon Press, 1998).

Waldron J, 'Moments of Carelessness and Massive Loss' in David G Owen (ed), *The Philosophical Foundations of Tort Law* (Oxford University Press, 1997).

Whelan P, 'Competition Law and Criminal Justice', Galloway (ed), *The Intersections of Antitrust: Policy and Regulations* (Oxford University Press, 2019).

Wright RW, 'The Nightmare and the Noble Dream: Hart and Honore on Causation and Responsibility' in Matthew Kramer and others (eds), *The Legacy of H.L.A. Hart: Legal, Political and Moral Philosophy* (Oxford University Press, 2008).

'Proving Causation: Probability versus Belief' in Richard Goldberg (ed), *Perspectives on Causation* (Hart, 2011).

'The NESS Account of Natural Causation: A Response to Criticisms' in Richard Goldberg (ed), *Perspectives on Causation* (Hart, 2011).

JOURNAL ARTICLES

Abele HA, Kodek GE and Schaefer GK, 'Proving Causation in Private Antitrust Cases' [2011] 7 *Journal of Competition Law and Economics* 847.

Afferni G, 'Azione Di Classe e Danno Antitrust' (2010) 3 *Mercato concorrenza e regole* 491.

'"Opt-In" Class Actions in Italy: Why Are They Failing?' [2016] 7 *Journal of European Tort Law* 82.

'Il Risarcimento dei Danni per Violazioni del Diritto della Concorrenza: Prescrizione e Responsabilità Solidale' [2018] *Nuove leggi civili commentate* 171.

Allen RJ, 'A Reconceptualization of Civil Trials' [1986] 66 *Boston University Law Review* 401.

'The Nature of Juridicial Proof' (1991) 13 *Cardozo Law Review* 373.

'Factual Ambiguity and a Theory of Evidence' [1993] 88 *Northwestern University Law Review* 604.

'Burdens of Proof' (2014) 13 *Law, Probability and Risk* 195.

Allen RJ and Callen CR, 'The Juridical Management of Factual Uncertainty' [2003] 7 *International Journal of Evidence & Proof* 1.

Allen RJ and Leiter B, 'Naturalized Epistemology and the Law of Evidence' [2001] *Virginia Law Review* 1491.

Allen RJ and Stein A, 'Evidence, Probability, and Burden of Proof' [2013] 55 *Arizona Law Review* 557.

Bailey D, 'Presumptions in EU Competition Law' [2010] *European Competition Law Review* 20.

Bailey SH, 'Causation in Negligence: What Is a Material Contribution?' [2010] 30 *Legal Studies* 167.

Baker JB and Bresnahan TE, 'Empirical Methods of Identifying and Measuring Market Power' [1997] 27 *Journal of Reprints for Antitrust Law and Economics* 743.

Ball VC, 'The Moment of Truth: Probability Theory and Standards of Proof' [1960] 14 *Vanderbilt Law Review* 807.

Bastianon S, 'Tutela risarcitoria antitrust, nesso causale e danni "lungolatenti"' [2007] *Il Corriere Giuridico* 4.

Bear A and Knobe J, 'Normality: Part Descriptive, Part Prescriptive' [2017] 167 *Cognition* 25.

Besso C, 'La Vicinanza Della Prova' [2015] 70 *Rivista di diritto processuale* 1383.

Bitterich K, 'Elements of an Autonomous Concept of Causation in European Community Law Concerning Liability' [2007] *Zeitschrift für vergleichende Rechtswissenschaft* 12.

Botta M, 'The Principle of Passing on in EU Competition Law in the Aftermath of the Damages Directive' [2017] 25 *European Review of Private Law* 881.

Brealey M, 'The Burden of Proof before the European Court' [1985] 10 *European Law Review* 254.

Brennan TA, 'Causal Chains and Statistical Links: The Role of Scientific Uncertainty in Hazardous-Substance Litigation' [1987] 73 *Cornell Law Review* 469.

Broadbent A, 'Fact and Law in the Causal Inquiry' [2009] 15 *Journal Legal Theory* 173.

Bruner J, 'The Narrative Construction of Reality' [1991] 18(1) *Critical Inquiry* 1.

Buhart J and Lesur L, 'France: Private Antitrust Litigation' Getting the Deal Through [2014] *Global Competition Review* 60.

Buxton R, 'The Human Rights Act and the Substantive Criminal Law' [2000] *Criminal Law Review* 331.

Calabresi G, 'Concerning Cause and the Law of Torts: An Essay for Harry Kalven, Jr.' [1975] 43 *The University of Chicago Law Review* 69.

Carbonelli V, 'Private Enforcement of EU Competition Law between Public and Private Issues' [2012] 2 *International Journal of Public Law and Policy* 335.

Carnelutti F, 'Perseverare Diabolicum: A Proposito Del Limite Della Responsabilità per Danni' [1952] 75 *Il Foro Italiano* 97.

Carrier MA, 'A Tort-Based Causation Framework for Antitrust Analysis' [2011] 77 *Antitrust Law Journal* 991.

Bibliography

Cartwright N, 'Causation: One Word, Many Things' [2004] 71 *Philosophy of Science* 805.

Cartwright N, 'Counterfactuals in Economics: A Commentary' [2007] 4 *Causation and Explanation* 191.

Cartwright N and Reiss J, 'Uncertainty in Econometrics: Evaluating Policy Counterfactuals' [2004] *Economic Policy*.

Castelli L, 'La Causalità Giuridica Nel Campo Degli Illeciti Anticoncorrenziali' [2013] 18 *Danno e responsabilità* 1049.

Cengiz F, 'Passing-On Defense and Indirect Purchaser Standing in Actions for Damages against the Violations of Competition Law: What Can the EC Learn from the US?' [2007] University of East Anglia Centre for Competition Policy, Working Paper 07.

Chabas F, 'La Perte d'une Chance En Droit Français, Colloque Sur Les Développements Récents Du Droit de La Responsabilité Civile' [1991] *Centre d'études européennes* 131 ss.

Chen Z, 'Dominant Retailers and the Countervailing-Power Hypothesis' [2003] 34(4) *RAND Journal of Economics* 612.

Cheng EK, 'Reconceptualizing the Burden of Proof' [2012] 122 *Yale Law Journal* 1254.

Clermont KM, 'Standards of Proof Revisited' [2008] 33 *Vermont Law Review* 469.

Clermont KM and Sherwin E, 'A Comparative View of Standards of Proof' [2002] 50(2) *The American Journal of Comparative Law* 243.

Collingwood RG, 'Causation in Practical Natural Science' [1937] 38 *Proceedings of the Aristotelian Society* 85.

Connor JM, 'Forensic Economics: An Introduction with Special Emphasis on Price Fixing' [2008] 4 *Journal of Competition Law and Economics* 31.

Connor JM and Lande RH, 'Cartels as Rational Business Strategy: Crime Pays' [2012] 34 *Cardozo Law Review* 427.

Cooter R, 'Torts as the Union of Liberty and Efficiency: An Essay on Causation' [1987] 63 *Chicago-Kent Law Review* 523.

Cowling K and Waterson M, 'Price-Cost Margins and Market Structure' [1976] 43 *Economica* 267.

Craswell R, 'Passing on the Costs of Legal Rules: Efficiency and Distribution in Buyer-Seller Relationships' [1991] 43 *Stanford Law Review* 361.

Davidson D, 'Causal Relations' (1967) 64 *The Journal of Philosophy* 691.

Demougin D and Fluet C, 'Preponderance of Evidence' [2006] 50 *European Economic Review* 963.

Denozza F and Toffoletti L, 'Compensation Function and Deterrence Effects of Private Actions for Damages: The Case of Antitrust Damage Suits' http://papers.ssrn.com/abstract=1116324, accessed 12 May 2014.

Dewey J, 'The Historic Background of Corporate Legal Personality' [1926] 35 *Yale Law Journal* 655.

Dittrich LB, 'L'assunzione Delle Prove Nel Processo Civile Italiano' [2016] (3) *Rivista di diritto processuale* 589.

Dougan M, 'Addressing Issues of Protective Scope within the Francovich Right to Reparation' [2017] 13 *European Constitutional Law Review* 124.

Edgerton HW, 'Legal Cause' [1924] 72 *University of Pennsylvania Law Review and American Law Register* 211.

Engel C, 'Preponderance of the Evidence versus Intime Conviction: A Behavior Perspective on a Conflict between American and Continental European Law' [2008] 33 *Vermont Law Review* 435.

Epstein RA, 'Causation and Corrective Justice: A Reply to Two Critics' [1979] 8 *The Journal of Legal Studies* 477.

Ezrachi A, 'Buying Alliances and Input Price Fixing: In Search of a European Enforcement Standard' [2012] 8 *Journal of Competition Law and Economics* 47.

'Sponge' [2016] 5 *Journal of Antitrust Enforcement* 49.

Ferrari F, 'Burden of Proof under the United Nations Convention on Contracts for International Sale of Goods (CISG)' [2000] *Spring International Business Law Journal* 665.

Fox E and Sirkis P, 'Antitrust Remedies–Selected Bibliography and Annotations' [2005] American Antitrust Institute Working Paper No. 06-01, http://ssrn.com/abstract=1103601, accessed 12 May 2014.

Fox EM, 'What Is Harm to Competition-Exclusionary Practices and Anticompetitive Effect' (2002) 70 *Antitrust Law Journal* 371.

Friedman RD, 'Economic Analysis of Evidentiary Law: An Underused Tool, an Underplowed Field' [1997] 19 *Cardozo Law Review* 1531.

Frignani A, 'La Difesa Disarmata Nelle Cause Follow on per Danno Antitrust. La Cassazione in Guerra Con Se Stessa' [2013] 41 *Mercato Concorrenza Regole* 429.

Gavil AI, 'The Challenges of Economic Proof in a Decentralized and Privatized European Competition Policy System: Lessons from the American Experience' [2008] 4 *Journal of Competition Law and Economics* 177.

Geistfeld MA, 'The Doctrinal Unity of Alternative Liability and Market-Share Liability' [2006] 155 *University of Pennsylvania Law Review* 447.

Geradin D and Girgenson I, 'The Counterfactual Method in EU Competition Law: The Cornerstone of the Effects-Based Approach' [2011] (December 11, 2011) available at http://papers.ssrn.com/sol3/papers.cfm?abstract_id=1970917, accessed 25 August 2014.

Gilbert CL, 'LSE and the British Approach to Time Series Econometrics' [1989] 41 *Oxford Economic Papers* 108.

Gippini-Fournier E, 'The Elusive Standard of Proof in EU Competition Cases' [2009] 33 *World Competition*.

Goldberg R, 'The Role of Scientific Evidence in the Assessment of Causation in Medicinal Product Liability Litigation: A Probabilistic and Economic Analysis' [1998] 1 *Current Legal Issues* 55.

Gorla G, 'Sulla Cosiddetta Causalità Giuridica: Fatto Dannoso e Conseguenze' [1951] I (11) *Rivista di diritto commerciale* 405.

Gottwald P, 'Civil Procedure Reform in Germany' [1997] 45(4) *The American Journal of Comparative Law* 753.

Graziano TK, 'Loss of a Chance in European Private Law-All or Nothing or Partial Liability in Cases of Uncertain Causation' [2008] 16 *European Review of Private Law* 1009.

Gregory CO, 'Proximate Cause in Negligence: A Retreat from "Rationalization"' [1938] 6 *The University of Chicago Law Review* 36.

Haavelmo T, 'The Probability Approach in Econometrics' [1944] 12 *Econometrica: Journal of the Econometric Society* 43.

Hansberry D and others, 'Umbrella Effect: Damages Claimed by Customers of Non-Cartelist Competitors' (2014) 5 *Journal of European Competition Law & Practice* 196.

Harris RG and Sullivan LA, 'Passing on the Monopoly Overcharge: A Comprehensive Policy Analysis' [1979] 128 *University of Pennsylvania Law Review* 269.

Harvard Law Review Association, 'Is the Incidence of the Burden of Proof a Matter of Substantive or Procedural Law?' [1915] 29 *Harvard Law Review* 95.

Heckman JJ, 'Causal Parameters and Policy Analysis in Economics: A Twentieth Century Retrospective' [2000] 115 *The Quarterly Journal of Economics* 45.

Bibliography

'Econometric Causality' [2008] 76 *International Statistical Review* 1.

Heckman JJ, LaLonde RJ and Smith JA, 'The Economics and Econometrics of Active Labor Market Programs' [1999] 3 *Handbook of Labor Economics* 1865.

Hellner J, 'Causality and Causation in the Law' (2000) 40 *Scandinavian Studies in Law* 111.

Hellstrom P, 'A Uniform Standard of Proof in EU Competition Proceedings' [2009] *European Competition Law Annual* , available at http://papers.ssrn.com/abstract=2147705, accessed 20 November 2014.

Hitchcock C and Knobe J, 'Cause and Norm' [2009] 106 *The Journal of Philosophy* 587.

Hoover KD, 'The Methodology of Econometrics' [2006] 1 *New Palgrave Handbook of Econometrics* 61.

Hovenkamp H, 'The Indirect Purchaser Rule and Cost-Plus Sales' [1995] 25 *Journal of Reprints for Antitrust Law and Economics* 949.

'American Needle and the Boundaries of the Firm in Antitrust Law' [2010], available at SSRN: http://ssrn.com/abstract=1616625.

Hovenkamp HJ, 'American Needle and the Boundaries of the Firm in Antitrust Law' [2010], available at SSRN: http://papers.ssrn.com/sol3/papers.cfm?abstract_id=1616625, accessed 18 February 2015.

Inderst R, Maier-Rigaud FP and Schwalbe U, 'Umbrella Effects' [2014] 10 *Journal of Competition Law and Economics* 739.

Inderst R and Valletti TM, 'Buyer Power and the "Waterbed Effect"' [2011] 59 *The Journal of Industrial Economics* 1.

Jenny F, 'A Judge's Perspective on the Role of Economic Analysis in Damages Actions' *Oxera* www.oxera.com/Latest-Thinking/Agenda/2010/A-judge's-perspective-on-the-role-of-economic-anal.aspx, accessed 24 August 2014.

Kadner TG, 'Loss of a Chance in European Private Law "All or Nothing" or Partial Liability in Cases of Uncertain Causation' [2008] 16 *European Review of Private Law* 1009.

Kalintiri A, 'The Allocation of the Legal Burden of Proof in Article 101 TFEU Cases: A 'Clear'Rule with Not-So-Clear Implications' [2015] 34 *Yearbook of European Law* 232

Kaplow L, 'Burden of Proof' [2011] 121 *Yale Law Journal* 738.

Karner E, 'The Function of the Burden of Proof in Tort Law' [2009] 2008 *European Tort Law* 68.

Kaye D, 'The Limits of the Preponderance of the Evidence Standard: Justifiably Naked Statistical Evidence and Multiple Causation' [1982] 7 *Law & Social Inquiry* 487.

Koenig C, 'An Economic Analysis of the Single Economic Entity Doctrine in EU Competition Law' [2017] 13 *Journal of Competition Law & Economics* 281.

Kortmann J and others, 'The Draft Directive on Antitrust Damages and Its Likely Effects on National Law' [2014] *Serie onderneming en recht*.

Kosicki G and Cahill MB, 'Economics of Cost Pass through and Damages in Indirect Purchaser Antitrust Cases' [2006] 51 *Antitrust Bull* 599.

Landes WM and Posner RA, 'Should Indirect Purchasers Have Standing to Sue under the Antitrust Laws? An Economic Analysis of the Rule of Illinois Brick' [1979] 46 *The University of Chicago Law Review* 602.

'The Positive Economic Theory of Tort Law' [1980] 15 *Georgia Law Review* 851.

'Causation in Tort Law: An Economic Approach' [1983] 12 *The Journal of Legal Studies* 109.

'Tort Law as a Regulatory Regime for Catastrophic Personal Injuries' [1984] 13 *The Journal of Legal Studies* 417.

Bibliography

Legal H, 'Standards of Proof and Standards of Judicial Review in EU Competition Law' (Kluwer Academic Publishers, 2006), available at https://groupes.renater.fr/sympa/d_read/creda-concurrence/Art/Legal-Fordham2005.pdf, accessed 20 November 2014.

Lempert R, 'The New Evidence Scholarship: Analyzing the Process of Proof' (1986) 66 *Boston University Law Review* 439.

Leuken RV, 'Parental Liability for Cartel Infringements Committed by Wholly Owned Subsidiaries: Is the Approach of the European Court of Justice in Akzo Nobel Also Relevant in a Private-Law Context?' [2016] 24 *European Review of Private Law* 513.

Lewis D, 'Causation' [1973] 70 *The Journal of Philosophy* 556.

Lianos I, 'Competition Law Remedies in Europe: Which Limits for Remedial Discretion?' [2013] CLES Research Paper No. 2/2013, available at http://papers.ssrn.com/abstract=2235817, accessed 12 May 2014.

'Some Reflections on the Question of the Goals of EU Competition Law' [2013] CLES Working Paper Series 3/2013, available at http://papers.ssrn.com/abstract=2235875, accessed 12 May 2014.

'Causal Uncertainty and Damages Claims for the Infringement of Competition Law in Europe' [2015] 34 *Yearbook of European Law* 170.

'Polycentric Competition Law' [2018] 71 *Current Legal Problems* 161.

Lianos I and Genakos C, 'Econometric Evidence in EU Competition Law: An Empirical and Theoretical Analysis' [2012] CLES Research Paper series 06/12, available at http://papers.ssrn.com/abstract=2184563, accessed 26 August 2014.

Lombardi C, 'The Passing-On of Price Overcharges in European Competition Damages Actions: A Matter of Causation and an Issue of Policy' [2015] Discussion Paper, Europa-Kolleg Hamburg, Institute for European Integration, available at https://ssrn.com/abstract=2700042 or http://dx.doi.org/10.2139/ssrn.2700042.

Luminoso A, 'Possibilità o Necessità Della Relazione Causale' [1991] 1991(2) *Rivista giuridica sarda* 533.

Lyon A, 'Causality' [1967] 18 *British Journal for the Philosophy of Science* 1.

Maier-Rigaud FP, 'Toward a European Directive on Damages Actions' [2014] 10 *Journal of Competition Law and Economics* 341.

Majumdar AN, 'Waterbed Effects and Buyer Mergers' [2005] CCP Working Paper No. 05-7, available at http://papers.ssrn.com/sol3/papers.cfm?abstract_id=911574, accessed 15 July 2015.

Malone WS, 'Ruminations on Cause-in-Fact' [1956] 9 *Stanford Law Review* 60.

Marcheis CB, 'La Vicinanza Della Prova' [2015] 16 *Revista Eletrônica de Direito Processual-Procedural Law Electronic Review*.

McNaughton JT, 'Burden of Production of Evidence: A Function of a Burden of Persuasion' [1955] 68 *Harvard Law Review* 1382.

Ménard C, 'The Economics of Hybrid Organizations' [2004] 160 *Journal of Institutional and Theoretical Economics (JITE)* 345.

Meyer J and Cramon-Taubadel S, 'Asymmetric Price Transmission: A Survey' [2004] 55 *Journal of Agricultural Economics* 581.

Moréteau O, 'France: French Tort Law in the Light of European Harmonization' [2013] 6 *Journal of Civil Law Studies* 15.

'French Tort Law in the Light of European Harmonization' [2013] 6 *Journal of Civil Law Studies* 759.

Morris C, 'On the Teaching of Legal Cause' [1939] 39 *Columbia Law Review* 1087.

Narveson J, 'Collective Responsibility' [2002] 6 *The Journal of Ethics* 179.

Bibliography

Newberg JA, 'The Narrative Construction of Antitrust' [2002] 12 *Southern California Interdisciplinary Law Journal* 181.

O'Connor KJ, 'Is the Illinois Brick Wall Crumbling' [2000] 15 *Antitrust* 34.

Odudu O, 'The Wider Concerns of Competition Law' [2010] 30 *Oxford Journal of Legal Studies* 599.

OECD, 'The Objectives of Competition Law and Policy and the Optimal Design of a Competition Agency' [2003] 5 *OECD Journal: Competition Law and Policy* 7.

Oliphant K, 'Causation in Cases of Evidential Uncertainty: Juridical Techniques and Fundamental Issues' [2016] 91 *Chicago-Kent Law Review* 587.

Orbach BY, 'The Antitrust Consumer Welfare Paradox' [2010] 7 *Journal of Competition Law and Economics* 133.

Ottolenghi S, 'From Peeping behind the Corporate Veil, to Ignoring It Completely' [1990] 53 *The Modern Law Review* 338.

Page WH, 'Antitrust Damages and Economic Efficiency: An Approach to Antitrust Injury' [1980] 47 *The University of Chicago Law Review* 467.

Papineau D, 'Causal Asymmetry' [1985] 36 *British Journal for the Philosophy of Science* 273.

Parlak S, 'Passing-on Defence and Indirect Purchaser Standing: Should the Passing-on Defence Be Rejected Now the Indirect Purchaser Has Standing after Manfredi and the White Paper of the European Commission?' [2010] 33 *World Competition* 31.

Parmentier H and Descôte M, 'The French Commercial Supreme Court Validates the Passing-on Defence in a Follow-on Action Based on the Lysine Cartel' (Doux Aliments/Ajinomoto Eurolyne)' [2010] e-Competitions.

Patti S, 'La Responsabilità Degli Amministratori: Il Nesso Causale' [2002] 67(3) *Responsabilità civile e previdenziale*.

Pickering MA, 'The Company as a Separate Legal Entity' [1968] 31 *The Modern Law Review* 481.

Pollock EE, 'Injury and Causation Elements of a Treble–Damage Antitrust Action' (1962) 57 *Northwestern University Law Review* 691.

'The "Injury" and "Causation" Elements of a Private Antitrust Action' [1962] 21 *Section of Antitrust Law* 341.

'Standing to Sue, Remoteness of Injury, and the Passing-On Doctrine' [1966] 32 *Antitrust Law Journal* 5.

Posner RA, 'The Law and Economics of the Economic Expert Witness' [1999] 13 *The Journal of Economic Perspectives* 91.

'An Economic Approach to the Law of Evidence' [1999] University of Chicago Law School, John M. Olin Law & Economics Working Paper No 66, available at SSRN: http://papers.ssrn.com/abstract=165176, accessed 21 January 2015.

'Common-Law Economic Torts: An Economic and Legal Analysis' (2006) 48 *Arizona Law Review* 735.

Powell W, 'Neither Market nor Hierarchy' [2003] 315 *The Sociology of Organizations: Classic, Contemporary, and Critical Readings* 104.

'Quantifying Antitrust Damages: Towards Non-binding Guidance for Courts Study Prepared for the European Commission' [2009] *Luxembourg, Publications Office of the European Union*.

Rabin RL, 'The Pervasive Role of Uncertainty in Tort Law: Rights and Remedies' [2010] 60 *DePaul Law Review* 431.

Reddick EN, 'Joint Ventures and Other Competitor Collaborations As Single Entity – "Undertakings" Under US Law' [2012] 8 *European Competition Journal* 333.

Reiss J, 'Causation in the Social Sciences: Evidence, Inference, and Purpose' [2009] 39 *Philosophy of the Social Sciences* 20.

Ritter C, 'Presumptions in EU Competition Law' [2018] 6 *Journal of Antitrust Enforcement* 189.

Rizzo MJ, 'The Imputation Theory of Proximate Cause: An Economic Framework' [1980] 15 *Georgia Law Review* 1007.

Robins J and Greenland S, 'The Probability of Causation under a Stochastic Model for Individual Risk' [1989] *Biometrics* 1125.

Rodger BJ and MacCulloch A, 'Wielding the Blunt Sword: Interim Relief for Breaches of EC Competition Law before the UK Courts' [1996] 17 *European Competition Law Review* 393.

Rubin DB, 'Causal Inference Using Potential Outcomes' [2005] 100 *Journal of the American Statistical Association*.

Sacco R, 'Legal Formants: A Dynamic Approach to Comparative Law (Installment I of II)' [1991] 39 *The American Journal of Comparative Law* 1.

'Legal Formants: A Dynamic Approach to Comparative Law (Installment II of II)' [1991] 39 *The American Journal of Comparative Law* 343.

Samuelson PA, Koopmans TC and Stone JR, 'Report of the Evaluative Committee for Econometrica' [1954] 22 *Econometrica* 141.

Sanders J, Green MD and Powers Jr WC, 'The Insubstantiality of the Substantial Factor Test for Causation' [2008] 73 *Missouri Law Review* 399.

Savatier R, 'La Responsabilité Médicale En France (Aspects de Droit Privé)' [1976] 28 *Revue internationale de droit comparé* 493.

Schaffer J, 'Overdetermining Causes' [2003] 114 *Philosophical Studies* 23.

Schulin B, 'Der Natürliche, Vorrechtliche Kausalitätsbegriff Im Zivilen Schadensersatzrecht'.

Schwartz A, 'Causation in Private Tort Law: A Comment on Kelman' [1987] 63 *Chicago-Kent Law Review* 639.

Schwartz A and Scott RE, 'Contract Theory and the Limits of Contract Law' [2003] *Yale Law Journal* 541.

Seavey WA, 'Mr. Justice Cardozo and the Law of Torts' [1939] *Yale Law Journal* 390.

Severi C, 'Perdita Di Chance e Danno Patrimoniale Risarcibile' [2003] *Resp. civ. e prev* 296.

Shavell S, 'An Analysis of Causation and the Scope of Liability in the Law of Torts' [1980] *The Journal of Legal Studies* 463.

'Uncertainty over Causation and the Determination of Civil Liability' [1985] 28 *Journal of Law and Economics* 587.

Sibony A-L and Barbier de La Serre E, 'Charge de La Preuve et Théorie Du Contrôle En Droit Communautaire de La Concurrence: Pour Un Changement de Perspective' [2007] 43 *Revue Trimestrielle de Droit Européen* 205.

Singh N and Vives X, 'Price and Quantity Competition in a Differentiated Duopoly' [1984] 15 *The RAND Journal of Economics* 546.

Siragusa M, 'Action for Damages and Imposition of Fines' [2015] 2 *Rivista Italiana di Antitrust/Italian Antitrust Review* 103.

'Private Damages Claims: Questions Relating to the Passing-on Defence' [2011] *Oxera* http://www.oxera.com/Oxera/media/Oxera/downloads/Agenda/Private-damages-claims-%28Mario-Siragusa%29_1.pdf?ext=.pdf.

Smiley M, 'Collective Responsibility' [2017] *The Stanford Encyclopedia of Philosophy*, available at https://plato.stanford.edu/archives/sum2017/entries/collective-responsibility/, accessed 15 March 2019.

Spickhoff A, 'Folgenzurechnung Im Schadensersatzrecht: Gründe Und Grenzen' [2007] 39 *Karlsruher Forum.*

Stapleton J, 'Law, Causation and Common Sense' [1988] 8 *Oxford Journal of Legal Studies* 111.

'Choosing What We Mean by Causation in the Law' [2008] 73 *Missouri Law Review* 433.

'The Two Explosive Proof-of-Causation Doctrines Central to Asbestos Claims,' [2008] 74 *Brooklyn Law Review* 1011.

'Factual Causation' [2010] 38 *Federal Law Review* 467.

'Cause-in-Fact and the Scope of Liability for Consequences' [2003] 119 *Law Quarterly Review* 388.

Stone J, 'Burden of Proof and the Judicial Process' [1944] *Law Quarterly Review* 262.

Strand M, 'Indirect Purchasers, Passing-on and the New Directive on Competition Law Damages' [2014] 10 *European Competition Journal* 361.

Stucke ME, 'Reconsidering Antitrust's Goals' [2012] 53 *Boston College Law Review* 551.

'Should Competition Policy Promote Happiness?' [2013] 81 *Fordham Law Review* 2575.

Summers A, 'Common-Sense Causation in the Law' [2018] 38 *Oxford Journal of Legal Studies* 793.

Taruffo M, 'Rethinking the Standards of Proof' [2003] 51 *The American Journal of Comparative Law* 659.

'Towards a Coherent European Approach on Collective Redress' (2011) SEC (2011) 4.2.201 173.

Twining W, 'Evidence and Legal Theory' [1984] 47 *The Modern Law Review* 261.

Utzschneider Y and Parmentier H, 'The New Frontier of Antitrust: Damages Actions by Indirect Purchasers and the Passing on Defence in France and California' [2011] 32 *European Competition Law Review* 266.

Valcavi G, 'Sulla causalità giuridica nella responsabilità civile da inadempienza e da illecito' [2001] II *Rivista di diritto civile* 409.

Valente, 'Appunti in Tema Di Fatto, Nesso Causale e Danno' [1955] *Diritto e Giurisprudenza* 372.

Van den Bergh R, 'Private Enforcement of European Competition Law and the Persisting Collective Action Problem' [2013] 20 *Maastricht Journal of European and Comparative Law* 12.

Van Gerven W, 'Harmonization of Private Law: Do We Need It?' [2004] 41 *Common Market Law Review* 505.

Veljanovski C, 'Counterfactual Tests in Competition Law' [2010] 9(4) *Competition Law Journal* 436.

'Market Power and Counterfactuals in New Zealand Competition Law' [2013] 9(1) *Journal of Competition Law and Economics* 171.

Verboven F and Van Dijk T, 'Cartel Damages Claims and the Passing-on Defense*' [2009] 57 *The Journal of Industrial Economics* 457.

Volpin C, 'The Ball Is in Your Court: Evidential Burden of Proof and the Proof-Proximity Principle in EU Competition Law' [2014] 51 *Common Market Law Review* 1159.

Wagner-von Papp F, 'Implementation of the Damages Directive in England & Wales' (2015) 2 *Concurrences* 29.

Weinrib EJ, 'Causal Uncertainty' [2015] 36 *Oxford Journal of Legal Studies* 135.

Weinstein JB, 'Some Difficulties in Devising Rules for Determining Truth in Judicial Trials' [1966] 66 *Columbia Law Review* 223.

216   *Bibliography*

Whelan P, 'An Argument in Favour of the Passing-On Defence: A Response to Private
    Actions in Competition Law: A Consultation on Options for Reform' [2012] *Competition
    Law Journal* 211.
  'A Principled Argument for Personal Criminal Sanctions as Punishment under EC Cartel
    Law' [2007] 4 *Competition L Rev* 7.
Williams G, 'The Risk Principle' [1961] 77 *Law Quarterly Review* 179.
Williamson J, 'Causal Pluralism versus Epistemic Causality' [2006] 77 *Philosophica-Gent* 69.
Williamson OE, 'The Economics of Governance' [2005] 95(2) *American Economic Review* 1.
Wils WP, 'The Undertaking as Subject of E.C. Competition Law and the Imputation of
    Infringements to Natural or Legal Persons' [2000] 25 *European Law Review* 99.
  'Is Criminalization of EU Competition Law the Answer' [2005] 28 *World Competition* 117.
Wils WPJ, 'The Undertaking as Subject of EC Competition Law and the Imputation of
    Infringements to Natural or Legal Persons' [2000] 25 *European Law Review* 99.
  'Ten Years of Regulation 1/2003 – A Retrospective' [2013] *Journal of European Competition Law
    and Practice*, available at http://papers.ssrn.com/abstract=2274013, accessed 12 May 2014.
Wright CA, 'The Law of Remedies as a Social Institution, The' (1954) 18 *University of Detroit
    Law Journal* 376.
Wright RW, 'Actual Causation vs. Probabilistic Linkage: The Bane of Economic Analysis'
    [1985] 14(2) *The Journal of Legal Studies* 435.
  'Causation in Tort Law' [1985] 73 *California Law Review* 1735.
  'Causation, Responsibility, Risk, Probability, Naked Statistics, and Proof: Pruning the
    Bramble Bush by Clarifying the Concepts' [1987] 73 *Iowa Law Review* 1001.
  'The Grounds and Extent of Legal Responsibility' [2003] 41 *San Diego Law Review* 1425.
Wright RW and Puppe I, 'Causation: Linguistic, Philosophical, Legal and Economic' [2016]
    91 *Chicago-Kent Law Review* 461.
Young R, Faure M and Fenn P, 'Causality and Causation in Tort Law' [2004] 24 *International
    Review of Law and Economics* 507.
Zöttl J and Schlepper L, 'Die Private Durchsetzung von Kartellrechtlichen Schadensersat-
    zansprüchen – Status Quo in Deutschland' [2012] *Europäische Zeitschrift für Wirtschafts-
    recht* 573.
Zygimantas J, 'Obstacles in European Competition Law Enforcement: A Potential Solution
    from Collective Redress' [2014] *European Journal of Legal Studies*, available at http://
    cadmus.eui.eu/handle/1814/32274, accessed 26 January 2015.

REPORTS

Català P, 'Avant-Projet de Réforme Du Droit Des Obligations et Du Droit de La Prescription'
    (Documentation française, 2005), available at www.ladocumentationfrancaise.fr/rap
    ports-publics/054000622/.
Centre for European Policy Studies (CEPS), Erasmus University Rotterdam (EUR) and Luiss
    Guido Carli (LUISS), 'Making Antitrust Damages Actions More Effective in the EU:
    Welfare Impact and Potential Scenarios', available at http://ec.europa.eu/competition/
    antitrust/actionsdamages/files_white_paper/impact_study.pdf, accessed 8 May 2014.
Chagny M and Fourgoux J-L, Competition Law, Private Enforcement and Collective Redress
    in France, in AHRC Project on Competition Law: Comparative Private Enforcement
    and Consumer Redress, Led by Prof. Barry Rodger, available at www.clcpecreu.co.uk.
ESMA, 'Comparison of Liability Regimes in Member States in Relation to the Prospectus
    Directive' (2013) 619, available at www.esma.europa.eu/document/comparison-liability-
    regimes-in-member-states-in-relation-prospectus-directive, accessed 19 October 2017.

Bibliography

Gerner-Beuerle C and others, 'Study on the Law Applicable to Companies – Final Report' (2016), available at https://publications.europa.eu/en/publication-detail/-/publication/259a1dae-1a8c-11e7-808e-01aa75ed71a1/language-en, accessed 8 July 2019.

Komninos AP and Oxera, 'Quantifying Antitrust Damages: Towards Non-Binding Guidance for Courts' *Oxera*, available at www.oxera.com/Latest-Thinking/Publications/Reports/2010/Quantifying-antitrust-damages-Towards-non-binding.aspx, accessed 20 March 2014.

Organisation for Economic Co-Operation and Development, 'Safe Harbours and Legal Presumptions in Competition Law, Background Note by the Secretariat' (2017) DAF/COMP (2017) 9.

Organisation for Economic Co-operation and Development, *Monopsony and Buyer Power* (OECD, 2008).

Renda A, van den Bergh RJ and Pardolesi R, 'Making Antitrust Damages Actions More Effective in the EU: Welfare Impact and Potential Scenarios: Final Report' (2007) Contract DG COMP/2006/A3/012, available at http://ec.europa.eu/competition/antitrust/actionsdamages/files_white_paper/impact_study.pdf.

Waelbroeck D, Slater D and Even-Shoshan G, 'Study on the Conditions of Claims for Damages in Case of Infringement of EC Competition Rules (Ashurst Study)' (2004), available at http://ec.europa.eu/competition/antitrust/actionsdamages/comparative_report_clean_en.pdf.

LEGISLATION AND ACCOMPANYING DOCUMENTS

Antitrust.Modernization Commission Report and Recommendations VI 2007.

Act on Administrative Offenses (Ordnungswidrigkeitengesetz, OWiG) (German law)

Act against Restraints of Competition (Competition Act) – Gesetz gegen Wettbewerbsbeschränkungen (GWB) (German law)

Charter of Fundamental Rights of the European Union OJ C 303, 14.12.2007.

Civil Code (Bürgerliches Gesetzbuch, BGB) (German law)

Civil Code (Code civile) (French law)

Civil Code (Codice civile) (Italian law)

Civil Liability (Contribution) Act 1978 (English Law)

Civil procedure code (Codice di procedura civile) (Italian law)

Civil procedure code (Code de procédure civile) (French law)

Code de commerce (French law)

Code of Civil Procedure (Zivilprozessordnung, ZPO) (German law)

Competition Act 1998 (English law)

Competition Act 2002 (English law)

Commission Recommendation of 11 June 2013 on Common Principles for Injunctive and Compensatory Collective Redress Mechanisms in the Member States Concerning Violations of Rights Granted under Union Law OJ L 201, 26.7.2013, p. 60–65.

Commission Staff Working Document – Practical Guide on Quantifying Harm in Actions for Damages Based on Breaches of Article 101 or 102 of the Treaty on the Functioning of the European Union SWD (2013) 205 2013.

Commission Staff Working Paper Accompanying the White Paper on Damages Actions for Breach of the EC Antitrust Rules 2008 [COM (2008) 165 final, SEC (2008) 404].

Committee on Economic and Monetary Affairs, Amendments to the Proposal for a Directive on Certain Rules Governing Actions for Damages under National Law for Infringements of the Competition Law Provisions of the Member States and of the European Union (COM (2013) 0404 – C7-0170/2013 – 2013/0185 (COD)), PE516.968v01-00 2014.

Council Regulation (EC) No 1/2003 of 16 December 2002 on the Implementation of the Rules on Competition Laid Down in Articles 81 and 82 of the Treaty OJ L 001, 04/01/2003 2003.

Council Regulation (EC) No 1206/2001 of 28 May 2001 on Cooperation between the Courts of the Member States in the Taking of Evidence in Civil or Commercial Matters OJ L 174, 27.6.2001.

Damages Act 2017 (English law)

Directive 2014/104/EU of 26 November 2014 on Certain Rules Governing Actions for Damages under National Law for Infringements of the Competition Law Provisions of the Member States and of the European Union, [2014] OJ L349/1 2014.

EC 'Quantifying Antitrust Damages – Towards Non-Binding Guidance for Courts' ('the Quantification Study'). Page numbers quoted in this report refer to the electronic version of the quantification study: http://ec.europa.eu/competition/antitrust/actionsdamages/quantification_study.pdf.

European Convention for the Protection of Human Rights and Fundamental Freedoms as amended by Protocols Nos. 11 and 14 supplemented by Protocols Nos. 1, 4, 6, 7, 12, 13 and 16.

European Group on Tort Law, Principles of European Tort Law 2005.

Green Paper – Damages Actions for Breach of the EC Antitrust Rules SEC (2005) 1732 COM/2005, 672 2005.

Impact Assessment Report Accompanying the Proposal for a Directive COM (2013) 404, SWD(2013) 203 Final 2013.

Law 10 October 1990, n 287, Norme per la tutela della concorrenza e del mercato 'Law No. 287 Containing Rules on Protection of Competition', Gazzetta Ufficiale del 13 ottobre 1990, n 240.

Law No 2014-344 of 17 March 2014 'Loi Hamon'.

Law No 287 of 10 October 1990 Containing Rules on Protection of Competition ('Norme per la tutela della concorrenza e del mercato) G.U. 13 October 1990, no 240.

Law no. 287, 10 October 1990 (Legge 287/1990) (Italian law).

Legislative Decree no. 3, 19 January 2017 (Decreto Legislativo 19 gennaio 2017, n. 3) (Italian law).

Ordonnance n° 2017–303 relative aux actions en dommages et intérêts du fait des pratiques anticoncurrentielles, 9 March 2017 (French law).

Proposal for a Directive of the European Parliament and of the Council on Certain Rules Governing Actions for Damages under National Law for Infringements of the Competition Law Provisions of the Member States and of the European Union COM(2013) 404 2013.

Regulation 2017 on 'The Claims in Respect of Loss or Damage Arising from Competition Infringements' (Competition Act 1998 and Other Enactments (Amendment)) (SI 2017/385).

Regulation (EC) No 1049/2001 of the European Parliament and of the Council of 30 May 2001 regarding public access to European Parliament, Council and Commission documents OJ L 145, 31.5.2001.

Siebtes Gesetz zur Änderung des Gesetzes gegen Wettbewerbsbeschränkungen, Bundesgesetzblatt (BGBl.) 2005, Part I, 1954–1969 2005.

Treaty on European Union (consolidated version) OJ C 115,9.5.2008.

Treaty on the Functioning of the European Union (consolidated version) OJ C 115,9.5.2008.

White Paper on Damages Actions for Breach of the EC Antitrust Rules SEC (2008) 404–406.

Index

adequate causal link, 37
adequate causal theory
  adequate causation, 39
  in English law, 37
  in German law, 39
adequate causality
  scope of the risk, 37
adequate causation, 39
  in French law, 41
aims of competition law, 57
  consumer welfare, 58
  multiple objectives, 58
Allied Maples Group Ltd v Simmons & Simmons
  [1995] EWCA Civ 17, 97
all-or-nothing approach, 79, 108
antitrust injury, 48
apportionment of liability, 81
Arkin v Borchard Lines Ltd [2003] EWHC 687
  (Comm), 117, 139

balance of probability, 116, 122
balance of probability rule
  burden of proof and, 116
Barker v Corus (UK) plc [2006] UKHL 20, 37
BGH 6.7.1993 VI ZR 228/92, 156
BGH, 12.7.2016, KZR 25/14, 156
BGH, 17 February 1970 ('Anastasia Decision'), 125
BGH, 28.6.2005, KRB 2/05, NJW 2006, 155
BGH, 28/6/2011, KZR 75/10, 100
Broadcom Corp. v Qualcomm Inc 501 F.3d 297 (3d
  Cir. 2007), 46
Brunswick Corp. v Pueblo Bowl-O-Mat, Inc. 429
  U.S. 477 (1977), 48
burden of proof, 109
  allocation, 146
burden of persuasion, 109

causal uncertainty, 142
  departures, types of, 142
  English law, 122
  German law, 124
  in EU law, 112
  in French law, 127
  in Italian law, 129
  informational asymmetry, 143
  moral justification, 160
  probatio diabolica, 82
  relaxation rules, 142
  risk allocation, 109
burden of proof, 83

cartel. *See* anticompetitive agreements
Case C-6/74 Société Roquette Frères v
  Commission of the European Communities
  [1976] ECR 677, 52
Case C-8/08 *T-Mobile v Raad van bestuur van de
  Nederlandse Mededingingsautoriteit* [2009]
  ECR I-4529, 119, 147
Case C-12/03 P, *Commission v Tetra Laval* [2005]
  ECR I-987, 138
Case C-42/84, Remia [1985] ECR 2545, 39
Case C-49/92 P Commission v Anic Partecipazioni
  [1999], 147
Case C-56/65 [1966] ECR 235, 135
Case C-62/86 *AKZO Chemie BV v Commission*
  ECLI:EU:C:1991, 286, 147
Case C-73/95 P. *Viho Europe BV v Commission of
  the European Communities* [1996] ECR
  I-5457, 87
Case C-74/14 Eturas and Others ECLI:EU:
  C:2016:42, 144
Case C-97/08 P Akzo Nobel NV OJ C 128, 86
Case C-199/92 P Hüls v Commission [1999], 147

Index

Case C-453/99 *Courage Ltd v Bernard Crehan and Bernard Crehan v Courage Ltd and Others* [2001] ECR I-06297, 1, 97, 166
Case C-557/12 *Kone AG and Others v ÖBB-Infrastruktur AG*, 137
Case T-11/89 *Shell International Chemical Company v Commission* [1992] ECR II-757, 86
Case T-201/04 *Microsoft Corp. v Commission* [2007] ECR II-3601, 137
Case T-216/13 *Telefónica v Commission* ECLI:EU: T:2016:369, 112
CAT *JJB Sports Plc v Office of Fair Trading*, 123
causal contribution, 82, 85
causal inference, 143
  abductive inference, 143
  deductive inference, 143
  inductive inference, 143
  prima facie evidence, 144
  presumption, 145
  proof proximity, 159
causal presumption
  control, presumption of, 89
causal probability
  semantics, 75
causal proportional liability, 77, 89
causal proportional theories.
  See causal proportional liability
causal redundancy, 104
causal regularity, 44
  direct causal link, 43
  in English Law, 34
  in French law, 40
  in German law, 38
  in Italian law, 43
  quantitative or scalar, 23
  risk theory, 24
  risk, scope of, 37
causal uncertainty, 2, 4, 7–8, 10–11, 13, 16, 19, 43, 69–74, 77–79, 114–115, 117, 121, 142, 153, 161, 165, 192
counterfactual proof, 73
  definition, 69
  economic harm, 71
  factual uncertainty, 72
  general, 72
  in English law, 84
  in French law, 83
  in German law, 85
  in Italian law, 85
  indeterminate defendants, 79
  indeterminism, 73
  overdetermined causation, 81
  probabilistic causation, 74
  scientific uncertainty, 72

sources, 70
  specific, 72
  underdetermined causation, 82
causation
  all-or-nothing approach, 108
  and cumulative effects of contracts, 82
  decisive influence, 89
  empirical method, 8
  function of, 5
  in economic analysis of law, 11
  in EU law, 66
  in US antitrust law, 45
  regularity theories, 9
causation, proof of, 106
  discretionary power, 119
  statistical probability, 120
  standards of proof, 120
  economic evidence, 120
  in English law, 122
  in German law, 124
  in French law, 127
  in Italian law, 128
  informational asymmetries, 141
causation, proof of evaluation, 119
causation in fact
  material causation, 19, 25
causation test
  adequate causal theory, 37
  but-for test, 35
  NESS, 21
cause in fact
  but-for test, 35
claimants indeterminacy, 103
collective redress, 103
common sense, 31
comparator-based model, 138
compensatory principle, 1, 14, 59, 80
competition law infringement
  exclusionary offense, 18
  exploitative offense, 17
competition law liability
  causal contribution, 82
  comparative fault, 90
  contributory negligence, 89
  joint and several liability, 80
competition law liaibility
  apportionment of liability, 89
competition law objectives
  Damages Directive aims, 59
  liability, 57
concerted practice, 111
conditio sine qua non. See but-for test
consequential damages, 166
convergence of national rules, 64

Index

Cooper Tire & Rubber Co & Ors v Shell Chemicals UK Ltd & Ors [2009] EWHC 2609 (Comm), 87

Cooper Tire & Rubber Company Europe Limited v Dow Deutschland Inc [2010] EWCA Civ 864, 179

corrective justice, 1, 3, 5, 14, 26, 59, 74, 80, 88, 141, 152
 first-order duties, 6
 second-order duties, 6

Corte d'Appello Cagliari 23.1. 1999, Unimare S.r.l v Geasar S.p.a, 177

Corte d'Appello Turin 6.7.2000, Indaba Incentive Co v Juventus FC S.pA, 188

Corte di Cassazione civ., Telecom v Sign and Others, 16 May 2007, n 11312, 103

Corte di Cassazione Sara Assicurazioni v G.V., 30 May 2013, n 13667, 140

Corte di Cassazione sez. III, 4 marzo 2004, n 4400, 92

Corte di Cassazione, Allianz v Tagliaferro, 26 May 2011, n 11610, in Giust. civ. Mass. 2011, 5, 808 (2011), 140

Corte di Cassazione, Blasi v Az. cons. trasp. pubbl. Napoli, 22 April 1993, no 4725, 102

Corte di Cassazione, Fonsai v Nigriello, 2 February 2007, n 2305, 130

Corte di Cassazione, Montani et al v Lloyd Adriatico, 25 September 1998, no 9598, 101

Costner v Blount National Bank n 52 578 F.2d 1192 (6th Cir. 1978), 47

counterfactual, 20, 73, 132, 134–135

counterfactual buyer, 26

Cour d'Appel Paris, SNC Doux Aliments Bretagne etc v SAS Ajinamoto Eurolysine, 27 February 2014 No 07/10478, 176

Cour de Cassation civile, 1re, 12 November 1985, Bull. civ I, no. 298, 94

Cour de Cassation, comm., 15.6.2010, 09/15816, 176

Cour de Cassation, commercial division, Ajinomoto Eurolysine v SNC Doux Aliment Bretagne and Others No 09/15816 (15 June 2010), 95

Cour de Cassation, Doux Aliments v Ajinomoto Eurolyne 09-15816., 175

Cour de Cassation, JCB Services et al. v Central Parks, 6 October 2015, no. 13-24.854, 83

Cour de Cassation, Le Gouessant, 15 May 2012, 11-18495, 176

Cour de Cassation, Orange v Cowes, 25 March 2014, No 1313839, 95

Court of Appeal of Paris, M. Merhi Bassam v SNC Société Presse Paris Services – SPPS, No 08/21750, 27 April 2011, 96

Court of Appeal of Versailles, SA Concurrence v SA Aiwa France, No 01/08413, 9 December 2003, 96

Court of Cassation, Fonsai v Nigriello, 2 February 2007, n 2305, 146

Crehan v Inntrepreneur Pub Company CPC [2004] EWCA Civ 637, 34, 97

cumulative foreclosure effect, 90

damages action
 harmonization process, 66

damages actions
 in English law, 34
 in French law, 40
 in German law, 38
 in Italian law, 43
 liability standards, 54
 scope of, 61
 statutory duty in English law, 35

deterrence, 15

Devenish Nutrition Ltd v Sanofi-Aventis SA [2008] EWCA Civ 1086, 178

direct causal link
 in EU law, 52
 proximity principle, 52

direct purchaser, 167

Directive on damages actions 104/2014, 50

documentary evidence, 106

duplicative causes, 104

duty of consistent interpretation, 5

economic evidence, 131
 admissibility, 131

econometrics, 132
 probative value, 145

effectiveness, 2, 49, 53, 55–56, 58–60, 62–63, 65–67, 81–82, 97, 113, 118, 144, 148, 150, 156–157, 189

effectiveness, principle of, 50

Emerald Supplies Ltd & Anor v British Airways Plc [2010] EWCA Civ 1284, 178

Emerson Electric Co & Ors v Mersen UK Portslade Ltd & Anor [2012] EWCA Civ 155, 88

Enron Coal Services Limited v English Welsh & Scottish Railway [2011] EWCA Civ 2, 98

Enron Coal Services Limited v English Welsh & Scottish Railway Limited [2009] CAT 36, 139

equivalence, 2, 29, 53, 55–56, 59, 64–65, 68, 82, 118

equivalence, principle of, 50

evidence, 106
 circumstantial evidence, 146
 evaluation, 162
 value of the proof, 161

Index

evidence, disclosure of, 113
evidence, law of, 107
evidential burden, 109, 115
  scientific expert, 131
exceptional proof rules
  English law, 152
  French law, 158
  German law, 155
  Italian law, 158
exclusionary conduct, 165
exclusionary practice, 16
expert witness, 131
exploitative abuse, 16, 165
exploitative conducts, 8

factual causation
  in English law, 35
  in French law, 41
  in German law, 38
  in Italian law, 44
  in US law, 46
Fairchild v *Glenhaven Funeral Services Ltd* [2002]
  UKHL 22, 37
fairness, 141
false acquittals, 116
false condemnations, 116
foreseeability, 115
foreseeability test
  reasonableness, 36
French commercial court, 30 March 2011, SA
  Numericable et a. v. SA France Telecom
  Orange, 128
Fulton Shipping Inc of Panama v *Globalia
  Business Travel SAU (formerly Travelplan
  SAU) of Spain* (2014) EWHC 1547 (Comm),
  179

Gatt Communications, Inc. v *PMC Associates,
  L.L.C.* 711 F.3d 68, 76 (2d Cir. 2013), 48
general causation, 6, 72, 147

Hanover Shoe, Inc v *United Shoe Machinery Corp*
  392 US 481 (1968), 180
Healthcare at Home v *Genzyme Ltd* [2006] CAT
  29, 139
Higher Regional Court of Düsseldorf, 9 April 2014,
  VI-U (Kart) 10/12, 100

I Illinois Brick Co v *Illinois* 431 US 720 (1977),
  180
indirect purchasers' claims, 167
*In re Methyl Tertiary Butyl Ether (MTBE) Products
  Liability Litigation* (2010) 739 F. Supp. 2d 576
  (SDNY) 596, 46

indirect economic losses, 164
indirect harm, 44
  counterfactual buyer or customer, 17
  waterbed effect, 185
indirect loss, 116
inference, 112
  abductive reasoning, 144
indirect evidence, 144
information asymmetry, 113
inspections, 106
Italian Court of Cassation civ. Sez. Un.,
  4 February 2005, n 220, 14
Italian Court of Cassation, Comi/Cargest,
  judgment no 11564 of 4 June 2015, 130
Italian Court of Cassation, Division III, no 7026,
  2001, 129
Italian Court of Cassation SU, 11 January 2008,
  no 581, 129

Joined Cases C-6/90 and C-9/90, *Andrea
  Francovich and Danila Bonifaci and others* v
  Italian Republic [1991] ECR 5357, 52
Joined Cases C-295/04 to C-298/04 *Vincenzo
  Manfredi* v *Lloyd Adriatico* Assicurazioni SpA
  (2006) ECR I-06619, 1, 50, 165
joint and several liability, 80
  in English law, 84
  in French law, 83
  in German law, 85
  in Italian law, 85

KG 01.10.2009, 2 U 10/03 Kart NZG 2010,
  420, 173
KG 01.10.2009, 2 U 17/03 openJur 2012,
  11758, 173
Kone AG and Others v *ÖBB-Infrastruktur AG*, 188

legal causation
  and common sense, 28
  and corrective justice, 26
  and fairness concerns, 28
  and foreseeability, 27
  and legal policy objectives, 28
  foreseeability of the harm, 29
  generalizing theories, 27
  in French law, 41
  in Italian law, 44
  remoteness, 36
  remoteness in English law, 36
legal policy theory. *See* scope of the rule
LG Dortmund 01.04.2004, 13 O 55/02 Kart WuW/
  E DE-R, 1352, 173
LG Mainz, 15.01.2004, 12 HK.O 52/02 Kart
  NJW-RR 2004, 478, 172

Index

LG Mannheim 11.7.2003 7 O 326/02 GRUR 2004, 182, 172

LG Mannheim 29.04.2005, 22 O 74/04 Kart EWiR 659, 173

loss of chance, 91
  in English law, 97
  in French law, 94
  in general, 91
  in German law, 100
  in Italian law, 101
lost chances. *See* loss of chance
lost opportunities, 16
lost-volume effect, 16

material causation, 10, 169. *See also* factual causation
McGhee v National Coal Board [1972] 3 All E.R. 1008, 1 W.L.R. 1, 36
Miller v Minister of Pensions, 122
multiple defendants, 77, 79

Napp Pharmaceuticals Holdings Ltd v Director General of Fair Trading, 123

OLG Karlsruhe 11.06.2010, 6-U 118/05 Kart, 174
OLG Karlsruhe 28.1.2004, 6 U 183/03 NJW 2004, 2243, 172
overcharge, 1, 9, 16–17, 26, 29–30, 75, 95, 102, 105, 138, 149–150, 165–167, 169–170, 172–173, 175–176, 178, 180, 182–184, 186–188, 190–191, 196
overdetermined causation, 81

parallel behaviours, 111
Paris Court of Appeal, SNC Doux Aliments Bretagne etc v. SAS Ajinamoto Eurolysine, No 07/10478, 10 June 2009, 94
passing on, 167
  cause-in-fact, 169
  English law, 178
  EU law, 183
  French law, 175
  German law, 172
  Italian law, 177
  legal causation, 170
perte de chance. *See* loss of chance
preemption, 104
preponderance of the evidence, 116. *See also* balance of probability
presumption, 145
  carte harm, 148
  conclusive, 146
  EU courts, 147
  EU law, 148
  evidential, 146
  factual presumption, 145–146

in English law, 153
in EU law, 149
in French law, 158
in German law, 155
in Italian law, 159
irrebuttable, 145
legal presumption, 145–146
persuasive, 146
presumption of innocence, 150
provisional, 146
rebuttable, 145
price effects, 112
private antitrust enforcement, 116
protective scope of the rule, 59
probabilistic liability, 117
procedural autonomy, principle of, 119
proof, 107
proof proximity, 159
proportional liability, 81
protective scope of a law, 57
protective scope of the rule, 61
proximate cause, 46
punitive scope, 62, 111
pure economic loss, 11, 26, 69, 94, 132, 164
pure financial losses, 12

*Rambus Inc. v FTC.*522 F.3d 456 (D.C. Cir. 2008), 47
Regulation 1/2003, 64, 118
relaxation, proof rules, 111
responsibility in solidum. *See* joint and several liability
right of standing, 60
right to compensation, 1, 50, 55, 63, 65, 109, 113, 115, 150, 173, 182, 189
risk allocation, 141
risk-liability theory, 137

Sainsbury's Supermarkets Ltd v Mastercard Incorporated and Others [2016] CAT 11, 88, 187
scientific or economic uncertainty, 141
scope of the norm, 62
scope of the rule, 39
secondary harms, 116, 164
single economic entity principle, 85
singular causation, proof of. *See* causation, proof
solidary responsibility. *See* joint and several liability
specific causation, 6–7, 24, 39, 72, 88, 132, 137, 147, 160
standard of proof, 110, 114
  and balance of probabilities, 121
  free evaluation of the evidence, 124
  in English law, 122

Index

standard of proof (cont.)
in EU law, 114
in French law, 127
German law, 121, 124
in Italian law, 121, 129
in national systems, 116
intime conviction, 120–121, 125
relaxation of, 151
requisite legal standard, 115
statutorily protected interest, 11, 26, 38, 164
stochastic causality, 137
subjective right, 11, 26, 164

T-112/07 *Hitachi Ltd, Hitachi Europe Ltd and Japan AE Power Systems Corp.* v *European Commission* [2011], 147
Tele Atlas N.V. v *NAVTEQ Corp.* No C-05-01673, 2008 WL 4809441, at *22 (N.D. Cal. 2008), 46
Tribunal de Commerce de Nanterre *SA Les Laboratoires Pharmaceutiques Arkopharma* v *Ste Roche etc*, 11.5.2006, n. 02004F02643, 177
Tribunal de Commerce de Paris, *Société les Laboratoires Juva Production* v *SAS Roche*, 10 September 2003, No. RG2003048044, 176

Tribunale di Milano, 27 December 2013 *Brennercom Spa* v *Telecom Italia Spa*, no 22423/2010, 102
Tribunale di Milano, *Brennercom Spa* v *Telecom Italia Spa*, 3 March 2014 no 14802/2011, 102, 139
Tribunale di Milano, OK Com Spa c. Telecom Italia SpA, 13 February 2013, R.G. 76568/2008, 103
Tribunale Milan, *SEA* v *Swiss International Air Lines* 27.06.2016, n 7970/2016, 184

umbrella effect, 188
underdetermined causation, 82
United States v *Microsoft* 253 F.3d 34 (D.C. Cir. 2001), 46, 137

WH Newson Holding Ltd & Ors v *IMI Plc & Ors* [2013] EWCA Civ 1377, 178
witnesses, 106

Zenith Radio Corp. v *Hazeltine Research, Inc.* 395 U.S. 100 (1969), 46

2 Travel Group PLC (in liquidation) v *Cardiff City Transport Services Ltd* [2012] CAT 19, 30, 99, 139

Lightning Source UK Ltd.
Milton Keynes UK
UKHW022027141219
355411UK00005B/23/P